THE DAILY STUDY BIBLE

(OLD TESTAMENT)

General Editor: John C. L. Gibson

PSALMS

Volume 2

PSALMS

Volume 2

G. A. F. Knight

THE WESTMINSTER PRESS
PHILADELPHIA

Published by
The Saint Andrew Press
Edinburgh, Scotland
and
The Westminster Press ®
Philadelphia, Pennsylvania

Printed in the United States of America

4   5   6   7   8

Library of Congress Cataloging in Publication Data

Knight, George Angus Fulton, 1909–
    Psalms.

    (The Daily study Bible series)
    Bibliography: p.
    1. Bible. O.T. Psalms—Commentaries. I. Title.
II. Series: Daily study Bible series (Westminster Press)
BS1430.3.K64 1982   223'.2'077   82-20134

ISBN 0-664-21808-3 (v. 2)
ISBN 0-664-24575-7 (pbk. : v. 2)

"Why are you writing a commentary on the Psalms," asked a well-read churchwoman in today's society, "when they are just a collection of religious poetry?"

A professor in a famous University to his new lecturer in Biblical Studies: "You must never teach the Psalms; there is nothing in them."

GENERAL PREFACE

The series of Old Testament commentaries, to which this second volume on the *Psalms* by Dr. Knight belongs, has been planned as a companion series to the much-acclaimed New Testament series of the late Professor William Barclay. As with that series, each volume is arranged in successive headed portions suitable for daily study. The Biblical text followed is that of the Revised Standard Version or Common Bible. Eleven contributors share the work, each being responsible for from one to three volumes. The series is issued in the hope that it will do for the Old Testament what Professor Barclay's series succeeded so splendidly in doing for the New Testament—make it come alive for the Christian believer in the twentieth century.

Its two-fold aim is the same as his. Firstly, it is intended to introduce the reader to some of the more important results and fascinating insights of modern Old Testament scholarship. Most of the contributors are already established experts in the field with many publications to their credit. Some are younger scholars who have yet to make their names but who in my judgment as General Editor are now ready to be tested. I can assure those who use these commentaries that they are in the hands of competent teachers who know what is of real consequence in their subject and are able to present it in a form that will appeal to the general public.

The primary purpose of the series, however, is *not* an academic one. Professor Barclay summed it up for his New Testament series in the words of Richard of Chichester's prayer—to enable men and women "to know Jesus Christ more clearly, to love Him more dearly, and to follow Him more nearly." In the case of the Old Testament we have to be a little more circumspect than that. The Old Testament was completed long before the time of Our Lord, and it was (as it still is) the sole Bible of the Jews, God's first people, before it became part of the Christian Bible. We must take this fact seriously.

Yet in its strangely compelling way, sometimes dimly and sometimes directly, sometimes charmingly and sometimes embarrassingly, it holds up before us the things of Christ. It should not be forgotten that Jesus Himself was raised on this Book, that He based His whole ministry on what it says, and that He approached His death with its words on His lips. Christian men and women have in this ancient collection of Jewish writings a uniquely illuminating avenue not only into the will and purposes of God the Father, but into the mind and heart of Him who is named God's Son, who was Himself born a Jew but went on through the Cross and Resurrection to become the Saviour of the world. Read reverently and imaginatively the Old Testament can become a living and relevant force in their everyday lives.

It is the prayer of myself and my colleagues that this series may be used by its readers and blessed by God to that end.

New College   JOHN C. L. GIBSON
Edinburgh   General Editor

CONTENTS

ABBREVIATIONS

AV	Authorized, or King James, Version of the Bible
ftn.	Footnote to a verse in the RSV (a list of footnotes referred to will be found in Appendix 1)
LXX	The Septuagint or Greek Version of the OT
NAB	New American Bible
NEB	New English Bible
NIV	New International Version
NT	New Testament
OT	Old Testament
RSV	Revised Standard Version
RV	Revised Version, 1885
TEV	Today's English Version, or Good News Bible

INTRODUCTION

The Psalter is composed of five books. We studied Books I and II in our Volume 1 of *The Daily Study Bible*; that volume finished with Psalm 72. Books III, IV and V cover Psalms 73 to 150, and these we study now in Volume 2. The reader who has not read Volume 1 is advised to turn to the Introduction to that volume, since what is said there refers to all 150 psalms in the Psalter.

As we now study the second half of the Psalter, however, we are in a position to watch for the most important element of all in the psalms. There is so much more in them than just individual verses that speak home to us privately in our various moods. As we noted in Volume 1, the five books of the Psalter were probably read aloud in the Synagogue in Jesus' day in Nazareth, in parallel with the five books of the *Torah*. That word is the Hebrew name for the Law or Pentateuch, the first five books of the Old Testament, known to the Jewish people also as the five books of Moses. Genesis to Deuteronomy covers the whole story of Israel from the Creation, when Israel too was but an idea in the mind of God (Isa. 51:16), through Israel's growth and development as God's son (Exod. 4:22–23), when as God's people she was being trained and educated to be his servant. This education took place (1) through God's Revelation-Instruction, as the word *Torah* means, that is, revelation of himself, of his nature and purpose, and instruction for the way in which a servant people is meant to live and work together in harmony and love; (2) through the experience of living through God's "mighty acts" in Israel's history as these are narrated and interpreted in the *Torah*, and by which Israel discovered that these acts of God were actually terrible *for God*.

But the education went on after the *Torah* (3) via the pain and suffering that God's people had to undergo when their beloved city of Jerusalem was destroyed and they themselves had to depart into exile; through all of which they learned that to be God's servant was to be like God himself, and so to be his suffering servant. (4) This experience, Amos had declared beforehand, would be the "end" of Israel, in that Israel had rebelliously turned her back upon God and upon God's plan to use her for the redemption of the world. Ezekiel also described the events of 587 B.C. as the "death" of Israel. (5) But God is greater than both sin and death. It was through Ezekiel again that Israel learned the greatness of God; for this prophet interpreted God's unconquerable grace by speaking of Israel's coming "resurrection" from the grave, her restoration to serve God's plan once more. (6) Finally, Israel was trained and educated through her worship, as in the Temple she recalled all the "terrible acts" of God and each individual glimpsed through the liturgy something of the cost to God of his "steadfast love" both to him and to his family and friends, prompting him to make a response of deep faith and joy, and of a new dedication to serve God in fear and love. All Israel's history is reflected in the sequence of the psalms, as each in turn emerges from one or other of the great moments in her past.

Psalms 1–72 seem, generally speaking, to concentrate on the earliest period of the formation of the nation and the great days of David and Solomon, whereas Psalms 73–150 seem to reflect the later period of Israel's experience of God's steadfast love. That is the period of the great prophets of the eighth and seventh centuries, of the wiping out of the Northern Kingdom in 722 B.C., the siege of the Holy Land by Sennacherib around 700 B.C., the revival of faith and obedience in Judah in the days of Josiah, followed by the destruction of Jerusalem itself in 587 B.C. and the Exile in Babylon; then there was the Return to Judah, the rebuilding of the city and Temple, and the establishing of the redeemed people of God as a worshipping community once more in the new Jerusalem. This chronological sequence can be roughly traced behind the psalms we study in Volume 2. If an occasional psalm does not seem to fit into this progression, it only means that we do not see the wholeness of the pattern of God's activity as clearly as did the compilers. The fault evidently lies with us, not with them.

There are then two patterns in the Psalter, one following the five books of the *Torah* and one the whole story of God's dealings with Israel. Thus when we come to the last group of psalms we find that these illustrate what the last chapters of the *Torah* tell us about God. For example, the "Song of Moses" (Deut. 32), which long preceded our Psalter, had given Israel, even before David's day (around 1000 B.C.—three thousand years ago!) an interpretation in essence of all God's terrible acts, that is, of his terrible acts of love and creative purpose; while the whole *Torah* ends with an account of Moses' "ascension" to God on Mount Pisgah (Deut. 34:1), from which *the Lord showed him all the land.* In the same way, at the end of the Psalter, God has shown Israel the ultimate outcome of his purposes of redemption—of her rebirth and restoration after judgment and exile—so that Israel's response can only be one of praise and joyous thanksgiving. In fact Deuteronomy ends with the choice being laid before God's people of life and blessing, or death and curse, the latter seen as a reversion to the chaotic existence of greed, selfishness and violence that characterized the nations outside the Covenant fellowship. The Psalter too ends on this note, as it speaks of God's two-edged sword, but it lifts this vital issue out of past history and makes it relevant for all time.

Step by step, then, in the Psalms, Israel had been given a *theological* interpretation of the pattern of events that she had lived through as the people of God. But Israel was all the time composed of individual men, women and children, and it was they who worshipped God then as we do now. Because they belonged within the Covenant, each individual could actually undergo the same pattern of God's redemptive love in his own experience, of adoption, of learning by suffering, of death, and of the new creation and of a covenantal relationship with God. Paul makes all this plain for the Christian in, for example, 2 Cor. 5:17; 6:8–10. The individual Christian is now able to undergo such an experience only because Jesus has first acknowledged and then lived out in himself the pattern that we find in the Psalms and indeed in the Old Testament as a whole. The Psalms tell their readers to *remember* the mighty acts of God, that is, to recall them out of the past and to make them their own experience.

This is what Jesus did, and it is what we must and what, with his help, we can do.

The Psalms bring the mighty acts of God right into our own small lives as unimportant little soldiers in the army of the Lord.

PSALMS

LIFE ETERNAL

Psalm 73:1–20

A Psalm of Asaph.

[1]Truly God is good to the upright,
   to those who are pure in heart.
[2]But as for me, my feet had almost stumbled,
   my steps had well nigh slipped.
[3]For I was envious of the arrogant,
   when I saw the prosperity of the wicked.

[4]For they have no pangs;
   their bodies are sound and sleek.
[5]They are not in trouble as other men are;
   they are not stricken like other men.
[6]Therefore pride is their necklace;
   violence covers them as a garment.
[7]Their eyes swell out with fatness,
   their hearts overflow with follies.
[8]They scoff and speak with malice;
   loftily they threaten oppression.
[9]They set their mouths against the heavens,
   and their tongue struts through the earth.

[10]Therefore the people turn and praise them;
   and find no fault in them.
[11]And they say, "How can God know?
   Is there knowledge in the Most High?"
[12]Behold, these are the wicked;
   always at ease, they increase in riches.
[13]All in vain have I kept my heart clean
   and washed my hands in innocence.
[14]For all the day long I have been stricken,
   and chastened every morning.

15If I had said, "I will speak thus,"
    I would have been untrue to the generation of thy children.
16But when I thought how to understand this,
    it seemed to me a wearisome task,
17until I went into the sanctuary of God;
    then I perceived their end.

18Truly thou dost set them in slippery places;
    thou dost make them fall to ruin.
19How they are destroyed in a moment,
    swept away utterly by terrors!
20They are like a dream when one awakes,
    on awaking you despise their phantoms.

In all periods there are people who are more intellectually curious than the majority. The so-called "Wisdom" psalms were composed by people who longed to understand how God works in the world and in their own life. It is possible that the three following psalms have been placed together because they handle the same deep theological problem; but they do not do so in an abstract way but rather out of the writers' own human experience. This psalmist is deeply worried why evil men can "get away with it", so to speak, in that God doesn't seem to notice the evil that they do or the way they live. And so he has his doubts about the goodness and the justice of God. But he receives a wonderful answer from God, not an intellectual, "theological" one. Clearly God does not want only intellectuals to believe in him. Confidence in his love is meant even for little children, for simple unlettered folk, and even for the intellectually handicapped.

Verses 1–3, *Losing faith.* The first verse tells us what many people take for granted about God. It comes as an answer in an argument: "Oh, no," they exclaim, "God is good to good people." "If you are a good boy," some misguided parents say to their child today, "God will love you." But I cannot really accept that view, says our psalmist. It doesn't work out like that. It seems that God pays no attention when men are wicked. And so I almost lost what faith I had in God. I almost felt that it was unscrupulous people who have the best of things.

Unless it is pointed out to us, we may not realize how many of the great souls of the Bible experience deep doubts about the goodness of God. So we are in a great company if we share the doubts of our psalmist.

Verses 4–9, *Evil looks clever.* What a telling series of pictures we are given of arrogant and unscrupulous people! Let us remember, as we read on, that arrogance is the basic sin behind all others. They do not have pains in the belly, the psalmist says, they do not get incensed at the boastful, they wear their self-satisfaction like a *necklace* that all can see. *Therefore* they wear the violence of their nature like a gaudy, provocative overcoat, regarding it as a status symbol. Why *therefore*? For it follows naturally that they reveal their arrogance to others, though they are blind to what they are doing, just as the darkness cannot comprehend or put out the light (John 1:5). Vice oozes from their soul. "They have bright little pigs' eyes gleaming maliciously out of fat puffy cheeks," as G. R. Driver translates verse 7. The followers of pill-popping pop singers, of the James Bonds of today's films, of the demagogues of society, would regard these aberrant people as the prophets of the new age. "They never open their mouths without blaspheming against God, and arrogantly give orders to those human beings with whom they have to deal. They talk loftily as if they were gods in heaven."

Verses 10–14, *"Aren't they clever?"* Therefore God's people flock round them in admiration and suck the experience of such arrogant people dry. They do so because they notice that God does not rebuke evil men. Consequently they suppose that their way of life must be the best way. Such people win out, for their power and arrogance makes them rich.

So what can I get out of being faithful and good? It doesn't obviously pay to be good. All it leads to is pain and suffering.

Verses 15–20, *Looking for the answer.* If I had told people what I felt in this regard, that would have made it more difficult for young people to believe. In fact I came to realize the meaninglessness of the world's violence, and that it was not the answer, the intellectual answer to my quest—it was not the truth of God! We remember that later on in history Jesus said: "If your eye is not sound, your whole body will be full of darkness".

It was only when I began to take God into account and so to see things *sub specie aeternitatis*—with the eyes of eternity—that *I perceived their end.* Now suddenly this sceptical psalmist says: "Thou". *Truly thou dost set them in slippery places.* And suddenly he sees their activities as God sees them, and not just as man sees. He sees the outcome of their egotism. Slowly, perhaps rather than suddenly, he then discovers the two ways of being in some kind of relationship to God. The wicked live "theofugal" lives, that is, their actions send them flying off at a tangent from God, into outer space, so to speak, to where God is not, as the OT declares, that is to hell. But God really calls us to live "theocentric" lives, with our lives circling round him who is at the centre of all things. The word *shau* in verse 18, which describes the end of the line for the wicked, means emptiness, negation, vanity, meaninglessness. In fact, the arrogant are not real people. They are "hollow men", to use T. S. Eliot's term. When you rouse yourself, our psalmist discovered, and stop being sorry for yourself, you recognize that the wicked have no more reality than a dream. For of course only God is Reality (or Truth, as we can interpret the word—see John 14:6), so that those whose feet slide down the slope away from God cease to have any real being in themselves.

THE ANSWER IS GRACE

Psalm 73:21–28

21When my soul was embittered,
   when I was pricked in heart,
22I was stupid and ignorant,
   I was like a beast toward thee.
23Nevertheless I am continually with thee;
   thou dost hold my right hand.
24Thou dost guide me with thy counsel,
   and afterward thou wilt receive me to glory.
25Whom have I in heaven but thee?
   And there is nothing upon earth that I desire besides thee.
26My flesh and my heart may fail,
   but God is the strength of my heart and my portion for ever.

²⁷For lo, those who are far from thee shall perish;
  thou dost put an end to those who are false to thee.
²⁸But for me it is good to be near God;
  I have made the Lord God my refuge,
  that I may tell of all thy works.

Verses 21–26, *Finding the answer.* "I went through a terrible time of embitterment; it was (literally) as if teeth were biting into my kidneys. For to let doubts dominate me as I had done only showed that I had allowed 'the beast' to control me." This idea of a beast here probably refers to the monster Leviathan, the living power of evil and of darkness over against which God had created Light, right at the beginning (Gen. 1:2–3). In other words, this believing man here was only just discovering that he had allowed himself to be as guilty as those arrogant people whom he had envied.

Yet it was at this nadir of self-loathing and self-contempt that God gave back to the psalmist the gift of faith. That is to say, it was when this very human being went into the sanctuary of God, that is, when he returned to God in penitence, and approached him in awe and wonder, no longer secretly wanting to be like the arrogant persons he knew, that God answered his cry. God did so, not by giving him an intellectual answer to the problems of divine providence and to the existence of evil, but by helping him win the battle within his own soul for the very survival of his personal faith. *The arrogant* spoken of here may of course have been real people, whom the psalmist knew and encountered daily. But the word used in the Hebrew also describes his own inner egotistical view of life. But now the answer God gives him is not an argumentative one; rather, God gives him his own Self, his very Presence. By doing so he reveals to the psalmist his unspeakable love and grace. So that now, says the psalmist: "I have him!"

Since such unspeakable love is not of this world, it must belong in eternity. The opposite of arrogance is humility. The humble man alone has found freedom from the tyranny of his own egotism. He now possesses freedom to desire God more than anything else that this world can offer. Some day, the psalmist confesses, his frail body will reach the end of the road. But death cannot thwart that love which belongs in eternity, for eternity envelops death. And so he confidently declares that God and God's love will be his *portion,* the whole meaning of his being and of his existence both now and throughout eternity.

In the Middle Ages Spain stamped on its coins a picture of the Straits of Gibraltar with the words: "*Ne plus ultra*", "Nothing beyond". That, we know, is how some people think of death. But Spain herself went on to produce a few daring spirits who believed that there was indeed another world across the seas. Let us remain aware, as we read the Psalms, that the difference between the Testaments is not in content. It is only that the NT is the transfiguration of the OT.

We are constantly astonished at the depths of faith that we find in the Psalms. Since faith is the gift of God, we make the discovery that the God of the NT is also the God of the OT. Faith means putting oneself completely at the disposal of God and inviting him to continue his work of creation through oneself now and into all eternity. Whereupon God accepts one's offer, as only a heavenly Father could, and taking one by the hand, leads one forward into the unknown future.

Verses 27–28. It is an indisputable fact, however, that those who have deliberately chosen to fly off at a tangent from God as the centre of their lives, have at the same time separated themselves from eternal life. But, continues the psalmist, I have found that to live with God is *good for me,* as the Hebrew means, for he is now no less than the Rock of my heart (the literal meaning of "strength" in verse 26; see *ftn*). That is to say, he has found what David had discovered so long before and about which he had sung with such great joy (Ps. 18:2; 2 Sam. 22:2, 47).

What is it that has liberated our psalmist in this way? It is certainly not the discovery merely that "sin does not pay". For like Paul in the NT he is aware that he is not discussing the question of morals, of "being good", far less of being blessed by God as a reward for his good deeds. If it had been so, then he would not have had to ask, "Why should this happen to me?", or

"What have I done to deserve this?" Rather, he had found that to be near God, to have God at the centre, as the Rock foundation of his being, was to allow God to work through him his plan for his life. In fact, the word *counsel* in verse 24 means God's plan and purpose for the universe. God was prepared to use the psalmist to work out this plan for the universe, as he plans also to do through us!

So the very *nearness of God, the Rock that is my refuge,* actually induces me *to tell of all thy works.* This word *works* may mean two things. (1) It may mean the actual creative acts of God as the Almighty Craftsman. But (2) it may refer to the ministering angels of God. Or the two ideas may be put together as one, and so speak of God's creative acts that are aimed just at me. God gives his beloved meaning and purpose to life, by showing him what meaning and purpose it has for him.

THE ETERNAL WAR (i)

Psalm 74:1–23

A Maskil of Asaph.

[1]O God, why dost thou cast us off for ever?
　　Why does thy anger smoke against the sheep of thy pasture?
[2]Remember thy congregation, which thou hast gotten of old,
　　which thou hast redeemed to be the tribe of thy heritage!
　　Remember Mount Zion, where thou hast dwelt.
[3]Direct thy steps to the perpetual ruins;
　　the enemy has destroyed everything in the sanctuary!

[4]Thy foes have roared in the midst of thy holy place;
　　they set up their own signs for signs.
[5]At the upper entrance they hacked
　　the wooden trellis with axes.
[6]And then all its carved wood
　　they broke down with hatchets and hammers.
[7]They set thy sanctuary on fire;
　　to the ground they desecrated the dwelling place of thy name.

⁸They said to themselves, "We will utterly subdue them";
  they burned all the meeting places of God in the land.

⁹We do not see our signs;
  there is no longer any prophet,
  and there is none among us who knows how long.
¹⁰How long, O God, is the foe to scoff?
  Is the enemy to revile thy name for ever?
¹¹Why dost thou hold back thy hand,
  why dost thou keep thy right hand in thy bosom?

¹²Yet God my King is from of old,
  working salvation in the midst of the earth.
¹³Thou didst divide the sea by thy might;
  thou didst break the heads of the dragons on the waters.
¹⁴Thou didst crush the heads of Leviathan,
  thou didst give him as food for the creatures of the wilderness.
¹⁵Thou didst cleave open springs and brooks;
  thou didst dry up ever-flowing streams.
¹⁶Thine is the day, thine also the night;
  thou hast established the luminaries and the sun.
¹⁷Thou hast fixed all the bounds of the earth;
  thou hast made summer and winter.

¹⁸Remember this, O Lord, how the enemy scoffs,
  and an impious people reviles thy name.
¹⁹Do not deliver the soul of thy dove to the wild beasts;
  do not forget the life of thy poor for ever.
²⁰Have regard for thy covenant;
  for the dark places of the land are full of the habitations of
    violence.
²¹Let not the downtrodden be put to shame;
  let the poor and needy praise thy name.

²²Arise, O God, plead thy cause;
  remember how the impious scoff at thee all the day!
²³Do not forget the clamour of thy foes,
  the uproar of thy adversaries which goes up continually!

This psalm is a communal lament, such as is referred to in Zech.
7:1–6; 8:18–19. After the Return from Exile the Israelites were
accustomed to hold fast-days when they thought back together in
God's presence to the horror of the destruction of Jerusalem and

of the Temple by King Nebuchadnezzar, that is, to what happened on March 16, 587 B.C. It was an exact date in history, just as was Good Friday, A.D. 30. The peculiar horror of that event rested in the fact that what happened then was the destruction, not of Damascus or Nineveh, but of God's own chosen city, the city which God had promised would be the rallying point of all nations in accordance with his redemptive plan for the whole world. (See Isa. 2:2–4)

Verses 1–3, *Furious at God.* Why? Why? Why does Almighty God allow the destruction of his own city by a pagan army? Why has God broken faith with his own chosen people whom he had promised when he made Covenant with them to cherish and care for them for ever? "Take big strides, God, come and have a look at the ruins where your own sanctuary was, the Temple, the Altar, the Laver, the Ark of the Covenant, the courtyards, the choirs' music stores, the priests' quarters."

God had of course "*gotten Israel of old*", that is to say, he had begotten Israel at the foundation of the world. As Isa. 51:16 puts it: "While I was stretching out the heavens and laying the foundations of the earth, I was saying to Zion, 'You are my people'." The holy place that was in ruins was where the eternal God had promised to meet up with and confront eternal evil—and evil now had won the day! The "Abomination of Desolation" had in fact become a fact of history. That is the name Jesus used of the eternal war "become flesh", of evil becoming a moment in history, and winning the battle; the RSV translates it *the desolating sacrilege* (Mark 13:14).

Jesus' reference was to that other victory of evil over God that happened on December 6, 167 B.C., when the foreign king Antiochus offered the abomination of heathen sacrifice in the rebuilt Second Temple. Yet Jesus knew that the war was eternal. Consequently he was referring at the same time to that third destruction of the Holy City still to come, when, in A.D. 70 the Romans laid Jerusalem waste and desecrated the Temple for ever. But of course he also referred to the ultimate manifestation of the eternal war when the power of wicked men won the battle at Golgotha and put to death God's "holy one", as Paul called

Jesus. In the Garden of Gethsemane the night before it happened Jesus said to the Temple police who had come to arrest him: "But this is your hour, and the power of darkness" (Luke 22:53). Moreover, terrible as it appeared to the disciples, it was an "hour" that God had permitted to happen, even although, as Jesus put it, God had at his command "more than twelve legions of angels" (Matt. 26:53) ready to come to his aid.

THE ETERNAL WAR (ii)

Psalm 74:1–23 (*cont'd*)

Verses 4–11, *What happened.* These verses seem to be the record of a first-hand witness as much as are the Gospel accounts of the crucifixion of Jesus. The bestial destruction described here took place *in the midst of thy holy place.* The words *holy place* in the Hebrew are "in the holiness". Thus they could apply not just to the Holy of Holies in the Temple, but also either to God himself, or even to a man. For (1) God is the holy one (Ps. 99:5); (2) David, God's adopted son, is also described as *thy holy one* (RSV "godly") in Ps. 16:10. Then (3) Acts 2:27 quotes this passage and refers it to Christ. Yet the NT affirms that (4) all who are called to be sons of God through Christ are described as "holy". So here we meet with the eternal question—why does God allow himself to lose the war again and again, even in the final and crucial moment of the death of Christ? Does evil have the final word so that it occasions the horrible cry that we hear: *O God, why dost thou cast us off for ever?* (verse 1) or, as the words may mean, "right into eternity"? And was that cry not echoed in the words of Jesus: "My God, my God, why hast thou forsaken me?" (Matt. 27:46; Ps. 22:1)?

The activities of these vandals, declares verse 7, was not just a lust for destruction of an earthly building, it was actually the destruction of *the dwelling place of thy name.* See 2 Kings 25:9–10. In order to eradicate the worship of Yahweh completely, these vandals even burned the local shrines in the villages of Judah. There the priests or Levites were the interpreters of the mind of God to their flocks. The line of prophets had begun with Samuel; now it was at an end. *We do not see our signs*, the people were saying, such as the Ark, the Temple, the priest. In their place the Babylonians had actually erected their own pagan signs (verse 4). God's enemies, it seemed, had been successful in creating hell on earth, an unending interminable state of hell that would last to all eternity. Their blasphemous act was not done *with* God, but against his will, and so, not being within his eternal purpose, it belonged to his eternal detestation. So it should be. But was it so? For now, says the psalmist, there was no one left to *see*, no one left to be a witness to God's people; nor was there any left to interpret the meaning of the historical moment they were living through. So the basic question remained unanswered— How can it be that our good God should also be the all-powerful God and yet let this defeat take place?

Verses 12–17, *But what about history?* But now, with a rush of faith, an individual in the congregation declares: "But God is *my* King! Look back and see how he has never ceased to win the war in the end over the powers of evil." Then this man goes on to point out that God had done so in both earth and heaven. God had brought Israel safely through the Red Sea and he had routed the army of the Egyptians. God had continued to *work salvation* (or "win the victory", as it may mean) *in the midst of the earth*. He had done so, ever since creation began! For at that point he had overcome *Leviathan*. That was the name (along with others) of the personified chaos monster to which Gen. 1:2 refers. At that time, as always!, the psalmist notes, God had brought good into being over against evil, for he had brought Light into being and had separated it off from Darkness. In this way he had "put Darkness in its place". Then he had used the carcass of Leviathan (who had seven *heads*), or the *Dragon*, as he was variously called, as food for the creatures of the wilderness. That is to say, he let evil feed upon itself. Thus from the primal watery deep he had brought forth, not chaos, but *ever-flowing* streams of water for the good of man. And again, from the original chaos he had created the orderly succession of the seasons (verse 16), where we find the same terms used as in Gen. 1:14. All Nebuchadnezzar had been able to do in 587 B.C. was just to smash and create more chaos. He had not won against the creative purposes of God at all!

The point is that God is the eternal Creator. He creates good over against, perhaps even out of, evil, by employing evil to create what is good. (See how this basic reality is described in picture form in the book of Revelation, especially chapters 13 and 20.) So what the psalmist is really saying here is that God has always acted everywhere in grace, even though man may not be able to discern what God is doing at the moment of his complaint. But in God's own time, he will use the blasphemous activities of the world's Nebuchadnezzars to create a greater good than before.

Verses 18–19. So then, since this is true of you, God, and since this is what you always do, why don't you do it now? Or is this in fact that moment in history that is the final end to your creative purpose and plan? You chose us to be your special people, your instrument, through and in whom you planned to create a loving human society. We are your *poor*, your humble servants. You have even called us your *dove* (which is the word Jonah in Hebrew), for you intended us to proclaim the Good News to Nineveh, the capital city of the *wild beasts* of the east. But now, these very people, these beasts, are reviling *thy name*. Will you not act for your own name's sake, if for nothing else?

Verses 20–23, *You promised, Lord*. You made a Covenant with our forefathers at Mount Sinai. It ran, "I will be your God, and you will be my people." But the primal darkness at Creation seems to have descended again both on this chosen land and on the hearts of your people. So your honour is at stake, God. In a word, God, just remember Nebuchadnezzar, who called himself "king of kings and lord of lords", and surely that was the most arrogant thing any human being could say.

Martin Luther, that extraordinary, intense, totally committed Reformer, moved to the depths of his being by the seeming victory of eternal evil that was visible in his days also, wrote about one particular moment in his experience of life. "I flung my sack before his door, and rubbed his ears with all his promises, so that he must hear me, if I were ever again to trust him."

How many a prisoner in a Nazi extermination camp or in a Soviet psychiatric hospital must have echoed the violent reaction of Martin Luther as he too cried the awful cry of *O God, why dost thou cast us off for ever?*

The Psalms are Scripture for both Jews and Christians. Today the thoughtful Jew who may have lost his whole family in the Auschwitz holocaust asks of the thoughtful Christian, "You say that in Christ God has redeemed the world from its sin, that the Cross of Christ is effective for man's redemption. How is it then that the world is clearly not redeemed, since evil still rules the hearts of men?" This psalm should urge both the Jew and the Christian to seek ever more deeply for an answer to this basic theological as well as very practical problem of faith.

None of the psalmists of ancient days wrote anything like the "pap" that passes in some areas today in the guise of "religious uplift". The psalmists took God seriously, life seriously, and the problem of evil seriously. A century ago the poet Robert Browning wrote: "God's in his heaven; all's right with the world". I wonder what our psalmist would have said to that.

GOD IS ALWAYS IN CHARGE

Psalm 75:1–10

To the choirmaster: according to Do Not Destroy. A Psalm of Asaph. A Song.

¹We give thanks to thee, O God; we give thanks;
we call on thy name and recount thy wondrous deeds.

²At the set time which I appoint
I will judge with equity.
³When the earth totters, and all its inhabitants,
it is I who keep steady its pillars. *Selah*

⁴I say to the boastful, "Do not boast,"
and to the wicked, "Do not lift up your horn;
⁵do not lift up your horn on high,
or speak with insolent neck."

⁶For not from the east or from the west
    and not from the wilderness comes lifting up;
⁷but it is God who executes judgment,
    putting down one and lifting up another.
⁸For in the hand of the Lord there is a cup,
    with foaming wine, well mixed;
and he will pour a draught from it,
    and all the wicked of the earth
    shall drain it down to the dregs.

⁹But I will rejoice for ever,
    I will sing praises to the God of Jacob.
¹⁰All the horns of the wicked he will cut off,
    but the horns of the righteous shall be exalted.

This is a song of praise. The tune that the folk in the Second Temple period used for it was entitled "Do Not Destroy"— probably a popular ditty of the day connected with the grape harvest (see Isaiah 65:8). As we saw in Psalm 74 the name by which God has made himself known to Israel is Immanuel, that is, God-is-with-us. Now, as the footnote to our Ps. 75 at verse 1 expresses it, "Your Name is Near". (See Isa. 30:26–27.) No wonder, then, *We give thanks to thee, O God* with joy and rejoicing, even when the Temple is just like a little island of joy in a turbulent world. In this way the author of this psalm seems to answer the doubts of the author of Ps. 74.

Verses 2–5, *God speaks: "In my good time". I*, not you, will seize the moment when I decide to act. My decision is to wait until the very foundations of life totter, for unless I do so, you will imagine you have been able to save yourselves. So I say (a) to those who think this way, "Don't be cocksure and suppose that you can run your own life in a world of pain, cancer and earthquakes." Then I say (b) to the arrogant (whom we met in Ps. 73), "Don't be insolent, and suppose that I will allow you to ride rough-shod over other people's lives and get rich off the persons you harass."

Verses 6–8, *A Temple minister expounds the words of God*. Nothing in the whole wide world, this minister declares, will give you the help you need, not your lucky stars, not your mediums, not your magic or superstition. Nor will the *wilderness* help you. The point is that the wilderness of Judea, which lay only a few hours' walk from Jerusalem to the south-east, was a place haunted by wild beasts and snakes and demons and jinns; in fact it represented the chaos spoken of in Ps. 74. If man should penetrate it, he would meet with the horror side of human existence. So we note with interest that both John the Baptist and Jesus spent time in it in retreat.

Lifting up refers to the action of a king. When a suppliant lay prone before him in fear and trembling, he had to await the royal decision whether to have him put to death or restore him to favour. This latter the king showed by putting his hand under the suppliant's chin and lifting up his head. In like manner, it is God alone who can make a similar decision, as the divine Judge in your lives, if he but lifts up your chin to show that he has pardoned and renewed you.

But both those whose chin he has lifted up and those with whom he has not so acted must accept the cup of judgment at the hand of the Lord, for he is the King who stoops from his throne to hand it to all his suppliants. This figure is to be found at Job 21:20; Isa. 51:17; and Jer. 25:15. Unlike modern western man who drinks his wine neat, in the Biblical period people drank their good *foaming wine well mixed* with water, usually three or four parts of water to one of wine. This, by the way, would probably be the case with the wine offered at the marriage in Cana of Galilee. Seldom, then, did one get drunk on such a welcome and cooling drink. No mention is now made of those whose chin the divine Judge had lifted up. Evidently they drank gladly, and, refreshed, got up and went away rejoicing. But *the wicked of the earth*, in their arrogance and self-assurance, seem to have drunk the cup greedily right *to the dregs*, and so, inebriated, brought upon themselves their own destruction. St. Paul seems to have had this and the parallel passages we have cited in mind when he made his solemn judgment in 1 Cor. 11:27–29.

Verses 9–10. But the psalmist is one of those who stands up on his feet, forgiven, renewed, refreshed, and rejoicing. Consequently, as the *ftn* to v. 9 says, "I will declare, bear witness, for ever, that the God who forgave Jacob after judging him at Bethel is the God who has forgiven me now." But he seems to go further, for he declares that from the joy he possesses God has given him an insight into the answer which the author of Ps. 73 received at 73:17, as well as into the deep issue which was the subject of Ps. 74. Consequently he is able to make it part of his witness that, even as God will cut off the power (*horns*) of the wicked and by means of this prevent them from continuing in their arrogant ways, so the power (*horns*) of those whom God has put right with himself he will now surely increase.

EVEN THE WRATH OF MAN CAN PRAISE GOD

Psalm 76:1–12

To the choirmaster: with stringed instruments. A Psalm of Asaph.
A Song.

¹In Judah God is known,
   his name is great in Israel.
²His abode has been established in Salem,
   his dwelling place in Zion.
³There he broke the flashing arrows,
   the shield, the sword, and the weapons of war.   *Selah*

⁴Glorious art thou, more majestic
   than the everlasting mountains.
⁵The stouthearted were stripped of their spoil;
   they sank into sleep;
 all the men of war
   were unable to use their hands.
⁶At thy rebuke, O God of Jacob,
   both rider and horse lay stunned.

⁷But thou, terrible art thou!
   Who can stand before thee
   when once thy anger is roused?
⁸From the heavens thou didst utter judgment;
   the earth feared and was still,
⁹when God arose to establish judgment
   to save all the oppressed of the earth.   *Selah*

¹⁰Surely the wrath of men shall praise thee;
  the residue of wrath thou wilt gird upon thee.
¹¹Make your vows to the Lord your God, and perform them;
  let all around him bring gifts
  to him who is to be feared,
¹²who cuts off the spirit of princes,
  who is terrible to the kings of the earth.

In Judah God is well known—for what? For rendering the holy city safe! Perhaps this psalm was composed to celebrate the defeat of Sennacherib in 701 B.C. in the days of the prophet Isaiah. The LXX seems to think so, for it adds into the psalm heading the words: "Regarding the Assyrian". We all know Lord Byron's poem on this theme:

  The Assyrian came down like a wolf on the fold,
    And his cohorts were gleaming in purple and gold;
  And the sheen of their spears was like stars on the sea,
    When the blue wave rolls nightly on deep Galilee.

And how:

  The Angel of Death spread his wings on the blast . . .
    And the might of the Gentile, unsmote by the sword,
  Hath melted like snow in the glance of the Lord!

The romantic story of what was God's victory and not man's is told in full in both 2 Kings 18:13–19:37 and in Isa. 36–37.

When the Pilgrim Fathers set sail from Europe they left home with the psalms on their lips. When they arrived at what is now Cape Cod, they called their first settlement Salem (that is, Jerusalem) and even as they did so they sang together in joy and gratitude this psalm we are reading.

So then, by his victory, God consolidated his abode in Salem, the city whose antiquity was established even in the days of Abraham. Salem is another spelling of the word *shalom*, which means "peace"; and it is a name that occurs in parallel with the city's theological title of Zion. That is why we can now sing with verse 4, *All light art thou* (rather than "glorious"). For it was to continue to be the city of peace and of salvation and of the new life of love that God intends for all people. Does this mean then that the whole universe is full of the light of love and of joy and peace? We shall see in a moment. For the *ftn* to verse 4 speaks of the *mountains of prey* or booty abandoned by Sennacherib's soldiers when they slipped into a coma, as the word *sleep* here implies, that is to say, into unnatural unconsciousness as they suffered some kind of paralysis or torpor of their limbs. Moreover, the word rendered *arrows* here can also mean "plague".

God is indeed *terrible*. For God's judgment is quite peculiar as sinful man sees it. For God brings *shalom out of* the forces of evil, as we saw in Ps. 74, using them, employing them to his own glory! This is something he always does, moreover. Verse 6 is a quotation from the great poem in Exod. 15, which celebrates God's creative action some five hundred years earlier. Thus God would surely continue to "milk" the powers of evil in all the years ahead. God had planned the defeat of Sennacherib, verse 8 declares; could we then, with our advantage of historical hindsight, not say that God had also planned the defeat of Pontius Pilate? So that out of that defeat he might *save all the oppressed of the earth*?

In verse 10 the psalmist, in a vivid piece of imagery, goes on to describe in other terms what he has just been saying. True to the Biblical revelation, he does not present us with a theological argument; rather he presents us with a theological picture. This is what the authors of Genesis do when they interpret God's saving activity as he wars against the powers of evil that have "flooded" over the whole earth. So literally, then, we read: "The survivors of your wrath you will make into your belt", when you, the Victorious Warrior, buckle on your armour in your war against evil. God's people, it seems, are to be as close to God as a belt is round the body. Consequently God's people are to share with God in the pain and suffering the warrior must undergo on the field of battle. Yet with this thought in mind: that this Warrior, the Living God, is bound to win in the end.

After his terrible experience of being sold into slavery by his brothers, at the end of the story, Joseph said to them when all were gathered together: "As for you, you meant evil against me, but God meant it for good" (Gen. 50:20). We note also God's handling of Pharaoh, and how that poor silly vassal of God behaved in all his crudity. Pharaoh did what he did so that, through the Exodus still to come, "my name may be declared throughout all the earth" (Exod. 9:16). Finally, at Acts 2:23 we hear from the lips of Peter how God had actually planned to use the wrath of men against Christ for the redemption of the world. Could it be, then, we might well ask the psalmist as we look for his advice, that the black cloud of the threat of nuclear war that hangs over us all today may be God's opportunity to evangelize the world in a new way?

Verses 11–12, *What we are to do about it.* The defeat of Sennacherib is meant for us also to contemplate. The command here is addressed to us, for we too belong in the Covenant people. We belong *around him* (verse 11), we who are the "outcome" of his wrath, whom he has fastened around himself as his belt. Our God is *terribly* mighty. Thus we are to *bring gifts to him who is to be feared*—remember the story of the Flood! As Zech. 12:1 says: God puts the spirit of man within him in the first place. Therefore he can just as easily *cut off* the spirit of man, even of princes and kings. This life of ours is never our own possession to do with as we will; it always remains the property of God or, better still, it remains the "place" where God's creative love and activity can operate. As Psalm 73 has declared, it is only too easy for dictators, prime ministers, presidents and all national leaders to succumb to the temptation of thinking that "it all depends on me"; and so there can be born within them an arrogance that leaves no place whatsoever for the Spirit of God to work through them. Such leaders, then, find themselves specially under the judgment of this terrible God. (See Isa. 18:4–5 and Rev. 14:18–19)

A DEEP HUMAN CRISIS

Psalm 77:1–20

To the choirmaster: according to Jeduthun. A Psalm of Asaph.

[1] I cry aloud to God,
     aloud to God, that he may hear me.
[2] In the day of my trouble I seek the Lord;
     in the night my hand is stretched out without wearying;
     my soul refuses to be comforted.

³I think of God, and I moan;
  I meditate, and my spirit faints.   *Selah*
⁴Thou dost hold my eyelids from closing;
  I am so troubled that I cannot speak.
⁵I consider the days of old,
  I remember the years long ago.
⁶I commune with my heart in the night;
  I meditate and search my spirit:
⁷"Will the Lord spurn for ever,
  and never again be favourable?
⁸Has his steadfast love for ever ceased?
  Are his promises at an end for all time?
⁹Has God forgotten to be gracious?
  Has he in anger shut up his compassion?"   *Selah*
¹⁰And I say, "It is my grief
  that the right hand of the Most High has changed."

¹¹I will call to mind the deeds of the Lord;
  yea, I will remember thy wonders of old.
¹²I will meditate on all thy work,
  and muse on thy might deeds.
¹³Thy way, O God, is holy.
  What god is great like our God?
¹⁴Thou art the God who workest wonders,
  who hast manifested thy might among the peoples.
¹⁵Thou didst with thy arm redeem thy people,
  the sons of Jacob and Joseph.   *Selah*

¹⁶When the waters saw thee, O God,
  when the waters saw thee, they were afraid,
  yea, the deep trembled.
¹⁷The clouds poured out water;
  the skies gave forth thunder;
  thy arrows flashed on every side.
¹⁸The crash of thy thunder was in the whirlwind;
  thy lightnings lighted up the world;
  the earth trembled and shook.
¹⁹Thy way was through the sea,
  thy path through the great waters;
  yet thy footprints were unseen.
²⁰Thou didst lead thy people like a flock
  by the hand of Moses and Aaron.

The Psalms both teach us how to pray and also help us to pray as we ought. They appear to differ from other Scripture in that they are the words of men and women as they speak to God, while the rest of the OT claims to be the Word of God addressed to men and women. However, a thoughtful reading of the Psalms leads us to make the discovery that God must have inspired their writing just as much as any other Scripture is inspired. This is because once the psalmist has cried to the Lord he makes the "revealed" discovery that God is a God who cares.

This is a very ego-centred psalm. It is full of I, I, I . . . In other words it gives us the prayer of an ordinary person. But he is a sinful person who is in very great trouble. Perhaps the psalmist made this prayer when, as one of the exiles, he was taken off to Babylon in 587 B.C. Consequently he would feel that he had lost, not only his home, means of livelihood and place of worship, but God himself. At any rate, he places the blame for his situation firmly in God's lap. When he thinks of God he *moans*. When he *meditates*, his *spirit faints*; he cannot sleep—and he even blames God for that.

He remembers what it was like in the old happy days of long ago in Jerusalem. How different life is now in exile! For it seems that the psalmist is in exile, not just from his city, but actually from God himself, or worse still, that God is in exile from him! Has God altogether forgotten *the promises* he made through Moses when he said: "I will be with you" (see Ps. 73)? Has God repudiated his Covenant with Israel his own people that he also made in the days of Moses? Has he withdrawn his *hesed*, his loyal, covenantal, *steadfast love* that was meant to last for ever? Has he now *shut up his compassion*, his "mother-love", a thing which seems to be quite inconceivable of God? (Isa. 49:14–16). Finally, having ruminated on all this in prayer (see verse 1), we hear him declaring, virtually, "Without God's grace I shall go mad". *It is my grief* (even to think) *that the right hand of the Most High* (by means of which God reveals himself to his world) *could change*— that is to say, that God could be untrue to himself!

Verses 11–15, *Who is it that has changed?* It is at this point, however, that we begin to observe God answering the psalmist's prayer almost step by step. Even as the psalmist makes his dreadful accusations against God, he recognizes that the thoughts that arise in his mind are not his own thoughts but that they have been inspired and put there by God. Step by step he comes to recognize the stupidity of the saying that prayer is merely auto-suggestion, that it is merely a process of thought that does not need to presuppose the interference of God at all.

What happens to him is that it is *he* who changes; for in meditating upon what God has *done*—not speculating philosophically about the existence of God—he comes to see that, of course, it is not God who has changed from what he once was; rather it is he himself who has changed, changed from a man of faith into a man of doubt. So now *he calls to mind the deeds of the Lord.* That is evidently a good way to begin to pray! In fact Bible study and prayer are two sides to the one coin.

What is his order of thought? He declares (1) that *God is holy*, that is, utterly other than sinful, mortal man; (2) that God reveals himself in acts and deeds in human life—a thing that no other god does. (3) He recognizes that God is eternal. This is what he rediscovers by using the word *wonders*, for that word means "belonging to the other world".

(4) Next he "reckons up", which the word *meditates* means here, *all thy work*. Notice here also how his mind moves. Unconsciously he has jumped from (a) talking about God, to (b) talking to God. Then he finds himself in prayer (c) confessing God's greatness, and finally (d) he seizes on the fact that of course (how silly he has been to forget it!) he belongs to that *people* whom God has already *redeemed!*

All this happens in his mind, just because he sets himself off to *remember*. Happens, we ask? No, surely the God of all grace has aided his mind to take all these steps, each one following the other in a wonderful sequence.

Verses 16–20, *I belong in the cosmos*. These verses look like a separate psalm. But of course they are not. What has happened to him in prayer is that God has led him to make the ultimate discovery that, tiny, doubting, unimportant sinful creature that he is, nevertheless he is all-important to God, and that God cares for him as if the whole of his care for the mighty universe was focused like a laser beam onto this one tiny soul, now in exile in a foreign land.

The point is that these verses describe in the traditional way, as we have already seen in other psalms, the mighty acts of God (a) in creation and then (b) in redemption. The section verses 16–18 describes God's agonized wrestling with the powers of "non-being" at the creation of the world, when he brought order out of chaos, and accomplished this just by the utterance of his almighty Word. The word *deep* in verse 16 is a kind of superlative plural. We might render it in English by a phrase such as "the total chaos of the primal ocean of non-being" (Gen. 1:2, 7; Exod. 20:4). Then verses 19–20 speak of the creation of God's people at the time of the Exodus from Egypt and of the crossing of the "Reed Sea" (as its name means in Hebrew), now representing the waters of chaos, as indeed it was for that fleeing rabble. No man can see God and live, God himself had said to Moses when he marched just that one invisible step ahead of them as they entered the Wilderness. In a parabolic manner verse 19 speaks of God's voice not being heard by them as if it were "a step ahead". Moses and Aaron had only to place their feet where God had already trod. And so the poem ends in the peace and quiet of a pastoral idyll. For its writer has now rediscovered that God had led his flock from the realm of chaos into the *shalom* of the land of milk and honey, into the fold of his love and joy.

Perhaps these last five lines were added from a still more ancient hymn once the very personal prayer of the psalmist had been adopted and brought into use for public worship. But the effect has been a powerful one. What has happened is that all of us, both the Temple worshippers of those far-away days, and the church worshippers of our own day alike, find that when we have to face some kind of "exile" from God, whether it be loss of faith, the onslaught of cancer, the death of a child, the outbreak of war, through really earnest prayer God will lovingly lead us back, first to rediscover what he is like, and then to show how his almighty redemptive purpose for the whole cosmos is actually focused on me!

PICTURE THEOLOGY (i)

Psalm 78:1–8

A Maskil of Asaph.

¹Give ear, O my people, to my teaching;
　incline your ears to the words of my mouth!
²I will open my mouth in a parable;
　I will utter dark sayings from of old,
³things that we have heard and known,
　that our fathers have told us.
⁴We will not hide them from their children,
　but tell to the coming generation
the glorious deeds of the Lord, and his might,
　and the wonders which he has wrought.

⁵He established a testimony in Jacob,
　and appointed a law in Israel,
which he commanded our fathers
　to teach to their children;
⁶that the next generation might know them,
　the children yet unborn,
and arise and tell them to their children,
⁷　so that they should set their hope in God,
and not forget the works of God,
　but keep his commandments;
⁸and that they should not be like their fathers,
　a stubborn and rebellious generation,
a generation whose heart was not steadfast,
　whose spirit was not faithful to God.

Verses 1–8, *A sermon in verse.* Perhaps this sermon was preached to a crowded congregation at one of the national festivals. If so, it had been very carefully prepared, as a sermon ought to be. Most of the worshippers would be illiterate (just as most worshippers today are "Biblically illiterate"), but illiterates, like the blind, often have excellent memories. By turning his sermon into verse this preacher thus helped many people to go home remembering what he had said almost word for word. Then, in later centuries, when his sermon was included in "The Hymn Book of the Second Temple", countless other people—and now ourselves—are grateful to him for having produced a sermon that is easy both to remember and to sing.

We have already noted that almost certainly there were people of influence like the great Isaiah present at these festivals. We call them today "cultic prophets", but we might understand better what they were if we called them by our word "minister". For their function was to preach, teach, and give counsel to those who came up from the villages and asked for help in understanding the faith of their fathers. The priests had their own tasks to perform. They had to organize the sacrifices, look after, feed and clean up the animals in their stalls, and after the sacrifices were over, clean out the stalls where the animals had been! They probably also organized the processions which we have met with in earlier psalms, and saw to the choirs and orchestras, and looked after their music manuscripts and instruments. The ministers, then, had the task of explaining to simple, unlearned people what God had said and done in Israel's history. In the Middle Ages, in the same way, illiterate people learned their faith from looking at the stained glass windows in their cathedral churches.

Our minister now speaks to his congregation in a way that we might well copy. He tells them he is going to speak *in a parable*, as Jesus did centuries later. The word *mashal* means more than that however. Our Biblical book of Proverbs, for example, is called in Hebrew "The Book of Mashals". In fact a *mashal* was any form of teaching that the hearer could "see" with his mind's eye. As Martin Luther comments at this point, "There is more philosophy and wisdom in this verse than if Aristotle had written a thousand *Metaphysics*."

Parallel with the word *mashal* our preacher-teacher uses the word *dark sayings*. This is one word, *hidoth*. It might well be translated by "secrets". But these could not have been secrets in the literal sense if his generation had heard them and understood them sufficiently to be able to pass them on down the generations to come. What he means, of course, is that God's *glorious deeds* take on meaning only when seen by the eyes of faith. That is why it is our duty to open the eyes of our children to look beyond the literal story of events and so discover their eternal significance in the purposes of God. Moreover, none of us is an isolated individual, nor are our children. It is only as members of a believing family that children discover the reality of faith. For faith is something you "see" or "feel" parabolically in the family situation. And especially is this so when parents and children grow together in grace and understanding. It is God's supreme "secret", known only to those who grow up within the Covenant of grace.

To that end God, says our preacher, had taken the initiative. He first *established a testimony in Jacob, and appointed a law in Israel*, Jacob and Israel being the same character, the progenitor of the whole people of God. *A testimony* means something that is an aid to memory or a warning that what it represents comes from God (Exod. 16:34). The two tablets carrying the Ten Commandments are given this name at Exod. 31:18. And then the word *law* is the same as that translated in verse 1 by *teaching!* When we recognize that this is so, our eyes are opened to the significance of the "five books of Moses". Because in the *Torah* God has revealed his will, so that coming generations might learn what that is, from the experience of the past. For example, God's people are not to be self-centred as their fathers had been of old, but are to walk humbly with their God, as Mic. 6:8 puts it. So then, says our preacher, God first acted, and then he taught. (We should note that that is what Luke says about Jesus in Acts 1:1).

PICTURE THEOLOGY (ii)

Psalm 78:9–31

⁹The Ephraimites, armed with the bow,
  turned back on the day of battle.
¹⁰They did not keep God's covenant,
  but refused to walk according to his law.

¹¹They forgot what he had done,
and the miracles that he had shown them.
¹²In the sight of their fathers he wrought marvels
in the land of Egypt, in the fields of Zoan.
¹³He divided the sea and let them pass though it,
and made the waters stand like a heap.
¹⁴In the daytime he led them with a cloud,
and all the night with a fiery light.
¹⁵He cleft rocks in the wilderness,
and gave them drink abundantly as from the deep.
¹⁶He made streams come out of the rock,
and caused waters to flow down like rivers.

¹⁷Yet they sinned still more against him,
rebelling against the Most High in the desert.
¹⁸They tested God in their heart
by demanding the food they craved.
¹⁹They spoke against God, saying,
"Can God spread a table in the wilderness?
²⁰He smote the rock so that water gushed out
and streams overflowed.
Can he also give bread,
or provide meat for his people?"

²¹Therefore, when the Lord heard, he was full of wrath;
a fire was kindled against Jacob,
his anger mounted against Israel;
²²because they had no faith in God,
and did not trust his saving power.
²³Yet he commanded the skies above,
and opened the doors of heaven;
²⁴and he rained down upon them manna to eat,
and gave them the grain of heaven.
²⁵Man ate of the bread of the angels;
he sent them food in abundance.
²⁶He caused the east wind to blow in the heavens,
and by his power he led out the south wind;
²⁷he rained flesh upon them like dust,
winged birds like the sand of the seas;
²⁸he let them fall in the midst of their camp,
all around their habitations.

²⁹And they ate and were well filled,
   for he gave them what they craved.
³⁰But before they had sated their craving,
   while the food was still in their mouths,
³¹the anger of God rose against them
   and he slew the strongest of them,
   and laid low the picked men of Israel.

Verses 9–16, *Tell them the old, old story*. Each generation of children was thus to learn the old, old story. But they were not to hear of it as a series of mere events. In verses 9–11 we are not even told all the facts about what the Ephraimites did. These were that northern half of the people of God who had formed themselves into a separate nation after the death of Solomon. What they did was evidently contrary to the will of God within the Covenant. Our minister declares that they forgot God's *miracles that he had shown them* and relied only on their own resources. That, then, he said, was the "secret" of the events that parents were to tell their children, the "secret" that God is involved in all that happens. It was the same too with the whole story of the Exodus and of the Wilderness wanderings; God's actions then were all *marvels*. What happened in them was not just a series of natural events; rather they were parabolic pictures of God revealing himself in his living purpose for Israel.

Verses 17–31. The preacher now declares that his people's forefathers had been blind to the *meaning* of the events they were living through. They had not grasped, for example, the *meaning* (not the fact!) of the Covenant he had given them. We see from this the danger of allowing good-hearted, believing girls of sixteen years of age to teach children in Sunday School without having received very careful instruction in the Gospel. Such girls may, indeed, "know their Bibles", know the literal facts of the story they are telling. But are they able, as our preacher emphasizes, to solve the riddle, the secret, of these facts? A literal understanding of God's mighty acts may (and did, in Israel's case) lead to mere suffering and disbelief. "How could God spread a table in the wilderness?" old Israel had asked, just as the modern schoolboy asks with scorn, "How could Jesus have walked on the water?" Is our sixteen-year-old Sunday School teacher able to explain to her class the parabolic nature of these two stories and so be able to unravel the secret (*the dark sayings from of old*, as verse 2 put it) of how God used his mighty acts to reveal himself in love?

For example, at verse 13 we hear (and let us remember we are reading poetry) that God made the *waters* of the Red (or rather Reed) Sea *stand like a heap*. That is *mashal* language, that is theology in picture language, that is indeed parable in the way our present-day hymn is parable: "In the beauty of the lilies Christ was born across the sea". Literally the statement is nonsense. But behind such poetry, surely there lies a "secret".

When the book of Exodus was finally edited after this psalm was written, this line of poetry (verse 13) was incorporated into the description of the crossing of the Sea as it is told us in Exodus, in order to explain the *mashal* involved. The basic story, reported as an incident in history, runs: "And the Lord drove the sea back by a strong east wind, and made the sea dry land..." (Exod. 14:21). But the editor then added here: "The waters were a wall to them on their right hand and on their left". He used picture language, because of course God had always been a wall to his people on the right hand and on the left, in the same way that David had discovered that God had always been his Rock. It is a pity that Cecil B. de Mille, having had a modern scientific education, could not understand how God could be either a Rock or a Wall. He supposed that, since the Bible is inspired, there could only be one literal meaning. And so that mighty "Hollywood spectacular" of his showed the world two great vertical walls of glass holding back the waters of the Red Sea. The unfortunate result of such manipulative photography was that it made stronger rather than weaker the view of so many people today that the Bible is "just a lot of fairy tales".

Then in the Wilderness, the minister goes on to say, God gave Israel pure water to drink that had surged up from "the waters under the earth". This language is part of his *mashal*. For he is telling us that the goodness of God showed itself when he gave his people the water of life that had been transformed out of the chaos of evil that lies under the earth (Exod. 20:4). Even then, however, they *demanded* food instead of trusting in God. So God gave them *the bread of angels* (more *mashal* surely), *and rained flesh upon them like dust, winged birds like the sand of the seas.* But the Israelites refused to regard even such manifestations as evidence of the love and care of God.

So of course it followed that God had to *kindle a fire against Jacob.* (See how this verse is taken up in Matt. 3:11 with still more *mashal* language.) They had committed the intolerable sin of not taking God seriously (verse 22). They could not see that the "secret" of the fire was the burning heat of God's lovingkindness and care for his own beloved people.

REVELATION THROUGH TRADITION (i)

Psalm 78:32–55

> ³²In spite of all this they still sinned;
>   despite his wonders they did not believe.
> ³³So he made their days vanish like a breath,
>   and their years in terror.
> ³⁴When he slew them, they sought for him;
>   they repented and sought God earnestly.
> ³⁵They remembered that God was their rock,
>   the Most High God their redeemer.
> ³⁶But they flattered him with their mouths;
>   they lied to him with their tongues.
> ³⁷Their heart was not steadfast toward him;
>   they were not true to his covenant.
> ³⁸Yet he, being compassionate,
>   forgave their iniquity,
>   and did not destroy them;
>   he restrained his anger often,
>   and did not stir up all his wrath.
> ³⁹He remembered that they were but flesh,
>   a wind that passes and comes not again.
> ⁴⁰How often they rebelled against him in the wilderness
>   and grieved him in the desert!

⁴¹They tested him again and again,
  and provoked the Holy One of Israel.
⁴²They did not keep in mind his power,
  or the day when he redeemed them from the foe;
⁴³when he wrought his signs in Egypt,
  and his miracles in the fields of Zoan.
⁴⁴He turned their rivers to blood,
  so that they could not drink of their streams.
⁴⁵He sent among them swarms of flies, which devoured them,
  and frogs, which destroyed them.
⁴⁶He gave their crops to the caterpillar,
  and the fruit of their labour to the locust.
⁴⁷He destroyed their vines with hail,
  and their sycamores with frost.
⁴⁸He gave over their cattle to the hail,
  and their flocks to thunderbolts.
⁴⁹He let loose on them his fierce anger,
  wrath, indignation, and distress,
  a company of destroying angels.
⁵⁰He made a path for his anger;
  he did not spare them from death,
  but gave their lives over to the plague.
⁵¹He smote all the first-born in Egypt,
  the first issue of their strength in the tents of Ham.
⁵²Then he led forth his people like sheep,
  and guided them in the wilderness like a flock.
⁵³He led them in safety, so that they were not afraid;
  but the sea overwhelmed their enemies.
⁵⁴And he brought them to his holy land,
  to the mountain which his right hand had won.
⁵⁵He drove out nations before them;
  he apportioned them for a possession
  and settled the tribes of Israel in their tents.

However, there were times, this sermon declares, when the children of Israel did repent and run for refuge back home to *God their Rock* (David's old *mashal!*), viz. the Most High God. Not just to Yahweh, let us note, their own Covenant Lord, but the

Lord God Almighty. They supposed they were flattering him by giving him such a title. The Most High God, however, ended their *days* in a puff, and their *years* in a stampede (a telling pun in the Hebrew). So then the Wilderness generation died right out. They had been disloyal to the God who had given them his Covenant. Then came the next generation. Moved by his "mother love" (verse 38) God forgave them, however, holding back his righteous *wrath* time and again, *remembering that they were but flesh*. Once, when it came time for an old minister to retire, he was asked, if he had his days of preaching over again, what would be his main theme. To which he replied simply, "The forgiveness of God".

The psalmist now virtually repeats his sermon which he had given from verse 12 on, in order that his congregation should really take it all in. The forgiveness of God! It was now a new generation, of course, that was listening to his words. So they in their turn had to be told the old, old story. And so he told them of the plagues in Egypt, and of the *signs* that God had worked for their ancestors and the miracles he had wrought at the Red Sea. He says a new thing, however. He tells us that God sent against the Egyptians *a company of destroying angels, and gave their lives over to the plague* (verse 49). The old AV misled our fathers before the RSV was produced by translating "he sent evil angels". Angels are neither good nor bad. They are only messengers, ministers of God, and convey God's loving caring concern for mankind. This care had to be shown to the Egyptians by turning upon them God's heated, fiery love and reconstructive purpose. With this, then, our poet continues the story, the history, of Israel up till the time when they entered the Promised Land.

REVELATION THROUGH TRADITION (ii)

Psalm 78:56–72

56Yet they tested and rebelled against the Most High God,
    and did not observe his testimonies,
57but turned away and acted treacherously like their fathers;
    they twisted like a deceitful bow.

⁵⁸For they provoked him to anger with their high places;
    they moved him to jealousy with their graven images.
⁵⁹When God heard, he was full of wrath,
    and he utterly rejected Israel.
⁶⁰He forsook his dwelling at Shiloh,
    the tent where he dwelt among men,
⁶¹and delivered his power to captivity,
    his glory to the hand of the foe.
⁶²He gave his people over to the sword,
    and vented his wrath on his heritage.
⁶³Fire devoured their young men,
    and their maidens had no marriage song.
⁶⁴Their priests fell by the sword,
    and their widows made no lamentation.
⁶⁵Then the Lord awoke as from sleep,
    like a strong man shouting because of wine.
⁶⁶And he put his adversaries to rout;
    he put them to everlasting shame.

⁶⁷He rejected the tent of Joseph,
    he did not choose the tribe of Ephraim;
⁶⁸but he chose the tribe of Judah,
    Mount Zion, which he loves.
⁶⁹He built his sanctuary like the high heavens,
    like the earth, which he has founded for ever.
⁷⁰He chose David his servant,
    and took him from the sheepfolds;
⁷¹from tending the ewes that had young he brought him
    to be the shepherd of Jacob his people,
    of Israel his inheritance.
⁷²With upright heart he tended them,
    and guided them with skilful hand.

Verses 56–66. Even then, however, having received from God's hand the land of milk and honey, *they rebelled against the Most High God*, just as their fathers had done before them. And so we hear next of the period of the Judges, and of how the newcomers took to the worship of the gods of the Canaanites. *God heard* (verse 59) their worship and counteracted, so to speak. To use a modern *mashal*, he overflowed in *wrath* like a volcano erupting.

Full of wrath he utterly rejected Israel, his chosen people, his first-born son (Exod. 4:22)—or did he do so? Note what Hosea has to say on this at Hos. 11:8–9. Hosea had realized that there is another factor in the situation which is no less than the cross that is there in the heart of God. So our poet was aware that, when Samaria fell to the enemy in 721 B.C. (the probable date of the first edition of our psalm) and many of its inhabitants were murdered and others were taken off into exile far away (verses 62–64), God himself was grieved to the heart. All Israel mourned as in the poem of Jane Elliott about the Battle of Flodden: "The flowers o' the forest are all wede away".

But there was more to it than that. God had now *removed his glory*, that is, the visible expression of his loving, saving purpose, removing it from Israel, and so leaving her empty and hollow, and had placed it *into the hand of the foe!* In other words, God did this terrible thing—to himself! For his glory in the last resort was his unique relationship to this sinful son of his, this sinful bride. For Hosea had drawn the two *mashals*, that of God's son and that of God's wife, in picture expressions to indicate the two deepest possible relationships known to man. And God had given his Self into the hands of Israel's enemies! What an extraordinary God this is! What sinful human being could ever have created the God of the Bible out of his own sinful ideas of what a god should be like?

The redeemed people, redeemed from Egypt, had committed the basic sin of breaking the First Commandment (verse 58). Note, when examining the other nine, how all of them depend upon keeping the first one, upon remaining loyal to God, the only God. That was how Hosea and then Jeremiah could picture Israel's "going awhoring after other gods" as adultery (Hos. chs. 1–2, 11:1–4; Jer. 31:20, 32). The word *jealousy* describes the passionate reaction of the husband when he discovers that his wife has been consorting with other lovers behind his back (verse 58). As a result, then, God *forsook his dwelling at Shiloh* (verse 60), the place where he was first worshipped before Solomon built the Temple in Jerusalem (1 Sam. chs. 1–3; Jer. 7:12–14; 26:6). It was *the tent where God had caused his name to dwell among men*, and it had been destroyed by the Philistines. That is to say, God had let Shiloh be destroyed. The divine plan of love for the whole of mankind seemed to have reached a full stop.

Then the Lord awoke as from sleep (verse 65). What a daring *mashal* to use! But more so even the second line! Clearly God had not *utterly rejected Israel* after all. What a strange God this is, to reveal himself to his chosen people, first by suggesting that he had given his Self into the hands of Israel's enemies, and then by making them imagine he was asleep or in a drunken stupor! But God was showing them that he waited to the last possible moment *to awake from sleep*, in order to let Israel see that she was absolutely worthy of the final punishment, which is death. So it was only *at that moment* that God revealed once again that he can only be true to his Covenant. God keeps holding on to mankind even when they are *in extremis*, for his grace lies behind all that he does—or does not seem to do.

Verses 67–72. In 721 B.C. the Northern Kingdom, Samaria, that is *the tribe of Ephraim* (who was the son of *Joseph*), was taken by the Assyrians. So God *rejected the tent of Joseph*, the word *tent* reminding us that God's people are always on the march through history. "Rejected", however, does not mean "repudiated". It means that, instead of Joseph, whom he saw was of no use to him in his purposes, *he chose the tribe of Judah* to the south, where Jerusalem lay and where *Mount Zion* was. He tells us that it was in *Mount Zion* that *God* had built his Temple (not Solomon!) and had "built it up to the sky", a *mashal* again, surely, meaning that all men would one day turn to it, recognizing it to be the place of his glory (Isa. 2:2–3). And there he *chose* and installed *David*, turning him from being the shepherd of sheep into the shepherd of the flock of God. Finally, the last line declares that David *did* God's will with complete devotion.

That, of course, is an idealization of the situation, for David was a great sinner. Yet the point is, he was always faithful to the Covenant, despite his personal sins. And so God called him a *saint*, as he called the whole people of God saints while they were faithful to the Covenant.

This psalm is about history. A Dutch theologian has written:

"When we can no longer find meaning in history, it means that we do not understand ourselves". It is a tremendous thought that the whole history of God's people, right since the days of Abraham and David, now passes through me. The ongoing movement of God in history is like a skewer that picks up and passes through a whole line of pieces of meat, so that the whole shish-kebab is connected by the metal skewer. So the history of God's activities, begun with the Exodus, now picks up and passes through me, and then through my children, and then through my children's children. What a responsibility I have then to ensure that my children are securely in the Covenant of Grace!

OH HORROR!

Psalm 79: 1–13

A Psalm of Asaph.

¹O God, the heathen have come into thy inheritance;
    they have defiled thy holy temple;
    they have laid Jerusalem in ruins.
²They have given the bodies of thy servants
    to the birds of the air for food,
    the flesh of thy saints to the beasts of the earth.
³They have poured out their blood like water
    round about Jerusalem.
    and there was none to bury them.
⁴We have become a taunt to our neighbours,
    mocked and derided by those round about us.

⁵How long, O Lord? Wilt thou be angry for ever?
    Will thy jealous wrath burn like fire?
⁶Pour out thy anger on the nations
    that do not know thee,
  and on the kingdoms
    that do not call on thy name!
⁷For they have devoured Jacob,
    and laid waste his habitation.

[8]Do not remember against us the iniquities of our forefathers;
   let thy compassion come speedily to meet us,
   for we are brought very low.
[9]Help us, O God of our salvation,
   for the glory of thy name;
 deliver us, and forgive our sins,
   for thy name's sake!
[10]Why should the nations say,
   "Where is their God?"
 Let the avenging of the outpoured blood of thy servants
   be known among the nations before our eyes!

[11]Let the groans of the prisoners come before thee;
   according to thy great power preserve those doomed to die!
[12]Return sevenfold into the bosom of our neighbours
   the taunts with which they have taunted thee, O Lord!
[13]Then we thy people, the flock of thy pasture,
   will give thanks to thee for ever;
   from generation to generation we will recount thy praise.

Verses 1–4. In this psalm we have moved forward in time to the final and complete END, not only of Israel's history, but also of Israel as a corporate body, the people of God. Amos had foreseen it coming. It is his word for *end* that is used here (Amos 8:2–3). But the end was delayed through God's grace and long-suffering. Two centuries after Amos, Ezekiel used the same word, at Ezek. 7:2, 3, 6, and declared that the end had come! For in the year 587 B.C. Nebuchadnezzar and his vandals, *the heathen*, did to Jerusalem just what verses 1–4 describe so excruciatingly. But the cry of horror raised in that year has been echoed again and again in history. Read 2 Kings 25:8–21 and the Book of Lamentations to learn about the destruction of Jerusalem referred to in this psalm. But then read 1 Maccabees at chapter 1 and chapter 3:45 to find that horror repeated by Antiochus Epiphanes only a century and a half before the birth of Christ. But then again the Romans obliterated Jerusalem in A.D. 70, the Huns sacked "the eternal city" of Rome in A.D. 410, the Marxists in this century stripped the churches of Russia and turned them into museums, and so on.

The horror described here brought about more than mere terror, for it was an act of both profanity and of blasphemy. Note the pronoun in *"thy* holy temple"; these words speak of profanity against God. *They have given the bodies of thy servants* . . *the flesh of thy saints* (those whom God had redeemed and whom he had "put right" with himself) *to the beasts of the earth.* That was profanity against man. For one always gave proper burial even to one's worst enemies (see Jer. 22:18–19). One hears an echo of this indictment when the name Hiroshima crops up in conversation.

Verses 5–7, *Have mercy, Lord.* Why ask God for mercy? Because what had happened to the holy city was *God's* choice of action, not just man's. As Jeremiah, who lived through the sack of the city, had declared, speaking for God, "It was done by *my servant Nebuchadnezzar"* (Jer. 25:9). Why had God picked on Israel in this way? Why hadn't he turned his wrath upon those heathen vandals? For it was they who had desecrated *his* holy city and *his* holy Temple. Moreover, they had also *devoured Jacob.* This phrase means what today we would describe as "total war". The heathen had destroyed Jerusalem's buildings, looted its treasures, cut down the fruit trees and stopped up the wells of the surrounding suburbs and countryside (see Jer. 10:25).

Verses 8–13, *Have we deserved all this*? Or did God act thus because our forefathers sinned before us? When the Crusaders swarmed over the Christian city of Constantinople in 1203–4, and when the Turks sacked it in 1453, or when Lenin proscribed the Christian faith in the Soviet Empire, or when the Allied bombers almost obliterated the city of Dresden with its many beautiful churches and art galleries, did those suffering such horrors ask the same questions as our psalmist does now? The psalmist of course seeks an answer to his own question. He tries other tacks: (1) God, he says, you are not being true to yourself. You call yourself the Saviour God (Isa. 43:3, 11). Well, then, why don't you save us? *For your name's sake*, at least, for it is "Saviour". Then (2) he reminds God that, just as Joel had already pointed out (Joel 2:17), he was upsetting his own plan of letting the heathen know about his saving love! Consequently (3) God should let the nations see that he was actually a God of vengeance! A God of justice should not only be just, he should let the world see his justice being done. Finally (4) he argued, God was the God who was ever mindful of the poor, and who heard the cry of the prisoner. But clearly he was not listening now.

There is a bas-relief from Egypt showing prisoners of war being led up to Pharaoh to be beheaded. That is what the Israelites now felt like. From Babylonian documents we learn of prisoners in stinking dungeons, *doomed to die*, "on death row". In the Middle Ages prisoners of war were normally held in filthy damp dungeons and kept deliberately at starvation level, in almost total darkness, chained to a wall. G. G. Coulton, the historian, so describes the dungeons of Carcassone in France, in the days of the Inquisition. Then there was the so-called bottle dungeon in St. Andrews, Scotland, and the dungeons of Mont St. Michel on the French side of the English Channel, that gloriously beautiful building—on the outside—but which was hell within. Could it be the plan of God to keep Israel in such a state?

The psalmist ends his cry with still two other suggestions he puts to God. One is that God should take vengeance upon *his* enemies sevenfold, because God is so much more, seven times more, powerful than man. The other is that *we, thy people, would then give thanks to thee for ever and recount thy praise from generation to generation.*

We today have no right to judge our psalmist for his evident misunderstanding of God's ways with Israel. He had prayed that *the outpoured blood of thy servants be known among the nations* (see verse 10). He was more right than he knew. For only thus could the world discover the creative, redemptive power of suffering love; and only thus, St. Paul might add, would the people of God be given the strength to share in the suffering of Christ, "becoming like him in his death" (2 Cor. 1:5; Phil. 3:10; see also 1 Peter 4:13) or, to use the thought of this psalm, "becoming like him in his END", thereby attaining *the subsequent glory* (1 Peter 1:11).

All unwittingly the psalmist has presented us in his psalm with a theology of the work of Christ.

SHEPHERD OF ISRAEL

Psalm 80:1–7

To the choirmaster: according to Lilies.
A Testimony of Asaph. A Psalm.

¹Give ear, O Shepherd of Israel,
  thou who leadest Joseph like a flock!
 Thou who art enthroned upon the cherubim, shine forth
² before Ephraim and Benjamin and Manasseh!
 Stir up thy might,
  and come to save us!

³Restore us, O God;
  let thy face shine, that we may be saved!

⁴O Lord God of hosts,
  how long wilt thou be angry with thy people's prayers?
⁵Thou has fed them with the bread of tears,
  and given them tears to drink in full measure.
⁶Thou dost make us the scorn of our neighbours;
  and our enemies laugh among themselves.

⁷Restore us, O God of hosts;
  let thy face shine, that we may be saved!

We jump back a century with this psalm, to the period after 721 B.C., when the area named *Joseph*, comprising *Ephraim, Benjamin, Manasseh*, and more not named here, all components of the northern tribes, were removed into exile by the Assyrians (compare Ps. 78:67). So it is a group of *us* (note the word), we poor exiles from the north, who write this pitiful psalm. The exiles do not take God's action in using the Assyrians in this way (see Isa. 5:24–30) lying down. They make a fighting, prayerful response. We hear the words: "My God, why...? How long...?" as in Ps. 22. The exile of God's son Israel (Exod. 4:22), happening as it did in three stages, in 721, 597, and 587 B.C., forms a historical situation of such a terrible nature that it compels and demands an answer in the same way as does the crucifixion of Jesus in the NT.

One issue is the extreme complexity of human relationships, the, humanly speaking, inexplicable relativities of history. The OT writers show that God handles these with ease and weaves them all into his purposes. For example, iron-smelting began somewhere in Asia Minor about 1400 B.C. The Hittites who lived there were thus the first to use iron weapons, with which they easily routed opposing forces armed merely with bronze swords; for iron swords could cut through bronze. Then the Assyrians succeeded the Hittites. By 800 B.C. they had a completely iron-ized army. With it they dominated their neighbours for two and a half centuries; with it they overran the whole of the Levant, including little Israel and Judah.

Verses 1–3, *The first prayer.* This sensitive people, this group of exiles, prays to the God whom David, in the 23rd Psalm, knew to be his living *Shepherd.* At Gen. 48:15 and 49:24 their ancestor Joseph, in the days of his wanderings, had declared that God had shepherded him all his days. But after the break between the north and the south in 921 at the death of Solomon, the southern kingdom had become known politically as Judah, and had allowed the northern group of tribes to use the name Israel politically for itself. This was despite the fact that "Israel" continued to be the theological name for the whole people of God, both north and south. But God was their transcendent Shepherd, enthroned, as Isaiah (chap. 6) had discovered, high and lifted up. In his vision Isaiah had seen seraphim attend God. This psalm speaks rather of *cherubim.* These watched over the Ark of the Covenant (Exod. 25:18–22; see also Ps. 99:1) which God had given to his people in the days of Moses.

Yet, as an eastern shepherd was expected to do, Israel's Shepherd must have gone ahead of his sheep and been watching over his forlorn people, scattered now as they were (see Ezek. 34:11) on the plains of Mesopotamia. Now, Jesus admired and told us to emulate in our prayers the importunate widow (Luke 18:1–8). In the spirit of that poor woman, this group of "us" were flinging at God the challenge: "Shake yourself, God; bestir yourself! All

you have to do is to smile on us and we shall be saved." They are
referring, of course, to the words of the Aaronic blessing to be
found at Num. 6:24–26.

Verses 4–7, *The second prayer*. Then they tell God how heart-
broken they are that he should actually *be angry* at their *prayers*.
Their condition had the opposite effect, they claim, upon their
enemy neighbours, for the latter *laugh among themselves*, laugh,
of course, not from simple pleasure but from glee at the plight of
Ephraim. Now that these two prayers have been edited for use in
public worship, the second ends with the same congregational
response as the first, and this response is repeated finally at the
end of the whole psalm.

THE PARABLE OF THE VINEYARD

Psalm 80:8–19

> 8Thou didst bring a vine out of Egypt;
>   thou didst drive out the nations and plant it.
> 9Thou didst clear the ground for it;
>   it took deep root and filled the land.
> 10The mountains were covered with its shade,
>   the mighty cedars with its branches;
> 11it sent out its branches to the sea,
>   and its shoots to the River.
> 12Why then hast thou broken down its walls,
>   so that all who pass along the way pluck its fruit?
> 13The boar from the forest ravages it,
>   and all that move in the field feed on it.
>
> 14Turn again, O God of hosts!
>   Look down from heaven, and see;
>   have regard for this vine,
> 15   the stock which thy right hand planted.
> 16They have burned it with fire, they have cut it down;
>   may they perish at the rebuke of thy countenance!
> 17But let thy hand be upon the man of thy right hand,
>   the son of man whom thou hast made strong for thyself!

¹⁸Then we will never turn back from thee;
  give us life, and we will call on thy name!

¹⁹Restore us, O Lord God of hosts!
  let thy face shine, that we may be saved!

Verses 8–13. That we are being presented with a theological interpretation of the Exile, and are not just being told mere fact, is shown (in the Hebrew) by all the verbs to follow occurring in the imperfect (incomplete) tense. This means that what is described here has happened again and again in history.

The section begins by placing God's redemptive act at the Exodus firmly as the basis of all that is to follow. Isaiah had already produced a parable in which he described God as the Vinedresser and Israel as his favourite vineyard (Isa. 5:1–7); in fact Israel was even the vine that grew in God's vineyard. Before Isaiah's day Hosea had already called Israel God's vine (Hos. 10:1). Then later, Jeremiah (at 2:21) picks up the allegory: *Yet I planted you a choice vine.* In the LXX this is translated by the words "true vine". Yet, as God says in the same verse, *You have turned degenerate and become a wild vine*, one that was not true to its root. Isaiah goes further in his parable and declares that Israel had become a "stinking" vine. God had intended Israel to be his instrument to give the wine of joy to the world. But in reality Israel had become the vine that failed. Without a doubt Jesus built upon this OT allegory when in John's Gospel he uses the exact words of the LXX, in the phrase, "I am the true vine, and my Father is the vinedresser" (John 15:1). Jesus, it seems, was not just the stem of the vine, with "you" as the branches. He was the whole vine and included the branches in himself, even as Israel had been the whole vine along with all its many branches and tendrils.

Next we hear the story of the vine as it grew and developed throughout the period of Joshua–Judges, when Israel struck deep roots in the land of Canaan. The reigns of David and Solomon that followed saw the great expansion of empire mentioned here when it reached from *the sea* (the Mediterranean) *to the River* (the Euphrates). But foreign armies, say verses 12–13, had now *ravished* the Promised Land.

Verses 14–19, *The third prayer.* The word *turn* is actually that used elsewhere of human repentance. How daring, but also how demanding this challenge to God necessarily is! Fancy telling God to repent! In the poetic parallelism by which much of Hebrew poetry is built up, we note that *stock* is intended to be another word for *vine.* So then, first, God is challenged to leave the seclusion of his *heaven* and come down and *see* for himself, and pay a *visit* to *this vine*, in other words, to remember that he is immanent (or Immanuel, God-with-us) as well as being transcendent. The Hebrew (see RSV verse 15 *ftn*) has another line of verse here, which we should keep: *and upon the son whom thou hast reared for thyself.* This is a direct reference, of course, to Exod. 4:22 and to Hos. 11:1. The OT delights to use such imaginative expressions to show by means of a *mashal* (see Ps. 78:2) the theological meaning of what cannot be expected to be taken literally.

Next, as is common in Hebrew style, we have in parallel to the words *the son whom thou has reared for thyself*, a line that runs *the son of man whom thou hast made strong for thyself.* This last verb here means to feed and educate and look after so that the young man grows up strong to be a good man. Moreover, this title *son of man* occurs here in parallel with the words *the man of thy right hand.* We found this also at Ps. 8 where *man* and *son of man* meant virtually the same thing. We have seen also in the so-called Royal Psalms that it was said of the king when he was crowned on Mount Zion that he was God's son (e.g. Ps. 2) and the man set at God's right hand (e.g. Ps. 110). That is, he was anointed to be God's agent and to work God's will in the world.

Here, then, we find all Israel is meant to possess just such "messianic" significance. God had (1) raised his son Israel up and had fed him and made him strong (compare Isa. 50:4–9). Then (2) God had done so in order to let him act as his right hand man to bring about the redemption of the world. David, it would seem from other psalms (but this is not discussed here), was to be the "head" of the whole body of Israel to act in this way for God (e.g. Ps. 110). The son of God was thus a title applied not only to David (2 Sam. 7:14; Ps. 2:7), but also to the whole people of

God. "If then, God," says our lonely group in exile, "if you would just let your hand rest upon us, your 'right hand man', we won't ever turn away from you. Just *give us* back our real life purpose, and we will call *upon your name*", that is, we will worship you in loyalty and obedience.

But in the wisdom of God this kind of repentence was not acceptable. God saw that Ephraim was not sincere. Ephraim had no intention of becoming God's suffering servant in exile. Ephraim was clearly only filled with self-pity. Thus this psalm tells the story of the vine that failed. It comprised the ten northern tribes who never in fact returned from exile. Yet we must take into account Ezekiel's hope that some would return, that some of their descendants would join with the descendants of the exiled Judah-ites, a remnant of whom had accepted their election to be obedient to God's plan (see Ezek. 37:15–17). But Ephraim was that son of man who could not grasp the meaning of his calling. Our author could not know, of course, that God would eventually use all the language to be found in Ps. 80 about another Son of Man, the one who was the true Vine. His coming was still a long way off.

Is it the case, then, that God goes back on his word and rejects at least some of those with whom he has made Covenant? Surely God's Covenant has been made to last for ever. No, that is not what the Bible has to tell us. What we meet with in both Testaments is that some men and women reject the Covenant which God has offered them, it is not God who rejects them. Nevertheless, just as God makes positive use of the obedience of those who remain faithful to him, so he makes positive use of those who turn their back on him. The message hidden in this Psalm is found again in John 6:70–71. If Judas Iscariot had not betrayed Jesus to be crucified, how then could God have brought about the world's redemption? This could come about only through the Cross. But woe to him who did the betraying!

A NEW YEAR SERMON IN VERSE

Psalm 81:1–16

To the choirmaster: according to The Gittith. A Psalm of Asaph.

¹Sing aloud to God our strength;
  shout for joy to the God of Jacob!
²Raise a song, sound the timbrel,
  the sweet lyre with the harp.
³Blow the trumpet at the new moon,
  at the full moon, on our feast day.
⁴For it is a statute for Israel,
  an ordinance of the God of Jacob.
⁵He made it a decree in Joseph,
  when he went out over the land of Egypt.

I hear a voice I had not known:
⁶"I relieved your shoulder of the burden;
  your hands were freed from the basket.
⁷In distress you called, and I delivered you;
  I answered you in the secret place of thunder;
  I tested you at the waters of Meribah.   *Selah*
⁸Hear, O my people, while I admonish you!
  O Israel, if you would but listen to me!
⁹There shall be no strange god among you;
  you shall not bow down to a foreign god.
¹⁰I am the Lord your God,
  who brought you up out of the land of Egypt.
  Open your mouth wide, and I will fill it.

¹¹"But my people did not listen to my voice;
  Israel would have none of me.
¹²So I gave them over to their stubborn hearts,
  to follow their own counsels.
¹³O that my people would listen to me
  that Israel would walk in my ways!
¹⁴I would soon subdue their enemies,
  and turn my hand against their foes.
¹⁵Those who hate the Lord would cringe toward him,
  and their fate would last for ever.

¹⁶I would feed you with the finest of the wheat,
and with honey from the rock I would satisfy you."

This "sermon" may have been prepared specially for use at the Feast of Tabernacles. This seems to be indicated at verse 3. As time went by three different reasons for holding this festival developed and coincided. (1) It formed the last of the three Harvest Festivals, that for the grape harvest, which fell near the end of September. (2) It included thanksgiving that God had brought his people out of Egypt, referred to at verse 6, out of slavery into freedom. To mark this, the people lived in "tabernacles" or booths made from the boughs of trees to remind them of the life they had lived after crossing the Red Sea in the Wilderness of Sinai, for they were still "pilgrims on the way". (3) The hot summer was now over, and the rains were due to begin. Only if these came could the whole cycle of the new agricultural year begin again. Accordingly New Year's Day was added on to the other two celebrations. This additional day was what John 7:37 refers to: *On the last day of the feast, the great day, Jesus stood up and proclaimed, "If any man thirst, let him come to me and drink"*. The point is that when, in the days of the psalmists, Israel prayed to God to send the rain that they could not do without, they included a petition that God might also pour out his Spirit upon his people.

You cannot hold a festival all by yourself. It is God's will, however, that we should hold festivals. These verbs *sing aloud, shout for joy* and so on are all expressed in the plural. These are activities a congregation should do, not an individual. Fifteen days is a lengthy period. The festivities began at a New Moon and ended with the Full Moon, with the ram's horn, the *shophar*, sounding loud, first to open the convocation and then to close it (verse 3). Read in more detail about these festivals in the Daily Study Bible for Leviticus at chapter 23. There we also learn how the Day of Atonement was later attached to this great season of the year.

Verses 1–5a. This section forms an invitation to all God's people to "come and worship". *Ki* is the first word of verse 4. As

we have seen, this little word means "that", rather than *for*. So
this preacher is saying: "(We believe) that God has *decreed* we
should do so." This word in italics is *hoq*. It refers in its original
usage to something that is meant to be imperishable for it has
been chiselled in stone. God then "demands" our regular worship. In his wisdom he knows that it is our regular participation in
congregational worship that keeps us right with himself. Public
worship is God's good idea, not ours.

Verses 5*b*–7, *I hear a voice.* Our preacher had, of course, read
the story in the book of Exodus of how God *had relieved your
shoulder of the burden* when he set his people free. But God had
also whispered the meaning of it all to him in his heart, as if he and
his congregation had been there in Egypt to experience it—and to
murmur and complain as Israel did then in the Wilderness. God's
thunder, once heard on Mount Sinai, was now sounding in their
ears. A clash of cymbals—*Selah*—emphasizes the drama of the
moment.

Verses 8–10, *The voice admonishes.* The people had asked God
to listen to them, but now, says God, "Now I want *you* to listen to
me." The preacher may have enlarged at this point upon the
meaning of the First Commandment. We should remember that
this whole sermon has been condensed into a short poem for later
use in worship. Thereupon he completes this first part of his
sermon with a thrilling appeal, letting it be heard as the very voice
of God: *Open your mouth wide, and I will fill it.* This is what we
today might call the great Gospel invitation. It reminds us of
God's own words spoken again at Isa. 55:1–2: "Ho, everyone
who thirsts . . ."—and of the words that Jesus was to use on that
"great day of the feast" in the future.

Verses 11–16, *The voice appeals.* As at Ps. 95:7*b*–9, which is
also written as the direct speech of God (and which is so well
known from its inclusion in the Anglican Prayer Book), the
preacher continues to be the mouth of God: *Israel would have
none of Me.* How tragic, how preposterous, how blasphemous!
"Consequently," says God, "I had to send them off to 'stew
in their own juice'" (compare Rom. 1:24). Despite his having
to do so, however, God still calls out: "*O that my people would*

listen to Me!", for then I would still be their Guide and Friend.

We witness in this psalm what every preacher prays God to enable him to do, even if it should happen only once in a long while in his ministry. It is that he should not just talk about God, but that through his very human words he may actually *confront* his people with the living Word of God. When that happens, two things result. Some of those present will turn away in horror at the demands of the gospel; but others will receive sustenance that will carry them into eternal life.

The words *their fate* in verse 15 are very solemn. Here is no Greek idea found in an Israelite psalm; far from it. The Hebrew word is *eth*, meaning "time", though not clock time. It refers to that eschatological moment upon which the whole "fate" of the soul will depend for all eternity. Listening to that one particular sermon, then, those present meet with God as he confronts them with their fate. It is the moment when they must turn either to the right hand or to the left hand. This sermon was saying to its first hearers, just as it is saying to us now, what Deut. 30:19 says in different words: "I call heaven and earth to witness against you this day, that I have set before you life and death ... therefore choose life."

THE TWILIGHT OF THE GODS

Psalm 82:1–8

A Psalm of Asaph.

¹God has taken his place in the divine council;
  in the midst of the gods he holds judgment:
²"How long will you judge unjustly
  and show partiality to the wicked?   *Selah*
³Give justice to the weak and the fatherless;
  maintain the right of the afflicted and the destitute.
⁴Rescue the weak and needy;
  deliver them from the hand of the wicked."

⁵They have neither knowledge nor understanding,
  they walk about in darkness;
  all the foundations of the earth are shaken.

⁶I say, "You are gods,
  sons of the Most High, all of you;
⁷nevertheless, you shall die like men,
  and fall like any prince."

⁸Arise, O God, judge the earth;
  for to thee belong all the nations!

The best way to view Michelangelo's magnificent paintings on the ceiling of the Sistine Chapel at the Vatican is to lie down on the floor and look straight up. Here the psalmist is lying flat on his back, so to speak, and is gazing straight up at the sky above him. Amongst other themes Michelangelo sought to express God's creation of Adam. To do so he made use of a picture on the level that the human mind can understand. He drew the Father with his finger just touching the finger of his child, man. In just such a manner, then, our psalmist offers us a picture of what, with the eye of faith, he saw in the heavens above. He saw the Most High God (verse 6) exercising rule over his whole universe, none of which is dead matter, but all of which is alive.

At Isa. 6:1–7 the prophet describes in picture language his vision of *the Lord, high and lifted up*. What he sees is God surrounded by the *seraphim*. Here in our psalm, on the other hand, ELOHIM (God) is surrounded by *elohim* (gods). The picture is of a session of the "Council of the Universe", with the Most High taking the chair. Such a picture, though strange to us, would have been fully understandable to the people of those days. For they knew that the great overlords of the east, whether Assyrians in Isaiah's day, or the neo-Babylonians in Jeremiah's day, called themselves King of kings, and Lord of lords. All the lesser kings of the small nations therefore had to sit in council (in imagination!) under the Great King (Isa. 36:4) and learn what their duties were as subordinates. But here it is the Judge of all the earth, the Mighty Lord, the Most High God, who takes the chair. This Council, then, under its Moderator, has been set up with the one and only purpose of administering justice to all the kingdoms and nations of the earth.

But the lesser kings, who were all regarded as gods by their subjects, had failed to administer equal justice. They had continued to favour *the wicked*. So the divine Moderator admonishes them, and orders them to show equal justice to *the poor*, and *the orphan*, *the afflicted* and *the desolate*. This is something that any eastern king or ruler or dictator never thought of doing, and so this judgment made by God marks off the uniqueness of the Biblical revelation. The Moderator makes his judgment in the Council very positively: the divine-king-rulers were not just to stop being unjust, they were to take positive action to *rescue the weak and the needy*, perhaps from the power of the bureaucrat, or of the money-lender, or of the hatred of the Ku Klux Klan, and to *deliver them from the hand of the wicked*, such as, for example, the successful farmer who forced his impoverished neighbour to give up his ancestral property in payment of a debt (compare Isa. 3:13–15; 5:8).

In Biblical thinking no line can be drawn between this world and "the other world", between the gods above and the god-kings below. If the one is evil, the other is too. In this great council-scene, then, the Most High God does what none of the religions of the world even suggest that their god should do. Our psalmist answers the question, not, "Who is God?", but, "What is God for?", by revealing that he is the God of the underdog and of the suffering masses of humanity, that in fact he is the God (as we would say today) of social justice.

Then we are to remember that "the gods" are all mere figments or creations of the human mind. In this council meeting they represent man's hand-made idols and man's mental images or ideologies. They include our humanly created power-blocks, the nationalistic aspirations to world dominion of this world's rulers, race prejudice, the outreach of multinational foundations for whose direction no one person is responsible, impersonal drifts towards war that no one can control, and such like. All of these forces actually rule our lives today, even when we have committed our individual lives to God in obedience. Like the gods, these movements, forces or ideologies, seem to exist outside of our control, so that our world appears to be headed for destruction.

But both the OT and the NT proclaim the profoundly good news that God is Lord over all the gods of both heaven and earth. The day is coming, says Isa. 24:21, when the Lord will pay a visit (rather than *punish*) to *the host of heaven in heaven, and the kings of the earth on the earth*. In God's sight, heaven and earth are one, and evil is evil, whether it be here or there. It is as if the High Court of the universe were already seated, when in walks the Most High to preside over it, inspect it, and to pass judgment upon both the gods above and the nations below. What does Paul call them? "The principalities, the powers, the world rulers of this present darkness, the spiritual hosts of wickedness in the heavenly places" (Eph. 6:12).

Despite being *sons of the Most High*, the gods shall *die* (that is the judgment!) just as *men must die*, and *fall like any prince*. (This verse is quoted by Jesus at John 10:34–36.) See Isa. 14:12 (where the same punishment is pronounced on a god); Ezek. 28:16–17 (where it is pronounced on a god-king); Luke 10:18 (where we have Jesus' vision of the fall of the gods); Luke 10:19–20 (where we learn of the results of the fall of evil on earth); Rev. 12:9 (where we have a picture of the final eternal outcome); Matt. 25:41 (where we see the same end coming on earth as in heaven).

In our day many people, even Christians, are obsessed with the idea that this world is out of control and is rushing to its doom. To further their argument they point to the violence, greed and bloody-mindedness they read of daily in the newspaper, to the helplessness small nations experience in face of financial and power-hungry forces which they cannot combat, to unemployment, recession, and the imminent collapse of the world's economy. To them our psalmist proclaims the Good News that is proclaimed in both Testaments. He is saying in reality what Jesus says in John 16:33 to all who have ears to hear: *Be of good cheer, I have overcome the world.*

That is why a famous theologian has described the era in which we are living as "the twilight of the gods". For we who have ears to hear know that their end is nigh.

THE COVENANT IN REVERSE

Psalm 83·1–18

A Song. A Psalm of Asaph.

¹O God, do not keep silence;
  do not hold thy peace or be still, O God!
²For lo, thy enemies are in tumult;
  those who hate thee have raised their heads.
³They lay crafty plans against thy people;
  they consult together against thy protected ones.
⁴They say, "Come, let us wipe them out as a nation;
  let the name of Israel be remembered no more!"
⁵Yea, they conspire with one accord;
  against thee they make a covenant—
⁶the tents of Edom and the Ishmaelites,
  Moab and the Hagrites,
⁷Gebal and Ammon and Amalek,
  Philistia with the inhabitants of Tyre;
⁸Assyria also has joined them;
  they are the strong arm of the children of Lot.   *Selah*

⁹Do to them as thou didst to Midian,
  as to Sisera and Jabin at the river Kishon,
¹⁰who were destroyed at Endor,
  who became dung for the ground.
¹¹Make their nobles like Oreb and Zeeb,
  all their princes like Zebah and Zalmunna,
¹²who said, "Let us take possession for ourselves
  of the pastures of God."

¹³O my God, make them like whirling dust,
  like chaff before the wind.
¹⁴As fire consumes the forest,
  as the flame sets the mountains ablaze,
¹⁵so do thou pursue them with thy tempest
  and terrify them with thy hurricane!
¹⁶Fill their faces with shame,
  that they may seek thy name, O Lord.
¹⁷Let them be put to shame and dismayed for ever;
  let them perish in disgrace.

¹⁸Let them know that thou alone,
  whose name is the Lord,
  art the Most High over all the earth.

Verses 1–8, *Don't be dumb, God; don't keep quiet in yourself.*
Those words sum up the resentment some poor individual is
feeling, living probably in the days of Isaiah, when the Assyrians
were continually harassing both Israel in the north and Judah in
the south. In fact, their armies even planned an act of genocide, *to
wipe them out as a nation.* And all the time, the psalmist declares,
God has said nothing. God has done nothing. The psalmist is
pointing to a very serious issue. The infallibility of God is at stake,
just as it was again when, in the 1940s, *the enemy* did more than
harass, it actually planned the extinction of a whole people and
the imposition upon it of what Hitler called "the Final Solution".
That people were the Jews and at Auschwitz and in other extermination camps of the Third Reich he nearly succeeded. At verse
3 Israel is called *thy people* (God's *am*); at verse 4, however,
"they" say that Israel is a mere *goi,* a heathen, a Gentile *nation.*

The theologian Paul Tillich, who died not many years ago,
escaped the holocaust himself and found refuge in the United
States. He pondered deeply upon this vital issue about God's
credibility. "Is the secular silence about God that we experience
everywhere perhaps God's way of forcing his Church back to a
sacred embarrassment when speaking of Him?", he suggested.
And yet people still dare to speak flippantly of God in such
phrases as "the Man upstairs", "the regular Good Guy", "the
livin' Doll", and suchlike nonsense. The point is, of course, that
we dare not be "pally" with the Most High God, even though he
is "our Father". He is that indeed, but he is " . . . who art in
heaven", and consequently transcendent, shrouded in mystery.
"Clouds and thick darkness are round about him". So it is too
with Jesus. He is not "my pal Jesus", "Are you running with me,
Jesus?" "A cloud took him out of their sight", as Acts 1:9
reminds us.

Or it may be, as Tillich suggests, that God purposely hides
himself when we look for him in the wrong places. The psalmist

expected God to reveal himself as Israel's Saviour by clubbing his people's enemies, for, as he implied, "God is on our side". But that is not necessarily the case. We are more likely to find God, we learn from the Bible as a whole, when we do not expect him to wield the big stick, but to be present in every human failure, in ugliness, in heartbreak, in fact, in the Cross. But, continues the psalmist, in the beginning of Israel's history God made a Covenant with his people to be their God; and now the nations round about have conspired to reverse God's plan, and have *made a covenant* to destroy the chosen people! In fact, Assyria has now joined this league and is acting as *the strong arm* that has urged *the children of Lot*, viz. *Moab and Ammon* (the *Hagrites* were desert Arabs), to the east of the Jordan, to destroy Israel. And there were all the other nations along the Mediterranean coast!

Verses 9–12. Unfortunately the psalmist thinks he knows better than God what God ought to do. He believes he is a good theologian. So he appeals to history, and reminds God how he had helped his people in the days of the Judges. He forgets, however, that in those "wild and woolly days" Israel was still a youth, so to speak. Now she has grown up, and has matured with the help of the great prophets, such as Amos, Hosea, Micah and Isaiah, all of whom had expressed vehemently much deeper views about the ways of God towards his Covenant people than anything known to Samson or Gideon.

Verses 13–18, *Curse them!* The psalmist's wild reaction gets worse and worse. He has clearly not listened to the prophets we have named. "O my God," he shouts, "make them like tumbleweed"—a very apt description of the utter helplessness and uselessness of a once living and green plant, now whirled along the countryside aimlessly with the wind. The demands he makes of God almost echo the words of Shakespeare in *Julius Caesar*: "Cry havoc! and let slip the dogs of war."

Then, suddenly, we come upon an amazingly different statement. In fact this is perhaps why this curious outburst of his has been turned into a congregational psalm. Out of the horrors of fire and tempest our writer now hopes that his nation's enemies will eventually *seek thy name, O Lord*. So he has learned something from Isaiah's preaching, after all! Yet he is still ambivalent in his prayer. In verse 17 he seeks the end of Israel's enemies. But in verse 18 he prays that they may eventually know *that thou alone . . . art the Most High over all the earth.*

Israel's God is the God *whose Name is the Lord,* whose name is "there is no Saviour but Me". That even the counter-covenanters, then, may yet know God as Saviour, is our psalmist's hope. Yes, the gate is always open. Even God's worst enemies may come in and acknowledge God as Saviour and Lord.

SINGING FOR JOY

Psalm 84:1–12

> *To the choirmaster: according to The Gittith.*
> *A Psalm of the Sons of Korah.*

¹How lovely is thy dwelling place,
  O Lord of hosts!
²My soul longs, yea, faints
  for the courts of the Lord;
 my heart and flesh sing for joy to the living God.

³Even the sparrow finds a home,
  and the swallow a nest for herself,
  where she may lay her young,
 at thy altars, O Lord of hosts,
  my King and my God.
⁴Blessed are those who dwell in thy house,
  ever singing thy praise!   *Selah*

⁵Blessed are the men whose strength is in thee,
  in whose heart are the highways to Zion.
⁶As they go through the valley of Baca
  they make it a place of springs;
  the early rain also covers it with pools.
⁷They go from strength to strength;
  the God of gods will be seen in Zion.

⁸O Lord God of hosts, hear my prayer;
  give ear, O God of Jacob!   *Selah*

⁹Behold our shield, O God;
  look upon the face of thine anointed!

¹⁰For a day in thy courts is better
  than a thousand elsewhere.
 I would rather be a doorkeeper in the house of my God
  than dwell in the tents of wickedness.
¹¹For the Lord God is a sun and shield;
  he bestows favour and honour.
 No good thing does the Lord withhold
  from those who walk uprightly.
¹²O Lord of hosts,
  blessed is the man who trusts in thee!

With us, New Year follows closely after Christmas. We make Christmas a religious festival, and then relax and think of New Year as merely a secular one. We even paganize it by celebrating it as a folk-festival, with song, dance and drunkenness, and paganize it even more by regarding it as a time for making good resolutions.

In Old Testament times, however, the New Year, which was celebrated towards the end of September, was a deeply religious occasion. For it marked the moment when God was remembered as the Creator God. Just as in Gen. 1:1, where we read *When God began to create* (see RSV *ftn*), so each New Year Israel remembered that God was beginning to recreate all things over again. New Year, in the September–October period, marked the beginning of the cycle of the agricultural year when God's love of creating was made visible again. Moreover, in respect of humanity, since God's love was a forgiving love, his love extended also to recreating people. The Israelites celebrated this truth about God by linking the celebration of his recreation of nature with his forgiving, renewing and recreating love throughout history in the life of his people by means of his "forgiveness". At this festival he "forgave" nature for going bone dry in Palestine in the period July to September, and brought about her renewal. But forgiveness and renewal cannot be mere sentiments in the mind of either God or man. They must be made visible, they must "become

flesh" in action. So at the New Year festival Israel prayed for (1)
the coming of the rains to recreate the dry soil; and (2) the
outpouring of God's Holy Spirit to recreate the hard and dry
hearts of his people Israel.

God did all this for both heaven and earth, for nature and for
man, by uttering his Word from just one small spot on earth, *his
dwelling place in Zion!* What a great mystery this is, one that finds
a parallel in the NT! For there God acts to recreate *all things* (the
time of universal restoration, Acts 3:21, NEB) through just one
man.

We have a picture in this psalm, then, of the families of Israel,
father, mother and children, leaving their scattered villages, all
wending their way up the hill to reach Jerusalem at the top. Their
hearts are overflowing with joy. They are longing to reach the
Temple precincts, *the courts of the Lord.* For there they will meet,
not just with God, but with *the living God.* (1) It is only the living
God who can create the cycle of nature out of the "deadness" of
the great heat of summer. (2) It is only the living God who can
create new life in the "deadness" of human hearts that have
rebelled against his Covenant love.

The sparrow is a sign of (1). She finds she can lay her eggs and
so create a new generation within the creative care of the living
Creator God. (We do not need to be literalists and ask if the nest
was made in a hole in the outer stone wall of the Temple, or in a
hole in an altar. (For there the baby birds might well have been
scorched!) Or in a wall of one of the courts. For we are reading
poetry!)

So also (2) those who *dwell in thy house* (not necessarily in a
literal sense again), those who walk with God in their daily lives
(Gen. 5:24; 6:9; Micah 6:8), have deep reasons for *ever singing
thy praise*; for the newness of the year is to be found in their
hearts.

All life is a journey. The literal trek of whole families and
villages *to Zion* becomes a sign in itself. *Baca* means "weeping".
Baca was an arid, waterless valley for much of the year. John
Bunyan must have understood this psalm well. He saw that *Baca*
symbolized that vale of tears that figured so much in the experi-

ence of life of many poverty-stricken Palestinian peasants, always subject to disease, hunger, and natural disasters as they were. But just as the rains brought life to that valley, so joy in the Lord brought new strength to the weary pilgrims. For they kept on repeating to each other the amazing exclamation: "The God of gods shows himself in Zion!" (verse 7, NEB).

Without laying too much stress on the significance of the word *strength*, we are to remember that in many places it is a synonym for the "power" of God's Holy Spirit. *They go*, it seems, *from* their own strength *to* God's *strength*. In Isa. 40:31 the prophet makes a similar promise to the exiles returning home from Babylon to Jerusalem. The symbolic nature of the annual pilgrimage as a description of the believer's journey through life as a whole is enhanced when we notice that the phrase *covers it with pools* can also be rendered "wraps it in blessings".

At verse 8 they have arrived. Their first prayer is not for themselves but for their king (our *shield*), *thine anointed*, for God has chosen to use this one man to exercise his creative purpose amongst his people. No wonder the very first words of the NT are: "Jesus Christ, son of *David*".

Verses 10–12, *Joy in believing* The poetry of these lines has satisfied the hearts of millions till this day. The use of *tents* keeps up the idea that all life is a pilgrimage, as it was for Israel in Moses' day. But even then God loved and cared for his people as their *sun and shield*. The last line of the psalm, consequently, does not tell us something *about* God. Rather, it is an exclamation made *to* God of wonder and joy, marvelling that, if only humanity (the word is *adam* meaning any man, all human beings, male and female, and not just Israel) would just *trust in thee*, then they would indeed be happy people.

Thus one can "lie at the threshold" (rather than *be a doorkeeper*) of *the house of my God* even when crossing a literal desert or when going through a desert of human experience. For a pilgrim can take Jerusalem with him all throughout his life. William Blake glimpsed this truth in his inspiring poem: "Till we have built Jerusalem in England's green and pleasant land."

Finally, God grants all these great blessings sung of here only to those who make the decision to go together to worship him; for it is only there and then in public, at that one spot and in fellowship with other people, that the individual human heart can find that it too can exclaim: *O Lord of hosts, blessed is the man who trusts in thee!*

A DIFFERENT KIND OF RETURN

Psalm 85:1–13

> *To the choirmaster. A Psalm of the Sons of Korah.*

¹Lord, thou wast favourable to thy land;
  thou didst restore the fortunes of Jacob.
²Thou didst forgive the iniquity of thy people;
  thou didst pardon all their sin.   *Selah*
³Thou didst withdraw all thy wrath;
  thou didst turn from thy hot anger.

⁴Restore us again, O God of our salvation,
  and put away thy indignation toward us!
⁵Wilt thou be angry with us for ever?
  Wilt thou prolong thy anger to all generations?
⁶Wilt thou not revive us again,
  that thy people may rejoice in thee?
⁷Show us thy steadfast love, O Lord,
  and grant us thy salvation.

⁸Let me hear what God the Lord will speak,
  for he will speak peace to his people,
  to his saints, to those who turn to him in their hearts.
⁹Surely his salvation is at hand for those who fear him,
  that glory may dwell in our land.

¹⁰Steadfast love and faithfulness will meet;
  righteousness and peace will kiss each other.
¹¹Faithfulness will spring up from the ground,
  and righteousness will look down from the sky.
¹²Yea, the Lord will give what is good,
  and our land will yield its increase.

¹³Righteousness will go before him,
 and make his footsteps a way.

Verses 1-3. "The long trek home from Babylon to Zion is a very important part of Israel's (and our) life-long pilgrimage to our home." We noted at Ps. 84 that God's forgiveness is offered and received as one of the "festal blessings" at the New Year festival. Here we learn about God's creative love in that in Ps. 85 God has now *restored the fortunes of Jacob*, rehabilitated Israel, *comforted his people* and brought them home from exile, just as the great prophet of Isaiah chs. 40–55 had proclaimed God was about to do. Such an action by God was what we might call "the sacramental sign and seal" of his *forgiving thy people all their sin.* So then, we learn, God had now *turned* from his *hot anger.*

Verses 4–7. One of the expressions used by many returning soldiers at the end of World War I was that they had fought to make their homeland "a land fit for heroes to live in". But as a fact of history many a man and woman later grew to be deeply disappointed about the prosperity of their country. The "millennium" had not dawned after all, it seemed, and so it was in the case of those exiles who had managed to make their way back home to Judah after the Persian King Cyrus had issued his famous edict in the year 538 B.C. (see Ezra 1:1–4). In it he gave permission for "the Jews", as he called the Israelite people who were now being named after their homeland, "Judah", to go home. The last section of the book of Isaiah, chs. 56–66 ("Third" Isaiah, it is sometimes called), offers us examples of the moments of pain and disillusionment, and yet of joy and confidence, that the returnees underwent as they sought to rebuild their ruined city and Temple.

Then why was God still angry with them? they wondered. Was it because there were the same old quarrels, the same old crop failures, the same old selfishnesses as there had been before? Why don't you show us your steadfast love and put us right with yourself once more?

Verses 8–9. You are looking in the wrong direction, a Temple minister exclaims. You are listening to the wrong voices. Listen to God before you open your silly mouths. *Let me hear what God the Lord keeps saying.* (I declare) that (*ki*) *he keeps on speaking peace to his people, to his saints,* that is, to his forgiven, Covenant people; thus to those who have not only returned from exile, but *who have also returned to him in their hearts.* It is as if this minister were explaining: You imagine that the Kingdom of God is to be understood in terms of perfect economic and social conditions. No, God's Kingdom is not of this world. It is marked by *shalom*, integrity of life, wholesomeness of family and national life, and these transcend all economic conditions. So he continues (verse 9): Not only so, but (*akh*, a strong expletive) *his saving love* is actually here now in our midst for those who *fear him* and so who worship him in awe and love. Yes, *his glory* has really "taken up its abode" *in our land.* Only the eye of faith could see that, of course. Israel's human eye could see only the ruins of their ancient city and Temple. So they must now get down to the task of rebuilding these (see Haggai 1:1–11; Zech. 2:1–5; 8:12).

So God had two words to say to these poor folk in their confused state of mind, now that they had completed a physical return to Jerusalem from Babylon. It was (1) that they had not yet completed their return until (2) they had done so spiritually.

Verses 10–13. Our speaker is truly a minister of the Word. His sermon continues: (a) God's *hesed* and (b) God's *emet* have now met. Note that in this passage the verbs are not in the future, as the RSV puts them. Our minister is speaking by faith and not by sight. He is saying that (a) God's steadfast, Covenant love, and (b) God's utter fidelity to his Covenant have now converged and have *met* at this point in history. The Return from Exile is thus the proof of the reliability of the Covenant. Then he adds that (c) God's *righteousness*, his saving love, and (d) his *peace*, have *kissed*, so as to show that his salvation and his peace are united for the same end, viz. the coming of his Kingdom. In other words, "The Kingdom of God is at hand!" An old Jewish mystic has said, "Prayer is the moment when heaven and earth kiss each other."

What will result then from this remarkable union? God's fidelity to the Covenant must surely have an effect on the other partner to the Covenant, viz. Israel, God's people. So he declares that (e) fidelity will spring up also from human hearts, actually, here, *from the ground*. But that is a way of saying "from human beings who live upon this earth". Thus God brings forth *emet* in Israel's heart by (f) his creative, saving love *looking down from the sky*; that is to say it will appear as sheer grace.

We see this two-way movement of grace and love described pictorially at Isa. 45:8. Both psalmist and prophet are seeking to express what St. Paul makes clear in the light of Christ. It is that God acts first in grace. He makes us *right* with himself (the word *righteousness* here). Paul calls this action of God "justification". But then as a result of it we who are justified receive power to respond to God, that is, love and faithfulness spring up within us, rendering us able to do to our fellows on earth what God has done for us. That is to say, we are rendered able to recreate other people in love, not as individuals so much as together as limbs in the Body of the Lord. This second step is what Paul calls "sanctification". It is God's gift to us, and not of ourselves. This "heavenly" love and compassion and self-forgetfulness is his gift through the Spirit. All other gifts of the Spirit are rendered secondary compared with this greatest gift of all, the gift of the power to love (1 Cor. 12:15; 13:13).

Yea, the Lord gives (g) what is *good for us*. (See the Introduction to Vol. I for a discussion of this word "good".) One result of his kindness will affect even inanimate nature; for "our land" (the Holy Land that God gave to us as a gift in the days of Joshua) *will yield its increase*, despite all appearances to the contrary. It had been ravaged by Nebuchadnezzar's army, its fruit trees cut down, its wells stopped up, the dikes and levees that held good soil together on the steep slopes of its hills, and which had taken generations to erect (as in South East Asia today), had been bulldozed away (see 2 Kings 3:25).

This grand visionary sermon ends with the same kind of language as Isa. 40:3 which had foretold the return from exile. God's creative, saving purpose (RSV *righteousness*) *will march ahead of him* (as it had always done ever since he gave it to Israel in the days of Moses); and he will *make his footsteps* the *way* where we are to plant our feet. Thus we are to step in the footsteps he has first made in the mud and dirt of life's highway leading onwards to what verse 1 has called *thy land.* What amazing grace!

ANYBODY'S PSALM

Psalm 86:1–17

A Prayer of David.

¹Incline thy ear, O Lord, and answer me,
    for I am poor and needy.
²Preserve my life, for I am godly;
    save thy servant who trusts in thee.
Thou art my God; ³be gracious to me O Lord,
    for to thee do I cry all the day.
⁴Gladden the soul of thy servant,
    for to thee, O Lord, do I lift up my soul.
⁵For thou, O Lord, art good and forgiving,
    abounding in steadfast love to all who call on thee.
⁶Give ear, O Lord, to my prayer;
    hearken to my cry of supplication.
⁷In the day of my trouble I call on thee,
    for thou dost answer me.

⁸There is none like thee among the gods, O Lord,
    nor are there any works like thine.
⁹All the nations thou hast made shall come
    and bow down before thee, O Lord,
    and shall glorify thy name.
¹⁰For thou art great and doest wondrous things,
    thou alone art God.
¹¹Teach me thy way, O Lord,
    that I may walk in thy truth;
    unite my heart to fear thy name.
¹²I give thanks to thee, O Lord my God, with my whole heart,
    and I will glorify thy name for ever.
¹³For great is thy steadfast love toward me;
    thou hast delivered my soul from the depths of Sheol.

14O God, insolent men have risen up against me;
   a band of ruthless men seek my life,
   and they do not set thee before them.
15But thou, O Lord, art a God merciful and gracious,
   slow to anger and abounding in steadfast love and faithfulness.
16Turn to me and take pity on me;
   give thy strength to thy servant,
   and save the son of thy handmaid.
17Show me a sign of thy favour,
   that those who hate me may see and be put to shame
   because thou, Lord, hast helped me and comforted me.

Almost every line of this psalm has been lifted out of other psalms in our collection or is a quotation from the *Torah*, the name of the first five books of the OT. We can discover in it no less than forty quotations. Yet the genius of its author shows itself as he welds all these scattered lines into a poem in praise of God. We too perhaps sing snatches of hymns as we go about our work, but not many of us could fit all these separate verses into one coherent whole, and then find that our patchwork had been adopted as Holy Scripture and sung in church! The psalm is in four parts.

Part I, verses 1–7, *I search for God*. The speaker is an ordinary, working-class (could we say?) citizen, a member of the church (for that is what *godly* means). "I need thee every hour," he says, as in Annie S. Hawks' well-known hymn. I know you are a forgiving God, and your Covenant love never lets you forget *all those who call on* you. However, he seems to have tried everything else before returning to God, all the various "isms" of his day. In contrast he declares seven times over in this psalm that he now knows God to be the sovereign Lord. He begins with a plaintive repetition of I . . . I . . . I . . . , but he quickly remembers to turn and say *Thou art my God* (verse 2). And so he quotes (verse 5) the great basic description of the nature of God himself revealed to us at Exod. 34:6–7.

The word *day* in verse 7 shows an interesting usage. It does not refer to clock time, any more than does the word "hour" as we have seen before. It speaks here of a terrible "moment", a crushing experience, when eternity breaks in upon a man's consciousness and he is overwhelmed with the horror of his *trouble*. This is no mere passing worry but is an experience of the eternal judgment of the living God. Thus he is compelled to *call upon God*, and he finds (*ki*) that *thou dost answer me*. So he finds God's amazing comfort right in the midst of his terror.

Part II, verses 8–10, *I have found him*. I know I have, because there can be no other God. Your divine majesty makes me feel as nothing. The things you do no other God could do. Consequently, he declares, not only my nation, Israel, but all the nations of the earth whom *thou hast made shall* one day *bow down before thee and shall glorify thy name*.

Part III, verses 11–13, *Teach me thy way, O Lord*. Thus he prays, so that the next step may be that *I may walk in thy truth*, or, "in responsive fidelity to your fidelity to me" (see at Ps. 85:10–13). To that end, he continues, "Please unite my heart", that is, integrate my personality so that I may become an uncomplicated person (compare Matt. 5:8). Then *I will give thanks to thee* "whole"-heartedly. I shall do so, for *thou hast delivered* my "whole" being (*soul* in the RSV) *from the depths of Sheol*. God has not, of course, raised him from the dead. *Sheol* represents something else that is "whole". It is in fact the "hollow place" down below the ground, down below the natural creation. But it is also the "sub"conscious of God's creature man. Deep within man's *sub*conscious (or, as the Biblical writers understood it, from the "heart" of man) there bursts up, as Jesus says, *all manner of evil thoughts, murder, adultery, fornication, theft, false witness, slander—these are what defile a man* (Matt. 15:19–20). And it is from these that God has evidently delivered our psalmist.

Part IV, verses 14–17, *My creed*. But that does not mean that I am immune from evil thoughts. *O God, insolent* "tendencies and habits" (there is no mention of *men* in the Hebrew) have risen up (out of the depths of my subconscious) once again *against me, a swarm of ruthless* "instincts" (again, there is no word for men) *that seek my life* (or "soul", or just "me"). How am I to deal with them? I am to declare defiantly: "*But thou, O Lord . . .*" and so to repeat my Creed that I have learned from Exod. 34:6–7. Words

from these verses occur again at Num. 14:18; 2 Chron. 30:9; Neh.
9:17; Pss. 103:8; 111:4; 112:4; 116:5; 145:8; Joel 2:13; Jonah
4:2. Just because this description of God is to be found so often
in the OT, we believe it was known to and used by most
worshippers, much as we today recite the Apostles' Creed in our
public worship. This gracious God, then, will save me from the
constant outbursts of my lower nature.

At verse 16 the psalmist calls himself *the son of thy handmaid*.
If this is the correct reading of the Hebrew, then it means "your
adopted son". But the words could also be vowelled to mean,
"the son to whom thou hast said Amen". The latter is an attractive possibility. He would then be saying that God had accepted
him just as he was, and had given him his loving blessing.
However, the mark of a careful Hebrew poet was that he could
make the one set of letters mean two things at once. Puns like that
cannot be conveyed in any translation; they can only be noted in a
commentary. Then at verse 17 the psalmist asks for a *sign*, a sign
that all would be well. He is not asking "Help me to believe", but
that *those who hate me* (are they real people, or are they his lower
nature?) *may see and be put to shame*; because at last they will
have recognized that it is *thou Lord, who hast helped* me before,
who will now *comfort me* again.

ZION, MOTHER OF US ALL

Psalm 87:1–7

> *A Psalm of the Sons of Korah. A Song.*

¹On the holy mount stands the city he founded;
²   the Lord loves the gates of Zion
  more than all the dwelling places of Jacob.
³Glorious things are spoken of you,
  O city of God.   *Selah*

⁴Among those who know me I mention Rahab and Babylon;
  behold, Philistia and Tyre, with Ethiopia—
  "This one was born there," they say.

⁵And of Zion it shall be said,
  "This one and that one were born in her";
  for the Most High himself will establish her.
⁶The Lord records as he registers the peoples,
  "This one was born there."   *Selah*

⁷Singers and dancers alike say,
  "All my springs are in you."

Verses 1–3. When the worshipper mounted up the long steep hill
to Jerusalem what did he see? Not just walls and houses, shops
and squares. He was looking at a city of joy and bubbling life.
This was because God *had founded* it, not man. It sat upon *the
holy mount.* That which is holy belongs to the holy God. It was
God who had founded Zion, and now, says the psalmist, God
loves the gates of Zion—not their bars of iron, of course, but the
people who congregated at the gate on all social occasions, and
who gathered to listen to the words of justice as the elders heard
their cases. "Glorious things of thee are spoken", we rejoice to
sing in the words of John Newton's fine hymn. But do we pause to
ask ourselves what the passive voice of this verb entails? Who did
the speaking? The meaning is, of course, that it was God, not so
much man, who rejoiced in his own beloved city. God had chosen
Israel as his people (Deut. 7:6–8), and he loved them. But God
had also chosen Jerusalem as his own city, and had declared
glorious things about her. What kind of things had he said? For
example, he had said at Isa. 14:32: *The Lord has founded Zion,
and in her the afflicted of his people find refuge.* That is what God
means by "glorious". Jerusalem was to be a city of compassion
and love. God was not interested in just Zion's towers and
battlements.
  Verse 4. Suddenly God himself speaks. As we listen we hear
from God's own lips what we might call the dawn of universal
salvation. "I am calling to mind," he says, "*Rahab* and *Babylon*
as amongst those who will know me." To *know*, as we have seen
before, is to be close in thought and life to another, in the way a
husband and wife "know" each other. *Rahab* was the name of the
monster of evil that floundered like a sick whale in the primal

ocean of chaos. But the name exactly fitted the case of Egypt. Egypt's civilization had been a "chaos of evil" at the time when Israel suffered under the lash of Pharaoh, that is to say, before God rescued his people and brought them out into freedom. Isaiah pictured Egypt therefore as a fat, blubbery sea-monster, stranded on the shore at the mouth of the Nile, absolutely useless for God's purposes in the world (Isa. 30:7). Then again, Babylon was that nation which similarly had held Israel captive in exile after the fall to Nebuchadnezzar of this very city of Jerusalem in the year 587 B.C. Yet now these two evil and hostile powers are God's first thought as he describes how the city will extend its population to take in all peoples. Then it will go on to take in Philistia and Tyre, next door, so to speak, and even Ethiopia, far away at the ends of the known world. Isaiah had believed that God would use Israel (the people known as Zion here!) to be his instrument of mission to those two great hostile and rival world powers of his day. Israel was to bring them into the Covenant fellowship that God had bestowed upon her alone—but which, of course, she was meant to share (see Isa. 49:6). The passage in question about the two world powers is to be found at Isa. 19:23–25. These peoples were now all to become citizens of the Holy City. Others would speak of them as though they had been born in it.

Verse 5. Is God still the speaker here? Or is it the psalmist? The issue, however, is clear. It is that grace comes first. All babies born within the now gloriously extended Covenant shall be accounted as "belonging", for God had acted first to *establish* the city before these peoples had even entered the world. What we have here is "picture theology" used to describe the meaning of prevenient grace.

We recall that Paul, in Gal. 4:26, declared free entry to Jerusalem. He declared that that city had been waiting to adopt us all as her children. This was because, in God's plan, she is the Mother of us all. Moreover, we recall that Paul regarded the Church as being one in continuity with the Israel of God of the OT, the Israel of the Psalms in other words. The Church was now the heir of the promises and the Covenants and everything else that God had bestowed upon her in his grace, even while the Jewish people also continued to be heirs of God's promises (Rom. 9:4–5; 11:1). Jews and Christians share in them together. Yet the Christian, he says, is now living in the period of *the New Covenant,* the one which Jeremiah had foreseen that God would bestow, which *God would make with the house of Israel and the house of Judah* (Jer. 31:31–34). He was not going to make it with some strange Gentile people, but with the one and only Israel, into whom all other peoples would be grafted. In the Scriptures the word Israel has no plural.

Here, then, we read that *the Most High himself will establish her.* This means, of course, that Zion can never be *un*-established! In the light of this verse, we can agree with the theologian who declared that "Jesus did not found a church; he found one."

Verse 6. Luke 2:1–5 tells us that Joseph went from Nazareth to Bethlehem to be enrolled or registered with Mary, his betrothed, because he was of the house and lineage of David, the founder, under God, of Jerusalem as the City of God. So here people from all nations are pictured as coming to Zion, where *the Lord* himself *records as he registers* them. Thereupon he hands the new convert a certificate, so to speak. On it are written the words: "*This one*, (Babylonian, Ethiopian, whose birth certificate says 'Born in Babylon', 'Born in Ethiopia'), *was born there*", that is, in Jerusalem, and so is now a member of the people of God.

Verse 7. A chorus tells us that Zion is the city of joy, for in it is to be found the water of life. We might better understand the psalm if we were to put verse 7 before verse 1 and use it as an introduction to the psalm as a whole. But we should also ask ourselves pointedly: Is our local Zion a "city of joy", and from it does "the water of life" really flow? (Isa. 12:3; Rev. 22:1–2). Each recurrent Lord's Day this miracle, by God's grace, *may* happen all over again (Ps. 30:11).

THE UNHAPPY CRY OF AN EXISTENTIALIST

Psalm 88:1–18

A Song. A Psalm of the Sons of Korah.
To the choirmaster: according to Mahalath Leannoth.
A Maskil of Heman the Ezrahite.

¹O Lord, my God, I call for help by day;
I cry out in the night before thee.
²Let my prayer come before thee,
incline thy ear to my cry!

³For my soul is full of troubles,
and my life draws near to Sheol.
⁴I am reckoned among those who go down to the Pit;
I am a man who has no strength,
⁵like one forsaken among the dead,
like the slain that lie in the grave,
like those whom thou dost remember no more,
for they are cut off from thy hand.
⁶Thou hast put me in the depths of the Pit,
in the regions dark and deep.
⁷Thy wrath lies heavy upon me,
and thou dost overwhelm me with all thy waves.   *Selah*
⁸Thou hast caused my companions to shun me;
thou hast made me a thing of horror to them.
I am shut in so that I cannot escape;
⁹ my eye grows dim through sorrow.
Every day I call upon thee, O Lord;
I spread out my hands to thee.
¹⁰Dost thou work wonders for the dead?
Do the shades rise up to praise thee?   *Selah*
¹¹Is thy steadfast love declared in the grave,
or thy faithfulness in Abaddon?
¹²Are thy wonders known in the darkness,
or thy saving help in the land of forgetfulness?

¹³But I, O Lord, cry to thee;
in the morning my prayer comes before thee.
¹⁴O Lord, why dost thou cast me off?

Why dost thou hide thy face from me?
¹⁵Afflicted and close to death from my youth up,
  I suffer thy terrors; I am helpless.
¹⁶Thy wrath has swept over me;
  thy dread assaults destroy me.
¹⁷They surround me like a flood all day long;
  they close in upon me together.
¹⁸Thou hast caused lover and friend to shun me;
  my companions are in darkness.

The key to understanding this psalm is to be found at verse 5 where we read, *I am like one forsaken among the dead.* In the psalm we have the thoughts and confessions of what today we would call a Christian existentialist.

The RSV has not properly understood the word which it renders *forsaken*. The old KJV (AV) is correct in rendering it "free". Moreover, the word *dead* is to be understood, not as merely physical death, but in the sense in which Jesus uses it, following the OT practice, when he declares, "Let the dead bury their dead".

It has been suggested that the psalmist was a Canaanite convert. He has entered the Covenant people, but has never fully understood what that entails; for in God's Covenant one is bound up with God and one's neighbour, and so loses one's basic freedom to be an individualist.

The modern existentialist is one who supposes himself to be completely free and autonomous, and to be the power-house of his own life and activities. He may still believe in God, but he rejects the way to God that the OT lays down, membership of the Covenant. The danger he faces is to use his humanly found freedom to emancipate himself from the God whom he may well believe to exist; but in so doing he comes to despise in a supercilious manner the common herd, and feels no obligation towards them. Yet these are the folk whom God loves. So he gradually becomes his own god, and makes his position of freedom into slavery to the service of his own ego.

In this psalm the writer declares both that he is a believer and that he needs God's *help* in life; but he dares to stipulate that God must accept him as an existentialist, and let him continue to be a free man. But things have not turned out right on his conditions, which are not God's conditions. For he tells us how he has not expected God to treat him as he has done. Now he is overwhelmed with a sense of God-forsakenness in terms of both physical death and of hell. How very telling this psalm has been therefore for countless tortured souls throughout Christian history! For it has taught them at what point they have gone wrong in their relationship to God.

Thoughtful people of all religions or none have known what it means to be *free*. "Stone walls do not a prison make, nor iron bars a cage." In the Spanish Civil War many a Leftist, even if he had no religious faith, gladly sacrificed his life for a cause he knew to be greater than himself. In that sense he was a free man. In olden times both the Greeks and the Romans produced many such heroic souls. It would seem that among the Hebrews the strong man Samson was also one such. These men and women were "transcendent", as the Dutch theologian Hendrikus Berkhof calls them: they could follow after ideals and overcome adversity with an inner integrity right unto death. They were free men— just as I am a free man, says our psalmist. But my tragedy, he adds, is that now I have discovered I am free only amongst the dead.

Poor man, although he is free, he is blind to the answer to his situation: *My soul is full of troubles; I am reckoned* (though I am free) amongst those who don't know the meaning of life. For since God is the living God, only those who have humbly accepted their station in God's Covenant, and who have given up their autonomous and transcendent freedom, and their distaste for all that living in a Covenant relationship entails ("I am the master of my fate; I am the captain of my soul", as W. E. Henley wrote), only such will ever be able to discover the meaning of life. *This day I have set before you life and death; therefore choose life* (Deut. 30:19). If you do not choose life, then you have already chosen death, as Jesus said of the mourners who were following the coffin of their friend (Luke 9:60; John 5:24).

Having rejected the bonds of the Covenant, then, these are the kind of people this psalmist finds himself associating with—people who are spiritually dead. He may cry as much and as often to God as he will; he may ask, *Are thy wonders known in the darkness, or thy saving help in the land of forgetfulness?* But God cannot answer his cry. For he has now enclosed himself within such a wall of egotism that the love of God cannot penetrate to his soul. So it is not that God *has cast me off* (verse 14). It is that he himself is *helpless* (verse 15). His is the cry of one who will not humble himself to accept the yoke of the Covenant. If he could have heard the call of Jesus, *Take my yoke upon you,* he would have scorned it as an insult to his "existentialist freedom".

And yet the very last line of the psalm reveals that he is becoming aware of the life of death he is living. *My companions are darkness* he finally admits. (The word *in* is not there.) Does this mean that he is beginning to realize that only *God*—the God of the Covenant, the God of the yoke—*is light, and in him is no darkness at all* (1 John:1)?

Perhaps *Heman the Ezrahite*, mentioned in the psalm's heading, wrote this psalm at a time of disillusionment. He was remembered in Chronicles as a great singer (1 Chron. 6:33 and elsewhere). In 2 Chron. 5:12–13 we meet with a man of his name all decked up in fine clothes and surrounded by 120 priests who were trumpeters, and others with cymbals, harps and lyres. Had all this "glory" perhaps gone to the head of this soloist? Had he never really heard the meaning of the Good News that was preached week by week, but thought of himself as a "performer" who was above such things as common worship? Had he now become an objectionable individualist without knowing what people felt about him, that *thou hast made me a thing of horror to them* (verse 8)? And did he despise the humble members of the congregation who were glad to accept the yoke of the Covenant which entailed loving God by loving one's neighbour? We can only speculate.

But if we are right in our interpretation of it, this black psalm is a warning to us all.

UNUSUAL FAITH AND CONFIDENCE

Psalm 89:1–18

A Maskil of Ethan the Ezrahite.

¹I will sing of thy steadfast love, O Lord, for ever;
    with my mouth I will proclaim thy faithfulness to all generations.
²For thy steadfast love was established for ever,
    thy faithfulness is firm as the heavens.
³Thou hast said, "I have made a covenant with my chosen one,
    I have sworn to David my servant:
⁴'I will establish your descendants for ever,
    and build your throne for all generations.'"   *Selah*

⁵Let the heavens praise thy wonders, O Lord,
    thy faithfulness in the assembly of the holy ones!
⁶For who in the skies can be compared to the Lord?
    Who among the heavenly beings is like the Lord,
⁷a God feared in the council of the holy ones,
    great and terrible above all that are round about him?
⁸O Lord God of hosts,
    who is mighty as thou art, O Lord,
    with thy faithfulness round about thee?
⁹Thou dost rule the raging of the sea;
    when its waves rise, thou stillest them.
¹⁰Thou didst crush Rahab like a carcass,
    thou didst scatter thy enemies with thy mighty arm.
¹¹The heavens are thine, the earth also is thine;
    the world and all that is in it, thou hast founded them.
¹²The north and the south, thou hast created them;
    Tabor and Hermon joyously praise thy name.
¹³Thou hast a mighty arm;
    strong is thy hand, high thy right hand.
¹⁴Righteousness and justice are the foundation of thy throne;
    steadfast love and faithfulness go before thee.
¹⁵Blessed are the people who know the festal shout,
    who walk, O Lord, in the light of thy countenance,
¹⁶who exult in thy name all the day,
    and extol thy righteousness.
¹⁷For thou art the glory of their strength;
    by thy favour our horn is exalted.

¹⁸For our shield belongs to the Lord,
  our king to the Holy One of Israel.

How different the tone of this psalm is from that of Ps. 88! Its
wording has expressed the faith and love to God of great souls all
down the centuries. St. Theresa made verse 1 her favourite
motto. The whole psalm forms a doxology, that is, a liturgical
formula of praise, and so it forms a fitting conclusion to the third
Book of the Psalter. This long poem is full of words, which we
shall need to examine carefully, that seek to express the miracle
of God's love to the people of his Covenant.

The psalm has been attributed to *Ethan the Ezrahite*. He was of
the tribe of Judah, one of the wise men of Israel (1 Kings 4:31; 1
Chron. 2:6). His name stands alongside that of the Heman we
met in Ps. 88. Perhaps the editor of Book III is arguing that a man
need not give up his faith just because he has educated himself
and become a philosopher. We note that the psalm is a *Maskil*,
and may therefore have a teaching function (see at 32:1).

Verses 1–4, *Introduction*. In verse 1 we hear the song-leader
declaring his faith in the Lord's acts (plural in Hebrew) that show
forth his *steadfast love* in the Covenant. He finds he must teach
what he has discovered to the young people in his charge, and
urge them to tell their children's children. Note that he says all
this to God, not to the children! That is to say, he is here making a
confession of faith. *Steadfast love, hesed*, is the kernel of God's
Covenant, for the latter is merely the shell of the coconut that
holds those who covenant together in unity. And so he refers
back to the Covenant that God had sworn to David, through his
court-chaplain, Nathan, which we read about in 2 Sam. 7. He
employs the pun that that chapter uses, where to *build a throne* is
to beget sons to sit upon it, in this case, *for ever*. Surely then this is
a good place to insert *Selah*—"Sound the cymbals!"

Verses 5–18, *A hymn declaring that the Lord is King*. "This
miracle of yours, Lord, let the heavens confess." The meaning of
God's free choice of the line of David is not confined to what .
happens on earth, that is, just to the history of Israel. It belongs to
both heaven and earth, or, to use our modern jargon, the line of
David has eschatological significance.

For the heavenly council, see Ps. 82:1. It is *the Lord of Hosts,* then, surrounded as he is by hosts of beings above, and hosts of human beings below (the armies of Israel led by David or by descendants of his) who is the real *Lord* and *God,* and no human king. He is *greatly terrible,* as the *ftn* to verse 7 puts it. Man lives under the wrath of God. He lives in terror that the Lord should ever forsake man. Yet this same God shows utter *faithfulness* in the lives of his Covenant people around him (see Introduction to Vol. 1). What then is this faithfulness like?

We see it in the way he regulates nature, and lets us do so too. He made a Covenant with Noah about this (Gen. 9:12–17). He is Creator (the word used at Gen. 1:1) of the heavens and the earth, the animals, and the hills, and these all *praise thy name* for the way he controls them, as do also the waves of the sea, even the swarms of locusts. *Thou hast a mighty arm* (verse 13). It is God's "arm" that acts for him within space and time, while he himself remains hidden in thick darkness (Exod. 20:21). So it was God, not Moses, *who didst crush Rahab,* as mighty Egypt was known to the prophets, Rahab being the very "incarnation"of the powers of evil (compare Ps. 74:12–17). There at the Exodus we see that *high is thy right hand,* when God won the victory over Pharaoh (Exod. 15:6). God also controls Mounts *Tabor* and *Hermon.* The name Hermon means very holy, taboo, untouchable, pointing to the horrible pagan practices carried out on mountain tops all around the "Holy" Land.

The *festal shout* of verse 15 is the cry "The Lord is King" (Ps. 93:1; 97:1; 99:1) at which time the people present receive the Aaronic Blessing (Num. 6:24–26). They raise the shout because—and what a telling expression this is!—*they walk* (they do not need to run) *in the light of thy countenance,* that is, in thy "saving love" (as "light" is pictured in both Testaments), the light of thy face, thy very presence. Naturally, then, they *exult in thy name,* that is, at the revelation God makes of himself to them, and they do it every day! Parallel with that great line we have: and they are *exalted* (verse 16 *ftn*), uplifted, thrilled to possess that compassionate love which is the gift of God to his redeemed ones, and which he has put in their hearts to use towards the poor and the needy. (See Introduction to Vol. 1 for this meaning of the feminine noun *righteousness*.) God is the God of the poor; *blessed* are those who now possess such divine love themselves. *For thou art the glory of their strength.* Note: (1) this love is of God; it is his glory, not man's; (2) the word *strength,* which his Covenant people receive from God, as we discover throughout the Psalter, is the power of the Holy Spirit. This fact the first Christians rediscovered at Pentecost, when the people of the "Way" were enabled to love the poor and feed the hungry, and to open the eyes of the blind. God began all this work when he raised up David, *our horn* (of strength), for *our king belongs to the Holy One of Israel.*

GOD'S PROMISE TO DAVID (i)

Psalm 89:19–37

¹⁹Of old thou didst speak in a vision
    to thy faithful one, and say:
"I have set the crown upon one who is mighty,
    I have exalted one chosen from the people.
²⁰I have found David, my servant;
    with my holy oil I have anointed him;
²¹so that my hand shall ever abide with him,
    my arm also shall strengthen him.
²²The enemy shall not outwit him,
    the wicked shall not humble him.
²³I will crush his foes before him
    and strike down those who hate him.
²⁴My faithfulness and my steadfast love shall be with him,
    and in my name shall his horn be exalted.
²⁵I will set his hand on the sea
    and his right hand on the rivers.
²⁶He shall cry to me, 'Thou art my Father,
    my God, and the Rock of my salvation.'
²⁷And I will make him the first-born,
    the highest of the kings of the earth.
²⁸My steadfast love I will keep for him for ever,
    and my covenant will stand firm for him.
²⁹I will establish his line for ever

and his throne as the days of the heavens.
³⁰If his children forsake my law
and do not walk according to my ordinances,
³¹if they violate my statutes
and do not keep my commandments,
³²then I will punish their transgression with the rod
and their iniquity with scourges;
³³but I will not remove from him my steadfast love,
or be false to my faithfulness.
³⁴I will not violate my covenant,
or alter the word that went forth from my lips.
³⁵Once for all I have sworn by my holiness;
I will not lie to David.
³⁶His line shall endure for ever,
his throne as long as the sun before me.
³⁷Like the moon it shall be established for ever;
it shall stand firm while the skies endure." *Selah*

What is all this, then, about the king *who belongs to the Holy One of Israel*? The answer is a lyrical poem about the place of David (and so about all the kings descended from him) in the divine plan for the redemption of the world. *Of old* the poem begins, that is, from the dawn of Covenant history, *thou didst speak in a vision to faithful* members of thy Covenant (plural, not as RSV). The reference is probably to both Samuel and to Nathan and their words about David (1 Sam. 13:14; 16:1–13; 2 Sam. 7:4–17). Then God declares: *"I have set the crown . . ."* This is not what the Hebrew says, however (see RSV *ftn*), though it is what later generations made of it. The word in Hebrew is "help". This word was used often enough when the source of help was God himself, in order to picture the work of the Holy Spirit in a human life (Deut. 33:26, 29). The picture is of David (or his successors) now inspired by God.

Then comes a delightful phrase, *I have found David.* (We should read at this point 2 Sam. 7:4–17 and 1 Chron. 17:3–15). Just as baptism is the sign that God has found us before we found him, so anointing is the sign that God had chosen David. His power, therefore, would be God's power, with the result that the

wicked (verse 22), meaning those who do violent deeds of in-
justice, the very opposite of what God does, would never get
David down. For God, being the exact opposite, is "violently"
creative! In his play *Measure for Measure* Shakespeare says:

> O! it is excellent
>> To have a giant's strength, but it is tyrannous
>> To use it like a giant.

This is the kind of violence God would use on David's behalf. The
secret of his success?—*My steadfast love shall be "with" him*
(compare Exod. 3:12 and contrast 2 Sam. 7:15).

The meaning of verse 25 is that David is to bear universal rule
from one end of the known world to the other, that is to say, from
the Mediterranean *Sea* in the west to Mesopotamia, the land of
the *rivers,* in the east. Then *he shall cry out to me* the following
words, meaning that he will have found out for himself what has
nappened to him as the result of God's initial act of grace: *"You
are my Father"* (see 2 Sam. 7:14), *my Rock*-fortress, you are he
who has put *salvation* (that is, the power to bring others to
salvation through love) in my heart.

We are to keep in mind that the king was the "head of the
body". Now, the "body" of Israel too God had claimed as his son
(Exod. 4:22; Jer. 31:20: Hos. 11:1). Thus when God *makes*
David *the first-born* he is only doing what he has already done to
his people Israel as a whole (Exod. 19:5). And when God swears
to keep *covenant* with David *for ever* and to be loyal to that
Covenant in *steadfast love,* he is only doing what he has already
done for Israel at Sinai. So it is also when we come to the "new"
Covenant in the New Testament. God does there only what he
has already done in the "ancient" Covenant, as Paul calls it. But
Israel too must be loyal to God in return. She dare not "profane"
(rather than *violate,* RSV verse 31) God's statutes. To profane
them is to declare that they are merely myths. Modern western
man does this constantly and lightheartedly, for example, with
reference to the Seventh Commandment in his attitude to the
sanctity of marriage. Now, to be disloyal means to rebel (not
transgress, as in the RSV verse 32), and rebellion against un-

merited grace is a shocking thing. It must inevitably call down
punishment upon the rebels. Nevertheless, despite the need God
sees to discipline Israel, he declares: *"But I will never profane
(treat lightly) my (side of the) covenant."*

At verse 27 there is a remarkable use of a "sacred" word. In the
Torah God is on occasions known as *elyon,* which we translate by
"the Most High God" (Gen. 14:18; Num. 24:16). But here God
hails David as the "most high" of the kings of the earth. This
usage therefore demands of us deep theological thought. We
should not suppose that this psalm "foretells" Christ, for many of
the details of it (e.g. verses 22–23) do not fit him at all. On the
other hand, we can confidently conclude that in Christ the
essence of this passage is fulfilled or "enfleshed" for ever. Not
David, not his successors, not Israel, but only he can match its
visionary sweep.

GOD'S PROMISE TO DAVID (ii)

Psalm 89:38–52

38But now thou hast cast off and rejected,
   thou art full of wrath against thy anointed.
39Thou hast renounced the covenant with thy servant;
   thou hast defiled his crown in the dust.
40Thou hast breached all his walls;
   thou hast laid his strongholds in ruins.
41All that pass by despoil him;
   he has become the scorn of his neighbours.
42Thou hast exalted the right hand of his foes;
   thou hast made all his enemies rejoice.
43Yea, thou hast turned back the edge of his sword,
   and thou hast not made him stand in battle.
44Thou hast removed the sceptre from his hand,
   and cast his throne to the ground.
45Thou hast cut short the days of his youth;
   thou hast covered him with shame.   *Selah*

46How long, O Lord? Wilt thou hide thyself for ever?
   How long will thy wrath burn like fire?

⁴⁷Remember, O Lord, what the measure of life is,
    for what vanity thou hast created all the sons of men!
⁴⁸What man can live and never see death?
    Who can deliver his soul from the power of Sheol?   *Selah*

⁴⁹Lord, where is thy steadfast love of old,
    which by thy faithfulness thou didst swear to David?
⁵⁰Remember, O Lord, how thy servant is scorned;
    how I bear in my bosom the insults of the peoples,
⁵¹with which thy enemies taunt, O Lord,
    with which they mock the footsteps of thy anointed.

⁵²Blessed be the Lord for ever!
    Amen and Amen.

Verses 38–45, *But now.* The historical reality, however, appears to be just the opposite of God's commitment to the Covenant. Says our psalmist: *He has* "disdained" (not *renounced,* for that would make God into a liar) *the Covenant with his servant,* and *defiled his crown* (see at verse 19), *breached the walls* of "the city of God" (!). You, God, he says, have caused the neighbouring nations (1) to scorn and gloat over this "son" of yours and (2) you have *exalted their right hand,* that is, you have let them plunder and burn the holy city. In the year 597 B.C. King Jehoiachin surrendered to the Babylonians when still a young man (verse 45); in fact he was only eighteen when he came to the throne, and was then taken into captivity (2 Kings 24:15). He remained in a Babylonian dungeon for the unthinkable period of thirty-seven years (2 Kings 25:27). And who did all these terrible things to the line of David? To use the voice of Jeremiah, who lived through the fall of Jerusalem in that year, it was, the Lord speaking, "My servant, Nebuchadnezzar" (Jer. 25:9).

We could not expect those who lived through this terror to understand what God was doing by it, any more than we could expect the disciples to see any meaning when God "put out the light" of him who had called himself the Light of the World. But that our psalmist was beginning to find God's extraordinary answer to this, the deepest problem in history, we can deduce from the language which he finds himself using. At verse 32 the word *scourges* is used. It is identical with the word *stricken* which we find at Isa. 53:4, where it is used of the Suffering Servant. Then the word *rebellion* is the word *transgression* used also at verse 32, and is the word that is emphasized at Isa. 53:12. At verse 39 emphasis is laid on the word *servant,* rather than on son, as is the case in Isa. 53. Moreover, at verse 50 (see RSV *ftn*), the word *many* is used to describe the sinners of the earth as in Isa. 53:11, 12. Was the answer then to the "unthinkable" problem of the "crucifixion" of Israel and of "David" its king that God had, through "his servant Nebuchadnezzar" turned Israel into his Suffering Servant for the sins of the world?

Verses 46–48. The heathen nations now join in, that is, *all the sons of men.* They perform here like a Greek chorus. They declare on behalf of the psalmist what he would like to say himself, but hardly dare. "The whole world needs to be re-deemed. All men live short and vain lives, and then go straight down to death. Moreover, none of the religions of the world can save their followers from death. So, Lord God of Israel, why are you taking so long to work out the salvation of the world if that is indeed your plan?"

The psalmist cannot have known the words of the great prophet of the Exile whom we call "Second" Isaiah, for the latter uttered his mighty words in Babylon; nor could he know that there would be an end to the Exile, and that God's people would return home to Jerusalem. At Isa. 54:10 we read: *The mountains may depart, and the hills be removed, but my steadfast love shall not depart from you, and my covenant of peace* (*shalom* probably means "comprehensive" here) *shall not be removed*—despite all appearances to the contrary! Again, at Isa. 49:8 (spoken, remember, during the Exile) *In a time of favour* (that is, at God's chosen moment) *I shall answer you... I have kept you* (in exile) *as a Covenant to the people* (that is, as God's Covenant instrument for the salvation of the nations of the earth). And at Isa. 45:14–15 we hear the nations declare: *God is in you only* (not *with* you, as RSV); *truly thou art a God who hidest thyself, O God of Israel, the Saviour.* They meant—what a funny place for the God of gods to hide himself!—in Israel. And that too when Israel was called upon to be the Suffering Servant!

Verses 49–52, *The congregation prays.* "In light of the above, Lord, what can we say?" OT man, let us remember, would have nothing to do with mysticism in any form. He hated to see King Saul speaking in tongues (1 Sam. 10:11) like the wild prophets to whom, later on, Jeremiah violently objected. He refused to try any means to hear God speak except sober reality. If God is hiding himself, then he is hiding himself, and there is nothing we can do about it.

On the other hand, as a well-known modern novelist has put it: "I happen to believe that God does not prophesy. It is man who prophesies. God promises. God has promised to use his Covenant, no matter what the appearances may be." In the same way, says the psalmist, I cannot accept the argument that God's Covenant has come to an end. If it had, then life would have no meaning. As to modern man, then, dare he ever claim that the Covenant which God made in OT times came to an end when, despite God's awesome promise, the ultimate Suffering Servant was crucified (verse 28, verse 34)?

So at verse 52 the congregation affirms that, though it cannot see, yet it believes: *Blessed be the Lord for ever! Amen and Amen.* In fact, this end to Book III of the Psalter might well serve as the end, in faith, to the whole of the OT itself.

O GOD OUR HELP IN AGES PAST (i)

Psalm 90:1–17

A Prayer of Moses, the man of God.

¹Lord, thou hast been our dwelling place
  in all generations.
²Before the mountains were brought forth,
  or ever thou hadst formed the earth and the world.
  from everlasting to everlasting thou art God.

³Thou turnest man back to dust,
  and sayest, "Turn back, O children of men!"
⁴For a thousand years in thy sight
  are but as yesterday when it is past,
  or as a watch in the night.

⁵Thou dost sweep men away; they are like a dream,
  like grass which is renewed in the morning:
⁶in the morning it flourishes and is renewed;
  in the evening it fades and withers.

⁷For we are consumed by thy anger;
  by thy wrath we are overwhelmed.
⁸Thou hast set our iniquities before thee,
  our secret sins in the light of thy countenance.

⁹For all our days pass away under thy wrath,
  our years come to an end like a sigh.
¹⁰The years of our life are threescore and ten,
  or even by reason of our strength fourscore;
 yet their span is but toil and trouble;
  they are soon gone, and we fly away.

¹¹Who considers the power of thy anger,
  and thy wrath according to the fear of thee?
¹²So teach us to number our days
  that we may get a heart of wisdom.

¹³Return, O Lord! How long?
  Have pity on thy servants!
¹⁴Satisfy us in the morning with thy steadfast love,
  that we may rejoice and be glad all our days.
¹⁵Make us glad as many days as thou hast afflicted us,
  and as many years as we have seen evil.
¹⁶Let thy work be manifest to thy servants,
  and thy glorious power to their children.
¹⁷Let the favour of the Lord our God be upon us,
  and establish thou the work of our hands upon us,
  yea, the work of our hands establish thou it.

Isaac Watts' hymn, which opens with the lines at the head of this daily portion, has been hailed as perhaps the finest hymn in the English language. But then it was based upon this finest of psalms. Ps. 90 is the only psalm we have that has been attributed to Moses. We are to remember that all theology begins with the passage Exod. 3:1–14. For there the God of both the OT and the NT, the God of the whole Bible, reveals himself (1) as the "holy"

God; and (2) as the creating God. This God also (3) reveals himself through his Word, by speaking out of the fire, that is out of the pain and suffering, and the chaos that are endemic in this world. (4) He "comes down" to deliver his people; as he did in the days of Moses, so he does always, in the person of Christ 2,000 years ago, in the power of his Spirit to us in our day. (5) He offers *himself* to us in his Word and Teaching (*Torah*) through the Covenant relationship of steadfast love which he gave to Israel through Moses; and God expects his people to show him obedience, love and loyalty in return for the forgiving nature of his love. And then, most wonderfully, this God (6) offers to be "with" us in a personal mannner, and (7) seals his offer by telling us his "personal" name.

The psalm has two poles, so to speak. The one is the pathetic shortness of human life; the other is the miracle of the eternity of God. But our psalmist begins right away by closing the gap! He begins by addressing the Lord himself, using God's personal name, Yahweh, the Hebrew word that lies behind the English word Lord, and he uses that name as the first word he utters. He tells Yahweh how wonderful it is to have him "with" us, his poor creatures, despite the awesome chasm that separates God and man. Moreover, he continues, this "witness" is to be found *in all generations*. So there is no reason why we in our day cannot repeat this wonderful first exclamation to be found here, and apply it to what we now know of God as our dwelling place, our "home", both in Christ and in the life of the Church (see also Deut. 33:27). For God does not change. He is the same God *who formed* ("travailed with") *the earth and the world* when it was born from the womb of time (see Job 38:8).

O GOD OUR HELP IN AGES PAST (ii)

Psalm 90:1–17 (*cont'd*)

And what of *man* (verse 3)? *Thou turnest enosh back to the dust*, declares our psalmist—not *adam*, let us note. "Adam" had failed God's loving plan for his life. Chapter 4 of Genesis shows how *adam*, humanity, in the persons of Cain and Lamech, and Adah and Zillah (both men and women) had become what unredeemed humanity is to this day, egocentric and mean, and unconcerned about the needs of their neighbour. But Gen. 4:26 went on to speak of the birth of Enosh, another word for man or humanity, a new kind of man, humble and sincere, "worshipping man", "man who calls upon the name of the Lord". But Mr. and Mrs. Enosh must not forget that they also belong to our common humanity that needs redemption from the stranglehold of sin. God cries to *all* humanity: "*Turn back* home, *O children of Adam.*" "Enosh", of course, has already discovered how wonderful the going back home is. In Ps. 8:4 the psalmist gazes in awe at the heavens and exclaims: "What is *enosh* that thou art mindful of him?" "Adam" was too self-centred ever to make such a cry. But this psalm is meant for the sons of the Covenant that God had made with Israel through Moses.

The nations of old, including the philosophically-minded Greeks (whom Paul addresses in 1 Cor. 1) all regarded space as what separated God from man. Israel, alone in all the world, declared that it was sin that did so; to her God was not "up there". If fellowship with God could be pictured as life lived together in a Garden, then it was sin that had excluded humanity from such a wonderful life (Gen. 3:22–24). Accordingly man now lives outside the Garden under the *wrath* of God, to the extent that man is *overwhelmed* (verse 7), baffled, dismayed, by the thought that God, who knows even *our secret sins* (verse 8) could possibly have forsaken mankind altogether. God even flaunts these sins, the same verse suggests, parades them before himself, pointing to each of them in turn like at a police identity parade. So our sins are no longer *hidden*; they are spotlighted and illuminated in the *light of thy countenance*.

So it is *sin* that spoils our lives, and not natural decay. This means that, since we are sinners, once we reach our allotted span, then that is in fact the end. *Our years come to an end like a sigh.* How sad it all is!

Verses 9–12 raise a good question. The great majority of humanity consider man's inevitable death in scientific terms.

They see it as the running down of the natural functions of the body till these reach a full stop. But *the heart of wisdom* which the psalmist prays for (and which Paul speaks of in 1 Cor. 1) is one that understands his coming death to be the result of God's *wrath* at his sinful, rebellious nature. His rebellious state prevents him from standing still in awe and wonder, and being overwhelmed by what is the wholly Hebraic, but certainly not the Greek, idea that God loathes sin.

Verses 13–17. The psalmist ends his poem in a way that no "Greek", ancient or modern, would think of doing; for modern western man has emancipated himself from all ideas that there is a God and that religion is anything other than superstition. Note that the psalmist does not beg God for a long life, far less for immortality. We saw at verse 3 that God says to man: "Come back home (to where you belong) for sin has separated you from me." Now, however, the psalmist addresses the same word back to God! "Come back to us, O Lord," he begs. "How long will it be till you change your plan about your servants? Tomorrow morning (don't wait any longer) please satiate (!) us with your *hesed*, your *steadfast love*, *that we may rejoice and be glad all our days*. If such should happen, then we need not worry about death any more. For your *hesed* is stronger than death" (see S. of Songs 8:6).

Finally he prays for four things: (1) Make the sum of joy in our hearts equal to the sum of *the evil we have seen*. (2) Make that love of yours plain to us *your servants* now. And (3) do not forget our children—for surely little children too can experience your Covenant. Let this *work* of yours be *manifest to*, "seen by", your servants. "My Father is working still," said Jesus, "and I am working" (John 5:17). God's work has been to create, first, the heavens and the earth, and all that is in them, including humanity; and then, second, it is to recreate and make new heavens and a new earth, and so to recreate new men and women (Isa. 66:22). You have promised to do this by redeeming us from the power of sin and so of death. Do it then for us and those who follow us! Then the psalmist asks: (4) Let your *favour*, your graciousness, your beauty enable us in our turn to do *your* will.

"Beauty" is the translation found in the AV, rather than the RSV's *favour*, and how right it is! For graciousness is beautiful. Charles Kingsley was overheard in his last illness murmuring quietly to himself: "How beautiful God is, how beautiful God is!"

No more talk, then, of horror at inevitable death! The living, loving, kind, gracious and beautiful God, through his forgiving love, creates in us his own fulness of life. And this *glorious power* is what prevails even over death itself.

> Change and decay in all around I see:
> O thou who changest not, abide with me.   (H. F. Lyte)

The editors of the Psalter placed Ps. 90 immediately after Ps. 89. The latter finished with a declaration of faith that God's steadfast love must necessarily reach beyond the "end" of Israel as marked by her exile. With this, Book III ended. But, learning from the historical fact that God has now restored his people to life, Book IV can begin with a psalm which declares that God's *glorious power* does indeed prevail not only over "exile", but over death itself.

GOD IS MY HOME

Psalm 91:1–16

> ¹He who dwells in the shelter of the Most High,
>   who abides in the shadow of the Almighty,
> ²will say to the Lord, "My refuge and my fortress;
>   my God, in whom I trust."
> ³For he will deliver you from the snare of the fowler
>   and from the deadly pestilence;
> ⁴he will cover you with his pinions,
>   and under his wings you will find refuge;
>   his faithfulness is a shield and buckler.
> ⁵You will not fear the terror of the night,
>   nor the arrow that flies by day,
> ⁶nor the pestilence that stalks in darkness,
>   nor the destruction that wastes at noonday.

⁷A thousand may fall at your side,
  ten thousand at your right hand;
  but it will not come near you.
⁸You will only look with your eyes
  and see the recompense of the wicked.

⁹Because you have made the Lord your refuge,
  the Most High your habitation,
¹⁰no evil shall befall you,
  no scourge come near your tent.

¹¹For he will give his angels charge of you
  to guard you in all your ways.
¹²On their hands they will bear you up,
  lest you dash your foot against a stone.
¹³You will tread on the lion and the adder,
  the young lion and the serpent you will trample under foot.

¹⁴Because he cleaves to me in love, I will deliver him;
  I will protect him, because he knows my name.
¹⁵When he calls to me, I will answer him;
  I will be with him in trouble,
  I will rescue him and honour him.
¹⁶With long life I will satisfy him,
  and show him my salvation.

Verses 1–8. The rendering of verse 1 in the AV is most attractive:
"He that dwelleth in the 'secret place' of the Most High". Ps. 90,
as we have seen, had been about the awesomeness and the
greatness and the everlastingness of the Most High God over
against man's smallness and the brevity of his life. Yet, says the
psalmist, this mighty God invites even such little persons as we
are to share the secret of his love with him.

The Jewish Prayer Book suggests that this psalm be read "before retiring to rest". Yet it is not so much a prayer as a sermon in
verse. It appears to be the voice of a Temple minister assuring a
private enquirer (for this idea see Ps. 27:4) that God can and will
protect him or her from all, even the most sinister, threats of evil,
the evil that leads to the death of the human spirit. In his talk with
this ordinary person he explains that the opposite of fear is not
courage, but faith.

The word *abides* in verse 1 means "to spend the night" as in a room in an inn. As Jesus put it, "In my Father's house are many rooms" (John 14:2). "Keep on coming back into the care of the Almighty each evening," this minister is recommending his enquirer, then you will find yourself saying to the Lord, *"My refuge and my fortress, my God, in whom I trust."* For you will have discovered that God has delivered you from what is threatening your life. *His faithfulness*, his unshakeability, is impregnable, it is *a shield and buckler.*

The subsequent poetic descriptions of the attacks of evil from outside of us are far more telling than any mention of wild dogs, or of thugs, or of "things that go bump in the night", or, to be up to date, of bombs, flying-saucers, bacteria, or even the secret police. That eastern man did live in terror of evil powers outside of himself, even when he had locked his doors against them, is evidenced by an Assyrian bronze statuette now to be seen in the Louvre in Paris. It is of a demon with wings, naked, and with a malicious face. In contrast, the Lord too has wings (poetically speaking!, verse 4). Then the LXX, the Greek version of the OT, translates verse 6b as "the demon of midday", possibly suggesting sunstroke. In a word, what our Temple minister is saying is "This is a risky world. You may quite possibly be hit by one of the arrows of the powers of evil (faith is not an insurance policy against sickness and death), but don't *fear* these things when they come." As Paul puts it at Rom. 8:28, "We know that in *everything* God works for good", through nakedness, peril and all the rest. Consequently the language of this psalm is far removed from the silly self-centred cry of the person saved from the shipwreck when all others perished—"Now I have received proof of the existence of God, for he answered my prayer when I was struggling in the water."

What has all this got to do with us today? Jung, the great psychologist, has written: "All one's neighbours are ruled by an uncontrolled and uncontrollable fear just like oneself. In lunatic asylums it is a well-known fact that patients are far more dangerous when suffering from fear than when moved by wrath or hatred." Or, as J. B. Priestley writes: "Heads of governments know that a frightened people is easier to govern and will agree to millions and millions being spent on 'Defence'." God knows all this about our frightened human nature. If we were but to look in a concordance to the Scriptures under the word "angel", we would discover that, when the eternal world breaks in upon our human consciousness, the very first words that man hears with his heart and mind are "Do not be afraid".

We have a picture here of a little child looking up trustingly into his father's face, knowing that *under his wings* "it will all be all right". The idea of God's caring wings is as ancient as the earliest passages in the OT—see Exod. 19:4; 25:20; Deut. 32:12. In fact, the picture is as much that of God's mother-love as it is that of his father-love.

Verses 9–13, *Because*. Why then should you fear? It works two ways: (1) *Because thou, Lord, art my refuge* (see RSV verse 9 *ftn*). God, in other words, has acted first, for he has invited me to come home to the place he has prepared for me. (2) *Because you have made the Most High your "home"* (compare Deut. 26:15); in other words, you have responded to God's loving invitation by faith. You may be living in a tent (the "home" of the pilgrim in all ages), but God is in truth your real home. And he has always been so! Here we have the deliberate use of ancient epithets for God. This reminds us of two things: (1) It reminds us of what Ps. 90 has been saying about the "ancientness" of God, and (2) it reminds us that the Church of today is many thousands of years old, and not just a mere two thousand. But (3) he adds: "Don't imagine that you have been 'saved' just in order 'to be saved'." God has now turned you into a St. George, as we might put it, and has enabled you to fight with all the dragons that haunt the life of human beings (verse 13), whatever they be, subtle temptations or powerful forces of communal evil.

Verses 14–16, *Because, once again*. This time God himself speaks: *Because* he clings *to me in love*, even "hugs" me, as the verb can mean, I will be to him what I promised to be to Abraham a thousand years before this period of the psalmist. "Don't be afraid, Abraham, I myself am your shield; I myself am your very great reward" (Gen. 15:1). See also Ps. 34:7; Gen. 24:7, 40; Exod. 23:20; Matt. 4:6.

Then God adds: *I will be with him in trouble*, as we hear God say again at Isa. 43:1–3. There God proclaims, "I have called you by name, you are mine". But here God says, *"Because he knows my name"*. So this very small human person is actually in intimate fellowship with Almighty God! (verse 1). We can say this with confidence, because to know the name in olden days meant to know the very essence of the personality of its owner. Faith then in this psalm is not an act of the intellect. If it were so, then many of us would be excluded, including all the mentally handicapped folk in our society. Faith is a passionate relationship of love that even a child can know.

This section uses powerful language. God promises an eight-fold blessing. Perhaps we might count these up for ourselves. One of them is: *With long life I will satisfy him.* The idea of long life was meant to be understood as a sacramental promise of eternal life. God will actually "satiate" him with life! Jesus said: "I came that they may have life, and have it abundantly" (John 10:10), that is to say, be satiated with life. Another is when in the last line of the psalm we move even beyond faith to revelation: *I will show him*, or rather, "let him see into" my *salvation*, my saving love. That has always been the excited hope of the believer, that beyond death he will see into, see the meaning of, God's saving love, and see it from within that home which God will give him for all eternity.

ENJOYING GOD

Psalm 92:1–15

A Psalm. A Song for the Sabbath.

¹It is good to give thanks to the Lord,
　to sing praises to thy name, O Most High;
²to declare thy steadfast love in the morning,
　and thy faithfulness by night,
³to the music of the lute and the harp,
　to the melody of the lyre.
⁴For thou, O Lord, hast made me glad by thy work;
　at the works of thy hands I sing for joy.

⁵How great are thy works, O Lord!
   Thy thoughts are very deep!
⁶The dull man cannot know,
   the stupid cannot understand this:
⁷that, though the wicked sprout like grass
   and all evildoers flourish,
 they are doomed to destruction for ever,
⁸   but thou, O Lord, art on high for ever.
⁹For, lo, thy enemies, O Lord,
   for, lo, thy enemies shall perish;
   all evildoers shall be scattered.

¹⁰But thou hast exalted my horn like that of the wild ox;
   thou hast poured over me fresh oil.
¹¹My eyes have seen the downfall of my enemies,
   my ears have heard the doom of my evil assailants.

¹²The righteous flourish like the palm tree,
   and grow like a cedar in Lebanon.
¹³They are planted in the house of the Lord,
   they flourish in the courts of our God.
¹⁴They still bring forth fruit in old age,
   they are ever full of sap and green,
¹⁵to show that the Lord is upright;
   he is my rock, and there is no unrighteousness in him.

This psalm makes a good sequel to Ps. 91. It is spoken by one who has done what Ps. 91 advises, who has made his home in God. And now, on a Sabbath Day, the day for the public worship of *the Most High God*, he lets his thoughts be known. For the Sabbath is a "sacramental" day. It reminds us week by week of the Sabbath satisfaction that God knows in eternity (Gen. 2:3), and which he seeks to share with us in the here and now.

Verses 1–4, *A call to worship*. We sometimes use these words today to open an act of public worship. This is understandable. Just as God's satisfaction is eternal, so our experience of worship need never vary, whether it be carried on in 1000 B.C. or A.D. 2000. And worship begins with an act of recognizing God's love and of *giving thanks* to him for it. Ps. 91 has shown us why we should want to do so. There we saw that it is God's *work* to have brought me "home" to himself (Ps. 91:1, 9). So then, for *all the works of thy hands I sing for joy*. The psalm, we note, begins with God, and as we shall see, it ends with God.

Verses 5–9, *The wonder of his works*. The boorish (RSV *dull*) man cannot see any meaning in life. The *stupid* fool (RSV merely *stupid*) cannot see God's works issuing from *the deep thoughts* of the Lord in the intricacies of the social life of mankind. He cannot therefore "enjoy" tracing the works of God all round him in the life and interaction of human communities. He simply cannot see that the wicked flourish, only to end in *eternal destruction. But thou, O Lord, art on high for ever,* that is, transcendent in eternity.

Verses 10–15. How do I know this to be so? Out of my own experience! I feel a delirious sense of joy, and can toss my head with a sensation of power, of possessing the Spirit of God. This is because you, God, selected *me*(!) for this, anointing me as you would anoint a king. I have also witnessed the reverse of this among those who attacked me because I witnessed to your love.

In verse 12 two trees are mentioned. (a) The *palm tree* grows very tall, it is "upright". It is useful, for it provides food for man. It also provides the materials man needs for making ropes, mats and roofing. Its genius is that it can bend before the hurricane, and survive the worst of the storms. (b) The *cedar of Lebanon* is the most magnificent of all the trees of the Levant. It can grow to be 120 feet tall and forty feet in girth. There are cedars growing there today that are 2,000 years old. It was the privilege of the cedar to provide the inner walls and adornments of Solomon's Temple. So then, the righteous man, says our poet, feels like these trees. When the theologian Karl Barth reached the age of eighty he wrote to another elderly theologian: "It is wonderful to feel hilarious joy—even an old tree!" Barth was referring to 2 Cor. 9:7, where the word *cheerful* ought to be rendered, as he renders it, by "hilarious". Barth knew, even in old age, that he could still give prodigally and thrillingly of his best for the world to read, as he interpreted for this generation the wondrous works of God.

Now we jump into using plural verbs (verse 13). The palm tree and the cedar have seeded, and have begotten many young new plants around them. Even in their full maturity, even in their *old age*, they can still bear *fruit* (compare John 15:16), and show forth the grace and vitality of love. This showing forth, however, is not an end in itself. What even an old tree must do is to tell others how good God is, and how good life is when, to quote the answer to the first question of the Shorter Catechism, he can declare with certainty, "Man's chief end is to glorify God and to enjoy him for ever."

GOD'S VICTORY OVER EVIL

Psalm 93:1–5

¹The Lord reigns; he is robed in majesty;
   the Lord is robed, he is girded with strength.
 Yea, the world is established; it shall never be moved;
² thy throne is established from of old;
   thou art from everlasting.

³The floods have lifted up, O Lord,
   the floods have lifted up their voice,
   the floods lift up their roaring.
⁴Mightier than the thunders of many waters,
   mightier than the waves of the sea,
   the Lord on high is mighty!

⁵Thy decrees are very sure;
   holiness befits thy house,
   O Lord, for evermore.

We have met psalms like this before (e.g. Ps. 47) and we shall meet more like it soon (Pss. 95–99). These psalms all proclaim the good news of the reign, not of the earthly king who sat enthroned before the eyes of his people in Jerusalem, but of God. In fact, *The Lord reigns* may equally well be rendered "The Lord is King". There he is, *robed,* as was the human king—but not in purple, but *in majesty* and *girded with strength,* that is, with the power of his Spirit.

Some scholars suggest that the Davidic king was re-enthroned each year. Such a ceremony was designed to keep him humble. It reminded him of two things: (1) that his people might not want him to remain king for life unless he behaved himself, and (2) that God was the real King of Israel, not he. How exciting this acted drama must have been, accompanied as it was by processions, the reciting of poems (as when John Kennedy was inaugurated as President of the United States), the beat of drums, the sound of martial music, and the fanfares of trumpets.

The Lord is King, then, King *from of old,* and King to all eternity. The *floods* have tried their utmost to overcome the world. But the Lord is *mightier* than the waves of the primal *sea* in his transcendent majesty.

Our psalmist declares, then, that God has shown himself to be King (a) in the *past* when he established the world; (b) at the *present* moment at this sacramental act when the crown was placed on the head of the human king; and (c) for ever, since *the world shall never be moved.* In fact, God is Lord of ALL!

As to the *floods,* they are (a) the powers of evil seen in Gen. 1:2; (b) the power of sin that flooded the whole world in Noah's day; (c) the power of sin within my own soul. But God is Lord of ALL! At Gen. 1:3 God overcame the primal flood when he "spoke". At Gen. 8:1 God overcame the flood when he "remembered", took note of, Noah. So then at this moment in this public act of the worship of God I discover that he has overcome the flood of evil in my life, by forgiving me and restoring my soul (Ps. 23:3).

Thy decrees are therefore inviolable. These decrees are God's words of revelation, the Ten Commandments, his promises, his Covenant. At Exod. 3:14 God uttered the "absolute" Word: I AM who I AM. No wonder *holiness* suits *thy house.* (a) God *was* I AM in the days of Moses; (b) God *is* I AM in the days of this psalm; (c) God *will be* I AM *for evermore.* As an old saint once said: "The one fact is God. All other things are circumstances."

WE ARE ALL UNDER JUDGMENT

Psalm 94:1–23

¹O Lord, thou God of vengeance,
    thou God of vengeance, shine forth!
²Rise up, O judge of the earth;
    render to the proud their deserts!
³O Lord, how long shall the wicked,
    how long shall the wicked exult?

⁴They pour out their arrogant words,
    they boast, all the evildoers.
⁵They crush thy people, O Lord,
    and afflict thy heritage.
⁶They slay the widow and the sojourner,
    and murder the fatherless;
⁷and they say, "The Lord does not see;
    the God of Jacob does not perceive."

⁸Understand, O dullest of the people!
    Fools, when will you be wise?
⁹He who planted the ear, does he not hear?
    He who formed the eye, does he not see?
¹⁰He who chastens the nations, does he not chastise?
    He who teaches men knowledge,
¹¹   the Lord, knows the thoughts of man,
    that they are but a breath.

¹²Blessed is the man whom thou dost chasten, O Lord,
    and whom thou dost teach out of thy law
¹³to give him respite from days of trouble,
    until a pit is dug for the wicked.
¹⁴For the Lord will not forsake his people;
    he will not abandon his heritage;
¹⁵for justice will return to the righteous,
    and all the upright in heart will follow it.

¹⁶Who rises up for me against the wicked?
    Who stands up for me against evil-doers?
¹⁷If the Lord had not been my help,
    my soul would soon have dwelt in the land of silence.
¹⁸When I thought, "My foot slips,"
    thy steadfast love, O Lord, held me up.

¹⁹When the cares of my heart are many,
    thy consolations cheer my soul.
²⁰Can wicked rulers be allied with thee,
    who frame mischief by statute?
²¹They band together against the life of the righteous,
    and condemn the innocent to death.
²²But the Lord has become my stronghold,
    and my God the rock of my refuge.
²³He will bring back on them their iniquity
    and wipe them out for their wickedness;
    the Lord our God will wipe them out.

Verses 1–7. The word *vengeance* does not sound right to us. And rightly so, for the word should be "recompense", "remuneration", "deserts", even "reward". God is of course impartial in his judgment. He returns to every man absolutely objective judgment. He is not swayed by likes or dislikes, any more than a judge of integrity is when he passes sentence. The psalmist, unfortunately, wants God to "reveal his anger", or, as TEV translates it, "let it shine forth". But God is not like that.

What the psalmist does here is to inform God about what he is, of course, fully aware of already. He describes to God the way that proud, self-sufficient people behave towards those they hold in their power. But what is more, he tells God that such people get away with their activities. And he complains that God makes no move to rescue the sufferers.

Yet this is what the real world is all about in all generations and in all places. We think today of petty officials in what we call "Banana Republics" sadistically dismissing the complaints of simple people who have no influence and no money for bribes. We think of loan sharks, of the Mafia in Italy or the States, of the Yakusa in Japan, of "bent" police, and so on. Ill-treatment of the *widow* and *orphan* of course arouses our ire (verse 6). But we only too easily look the other way in the case of the *sojourner* (same verse). Today this is the refugee, the displaced person, the Gastarbeiter in Europe, the coloured youth in the slums of our big cities, the au pair girl, the stateless stowaway. The psalmist shows that he has the pity of God in his heart for such as these.

Perhaps we today overlook such problem people as a nuisance to our conscience. In fact, the psalmist notices that the public does not agree with him in feeling pity. This is because God does not appear to condemn the egotism and cruelty that is rampant in the world. Thoughtful businessmen can even speak of the business world today as "the Jungle"—even while God looks the other way.

Verses 8–11, *God's reply*. It was the risen Christ who said pointedly to the group of disciples on the road to Emmaus: "O foolish men, and slow of heart to believe all that the prophets have spoken! Was it not necessary that the Christ should suffer these things?" (Luke 24:25–26). Equally, here, was it not necessary for God to suffer these things? God replies: *Understand, O dullest of the people* (was the risen Christ actually using the language of this psalm?) *when will you be wise?* Of course God sees and hears all that goes on in the world, for he made us and he made man. He knows that the *thoughts of man* (on punishing the wicked) *are but a breath*. On the other hand, the thoughts of God are very different.

We might then pose the question in the language we have quoted from the NT: "Was it not necessary that God himself should suffer these things?" God had *planted the ear,* and God had *formed the eye.* God knows all that goes on, and God knows what he is doing. God "instructs" (NEB), rather than *chastens, the nations.* He it is who has taught them their various cultures and scientific skills (see Gen. 4:17–22). So it is he, not we, who will "correct" them (NEB), and correct them out of the pain he feels in his loving heart. "Vengeance is mine, and recompense," says one of the earliest poems in the OT about God (Deut. 32:35). For you do not have any idea what recompense really means. It is interesting that Paul quotes this verse from Deuteronomy at Rom. 12:19.

Verses 12–15. Then—how extraordinary! *Blessed is the man whom thou dost* "instruct", *O Lord.* This does not refer, we discover, to the violent bullies of the world. It refers to the people of God, that is, to us, for it could be we who actually disdain the coloured immigrant or the down-and-out. Therefore it is God, our partner in the Covenant, who is bound up with us in love, who feels the pain of what we are doing and suffers from it—even while we may be blissfully unaware of the hurt we are causing him. *Fools,* he says, *when will you be wise?* In his pity, therefore, God seeks to make us wise. *For the Lord will not forsake his people.* He will not let us get away with our folly. He is determined that *justice will return to the righteous,* that is, to God's chosen people whom he has already "put right" with himself. Then all responsible people, then and now, will do justice (Micah 6:8) and leave God to attend to the wicked as that is his prerogative alone.

Justice will return. It was Bonhoeffer who said: "The OT insists on justice being done now, *as if* there were no after life." For only in this way can life take on meaning. For it is only at each moment in life now, when justice is actually being done, that that moment creates justice in the life beyond. This is the theme of Jesus' parable of the Last Judgment (Matt. 25:31–46).

Verses 16–23. The psalmist goes back to his original question (verses 1–3). *Who stands up for me against evil-doers?* Like most people, he doesn't like having God's finger pointing at him with the accusation "You are the man" (see 2 Sam. 12:7). But he now knows the answer. In his infinite *hosed,* his *steadfast love,* God has *held me up* all the time when I behaved as a fool, and supposed that God's judgment was upon evil-doers only. But not on me! If he had not chastened me, out of sheer grace to me a sinner, then my *foot* would have *slipped* and I would now be *in the land of silence,* that is, not just in the grave, but actually in the land where I could no longer hear the voice of God. Moreover, I have discovered that when I feel ill with worry about these issues *thy consolations cheer my soul.*

Here's a question, then, that our psalmist puts (verse 20). The Lord has revealed his living purpose by *statute, hoq.* This word we have met before and found it to mean an immutable law, chiselled in stone (as the verb means), unchangeable as God himself is unchangeable (Exod. 18:16; Deut. 12:1; Ps. 81:4). Can it be possible, then, for wicked men so *to ally themselves with God* that they can announce their evil plans by *statute?* What a ludicrous idea! These men are not God. But now the Lord *has become my stronghold* (I admit I couldn't accept his loving care at first). But now I am convinced. So with a quiet mind I leave the whole question of the future of the wicked to him.

THE VENITE

Psalm 95:1–11

¹O come, let us sing to the Lord;
    let us make a joyful noise to the rock of our salvation!
²Let us come into his presence with thanksgiving;
    let us make a joyful noise to him with songs of praise!
³For the Lord is a great God,
    and a great King above all gods.
⁴In his hand are the depths of the earth;
    the heights of the mountains are his also.
⁵The sea is his, for he made it;
    for his hands formed the dry land.

⁶O come, let us worship and bow down,
    let us kneel before the Lord, our Maker!
⁷For he is our God,
    and we are the people of his pasture,
    and the sheep of his hand.

 O that today you would hearken to his voice!
⁸   Harden not your hearts, as at Meribah,
    as on the day at Massah in the wilderness,
⁹when your fathers tested me,
    and put me to the proof, though they had seen my work.
¹⁰For forty years I loathed that generation
    and said, "They are a people who err in heart,
    and they do not regard my ways."
¹¹Therefore I swore in my anger
    that they should not enter my rest.

This psalm is very well known. It is an integral part of the Anglican Morning Prayer Service. It forms, in its opening verses, an invitation to worship. *Venite* is, of course, the Latin for "O come".

By the end of the OT period the Temple covered a large area. One reached its first gates by ascending a broad flight of steps. Then, having gone through the gates at the top (Ps. 24) the worshipper entered the Court of the Gentiles. It was really a great open space, colonnaded round its walls. Into it anyone could enter, Jew or Gentile. Having crossed over this courtyard, one entered another court, into which Jewish women were allowed to accompany their menfolk. But only male Jews could go into the next court. The divisions between these three courts is what St. Paul maintains Christ broke down, for in Christ there is neither Jew nor Gentile, neither male nor female (Gal. 3:28).

The lay worshipper could go no further. Entry to the final court was the prerogative of the priests alone. The idea behind even this barrier, however, was broken down eventually. At the Reformation in Europe the railing was finally removed which had prevented the laity from approaching right up to the altar. This was not because the priests had all now become mere laymen. It was because, in conformity with God's *hoq* (see Ps. 94), all lay people were fully granted the status that was already theirs at the giving of the Covenant when God had called Israel to be his "kingdom of priests" (Exod. 19:6).

Verses 1–2. A group of villagers has come up to Jerusalem, perhaps taking several days to make the pilgrimage, and they are now excitedly gazing at the first set of gates at the top of the great staircase. They are all there, wearing their "Sunday best", children included. They are met by a Temple functionary, either a priest or a "cultic prophet" whom we would call a minister. With joy he welcomes them and invites them to come in: *O come*, he says, *let us come into his presence with thanksgiving and with songs of praise*. And so they sing their way into the Temple precincts.

Verses 3–5. When a line in the Psalms begins with *for (ki)* we can usually better translate it by "that", with a solemn declaration before the "that". So we have to add: "We declare", or "we believe", that . . . At verse 3, then, another minister takes over and preaches a little sermon to those who are still standing outside the gates. He declaims, and almost certainly he gets the group of worshippers to repeat after him, lines which are really a short creed: "We believe that the Lord is a great God... All things are *in his hand, the mountains, the sea,* and *the dry land too.*"

Verse 6. The group passes through Gate I. They stop at Gate II. Outside it the speaker at verse 1 invites them to penetrate further in, and in this way they approach ever nearer to the Holy God. *Come in,* he cries, and let us worship... *our Maker.*

Verse 7 (except the last line). Again we meet with *ki.* The whole group responds as the second minister invites them to go through Gate II by declaring loudly another little creed: "We believe that *he is our God.*" In these words they take one step beyond what the "creed" of verses 3–6 had contained. In it God was Lord of nature. Now here he is the Good Shepherd of his people, the God who cares for each member of his flock. For the shepherd knows each individual sheep as he touches it *by hand.*

Verse 7 (last line). The minister next says: "All right. You are now about to take part in a solemn act of sacrifice. Please *hearken,* listen, *to his voice.*" How good that we receive such a warning! This psalm is sung at a Jewish wedding as the bride comes up the aisle. We are to remember that for both Jews and Christians the marriage of two believers reflects the very nature of God himself. In the Synagogue a prayer is next sung in which the worshippers present are reminded that when God claimed Israel as his Bride and made Covenant with her (we too use the word "Covenant" in our marriage service) he rejoiced over her with the words, "I will never let you go". It was evidently to just such total fidelity that Jesus referred in Mark 10:11–12.

Verses 8–11. One of the most solemn elements of the Word that God speaks to us in the Scriptures is his warning to remember the past. The next verses are actually a lesson from history given us out of the mouth of God. This is because the minister, like Moses, when he speaks, speaks as the representative of God. For the names *Massah* and *Meribah* see Exod. 17:1–7. The passage there tells of how Israel had had the temerity to put *the Lord to the proof,* by saying, "*Is the Lord among us or not?*", even though they had lived through the miracle of their redemption from Egypt, that is, even *though they had seen my work.*

I loathed that generation (or, was disgusted with it), God continues, *for forty years*, that is, right through the whole Wilderness Wandering (see Num. 14:34). For *they are a people whose hearts* have "wandered away" from me, and not wandered *with* me, for they are *not* "aware of" *my ways*. How can you enter these courts to worship, is the point of God's sermon, except you do so with a "whole heart", that is, with integrity of mind and spirit? Or, as Jesus put it, how dare you enter his courts (or, in our case, come to church on Sundays) unless you have first forgiven your brother and have learned to love him with your whole heart (Matt. 5:22-24)?

To find one's home in God's love, as we saw at Ps. 91, means to enter into his peace and joy. But those who rebel against his loving guidance exclude themselves from that rest. That is what *I swore in my anger* refers to.

This psalm thus takes its rightful place in any call made to man to worship the Living God. For it warns us that we dare not take God's majesty for granted, or enter his courts insouciantly, rashly, or in a spirit of superficial superstition.

Says this psalm: (1) God is the great God; (2) God is the loving God; (3) God has always kept his Covenant promise even when your fathers rebelled against him; (4) therefore enter his presence in awe, wonder and gratitude; for you are going to share in a sacrificial act that reveals the very heart of God.

A NEW SONG

Psalm 96:1-13

¹O sing to the Lord a new song;
   sing to the Lord, all the earth!
²Sing to the Lord, bless his name;
   tell of his salvation from day to day.
³Declare his glory among the nations,
   his marvellous works among all the peoples!
⁴For great is the Lord, and greatly to be praised;
   he is to be feared above all gods.
⁵For all the gods of the peoples are idols;

but the Lord made the heavens.
⁶Honour and majesty are before him;
  strength and beauty are in his sanctuary.

⁷Ascribe to the Lord, O families of the peoples,
  ascribe to the Lord glory and strength!
⁸Ascribe to the Lord the glory due his name;
  bring an offering, and come into his courts!
⁹Worship the Lord in holy array;
  tremble before him, all the earth!

¹⁰Say among the nations, "The Lord reigns!
  Yea, the world is established, it shall never be moved;
  he will judge the peoples with equity."
¹¹Let the heavens be glad, and let the earth rejoice;
  let the sea roar, and all that fills it;
¹²   let the field exult, and everything in it!
  Then shall all the trees of the wood sing for joy
¹³   before the Lord, for he comes,
  for he comes to judge the earth.
He will judge the world with righteousness,
  and the peoples with his truth.

God is the God who makes all things new. That is why Israel feels
compelled to call upon *all the earth* to sing a new song (compare
Rev. 5:9; 14:3; 21:1, 5). For God is not only the Creator, he
keeps on recreating. So each new day requires a new song. The
LXX (the Greek version of the OT) suggests that this psalm
refers to the new beginning offered to Israel when God brought
the exiles home from Babylon, after they had been forced
labourers in that land for fifty years. To celebrate this event, the
psalmist commands (!) the whole earth (1) to *sing to the Lord*; (2)
to tell *the nations* about his *salvation*, the creative love of God
which he gives to those whom he has saved. Israel knows about it
already; it is the world that has yet to learn of it. (We should look
back at the Introduction to Vol. 1 for a discussion of the word
used here, viz "creative love".) (3) To *ascribe to the Lord the
glory due to his name*, saying, "Thank you God that you are who
you are"; and (4) to *bring an offering* when they come to worship.

Since the psalmist's day "bringing an offering" has remained an integral part of Christian worship. All this is to be done "in the beauty of holiness", as the AV has it, being perhaps the best of the various translations available to us (verse 9; RSV *in holy array*).

This whole psalm is to be found at 1 Chron. 16:23–33, where it is preceded by a long quotation from Ps. 105 and followed by some verses from Ps. 106. In addition verses 6–9 use very similar wording to what we find at Ps. 29:1–2. In Chronicles this psalm is used in the context of public worship in the Temple. We are given the clear understanding there that all peoples are to be reached with the Good News with the aim that eventually all may join in God's praise. In other words, this psalm has a missionary purpose, and to that end it even tells us what we are to say.

We note at verse 5 that the gods of the nations are called *elilim*, a distinct pun and parody of the word *elohim*, which means "God". This name that he uses for the gods actually means "uselessness". These gods get you nowhere, he is saying; they do not *act* any more than do the various "isms" men put their trust in today. These in the end are all just human ideas. Then we note that it is the peoples who are to praise God, not mere individuals with their selfish ideas of salvation, such as being rescued out of a wicked world.

In the beauty of holiness is a lovely expression that can mean several things—and deliberately so, it would seem. For these old Hebrews loved to pun as they spun their poetry. (1) We note that this whole psalm is made up of twenty-five quotations from the OT, ending with Isaiah 66, which was written about 516 B.C., when the Temple was re-established. Our poet by using these many quotations is seeking to worship God by creating, in fact recreating, a holy array of "proof-texts". (2) The phrase can mean copying on earth the "array" of God's holy angels above. (3) It can mean to establish in our human worship the mysterious, holy beauty of God, so that when we do so we discover also here and now something of the rapturous joy of heaven above. (4) The phrase can mean to honour God with the best we have in the way of the finest of robes, the greatest of music, the most beautiful of liturgies, the best ordered acts of worship we can work out, when all the ordinary worshippers appear before the Lord in their "Sunday best". (5) The holy array (compare Isa. 52:7) can refer to a mighty band of evangelists going forth with the Good News of God to the nations of the earth. It is because of this last emphasis that *the nations* are to rejoice. For it is the world of human beings, *tevel* (verse 10), whom nature also serves, not *ha-arets*, the earth, that *shall never be moved.* These are the human beings whom God has created and whom he longs to recreate when they enter within his loving care.

The Good News is to contain the announcement that Yahweh, the Covenant God of little Israel, is really King of all, and that *the Lord reigns.* Thus he is in control of all nature on the one hand, and on the other is the absolutely impartial *Judge of all peoples.* Nature should be glad, of course, that it is under God's control, else it might run rampant and break the rules of the universe. After all, light always travels at the same speed, and Nature always seems to find its own balance. On the other hand, the Lord of Nature is always making all things new—new days, new weeks, new seasons, new eggs, new lambs, new fruit on the trees. A traveller in New Guinea writes: "There is nothing like the Papuan bush in the early morning. Bright parrots shriek their excitement over the prospect of a new day."

But Nature is *here*, yet not just as an end in itself. It is here for man's sake, as Gen. 1 describes for us. Nature, moreover, is glad that this should be so. For it has produced the place where man can live, his food and his clothes, so that in his turn man may create fields out of the wild bush to grow his crops. In this way man reveals God's gift to him of being able to produce a new thing. He produces order out of chaos, a cultivated field out of wild scrub. Read Josh. 17:15 and 17–18, where Joshua commands the tribe of Joseph to do this very thing by the use of a form of the verb *bara*, found in Gen. 1:1, a verb that appears nearly everywhere in the OT with God alone as its subject. Thus, recreating nature from a wild state to one of *shalom*, peace, order, perfection, is a divine activity, one which God invites his believing people to share in.

The repetition of the phrase *for he comes, for he comes* means that God keeps on coming, creating something new each time, in this case making new judgments as he judges the inhabited world (the word *tevel* we saw above) with *righteousness, tsedeq.* This last word can mean "what is just and right", something that God has given to his people out of his grace. That is how the word comes to mean that whole new way of life that is sketched for Israel (and so is intended for the whole world of men) in the *Torah,* meaning Law, Revelation, Teaching that we find in the "Books of Moses". When God *judges,* then, he is offering this great thing as an act of justice. But is it justice? Surely rather it is an act of grace. Then, *his truth* means his faithfulness, upon which man can confidently rely. But here it is the feminine form of the word that occurs. And so it speaks of God's unfailing faithfulness in creating hearts of love and of compassion in those to whom he has first offered his "justice", which is no less than his gracious, recreative love.

The German philosopher Lotze once wrote: "To their contemporaries the Hebrews seemed like a race of madmen; but to us today, looking back, they seem to be the one sober people in a world of drunkards. For instead of fearing God's judgment, they could sing for joy that it was coming." We meet with the same idea in Isa. 35.

There is one other point to note about this psalm. In the Old Latin Version of the Bible made in the early Christian centuries we find this reading at verse 10: "The Lord has reigned from the tree", i.e. the Cross. We must agree that this is a Christian gloss, even though some of the Latin Fathers of the Church took it at face value. But it is worth asking whether, as a gloss, it is any more far-fetched than the addition by some branches of the Church today of the Trinitarian Gloria that is recited or sung when the congregation reaches the end of a psalm.

GOD IS EXALTED OVER ALL

Psalm 97:1–12

> [1]The Lord reigns; let the earth rejoice;
>   let the many coastlands be glad!

²Clouds and thick darkness are round about him;
  righteousness and justice are the foundation of his throne.
³Fire goes before him,
  and burns up his adversaries round about.
⁴His lightnings lighten the world;
  the earth sees and trembles.
⁵The mountains melt like wax before the Lord,
  before the Lord of all the earth.

⁶The heavens proclaim his righteousness;
  and all the peoples behold his glory.
⁷All worshippers of images are put to shame,
  who make their boast in worthless idols;
  all gods bow down before him.
⁸Zion hears and is glad,
  and the daughters of Judah rejoice,
  because of thy judgments, O God.
⁹For thou, O Lord, art most high over all the earth;
  thou art exalted far above all gods.

¹⁰The Lord loves those who hate evil;
  he preserves the lives of his saints;
  he delivers them from the hand of the wicked.
¹¹Light dawns for the righteous,
  and joy for the upright in heart.
¹²Rejoice in the Lord, O you righteous,
  and give thanks to his holy name!

Verses 1–4, *The Lord reigns*. God's people ought to find life to be thrilling, simply because God reigns. We recall that the people shouted these words at that moment, once a year, when the "Son of David" of that year re-ascended the throne and took his seat as the representative on earth, or even as the sacramental symbol, of the divine King. But there was no king in our poet's day. The people of Israel had newly returned from exile in far-off Babylon. There many of them must surely have listened to the comforting words of the great prophet of the Exile (Isa. chs. 40–55). The important thing they had learned from this great "voice" (Isa. 40:6) was that, by faith, they could still declare "the Lord reigns" even though the last Son of David was now dead (see Ps. 89). This was because, by faith, they had found that Yahweh himself had survived the death of the line of David! And he was still with them as their loving God.

In the mood of Ps. 96, the Mediterranean islands and coastlands to the west, and Babylon lying to the east, are to take up Israel's song and are to rejoice with her. Rejoice that God does not need a David now to represent him? Yes, *clouds and thick darkness are round about him*—clouds of doubt, perhaps, and the darkness of despair. Yet even in Babylon's dungeons (Isa. 42:22) our psalmist had reached the faith that *righteousness and justice are the foundation of his throne*, or, in other words, that law and order, or right, and the true way of life revealed in the *Torah*, are the basis of all reality.

The God of the Bible is the hidden God. The Second Commandment forbids Israel to try to make any representation of God at all. So it was left to "Second" Isaiah to make the tremendous discovery while the Israelites were in exile that (and he makes the Gentiles say this!) God had hidden himself *in* Israel! "God is in you only" (not *with you*, as the RSV), "certainly no other god. Indeed thou art Israel's God and Saviour, the God who hides himself" (Isa. 45:14–15). How then does God, as the God of judgment, hide himself in Israel? Here we have some great theological pictures.

(1) God hides himself in fire (compare Ps. 50:3). For fire destroys and so it burns up God's adversaries. (2) But fire also cleanses, purifies and redeems, in the way that silver is purified of its dross. This is what happened to Israel, and as Nature watched, it *sees and trembles*. For the prophet who spoke of God hiding himself *in* Israel, also declared to Israel: "When you walk through fire you shall not be burned, for I will be with you" (Isa. 43:2). So God had been, not just *with* Israel, but *in* Israel, in the "hellishness" of the exile experience; and he had been there as Israel's King!

Verses 6–9. God's judgmental fire is now explained. It is revealed as God's fiery, hot, passionate, saving love—and *that* fiery love of God is his *glory*! So even the sky (rather than *the heavens*) preaches God's love! On the other hand, as we saw at verse 2, the prophet of the Exile had sarcastically scorned *worthless idols* (see at Isa. 44:9–20; 46:1–2). But the Lord's sky seems to be able to open up at times and shout to us Good News about God! (Luke 2:8–15).

We recall that the word *Zion* began by being a name for the oldest part of upper Jerusalem, but that it developed to mean the place of the Holy God's abode on earth. In fact, it became the theological name for Jerusalem. In far-away Babylon this psalmist, in love and faith, had first taken up the thought of Jerusalem. He did not forget, however, that faithful believers before the Exile had lived also in the suburbs and villages round about Jerusalem. It is these villages that are *the daughters of Judah*. Though these were now desolate and in ruins, he can declare in faith that it is natural for them to *rejoice*. How can they possibly do any such thing? *Because of thy judgments, O God*. Because of the way God has worked things out in history. God had of course passed judgment on his people. He had sent them off into exile. But our psalmist now sees that that had been a good thing.

Verses 10–12, *The bliss of belonging to the Lord. You who love the Lord, hate evil* (verse 10, RSV *ftn*) is undoubtedly the correct text, as Artur Weiser insists in his commentary. So we who love the Lord are not just advised to hate evil, we are actually commanded to do so. For we are to be like our Lord who hates evil (Ps. 5:5, etc.). What an anaemic picture of God some people have in their minds today, when they balk at what the Psalter says of God—that he hates! But the psalmist goes on. *The Lord preserves* (or "shepherds") the souls or, *the lives of his* Covenant community, *his* "church"; *he delivers them from the hand of the wicked*, simply because they cannot do that for themselves. Finally, the difficult words that follow are best translated by the rendering of the NEB: "A harvest of light is sown for the righteous, and joy for all good men." The God who reigns, despite the "hellishness" of the Exile, and of all "exiles" ever since, is he who comes down like tomorrow's dawn for the believer (the *tsaddiq*). In other words he is the God of Advent, the God who is coming to judge the *upright in heart* with saving love (Ps. 96:13), the God who is going to do something new even with the ruins of Jerusalem.

It is the turn of the Jerusalem Bible this time to sum up the wonder of the final verse of our psalm: "Remember his holiness, and praise him!" For in his presence there is joy, joy, joy. To end our comments we might recall once again the words of the Westminster Shorter Catechism: "Man's chief end is to glorify God and to enjoy him for ever."

CANTATE DOMINO

Psalm 98: 1–9

A Psalm.

¹O sing to the Lord a new song,
    for he has done marvellous things!
His right hand and his holy arm
    have gotten him victory.
²The Lord has made known his victory,
    he has revealed his vindication in the sight of the nations.
³He has remembered his steadfast love and faithfulness
    to the house of Israel.
All the ends of the earth have seen
    the victory of our God.

⁴Make a joyful noise to the Lord, all the earth;
    break forth into joyous song and sing praises!
⁵Sing praises to the Lord with the lyre,
    with the lyre and the sound of melody!
⁶With trumpets and the sound of the horn
    make a joyful noise before the King, the Lord!

⁷Let the sea roar, and all that fills it;
    the world and those who dwell in it!
⁸Let the floods clap their hands;
    let the hills sing for joy together
⁹before the Lord, for he comes to judge the earth.
He will judge the world with righteousness,
    and the peoples with equity.

O sing to the Lord, as the Church has been summoned to do in these Latin words for many centuries. Always it is to be *a new song*, new in every age. The great prophet of the new thing that God was about to do during Israel's exile in Babylon (see Isa. 40–55, especially 41:25; 42:10–13; 48:20; 52:13ff; 54:1–3) is the inspiration of this poem. The psalmist declares: *God has done marvellous things*. This word is reserved for acts of God, such as science cannot account for. And so it is here. Isa. 45:1–7 has announced that God had *grasped* the right hand of King Cyrus, monarch of mighty Persia, and was about to lead him on a triumphal march throughout the whole of the Near East to finish up at the gates of Babylon. How "marvellous" that God was using the most powerful monarch of the known world just to allow a mere handful of miserable Israelites to get out of their situation of forced labour (Isa. 40:2 RSV *ftn*), and be free to return home to Jerusalem. That was indeed a marvel. Moreover, it did actually happen, in the year 539 B.C. By 516 B.C. the Temple was rebuilt. A few months later it was dedicated for worship. There was a whole new situation. Almost certainly this psalm was composed as a *new* song for this *new* situation, as part of the *new* liturgy to be sung by God's *renewed* people in the *new* Temple building.

God's *right hand* and *arm* are what he "dips down" into space and time. These *have gotten him the victory* over the might of the Babylonian Empire, an act which rocked the whole known world of the nations; for they had *seen the victory of our God*. Yet this word means more than merely victory in war by the hand of Cyrus. It speaks of a victory which recreates—makes *new*—the loyalty of *the house of Israel* in their daily living, in response to God's *steadfast love and faithfulness*. These had never failed all through the hard years of exile.

Our poet is aware that God is always making all things new. So he is referring here, not just to the events of 539 B.C.; he is acclaiming the reality that God's victory keeps on happening "marvellously", that is, without our human help or participation. And that each of these victories is but one event in a chain of events that will never end. That is why the Psalter is as truly Holy

Scripture for us today as are the psalms (not all that different in their thrust from this one) that appear in Luke 1–2.

The real "victory", however, was that Israel was now a changed people; that is a victory that can happen equally today. So wonderful is this victory that *the whole earth* is invited to praise God for it with all the instruments of music they can muster. Moreover, "the whole earth" must necessarily include the defeated Babylonians! That then is the world of mankind. But the world of Nature too is to acclaim God's miracle of grace. Fancy the sea "playing tunes" in joy at God's victory, and the floods *clapping their hands* just like we do!

The OT is a forward-looking book. It lives in the period of Advent. *For the Lord is coming*, as we saw at Ps. 96:13. And as we noted there, Israel has no fear of this coming judgment, for it too will be "marvellous", since it too will be a victory for justice and love.

HOLY, HOLY, HOLY

Psalm 99:1–9

¹The Lord reigns; let the peoples tremble!
  He sits enthroned upon the cherubim; let the earth quake!
²The Lord is great in Zion;
  he is exalted over all the peoples.
³Let them praise thy great and terrible name!
  Holy is he!
⁴Mighty King, lover of justice,
  thou hast established equity;
 thou hast executed justice
  and righteousness in Jacob.
⁵Extòl the Lord our God;
  worship at his footstool!
  Holy is he!

⁶Moses and Aaron were among his priests,
  Samuel also was among those who called on his name.
  They cried to the Lord, and he answered them.

⁷He spoke to them in the pillar of cloud;
   they kept his testimonies,
   and the statutes that he gave them.

⁸O Lord our God, thou didst answer them;
   thou wast a forgiving God to them,
   but an avenger of their wrong-doings.
⁹Extol the Lord our God,
   and worship at his holy mountain;
   for the Lord our God is holy!

Holy is he is the keynote of this psalm. We wonder what we are to
make of this word *holy*, especially when we realize that we
ourselves are so very unholy. Yet that is how we are to understand the word; for God is just what we are not! He is utterly
other than our sinful natures. That is why, thinking of the mystery
of God's holiness, the psalmist can call upon sinners of the whole
world to *tremble*, and upon even inanimate nature to *quake*
before him. That is to say, both Man and Nature are to remember
they are "fallen" (see Rom. 8:20–23), and that they should
not expect to exist in their own right in the presence of the holy
God.

Verses 1–3, *The first Sanctus.* We recall that the *cherubim* were
not angels. Angels are God's messengers. The cherubim represented the pagan gods of the day, and if we want to visualize what
they looked like we should think of the Sphinx in Egypt. Now, if
God *sits enthroned upon the cherubim*, then he is literally *sitting*
on them (cf. 1 Sam. 4:4; 6:2; 2 Kings 19:15). He has put the gods
of the nations "in their place", so to speak, under his feet, using
them as his footstool. We have seen that (1) Man is to declare the
holiness of God; (2) Nature is to do so too; and now (3) the gods
of the nations are to do likewise!

This conception of the gods being "put in their place" is evident
at 1 Kings 6:29. There Solomon built into the walls of the Temple
representative carvings (1) of Nature, and (2) of the gods. The
Second Commandment forbids all stupid human attempts at trying to create any image of absolute holiness. For how could sinful
man ever imagine what the sinless God could be like? In the same

way even the most reverent painting or film that seeks to show the person of Christ is doomed to failure. In fact, the lack of credibility of any Hollywood portrayal of Christ, however sincere it may be, actually becomes the proof of the sinlessness of Christ. Solomon could merrily create gargoyles and call them cherubim or any other gods he fancied, and he did so. Yet, what a paradox, that in the Temple was to be found absolute holiness: *Holy is he; God is great in Zion!*

Verses 4–5, *The Second Sanctus.* God as King is *might* itself, but might that *loves justice.* In the Middle Ages theologians used to argue whether an Almighty God could be almighty and at the same time allow evil to flourish. Our poet sees no problem here, for, as a matter of historical fact, Almighty God had already acted in history to create on earth his revealed way of life (i.e. his *mishpat,* justice) *in Jacob,* that is, *in* the life of Israel his people. God had revealed what *shalom* (peace) means in the life of the Covenant people. God's plan was that they should face up to the evil in the world realistically, and surmount it by using that creative, recreative love (*tsedaqah,* righteousness), which showed itself as the *might* or strength of God which he has given to his redeemed people. So, then, holiness means compassionate and creative love (Isa. 5:16). Thus Israel is to worship this kind of a God, *worship* him *at his footstool* (Isa. 60:13), that place on earth where the HOLY ONE has made himself known to us as our God.

In his book *Doctor in Papua* (1974) Berkeley Vaughan writes of his contact with the Kunikas, a tribe of mountaineers in the Owen Stanley range. No girl of this tribe would ever lower herself to marry her suitor until he had committed a murder. If he killed a man then he established his manhood. Consequently the men of those villages would stalk and kill a complete stranger on sight. How then to revolutionize this furtive, destructive taking of life in these mountains? Clearly it was not to rush in with ideas, doctrines or ethical teachings, or to lay down sets of rules. It could be done only by linking these wild men to the Great Spirit, as they themselves called their idea of God. This is how Vaughan expressed the challenge. There were no words for love or honesty or unselfishness in their language. But the missionaries could speak of friendship and unity, words these people did know, and demonstrate what they meant by living them out in their own lives. The days passed, and there came about a whole new way of life in those villages. For the men and women both gave up beating their children, and started to offer food to their hereditary enemies, and even to ask forgiveness for their former malicious, heated and violent acts. "A whole new way of life", Vaughan's phrase, exactly translates the word *mishpat* (RSV *justice*), and asking forgiveness and offering food to one's enemies exactly illustrates the word *tsedaqah* (RSV *righteousness*). The psalmist declares here that such are the acts of the *holy* God.

Verses 6–9, *The third Sanctus*. Long ago God had heard when Israel's ancestors had *cried to the Lord*, for he had *answered them*. Their worship had taken the form of intercession, for they had cried, not for themselves, but for others. (In Num. 14:13–19 Moses prays; at verse 20 God answers.) So also in the case of Samuel (1 Sam. 12:16–25). These men had cried passionately; and God had answered them passionately. He had *spoken to them in the pillar of cloud* (Exod. 13:21; Num. 12:5; 14:14; Deut. 31:15) in his loving care for his pilgrim people. In return these men had humbly sought to do God's will.

For they had discovered (1) another remarkable aspect of the word holiness. It was that God had "become to them" (Hebrew) as a forgiving God (Num. 14:20), even while (2) he continued to judge them for their *wrong-doings*. In face of this mystery the poet therefore invites us to praise that kind of God, not just because *our God is holy*, utterly other than sinful man, but also because his holiness means his love and forgiveness.

The world knows the Polynesian word "taboo", in one or other of the various spellings in which it has reached the West. This word, we are told, means "holy". In the Fijian language the Bible is called *Ai Vola Tabu*, the "taboo" book! "Don't touch—too sacred for that!" How difficult it is, we can see, to interpret the Christian faith to people whose concepts have no contact with *the new way of life*, God's *mishpat*, his justice! Human language cannot fully express the gospel. First and foremost the other man must see the meaning of the fullness of life in the life style of the evangelist. As Isa. 49:6 puts it, when God addresses his servant Israel: "*I will give you* (as a gift from himself) *as a light to* (of, for) *the nations, that* 'my creative love in human lives' may be seen in you and so may *reach to the end of the earth.*" God's holiness, then, is something that can be conveyed *in us* to all humanity, so that (to revert to verse 1) what happens at God's footstool in Zion will make even the people of New Guinea and Fiji *tremble* as they bow in awe and gratitude.

THE OLD HUNDREDTH

Psalm 100:1–5

A Psalm for the thank offering.

¹Make a joyful noise to the Lord, all the lands!
² Serve the Lord with gladness!
Come into his presence with singing!

³Know that the Lord is God!
It is he that made us, and we are his;
we are his people, and the sheep of his pasture.

⁴Enter his gates with thanksgiving,
and his courts with praise!
Give thanks to him, bless his name!

⁵For the Lord is good;
his steadfast love endures for ever,
and his faithfulness to all generations.

"The Old Hundredth" is the name of the tune that is sung around the world to the metrical version of this favourite psalm: "All people that on earth do dwell". It was composed by William Kethe of Scotland, a friend of John Knox the Reformer, in 1560. The great composer Arthur S. Sullivan last century declared that "The Old Hundredth" was the grandest tune ever written. It was composed by Louis Bourgeois and appeared first in the French

Genevan Psalter in 1551. Both words and tune have survived all changes in thought and fashion for four and a half centuries.

The point is, of course, that the psalm is meant for the whole world, and all people receive an invitation in it. It invites *all lands* to *make a joyful noise, to serve* Yahweh (the name of the God of little, unimportant Israel) *with gladness*, and *to come into his presence with singing*. How could this ever come about? The answer, of course, lies in the fact that this psalm has a missionary purpose. Then again, what does *come into his presence* mean?

In the first place it means to enter through the various courts of the Temple right to where God is to be found at the Holy Place. The word *presence* is derived from the word for "face" in Hebrew. One recognizes a fellow human being by looking at his face. It was in this sense that Jesus said: "He who has seen me has seen the Father". So, in the second place, the worshippers are now being invited to come in and worship, not a distant deity, but a very personal God.

It seems that our psalm was first used in a most interesting manner. We are to see a group of pilgrims arriving at the outer gate of the Temple, perhaps, as in Jesus' day, from as far away as Egypt to the west, or Mesopotamia to the east. They are met at the gate by an official whose task it is to greet them "liturgically".

Verses 1–2. This official asks the pilgrims to turn their backs on the Temple first of all. They are to face the nations from which they have come at the ends of the earth. Facing away, then, they repeat after him this invitation, nay, this command (!) to all people that dwell on the face of the earth, even the Egyptians who had once held them as slaves, and the Mesopotamians, the pagans of the east (as in the book of Jonah, ch. 3), the cruel Edomites to the south and the warlike Syrians to the north-east. The message of the psalm was that even the farthest of the nations were to "worship" (RSV *serve*) Yahweh, the God of Israel; they were to come to Jerusalem on pilgrimage, and to enter the Temple courtyards *with singing!* We understand this word *serve* the better when we see how it is used in the idea of a church "service". (For these nations around Israel, see Amos chs. 1–2.)

Then they are to shout to these nations symbolically (or to take back these words when they go home?): *Know that the Lord* ("alone"—is what the Hebrew means) *is God.* Thereupon the pilgrims turn round and face each other this time, and declare to one another: *It is he that made us and we are his* (see Isa. 51:16). In these words they remind themselves that they are God's own possession among all peoples (Exod. 19:5), actually words which God had spoken through Moses at the moment when he made his Covenant with Israel at Sinai. But God had not stopped there. Some modern Christians wish that he had. For he declared next that his people were to be his *kingdom of priests*, that is, priests who were to mediate the love of God to all other peoples, even those under whom they had suffered and died. Then finally the group of worshippers repeat to each other: *We are his*, meaning that we are not our own property—or, as they may have said, (see the RSV *ftn* and the older AV), *he made us and we did not make ourselves.* For it is the Lord who makes individual believers into a congregation; it is not we who say, "Come, let us create a church". So the expectant worshippers, like ourselves when we reach the church door on Sundays, are reminded of "whose we are and whom we serve", and that even the building itself is not ours, but his.

Verse 4. The priest or temple official now calls out to the group: *Enter his gates* (they are his, not ours!) *with thanksgiving.* Our church buildings often contain a stone inserted in the wall, or a brass plate in the porch, bearing the words: "Ad majorem Dei gloriam"—to the greater glory of God. So it is *him* we are to bless and praise once we enter in.

The psalm's heading runs: *A psalm for the thank offering.* If we refer back to Lev. 7:11ff. we discover what took place at the special offering known by this name, and what it was for. The equivalent for us today would be the celebration of the Eucharist. That word means "giving thanks". So what this psalm is teaching both ancient Israel and us now is that we must not blandly expect to rush in to partake of Holy Communion with God where angels fear to tread.

Verse 5. The word *ki* normally means "that", rather than *for* as here. It introduces direct speech, just as *hoti* does in NT Greek. Perhaps the group have now gone through the outer gate and are standing together in the Court of the Gentiles. If so, then it is there that the priest helps these folk to make profession of their faith. He tells them to repeat after him: "(We believe) *that the Lord is good*", and so also with the last two lines, where they proclaim their faith in the God who is utterly loyal to them in love, and who has chosen them to be members of his Covenant People.

Not only so, but God has chosen them to be his co-workers in Covenant that the world may learn of his love; and he will continue *to all generations* to maintain his loyalty to his people to this end.

A ROYAL PLEDGE

Psalm 101:1–8

A Psalm of David.

¹I will sing of loyalty and of justice;
   to thee, O Lord, I will sing.
²I will give heed to the way that is blameless.
   Oh when wilt thou come to me?

 I will walk with integrity of heart
   within my house;
³I will not set before my eyes
   anything that is base.

 I hate the work of those who fall away;
   it shall not cleave to me.
⁴Perverseness of heart shall be far from me;
   I will know nothing of evil.

⁵Him who slanders his neighbour secretly
   I will destroy.
 The man of haughty looks and arrogant heart
   I will not endure.

⁶I will look with favour on the faithful in the land,
    that they may dwell with me;
he who walks in the way that is blameless
    shall minister to me.

⁷No man who practises deceit
    shall dwell in my house;
no man who utters lies
    shall continue in my presence.

⁸Morning by morning I will destroy
    all the wicked in the land,
cutting off all the evildoers
    from the city of the Lord.

This psalm reads like a confession of faith made by a king and so either by David himself, or by a "son of David" in later centuries (2 Sam. 7:12–16). Perhaps the court chaplain invited the king to repeat these words after him in a public ceremony, either at his coronation or at a re-enthronement festival in later years. As we have it here, it is the king who declaims these words about himself and his people. But the words he uses have now been turned into a psalm to be sung by a whole congregation! This means that Israel understood her king to be "the head of the corporate body" of Israel, so that what he confessed, all Israel came to confess with him.

Verses 1–4. The song begins with words used in Israel's Covenant theology. *Loyalty* here is the Hebrew *hesed* which we have met so often in previous psalms, the word that attempts to describe God's unfailing loyal love ever since that great day described in 2 Sam. 7. It is *God's hesed* and *God's* "whole new way of life" (*mishpat, justice* in the RSV), which he has given to Israel that he affirms here in song. It does not have its source in man, he declares, far less in himself as king. In consequence he says: *I will give heed to* (i.e. learn the meaning of) *the way that is blameless*, that is, the way that God has already revealed to Israel, and so to me, through Moses. But the king is a humble man. He is like the person in the NT who comes to Jesus and declares, "I believe, help my unbelief." So he adds to his promise and pledge the plea, "Please, Lord, don't hold back from helping me".

Then follow four promises:

(1) He promises that he will be a good husband and father to his children. How many persons standing for high office, we wonder, ever realize that most voters look for just such integrity in the candidate's home life as the necessary basis for any public office? To this end, then, he will *walk* with God, as did both Enoch and Noah in days of old (Gen. 5:22–24; 6:9; Micah 6:8).

(2) Paul tells us to fill our minds with whatsoever is good, pure, gracious, true (Phil. 4:8), so that as a result there will be no room left in them for *anything that is base.* In other words, there is a sense of "noblesse oblige" in the king's second promise.

(3) He declares, "To do deeds that deviate (from the Way) I hate"; "I would shake it off like a scorpion." This is like promise 2. For walking with God prevents temptations from assailing us to do anything evil.

(4) "A perverted mind I'll have nothing to do with," he says: this becomes possible for him since, as he says, "I won't let myself even associate with evil."

Verses 5–8. Now the king makes seven pledges with respect to his subjects:

(1) Just as I pledge myself to be loyal to God's Way, I demand that my people should be also.

(2) I am going to stop my people from speaking evil of others behind their back.

(3) In the royal court there must have been scores of sycophants doing just that kind of thing. As well as this backbiting, there would be sure to be those who "sucked up" to the king, meanwhile scorning those who were lower down in the pecking order. Shakespeare depicts such horrid behaviour in his historical plays which deal with royal courts. But we find the like in modern social clubs just as much, or in factories and even parliaments. The king is determined that there shall be *shalom* at his court, a warm, loving fellowship, with no backbiting, snobbery or class distinctions.

(4) I shall watch over the stable and reliable element in the community, he says next, so that they and I may co-operate together.

(5) Those who follow the Way given us by God through Moses will then actually be serving me (even as I, the king, am trying to serve God). What he is implying is that those who are loyal to God make the best citizens.

(6) I am not going to tolerate amongst my employees in the palace anyone who acts deceitfully (else those who are below them will never receive proper justice).

(7) The king's concluding promise is that "I will convene the court first thing *every morning*. Those whom I discover to have been doing evil I will forbid in Jerusalem, *in the city of the Lord*."

What this psalm makes clear is that morality does not arise from social custom, as sociologists so often teach today, but in response to the *hesed*, the love and loyalty of God.

So then, this psalm, written with a nostalgic loyalty to the "old days" of David, teaches later Israel just what, under God, they are to make of their newly reconstituted society in rebuilt Jerusalem.

THE EXILE NEARLY AT AN END

Psalm 102:1–17

A prayer of one afflicted, when he is faint and pours out his complaint before the Lord.

¹Hear my prayer, O Lord;
  let my cry come to thee!
²Do not hide thy face from me
  in the day of my distress!
 Incline thy ear to me;
  answer me speedily in the day when I call!

³For my days pass away like smoke,
  and my bones burn like a furnace.
⁴My heart is smitten like grass, and withered;
  I forget to eat my bread.

⁵Because of my loud groaning
    my bones cleave to my flesh.
⁶I am like a vulture of the wilderness,
    like an owl of the waste places;
⁷I lie awake,
    I am like a lonely bird on the housetop.
⁸All the day my enemies taunt me,
    those who deride me use my name for a curse.
⁹For I eat ashes like bread,
    and mingle tears with my drink,
¹⁰because of thy indignation and anger;
    for thou hast taken me up and thrown me away.
¹¹My days are like an evening shadow;
    I wither away like grass.

¹²But thou, O Lord, art enthroned for ever;
    thy name endures to all generations.
¹³Thou wilt arise and have pity on Zion;
    it is the time to favour her;
    the appointed time has come.
¹⁴For thy servants hold her stones dear;
    and have pity on her dust.
¹⁵The nations will fear the name of the Lord,
    and all the kings of the earth thy glory.
¹⁶For the Lord will build up Zion,
    he will appear in his glory;
¹⁷he will regard the prayer of the destitute,
    and will not despise their supplication.

Verses 1–11, *My cry*. The first verse of this psalm is one we use in
our liturgies today. If we ask God to *let my cry come to thee*, we
ought not to isolate the verse, but continue reading on to see what
the cry is all about. We shall find that what the psalmist has to say
is quite familiar, for much of his cry is composed of quotations
from other psalms. That, of course, is a good way to pray, to
make full use of the psalms ourselves, and to apply their words
and ideas to our own situation.

At Ps. 86:7 we noted that the word *day*, as here, does not refer
to the next twenty-four hours. It refers to a moment in one's
experience which has meaning for all eternity, and is vital in our

own life. For example, we can all recall the exact day of our marriage. So then, this poor Israelite, thinking back to when he was many hundreds of miles from home, working as a forced labourer in Babylon, is depicted as being totally and utterly miserable, but worse, as believing that his misery comes from God, and so belongs to eternity. Compelled to work when his bones are burning with fever, his "mind" *(heart)* affected so that he cannot remember today even what happened yesterday, just as grass dies when there is no rainfall, he has no appetite, and is physically emaciated. The old translation of *vulture* (verse 6) was "pelican"; and so the phrase, "like a pelican in the wilderness" has passed into the realm of an English proverb. The pelican was even used by the mediaeval church as a symbol of Christ. But the word refers rather to an unclean bird that people shunned. Then the word *bird* (verse 7) is really sparrow. Sparrows are gregarious creatures. They invade our gardens, never singly, but always in flocks. But our poor exile lies awake at night, feeling himself inconceivably lonely as a single sparrow must do if it is abandoned *on the housetop*. And so, with continued eastern hyperbole, he describes his condition as *cursed* by man and *taken up and thrown away* by God.

We discover next that he has been brought so low, poor man, that he can even declare it is all God's fault. It is *thy indignation* that has done this to me, he says. He thinks of God (who is light) paradoxically binging him into the oncoming darkness of the evening, and just as without light grass cannot grow, so now, he declares, *I wither away like grass.*

Notice that we have not been given the background of this very sad poem. It is we who have placed this poor man among the exiles in Babylon. But for millions on this earth this picture could fit their case perfectly well today. As we look at films taken by relief workers among the refugee poor of many lands, with their emaciated frames and their pot-bellied babies, we are staggered to recall that large numbers of them are believing people and fellow-workers with us in the church—and that they may well have read this psalm themselves. So we gaze in consternation at people who are actually saying as the film is being taken, *because of thy indignation and anger; thou hast taken me up and thrown me away.* Can there be any hope for these poor brethren of ours in such intolerable circumstances not only of body but also of mind and spirit? Momentarily, it would seem, our poet had fallen into the trap set him by believers in false gods. "As flies to wanton boys, are we to the gods," as Shakespeare put it in his *King Lear.*

Verses 12–13, *But THOU wilt arise.* Out of the depths of his utter despair our poet has the courage to shout: *But thou, O Lord, art enthroned for ever.* The Lord is King, still. *Thy name* was the same to Moses and David as it will always be *to all generations.* Lamentations 5:19 was written during the Exile. Its author courageously says this very same thing. In days of old *Thou didst arise.* You will do it again. *The day of my distress* (verse 2), when I am at the end of my tether, becomes your "time", Lord, to *have pity* on, to exhibit your mother-love (as the Hebrew means) to *Zion*, the people of God. It was just at the very moment in history when God raised up King Cyrus, the Persian monarch, to set free his people from the bonds of Babylon (see Isa. 45:1–7) that God's people bewailed: "The Lord has forsaken me, my Lord has forgotten me." To which the Lord replies, "Can a woman forget her sucking child, that she should have no compassion on the son of her womb? Even these may forget, yet I will not forget you" (Isa. 49:14–15).

So then, *the appointed time has come*, literally, "the time of meeting has come", the time, the moment when God will meet with Zion, and will act within Israel's experience in space and time. We can now see why this psalm was placed here—*after* God had acted to set Israel free. For it is addressed to us also, whom God has also set free.

Verses 14–17, *First steps towards God's Advent.* The *for* of verse 14 does not follow from verse 13. Here we begin a new statement of faith. We have learned that *the time has come.* Now we can leave the rest to God. That is why our psalmist feels heart-free and is able quietly to reminisce.

The poor exiles, he recognizes, are *thy servants.* They *hold her stones dear*, and "yearn for" (rather than *have pity on*) the very *dust* of the fallen masonry of Zion. Ralph Connor graduated from

Toronto University in 1883. After completing his exam he lay on the grass and thought of this verse. "I had not dreamed," he wrote, "till that moment, how dear stones and dust could be." Zion is Yahweh's city. For his own name's sake, therefore, our psalmist believes, God simply must rebuild her before the eyes of the world, and *appear in his glory* in the rebuilt Temple. Included in that glory of his, therefore, he will surely *regard the prayer of the destitute*. This last word is actually a rare but very strong word meaning "those who have been stripped naked".

GOD DOES NOT CHANGE

Psalm 102:18–28

18Let this be recorded for a generation to come,
    so that a people yet unborn may praise the Lord:
19that he looked down from his holy height,
    from heaven the Lord looked at the earth,
20to hear the groans of the prisoners,
    to set free those who were doomed to die;
21that men may declare in Zion the name of the Lord,
    and in Jerusalem his praise,
22when peoples gather together,
    and kingdoms, to worship the Lord.

23He has broken my strength in mid-course;
    he has shortened my days.
24"O my God," I say, "take me not hence
    in the midst of my days,
thou whose years endure
    throughout all generations!"

25Of old thou didst lay the foundation of the earth,
    and the heavens are the work of thy hands.
26They will perish, but thou dost endure;
    they will all wear out like a garment.
Thou changest them like raiment, and they pass away;
27   but thou art the same, and thy years have no end.
28The children of thy servants shall dwell secure;
    their posterity shall be established before thee.

We pause to make two observations arising from the passage we have just read. (1) We have noted that the terrible picture given us of destitution and despair need not be tied in the providence of God to the horrors of the Babylonian Exile. This is in conformity with the whole method of Biblical revelation. The man who went down from Jerusalem to Jericho and fell among thieves might equally well have been going down any dangerous road anywhere, and the Good Samaritan might equally well be a Good Zulu or a Good Swede. So we may boldly apply the experience of the poet to any individual, ancient or modern, or to any nation, again ancient or modern. (2) What is it that finally reaches home to the poet and gives him hope even in his extremity? It is the fact that God does not change. God had rescued his loved ones in days of old, and so will undoubtedly do so again. Accordingly we are made aware that merely feeding the hungry in a refugee camp— good and necessary as that may be— is not God's answer to such people's need. "Do gooding" without the accompaniment of the "Good News" (something the secular world simply cannot grasp) is not in conformity with the revealed will of God.

Verses 18–22. *Let this be recorded*, then, not just to boost the faith of the lucky ones who will eventually see the city of Zion, but *for a generation to come, so that a people yet unborn may praise the Lord*. There must be something basically false about any economic programme that will compel future generations to pay up the debts incurred by the present generation. Rather, let this generation, says the psalmist, tell how God has in fact set them free so that their children may not have a mortgage hanging over them, a mortgage of fear, terror and suffering. This will mean that, in days to come, our children's children will be free persons, gathering together freely in Jerusalem to worship the Lord. So then, he says, let there be a written record that on such and such a date *the Lord looked down from his holy height . . . to set free those who were doomed to die* (see Ezra 1:1–4). Moreover, because of that others too will begin to believe! All men are sinners, and in consequence thereof all men are doomed to die. Therefore the psalmist sees this particular act of God of forgiveness and renewal as the first-fruits of the ingathering of all peoples (verse 22).

Verse 23–28. But God does not bring in his kingdom by a wave of his almighty hand. Right fair and square on the road before both our psalmist and ourselves there stands a Cross—right *in mid-course*. Verse 24 dares to use language such as this: "As I see it before me I cry, 'Why should I have to die when I am only thirty-three years of age? You live for ever, God, so why shouldn't I reach your prescribed limit of threescore years and ten?'" "Your kingdom can come only through the bearing of the Cross, yes, but why should it be me? Why should I have to take up my cross as well? Why cannot I live long enough to walk in peace straight home to Jerusalem instead of being met by a cross *in mid-course*?"

What our poet has done is to personalize the experience of multitudes. Alexander Solzhenitsyn has done the same thing in his book that describes the experience of the thousands who languish in *The Gulag Archipelago*. Consequently our own personal experience of the powers of evil in this world becomes interpreted for us by such a psalm.

But our psalmist swiftly regains his confidence, not by thinking of his own miserable little self, but of the greatness of God. And so, quoting some pre-exilic psalms that he would undoubtedly know off by heart (just as Jesus quoted Psalm 22 on the Cross) and which he could recite to his fellow-sufferers in their destitution, he remembers this basic reality—that God does not change. What was it that God had said to Moses? "The Lord, the Lord, a God merciful and gracious (a word that speaks of God's mother-love), slow to anger, and abounding in steadfast love *(hesed)* and faithfulness *(emet)*." *Thou art he.* Therefore we can be absolutely sure that our children's children *shall dwell secure*. The earth is transient. The sorrow of the Exile must therefore be transient too. But God is eternal, and so our children shall surely be secure "in thy presence" *(before thee,* RSV). We remember that this great passage of faith is quoted at Hebrews 1:10–12, where it is used to interpret the eternal work of Christ.

HOW GOOD GOD IS!

Psalm 103:1–12

A Psalm of David.

¹Bless the Lord, O my soul; and all that is within me,
   bless his holy name!
²Bless the Lord, O my soul,
   and forget not all his benefits,
³who forgives all your iniquity,
   who heals all your diseases,
⁴who redeems your life from the Pit,
   who crowns you with steadfast love and mercy,
⁵who satisfies you with good as long as you live
   so that your youth is renewed like the eagle's.

⁶The Lord works vindication
   and justice for all who are oppressed.
⁷He made known his ways to Moses,
   his acts to the people of Israel.
⁸The Lord is merciful and gracious,
   slow to anger and abounding in steadfast love.
⁹He will not always chide,
   nor will he keep his anger for ever.
¹⁰He does not deal with us according to our sins,
   nor requite us according to our iniquities.
¹¹For as the heavens are high above the earth,
   so great is his steadfast love toward those who fear him;
¹²as far as the east is from the west,
   so far does he remove our transgressions from us.

The much loved hymn, "Praise, my soul, the King of heaven", by Henry Francis Lyte, is built upon the words of this psalm. But the psalm itself found its appropriate place centuries ago amongst the Reformed Churches when it came to be used to conclude a celebration of Holy Communion. In the period when it was written, however, it was a festal psalm, showing some Aramaic dialectical influence evidently picked up in the Exile. Curiously, it begins with the author speaking to himself and not the assembled congregation; that comes only later.

Verses 1–5, *Wholehearted gratitude*. He begins by addressing his soul and uses the feminine gender for it, because soul is feminine in his own Hebrew language! His soul is his *nephesh*, his self, his personality. It includes *all that is within me*. By that he means his heart, kidneys, mind, stomach, since all these parts of the body are named throughout the Psalter when "I" am called upon to praise the Lord. They are to do so by *blessing* God, with special reference to blessing his *Name*. This is because it was through uttering his Name, as he did to Moses at Sinai (see Exod. 3:13–15; 33:19; 34:6–7) that God let us see what he is like. What then does the psalmist advise his "self" to do?

He begins, *first*, by advising his "self" to "count your blessings, name them one by one", in the words of the old hymn. Then, *second*, he blesses God because *he forgives all your iniquity*. Iniquity here means perversity, crookedness, a twisted nature. We might well ask ourselves when using this psalm whether we really think of such words as descriptive of our own state before God. Yet, *third*, he blesses God because *he heals all your diseases*.

God did not create man as a soul living in a body, as the Greek philosophers believed in antiquity, or as the eastern religions do today. Man is one entity, a *nephesh*, as we saw. Thus it is possible for us to sin with our body, or rather, with our mind and body acting as one. Jesus drew no line between healing a person's body and forgiving his twisted nature, as we see at Mark 2:9–12 and John 5:6, 14. But then, of course, Jesus was a "son of the Law", of the Old Testament, and he drew all his thoughts, inspiration and knowledge of God from its pages. When it came the time for one of the great preachers of this century to retire, he was asked: "If you could have your ministry over again, what would you make central in your preaching?" To which he replied, "The forgiveness of sins". For he too, of course, knew that a man is one whole being, so that a chip on the shoulder can be caused by a pain in the stomach.

The psalmist now goes on to tell his "soul" to bless God because, *fourth*, he *redeems your life from the Pit*. Clearly we are not to limit the meaning of this word just to the Pit of Sheol, the lowest place in the world of death. For the word gives us a picture of what we might call "perdition" in our modern thinking. It seems that those who edited the Psalter placed Ps. 103 where they did, immediately following Ps. 102, because they saw that God's creative forgiveness is the answer to the hope expressed at Ps. 102:13 with reference to the horrors of life—indeed of "death"—that the people of God had suffered in the Babylonian Exile.

Who crowns you is his *fifth* great statement, as if you were a king in his eyes. He crowns you with his *hesed*, that loyal, steadfast love of his into which you entered as a "son of the Law" yourself. Then, his *mercy*, his compassionate mother-love for you, whether you are a girl or a boy, reaches you through his Covenant with Israel, through his covenanted love with your parents before you were born. Finally, his *sixth* statement is that God is good, and that he *satiates* (it is a strong word) *you with good*, fills you full with goodness, not only at this moment when you are at worship but in all moments to come. He satisfies your deepest longings for eternal life so that you go through the experience of being "born again" to a fresh new life. The *eagle* in the ancient legend was thought to live a very long life, to keep on, as it were, renewing its youth. The "voice" that proclaimed Good News to the stricken Israelites in Exile also made use of this legend in parabolic language, as we can see at Isa. 40:31.

Verses 6–12, *Amazing grace*. The speaker then turns to the congregation and preaches a sermon to them. In it he invites his hearers to realize what God has done in the past for *all who are oppressed*. He quotes God's own description of himself to Moses at Exod. 34:6. As we have already seen at Ps. 86:15, this verse continues to emphasize God's ever-forgiving love. God does not deal with us as justice would demand, he continues, rather he deals with us in his amazing grace, grace that is far vaster than anything we poor human creatures can ever begin to conceive. (See Isa. 55:8–9, words spoken while Israel was still in exile.) *Steadfast love* means love that is utterly loyal, love that will never let us go. Then, *our transgressions* that *he removes from us* are actually our acts of rebellion against such amazing love (compare Micah 7:19).

GOD'S FATHERLY LOVE

Psalm 103:13–22

¹³As a father pities his children,
    so the Lord pities those who fear him.
¹⁴For he knows our frame;
    he remembers that we are dust.

¹⁵As for man, his days are like grass;
    he flourishes like a flower of the field;
¹⁶for the wind passes over it, and it is gone,
    and its place knows it no more.
¹⁷But the steadfast love of the Lord is from everlasting to everlasting
    upon those who fear him,
    and his righteousness to children's children,
¹⁸to those who keep his covenant
    and remember to do his commandments.

¹⁹The Lord has established his throne in the heavens,
    and his kingdom rules over all.
²⁰Bless the Lord, O you his angels,
    you mighty ones who do his word,
    hearkening to the voice of his word!
²¹Bless the Lord, all his hosts,
    his ministers that do his will!
²²Bless the Lord, all his works,
    in all places of his dominion.
  Bless the Lord, O my soul!

The psalmist has (a) spoken of God's Covenant love, and then (b) hinted at God's mother-love (the word *merciful* in verse 8 is connected with the Hebrew word meaning "womb"). Now (c) he describes God's father-love. This is a love that remembers the vast distance that lies between the divine and the human (at verse 15 we have the word *enosh* for "man", meaning frail, mortal man, as at Ps. 90:3). Yet it is a love which bridges the great chasm between the divine and the human—but from God to man, not from man to God. Each blade of grass has its own little *place* in the world. This is a striking fact when we remember that no two blades are alike. Human beings are like that. Each person's *place (maqom)* is that corner of the world where he can express his individual identity; for each separate blade of grass and each individual human being has his or her own "standing" (as the word means), that is, enough room on which to stand up and be counted. But yet, even *its place knows it no more*! J. B. Phillips once wrote a telling book entitled *Your God is too Small*. Perhaps he had been meditating on this psalm.

But Covenant man has to respond to God's advances in love by (a) *keeping his Covenant*, and (b) *remembering* to obey his "orders".

Verses 19–22, *Let all creation bless the Lord*. God has always been there first. *He established his throne in the heavens*. From it he rules over all. So the response of God's creation must be in the form of a reply to his authority as Father and King. Who then must praise and bless the Lord?

(1) *His angels*. No matter how we picture them, we are to remember what the word means. It means "messengers", "missionaries".

(2) *You mighty ones that do his word*. God is the great Warrior against the powers of evil. These are his lieutenants in the realm of the spirit. We have noted before that God's might was a way of speaking of the power of his Spirit. They do not act on their own initiative, because they do not exist in their own right. (We shall find out just what they are in the next psalm.) They exist only as they *do his word*, and are totally obedient *to the voice of his word*. In ch. 1 of Genesis we learn that God created both the heavens and the earth by uttering his Word (see also Ps. 33:6). So he continues to maintain them still by his Word. Paul's name for these *mighty ones* is "principalities and *powers*" (Eph. 1:21; 3:10; 6:12; Col. 1:16; 2:15).

(3) *All his hosts*. It may be that, in the first place, God's hosts were the multitude of stars in the night sky. To Israel these "hosts of the Lord" were not dead matter, but were alive through the Word of the Lord. That was one reason why God came to be called "the Lord of hosts". In the same vein we pray today, "with all the hosts of heaven we worship and adore thy glorious name". But *host* is also the ordinary word for "army", and so could refer

to God's people Israel as God's army on earth. At Exod. 12:41 we read: "At the end of four hundred and thirty years, on that very day, all the hosts of the Lord went out from the land of Egypt." It is in consequence of this way of thinking that the Church today can sing the great hymn, "Onward Christian soldiers, marching as to war".

(4) *His ministers*. No doubt his angels but, again, where can we draw the line between heaven and earth? Whoever *does the will of God* by obeying his Word is God's *minister*.

(5) *All his works*, even inanimate nature, even "black holes" in the heavens, even the fish in the sea!

(6) And even me.

The last line is identical with the first line of the psalm, and in this way it rounds off the poem. God's forgiveness is so unexpected (verse 3). Yet of old, through Moses, Israel had learned about his amazing grace. In Jesus' day, people thought that such teaching would make men both lazy and immoral, that God loved and had forgiven them even before they repented. Consequently some said of Jesus, "He is leading the people astray". The same is said even today. The psalmist's answer to the jibe is virtually to say, "Read your Bible, for there you will see what God is really like".

In the language of "Second" Isaiah (Isa. chs. 40–55), the word redemption, *ga-al*, refers to God's act in "redeeming" his people from the power of Pharaoh in Egypt. Yet our poet is blessing God here for "forgiving his people their sins". So now we see another equation to add to that of soul and body, heaven and earth. It would seem that the redemption from Egypt in the past (and, the psalmist might add, redemption from exile not long concluded) is what we today would call sacramental acts. God's saving act in redeeming Israel from slavery to Pharaoh was the outward and visible sign and seal (see Exod. 3:12) of his forgiving love for his people and of their redemption from slavery to the power of sin.

WE ALL DEPEND ON GOD (i)

Psalm 104:1–23

¹Bless the Lord, O my soul!
   O Lord my God, thou art very great!
Thou art clothed with honour and majesty,
²   who coverest thyself with light as with a garment,
who hast stretched out the heavens like a tent,
³   who hast laid the beams of thy chambers on the waters,
who makest the clouds thy chariot,
   who ridest on the wings of the wind,
⁴who makest the winds thy messengers,
   fire and flame thy ministers.

⁵Thou didst set the earth on its foundations,
   so that it should never be shaken.
⁶Thou didst cover it with the deep as with a garment;
   the waters stood above the mountains.
⁷At thy rebuke they fled;
   at the sound of thy thunder they took to flight.
⁸The mountains rose, the valleys sank down
   to the place which thou didst appoint for them.
⁹Thou didst set a bound which they should not pass,
   so that they might not again cover the earth.

¹⁰Thou makest springs gush forth in the valleys;
   they flow between the hills,
¹¹they give drink to every beast of the field;
   the wild asses quench their thirst.
¹²By them the birds of the air have their habitation;
   they sing among the branches.
¹³From thy lofty abode thou waterest the mountains;
   the earth is satisfied with the fruit of thy work.

¹⁴Thou dost cause the grass to grow for the cattle,
   and plants for man to cultivate,
that he may bring forth food from the earth,
¹⁵   and wine to gladden the heart of man,
oil to make his face shine,
      and bread to strengthen man's heart.

¹⁶The trees of the Lord are watered abundantly,
    the cedars of Lebanon which he planted.
¹⁷In them the birds build their nests;
    the stork has her home in the fir trees.
¹⁸The high mountains are for the wild goats;
    the rocks are a refuge for the badgers.
¹⁹Thou hast made the moon to mark the seasons;
    the sun knows its time for setting.
²⁰Thou makest darkness, and it is night,
    when all the beasts of the forest creep forth.
²¹The young lions roar for their prey,
    seeking their food from God.
²²When the sun rises, they get them away
    and lie down in their dens.
²³Man goes forth to his work
    and to his labour until the evening.

Verses 1–4. Psalm 103 ended with the words of command: (a) *Bless the Lord, all his works*, and (b) *Bless the Lord, O my soul!* In Ps. 104 we learn one of the reasons why *my soul* should bless the Lord, for we learn how *all his works* do that very thing! Yet it is God who is the real hero of this poem, not Nature, and certainly not me. As the poet Browning wrote: "God is the perfect poet. Who in his person acts his own creations?" I would suggest that the Anglican Prayer Book version of this psalm has captured the spirit of verse 1*b* better than most modern translations. It runs, simply, "Thou art become exceeding glorious" (by creating the universe!).

Man can think of the Divine Being only as a Person, because pure Spirit is beyond his comprehension. As a Person, then, God is clothed. The Creation that he has brought into being is here pictured as his outer garment, as it were, for of course God himself we cannot see; what we see is the revelation of his greatness, that is, the robe of light that is "worn" by the King of creation.

One wonders, in reading what follows, whether our poet had the first chapter of Genesis before him, as well as Job chs. 38–41, along with perhaps the story of the Flood. He certainly matches these magnificent passages in this magnificent hymn.

At Ps. 103:20 it was suggested that Ps. 104 could help us to understand who these heavenly beings were to whom the AV in verse 4 gives the name "angels". These exist only as the *messengers* and *ministers* of God's creative work. In themselves and of themselves they are nothing. Their existence depends upon their obedience. We can set fire to a rubbish heap, and then watch the flames doing our will. They leap forth, burn the rubbish, and then disappear. In the same way a storm of wind can die away quite suddenly. Thus, since there is no line between heaven and earth, no line can be drawn between angels above and ministers of the gospel below, here on earth, that is to say, all the members of God's Covenant people. They are what they are only through their obedience, for it is God who is all in all. This verse strikes home to us more if we word it rather, "*We* are what we are, only if we are obedient."

Verses 5–13, *The good earth.* Verses 5–9 bring together in colourful language the mystery of Creation, as seen in Gen. 1, and that of providence, as seen in Gen. 6–8. Then verses 10–13 deal with the orderliness of the earth, following upon God's Covenant with Noah in Gen. 9. With the regular advent of the seasons, says the psalmist, there is food and drink a-plenty for all God's little creatures. For God keeps chaos in check (verse 9), those waters that are pictured at Isa. 54:9 as "the waters of Noah". Chaos has become cosmos.

Verses 14–23, *All this is for mankind.* God controls and regulates those waters so that they are now "good for man". So we are helped to "see" God's never-changing way of creative love. For God turns the waters of chaos into waters of blessing. He makes them "good for" the life of culture and of creativity. To quote Browning again, verses 16–22 make us understand that "God must be glad one loves his world so much". Our poet's love for Nature extends to a detailed observance of the ways of Nature, as he recognizes that trees, wild goats, young lions, are all beloved of God. The stork, for example, as we know today, winters in South Africa, but returns each spring to Palestine and southern Europe, arriving at the same chimney she has nested on before. That is one instance of God's unfailing *hesed* or reliable control of his Creation. In fact, the word stork, *hasidah*, represents a kind of sacramental sign of God's *hesed* towards mankind as well. For it is in this setting of Nature, of rain, wind, day and night, growth and decay, that man finds his place. His "place" in God's scheme of things, his "ministry", his "obedience" (verse 4) is to work the Garden (Gen. 2:15) in harmony with all God's creatures. For these all obey God's established order (Gen. 1:14–18). Mankind is meant to do so in the same rhythm as is to be found in Nature, where night follows day, at which time there is rest for man from work.

WE ALL DEPEND ON GOD (ii)

Psalm 104:24–35

> [24]O Lord, how manifold are thy works!
>   In wisdom hast thou made them all;
>   the earth is full of thy creatures.
> [25]Yonder is the sea, great and wide,
>   which teems with things innumerable,
>   living things both small and great.
> [26]There go the ships,
>   and Leviathan which thou didst form to sport in it.
>
> [27]These all look to thee,
>   to give them their food in due season.
> [28]When thou givest to them, they gather it up;
>   when thou openest thy hand, they are filled with good things.
> [29]When thou hidest thy face, they are dismayed;
>   when thou takest away their breath, they die
>   and return to their dust.
> [30]When thou sendest forth thy Spirit, they are created;
>   and thou renewest the face of the ground.
>
> [31]May the glory of the Lord endure for ever,
>   may the Lord rejoice in his works,
> [32]who looks on the earth and it trembles,
>   who touches the mountains and they smoke!
> [33]I will sing to the Lord as long as I live;
>   I will sing praise to my God while I have being.
> [34]May my meditation be pleasing to him,
>   for I rejoice in the Lord.

³⁵Let sinners be consumed from the earth,
    and let the wicked be no more!
Bless the Lord, O my soul!
Praise the Lord!

Verses 24–26, *He gazes over the sea.* Perhaps the psalmist planned this section of his poem when standing on the top of Mount Carmel. The summit is easily reached. It was from there that Elijah's servant stood and gazed out to sea to bring back news of a change in the weather (1 Kings 18:42–44). Consequently, in his imagination, our poet marvels at the mysteries of God's ways in the great deep. But *the earth* too, he says, *is full of thy creatures*, or, as the children's hymn puts it, "All creatures great and small . . . The Lord God made them all."

It is at this point that the poet bursts into a doxology of praise to God. And no wonder, if we have been able to join in spirit with this man who stands in such awe at God's wisdom, or, as we might prefer to put it today, at the wonders and complexities of the world of science. Amongst these there is that mysterious sea monster that you can see playing in the Mediterranean Sea. It has a number of names in the OT, Leviathan, Rahab, and more. In Gen. 1:21 we read that God created all the great sea monsters of the deep, and that he "saw that it was good". But Leviathan is not a crocodile, or a whale, or any other monster known to man. He is the "animalizing" of the Monster of the Deep (the chaos that was there in the beginning—Gen. 1:2). This can only mean that God saw the Monster as good *for* his purposes. God gave Leviathan freedom and free will just as he gave it to us. For God loves freedom. In fact, God enjoys watching this Monster *sport in* the sea—playing with God.

Verses 27–30, *Creation.* In Ps. 103 we were reminded that man is like the grass of the field, since he is but the creature of a day. Now we learn that Nature likewise has no basis of existence in itself. It is God who clothes the lily; as Jesus reminds us, the lily does not clothe itself. Any theory of evolution that we modern scientific people feel bound to accept therefore is not sufficient in itself, unless it takes into account the continuing generations of birds, beasts and fishes which this earth has seen over the centuries. These all exist only because God has first created them. *Thou sendest forth thy Spirit, they are created.* This is the verb we meet with at Gen. 1:1, a verb which is found with only God as its subject. Consequently we can speak of creation with awe and describe it in picture language. Moreover, *thou renewest the face of the ground*, that is to say its flora and fauna, its vegetation and its animal life, by ever new creative acts within the process of evolution. God has to do so, because each new generation *dies and returns to their dust.* Thus the death of Nature is not regarded here as a tragedy, because every single death of even the smallest creature occurs within the providence of God.

Verses 31–35. *May the glory of God endure for ever*, then, this glory that we are privileged to see with our eyes. Not only so, but *may the Lord* continue to *rejoice in his works*, even when the tops of the mountains are blown off in violence in volcanic activity! (Amos 9:5). How could God rejoice in them if death were the end of them? This is what it was like "at the beginning", says Job, *when the morning stars sang together, and all the sons of God shouted for joy* (Job 38:7). May it then be so *for ever!*

Consequently, in my own small way, he continues, I feel I can only echo that joy: *I will sing to the Lord as long as I live.* I hope, then, that this "composition" of mine (rather than RSV *meditation*) may please God, for it only echoes *my joy in the Lord.* How good it is to know that just as Nature depends utterly upon God, so do I!

God's Creation exhibits perfect order—except in one area, and that is the area of the life of mankind. Where were order and *shalom*, peace and harmony, to be found amongst God's people in the sad days of the Babylonian Exile? All people are sinners, including myself, he declares. Therefore, he goes on, *Let sinners be consumed from the earth*, for they corrupt its perfect harmony. The hymn "From Greenland's icy mountains" is not in fashion today, for, as a missionary hymn, it suggests that only other lands and not our own need deliverance from "error's chain". But our psalmist openly included himself as being bound in that chain. Nevertheless he finishes his poem with the words *Praise the Lord.* For having built his psalm to follow upon the contents of Ps. 103, he knows that God is the kind of God who is himself the answer to the sinfulness of mankind. The words *Praise the Lord* are the English of the Hebrew word *Hallelujah.* This exclamation is now used internationally and in all languages. Perhaps the great soul who penned this psalm is one with us in spirit today when we sing the Hallelujah Chorus in any of the many languages of the children of men.

The two great psalms 103 and 104 form a beautifully balanced pair, the first having as its theme the providence of God in the life of man (showing itself particularly in his forgiveness of their sins), the second the providence of God in the world of Nature (showing itself particularly in its order and harmony). The poetry of praise alone can compass these themes adequately. It is doubtful whether in any literature poetry has ever been used to such devastating effect.

GOD'S COVENANT WITH ISRAEL

Psalm 105:1–22

1O give thanks to the Lord, call on his name,
    make known his deeds among the peoples!
2Sing to him, sing praises to him,
    tell of all his wonderful works!
3Glory in his holy name;
    let the hearts of those who seek the Lord rejoice!
4Seek the Lord and his strength,
    seek his presence continually!
5Remember the wonderful works that he has done,
    his miracles, and the judgments he uttered,
6O offspring of Abraham his servant,
    sons of Jacob, his chosen ones!

7He is the Lord our God;
    his·judgments are in all the earth.
8He is mindful of his covenant for ever,
    of the word that he commanded, for a thousand generations,
9the covenant which he made with Abraham,
    his sworn promise to Isaac,
10which he confirmed to Jacob as a statute,

to Israel as an everlasting covenant,
¹¹saying, "To you I will give the land of Canaan
as your portion for an inheritance."

¹²When they were few in number,
of little account, and sojourners in it,
¹³wandering from nation to nation,
from one kingdom to another people,
¹⁴he allowed no one to oppress them;
he rebuked kings on their account,
¹⁵saying, "Touch not my anointed ones,
do my prophets no harm!"

¹⁶When he summoned a famine on the land,
and broke every staff of bread,
¹⁷he had sent a man ahead of them,
Joseph, who was sold as a slave.
¹⁸His feet were hurt with fetters,
his neck was put in a collar of iron;
¹⁹until what he had said came to pass
the word of the Lord tested him.
²⁰The king sent and released him,
the ruler of the peoples set him free;
²¹he made him lord of his house,
and ruler of all his possessions,
²²to instruct his princes at his pleasure,
and to teach his elders wisdom.

Verses 1–6, *Come and seek the Lord.* This psalm begins, as do so
many psalms, with a summons to the poet's own people, *sons of
Jacob, his chosen ones*, to keep on coming to worship regularly
(verse 4). They are to do so in order to *seek the Lord*, and to gain
in their lives the *strength*, or power, of his Spirit. At Acts 6:8 we
read that Stephen was full of faith and power (or strength). The
Spirit that "rushed" upon the assembled Church at Pentecost
(Acts 2:1–4) was this same power, of course (it could not be
other!), that the psalms speak of. But God's power is not mere
naked strength; it is the power of the love which is the essence of
his nature.

So the people are (a) to come, (b) to seek, (c) to remember.
They are not to do all this merely for the good of their souls. *His*

chosen ones have been chosen to entertain a missionary intention; they are to do what they do so as *to make known his deeds
amongst the peoples, the wonderful works that he has done.*

These verses were penned to be used at a particular period in
history. Perhaps that moment is the one related in 1 Chron.
16:1–22 which tells how the Ark was placed in the Tent in
Jerusalem to the accompaniment of this psalm. Or perhaps the
account in Chronicles reflects the liturgy of the Second Temple
which used this psalm when the significance of that great moment
in David's day was recalled. As W. Herberg says: "Dehistoriciz-
ing biblical faith is like paraphrasing poetry. This is because
biblical history is a dramatic recital and a call to action. It is a call
to us and to others to join us. We dare not remain cosy spectators.
We dare not say, 'I don't want to get involved'. We are to leap
onto the stage, and join in the drama." It is interesting that the
verses we are looking at were understood by some early Christians quite differently from the modern person who "doesn't
want to get involved". For, shouting them aloud in defiance, they
used them to challenge the order of the Roman Emperor to
sacrifice to Caesar.

Verses 7–15, *What do we see to be God's wonderful works?* (1)
His judgments, says the psalmist, his acts of love and correction
by which he brings about his revealed way of life; these are to be
found *in all the earth.* Let us note, not just in the Holy Land! (2)
He is mindful of his Covenant for ever (compare Gen. 9:15–16). It
is extraordinary how today there are many Christians whose faith
sees no need for God's Covenant and who are virtually ignorant
of what it stands for. They think of the Biblical faith as having to
do only with their own personal salvation and with their own
private religious experience. So their faith becomes progressively
more narrow and loveless. (3) *The Word that he commanded* is a
phrase which brings the Covenant truly alive. It is as if God sent
off his Word into the world like an angel, as we saw in Pss. 103 and
104, as a kind of missionary, and as if it was *commanded* to work
away like a leaven in the life of the world, and to do so for *a
thousand generations*!

But now, especially at (4) we meet with the words, *the covenant which he made with Abraham* (see Gen. 15:18; 17:1–8;

26:1–5; 28:10–15). In Luke 1:72–73 we find Zechariah declaring
of that Covenant that in his day it already went right back for two
thousand years, and that it still stood! Then, one element in the
ancient Covenant is emphasized—(5) God's sworn *promise* to
Isaac, confirmed later to *Jacob-Israel*, that the *land of Canaan*
should belong to Israel *as your portion for an inheritance.* The
word *your* is plural, so it refers to each and every Israelite. It is
interesting that the word *portion* can also mean "rope". So, in the
delightful manner of Semitic poetry, both meanings may be en-
tertained together. Canaan, as God's gift, is the "portion" that
God had "roped off" to be Israel's *inheritance* (see Josh. 2:9,
where this fact was known to a Canaanite woman). Consequently, if *the land* should suffer any set-backs by being
occupied by an enemy, or be devastated and ravaged by an alien
army, such crises would not be permanent (see the Commentary
on Lev. 26:31–35 in this series). For God's saving love is greater
than any such seemingly final set-back (verse 15).

The psalm began by expressing God's missionary purpose for
Israel. God's plan in giving Israel a land of her own, then, was
that she might have a pied-à-terre, in which to gather her strength
(the power of the Spirit) and from which she might go forth to be a
light to the nations.

To explain this, the poet first recounts some of the traditions of
his people. Thus, verses 12–15 speak of the days of the *wandering*
of Abraham and the other Patriarchs; and verses 16–22 tell of
how a slave, by God's grace, became a teacher of God's ways to
pagan foreigners; then in verses 23ff. the psalm goes on to show
how God had led Israel into the Promised Land.

Only here in the OT are the Patriarchs given the title of
anointed ones (verse 15), presumably because, at Gen. 20:7,
Abraham is called a prophet. The marvel is that the Covenant is
made with only a "handful" (verse 12, and see Gen. 34:30) of
people. The psalmist is therefore emphasizing the un-
touchability, the eternal nature, of God's Covenant, for the
Patriarchs lived such a very long time before his day. However,
Deut. 4:27 may also lie behind our verse 12, in which case the
"they" of *they were few in numbers* takes in all Israel in her later

history as well. If so, then all God's people are *my anointed ones*, with the implication that all God's people are called to be *my prophets* too.

Verses 16–22, *The story of Joseph.* As we have newly pointed out, the "chosen land" is not immune from harm, any more than is the "chosen people". *A famine* does not just "occur" there. What happens is that God *summons* it to be the instrument he has decided to use to effect his eternal purpose in the world. But along with such an act of judgment God always *sends* a way out— here he sends a man sold as a slave! How odd is God!

The words in verse 18 refer not merely to the pain that a person suffers in his body when thrown into an ancient prison, but also in his "soul"; for verse 18*b* can well be translated by the old rendering of the Prayer Book (now become an English proverb), "the iron entered into his soul". Moreover, God was behind all these happenings! The story of Joseph is evidently no mere folk tale from of old. It is history become the vehicle of the revelation of the providence of God.

But God continued to send his Word, to *test* Joseph, *until what he* had *commanded* actually *came to pass* (see Gen. 45:5, 7; 50:20). Finally God bade a *king* release a *slave* (just as later on he "bade" Pharaoh release his enslaved people)! The tables were turned with a vengeance. The slave Joseph, we recall, became the Grand Vizier.

GOD'S PROMISE OF THE LAND

Psalm 105:23–45

23Then Israel came to Egypt;
   Jacob sojourned in the land of Ham.
24And the Lord made his people very fruitful,
   and made them stronger than their foes.
25He turned their hearts to hate his people,
   to deal craftily with his servants.

26He sent Moses his servant,
   and Aaron whom he had chosen.

²⁷They wrought his signs among them,
  and miracles in the land of Ham.
²⁸He sent darkness, and made the land dark;
  they rebelled against his words.
²⁹He turned their waters into blood,
  and caused their fish to die.
³⁰Their land swarmed with frogs,
  even in the chambers of their kings.
³¹He spoke, and there came swarms of flies,
  and gnats throughout their country.
³²He gave them hail for rain,
  and lightning that flashed through their land.
³³He smote their vines and fig trees,
  and shattered the trees of their country.
³⁴He spoke, and the locusts came,
  and young locusts without number;
³⁵which devoured all the vegetation in their land,
  and ate up the fruit of their ground.
³⁶He smote all the first-born in their land,
  the first issue of all their strength.

³⁷Then he led forth Israel with silver and gold,
  and there was none among his tribes who stumbled.
³⁸Egypt was glad when they departed,
  for dread of them had fallen upon it.
³⁹He spread a cloud for a covering,
  and fire to give light by night.
⁴⁰They asked, and he brought quails,
  and gave them bread from heaven in abundance.
⁴¹He opened the rock, and water gushed forth;
  it flowed through the desert like a river.
⁴²For he remembered his holy promise,
  and Abraham his servant.

⁴³So he led forth his people with joy,
  his chosen ones with singing.
⁴⁴And he gave them the lands of the nations;
  and they took possession of the fruit of the people's toil,
⁴⁵to the end that they should keep his statutes,
  and observe his laws.
  Praise the Lord!

Verses 23–36, *The story of the oppression.* Egypt is known as *the land of Ham* (from Gen. 10:6). The *fruitfulness* of the people of Israel is described at Exod. 1:19–20. There we read also of the reaction of the Egyptian people—one that God had caused in the same way that God had caused Joseph's reaction when he was in prison! For it is by means of catastrophes that God creates good. The title *his servant Moses* comes from Exod. 14:31; and God's choice of Aaron from Exod. 7:1. But here we meet with no glorification of either Moses or Aaron. The emphasis is upon God's choice of them, and upon the fact that they did only what he told them to.

What follows is based on Exod. 4–11, chapters which should be studied at this point; for there we read how these two men *wrought his* (God's) *signs upon them* (the Egyptians), that is, the plagues and all the rest. That, then, is the emphasis the psalmist makes. He declares that the signs were mysterious, for they were not the kind of signs that a scientist could analyze. A modern reader could niggle at the fact that the list of plagues is not complete here, and that those that are mentioned are not placed in their correct order. He should remember that this is poetry.

Finally, verse 36 refers to the most important plague of all. For it happened in the light of God's great statement made to Moses at Exod. 4:22: "Israel is my first-born son".

Verses 37–42, *The Exodus.* This passage begins with an idealized statement about that incident which the book of Exodus describes as "spoiling the Egyptians" (Exod. 3:22; 12:36). Here it is seen in a glorified light. At verse 38 we even hear a chuckle coming from the poet's throat. For the Exodus is shown not to be the flight of a rabble of slaves, but the ordered movement of "the army of the Lord" from slavery to freedom. The Wilderness period and its miracles is then briefly recalled. For *God remembered his holy promise, and Abraham his servant.*

Verses 43–45. *And so they arrived*—just as did Abraham at Gen. 12:5 where the AV reads: "They went forth to go into the land of Canaan, and into the land of Canaan they came." As easy as that! Yes, because it was the Lord's doing. Despite all the setbacks we read about in the books of Exodus and Numbers, the people of God arrived at the Promised Land with *joy* and *singing*. But God had a purpose in doing all this on their behalf. It was that they might let the world see a people living in obedience to the *laws* of God.

We should note a number of issues here:

1. Liberation must not and cannot be an end in itself. We are set free from whatever oppression we may be suffering under, not for the sake just of being free, but in order to serve God as he commands, in fact to find that "in his service is perfect freedom". That is what our poet emphasizes in his last verse.

2. Israel's neighbours all held to a cyclical view of history. Just as the seasons of the year go in a cycle, reach an end and begin all over again, so it is, they believed, with the affairs of men. The Greeks produced a new way of recording history. Their historians learned to be scrupulously objective in order to record events as if from the outside, quite unlike the boastful records of almost every eastern monarch that we possess. Thus, if they were reporting a war, for example, the reader could not tell easily whose side the historian was on. But as to the meaning of history, of the battle that they were recording, the Greeks possessed few clues. In general they looked to the past, to the heroic era. They rarely tried to look to the future. Thus it was that for them time meant merely transitoriness, without containing in it any overwhelming purpose.

The psalmists, however, unlike contemporary Greek historians, could "hope in God", as they delight to say to each other within the Covenant. We see such history writing in the case of "The Court History of David" in the OT book of 2 Samuel. In the spirit of such writing, then, the poet here deliberately indicates the hand of God as it leads his people through their history to the end that God alone has in view, not they.

3. To help him indicate "meaning" in history writing, instead of repeating a mere list of facts, the psalmist remembers that he is a poet. The "eschatological significance" of the facts which cannot be described in ordinary prose terms he points to in this poem by openly employing poetic imagery.

4. As a further issue, we examine, in the light of history, God's

unconditional promise to Israel of the land of Canaan. On this the Jew and the Christian find it hard to agree. During the Exile in the OT period Israel lost her land for fifty years; and as this psalm explains, that temporary loss of it was for remedial and educative purposes. But Israel lost her land again in A.D. 70 when the Romans first destroyed Jerusalem, and then sixty years later finally forbade them even to live within the bounds of the Holy Land. Moreover, this situation lasted right till the year 1948, even though in the last century the Turkish overlords of the Levant allowed a few Jews to trickle back there to die. Today, then, the Jew lays claim to the whole of the "Promised Land" on the basis of God's promises recorded in the Bible, as in this psalm.

The Christian, however, sees the issue otherwise, no matter how much he may sympathize with the Jew. The Christian sees the Holy Land as that soil which nourished Jesus. Jesus ate the food that came out of it, his physical body was built from it. His body was *of* that "holy" land and of no other. Just as he summed up in himself, the Christian would declare, all the promises of God made ever since the days of Abraham, so too his body summed up and "extrapolated" the particular promise recorded here. May I then make the point, which may appear strange to some readers, that in the resurrection of the "whole" Christ God raised to his right hand the soil of the Promised Land in the body of Christ. (See the article on this issue by myself in the volume *The Witness of the Jews to God*, edited by David W. Torrance, 1982.) The Resurrection of Christ, as the first-fruits in promise of the resurrection of all who are "in Christ", is thus the first-fruits of the promise of God to create a new heaven and a new earth. That is the Promised Land to which we Christians now travel.

THE MAGNALIA DEI (i)

Psalm 106:1–15

[1]Praise the Lord!
O give thanks to the Lord, for he is good;
for his steadfast love endures for ever!

²Who can utter the mighty doings of the Lord,
  or show forth all his praise?
³Blessed are those who observe justice,
  who do righteousness at all times!

⁴Remember me, O Lord, when thou showest favour to thy people;
  help me when thou deliverest them;
⁵that I may see the prosperity of thy chosen ones,
  that I may rejoice in the gladness of thy nation,
  that I may glory with thy heritage.

⁶Both we and our fathers have sinned;
  we have committed iniquity, we have done wickedly.
⁷Our fathers, when they were in Egypt,
  did not consider thy wonderful works;
 they did not remember the abundance of thy steadfast love,
  but rebelled against the Most High at the Red Sea.
⁸Yet he saved them for his name's sake,
  that he might make known his mighty power.
⁹He rebuked the Red Sea, and it became dry;
  and he led them through the deep as through a desert.
¹⁰So he saved them from the hand of the foe,
  and delivered them from the power of the enemy.
¹¹And the waters covered their adversaries;
  not one of them was left.
¹²Then they believed his words;
  they sang his praise.

¹³But they soon forgot his works;
  they did not wait for his counsel.
¹⁴But they had a wanton craving in the wilderness,
  and put God to the test in the desert;
¹⁵he gave them what they asked,
  but sent a wasting disease among them.

This psalm is a companion to Ps. 105. It speaks "the gospel". Originally this word was "god spell", or "good story", good because it is God's story. "History", to the Hebrews, was the process of telling and retelling the Israelite "story". The psalmist realizes that God revealed himself in the *mental* appreciation of the events of his history as well as in the events themselves. As L. Gilkey puts it: "The majority of divine deeds (in the OT) become what we choose to call *symbols*, rather than plain historical facts". So Ps. 106 could be entitled the *Magnalia Dei*, being the Latin for the words we find at verse 2*a*. It forms a fitting doxology to Book IV of the Psalter.

What did Gilkey mean in that sentence of his? He meant that if God were to be totally involved in history, then he would be like a Hindu god, all arms and legs and sex symbols. If he were totally outside of history, again, he would be like Allah in the Qoran, ineffable, impassible, unknowable. But the God of the psalmist does not dwell in a timeless realm. He dwells "from age to age". Nor is he the object of scientific enquiry such as when some diffident person declares today "I believe in only what I can touch." He makes himself known to us by stooping down from the stage, to use Will Herberg's telling analogy, beckoning to the audience, and saying: "Don't remain a spectator, uncommitted, irresponsible. Come up here beside me and join me in the vigour of the drama through which I am working out my redemptive purpose for the world."

This psalm breathes the spirit of Solomon's prayer at 1 Kings 8 where "Israel's history", being recounted in words of prayer, and within an act of worship, actually becomes "God's history". How boring the history of the Wars of the Roses can be to generations of children at school! On the other hand, this history here is highly exciting, because it is bound up with the power of prayer. Yet there is one discordant note that runs right through it, and that is, as we recognize at once, the unfaithfulness of God's people Israel. It is extraordinary that this people should be described consistently as such *along with* descriptions of the greatness of God. But then the greatness of God is shown to be his never-failing love for unfaithful Israel.

Verses 1-3. The poem begins with a *Hallelujah*; for God's goodness and eternal *hesed* are focused on us! Happy then are those who echo those two great aspects of God, (a) who do what God does, that is, not just be good, but rather do good, and (b) who *do tsedaqah*, "righteousness" (the feminine noun we discussed in the Introduction to Vol. 1), that is, act in creative love to their neighbours, and do it *at all times*!

Verses 4–5. The psalmist interjects a little personal prayer, as if he were saying, "And this includes me, Lord." We have instances of such prayers at Neh. 5:19; 6:14; 13:14. Our poet thus shows us how a national psalm, designed for use in public worship, can be used by an individual in his private approach to God.

Verses 6–15, *Confession*. Note, *Both we and our fathers have sinned*. That is to say, we are no different from them. Their great sin was in not recognizing your mighty hand in the events they were living through. To be blind this way is to "create evil" (rather than RSV *done wickedly*.) "He that is not with me is against me," as Jesus said. He who does not remember the abundance of your *hesed* is not merely neutral, he actually creates evil!

Yet he saved them, because it is his nature to save, despite their creating evil. *He led them through the deep as through a desert* is a phrase that links theology with geography, for God revealed himself in that particular event of history. The Reed Sea (rather than *Red Sea*, because *suph* means "reeds") became the symbol of the deeps of chaos (Gen. 1:2) that are eternally at war with God, but so also is the desert. It too is a symbol of this kind. That is why the host (the army) of the Lord is so-called throughout the forty years that it "fought" its way against *the power of the enemy*, the powers of evil, right into the Promised Land. Yet their loyalty to their Commander-in-Chief was always in question, for they kept *putting God to the test* (verse 14). They did not notice that God had *led them* (verse 9), this army, not from the sky, but from their front, their head. When he revealed that his judgment against their enemies was total (verse 11) only *then* did they *believe and sing his praise*—but *they soon forgot his works*, unimaginable as it may seem. They forgot that God has a plan working through their lives and through their history, so that God knows better than they. How sad it all is! *He gave them*, however, *what they asked*—and what he gave them made them sick. Here again then, as at verse 4 and verse 6, the poet is saying, "This means me too."

THE MAGNALIA DEI (ii)

Psalm 106:16–48

16When men in the camp were jealous of Moses
   and Aaron, the holy one of the Lord,
17the earth opened and swallowed up Dathan,
   and covered the company of Abiram.
18Fire also broke out in their company;
   the flame burned up the wicked.

19They made a calf in Horeb
   and worshipped a molten image.
20They exchanged the glory of God
   for the image of an ox that eats grass.
21They forgot God, their Saviour,
   who had done great things in Egypt,
22wondrous works in the land of Ham,
   and terrible things by the Red Sea.
23Therefore he said he would destroy them—
   had not Moses, his chosen one,
 stood in breach before him,
   to turn away his wrath from destroying them.

24Then they despised the pleasant land,
   having no faith in his promise.
25They murmured in their tents,
   and did not obey the voice of the Lord.
26Therefore he raised his hand and swore to them
   that he would make them fall in the wilderness,
27and would disperse their descendants among the nations,
   scattering them over the lands.

28Then they attached themselves to the Baal of Peor,
   and ate sacrifices offered to the dead;
29they provoked the Lord to anger with their doings,
   and a plague broke out among them.
30Then Phinehas stood up and interposed,
   and the plague was stayed.
31And that has been reckoned to him as righteousness
   from generation to generation for ever.

³²They angered him at the waters of Meribah,
and it went ill with Moses on their account;
³³for they made his spirit bitter,
and he spoke words that were rash.

³⁴They did not destroy the peoples,
as the Lord commanded them,
³⁵but they mingled with the nations
and learned to do as they did.
³⁶They served their idols,
which became a snare to them.
³⁷They sacrified their sons
and their daughters to the demons;
³⁸they poured out innocent blood,
the blood of their sons and daughters,
whom they sacrificed to the idols of Canaan;
and the land was polluted with blood.
³⁹Thus they became unclean by their acts,
and played the harlot in their doings.

⁴⁰Then the anger of the Lord was kindled against his people,
and he abhorred his heritage;
⁴¹he gave them into the hand of the nations,
so that those who hated them ruled over them.
⁴²Their enemies oppressed them,
and they were brought into subjection under their power.
⁴³Many times he delivered them,
but they were rebellious in their purposes,
and were brought low through their iniquity.
⁴⁴Nevertheless he regarded their distress,
when he heard their cry.
⁴⁵He remembered for their sake his covenant,
and relented according to the abundance of his steadfast love.
⁴⁶He caused them to be pitied
by all those who held them captive.

⁴⁷Save us, O Lord our God,
and gather us from among the nations,
that we may give thanks to thy holy name
and glory in thy praise.

⁴⁸Blessed be the Lord, the God of Israel,
from everlasting to everlasting!

And let all the people say, "Amen!"
Praise the Lord!

Verses 16–23. Envy is a sickness, and a very ugly one too, and one which deserves the judgment of God (see Num. 16; 26:9–11; Deut. 11:6). Israel was meant to be a *company*, a fellowship (verse 18), but now envy had destroyed that fellowship.

The story continues with Israel's rebellion at Horeb (i.e. Mount Sinai). We read of it in Exod. 32. There, like silly school children, they "swapped" *the glory of God for the image of an ox*! But God was not their "Führer", their divine Boss, he was *their Saviour*. Moses alone knew this to be so, so that his intercession for his rebel people prevailed. The judgment which God *said* was that he would have to *destroy* (verse 23), actually "exterminate" his chosen (!) people (Exod. 32:10–14). But Moses stepped into *the breach*. He reminded God of his own essential nature (Num. 14:18) by accepting the possibility that God's holy detestation of sin might fall upon him as substitute for Israel (Exod. 32:32). Jesus commented on this: "Greater love has no man than this . . . " (John 15:13), surely with the example of Moses as well as his own example in mind. Moses, we read in Num. 16:48, *stood between the dead and the living*.

Verses 24–39. In Ps. 105 we saw how unconditionally gracious God was in *giving* the Promised Land to his chosen people. Now we learn that Israel *despised the pleasant land* when they saw it! *They had no faith in God's promise. Therefore he raised his hand* (what you do when you utter a terrible oath). (See Num. 14:1–35; Deut. 4:27.) Thereupon they broke the First Commandment and worshipped the local god of vegetation. Each hot summer season the god Baal died and went down below the ground into Sheol, coming to life with the rains of autumn. Fancy the people of the Living God worshipping and having communion with a god who was dead for half the year! Phinehas it was who this time interceded on their behalf (Num. 25:1–13), and with effect. For *that has been reckoned to him as righteousness*, that is as an act of saving love, creative love, that all generations have acknowledged and witnessed. And since it was *for ever*, it was an act that belonged in the sphere of the everlastingness of the Living God.

In Ps. 95 the congregation is warned, before they dare set foot in the sanctuary, to remember what happened at Massah and *Meribah* (Num. 20:2–13). That warning was aimed at the contemporary individual worshipper, and has been so aimed till the present day. So it is also with this reference (verses 32–33). Poor Moses! Three reasons have been adduced why *it went ill with Moses*. (1) As here, and at Deut. 1:37; 3:26; 4:21, because of the unbelief of the people. (2) Moses could evidently sometimes speak stupidly and irresponsibly, and not seriously, about God's will for his people. (3) As we saw at Ps. 105:26, Moses was no "plaster saint". He lost his temper at Meribah, being impatient and presumptuous at the leading of God. He "presumed" in other words on his special relationship to God as God's *servant*.

So the story goes on, right into the period of the settlement under Joshua. The psalmist's indictment is that instead of opposing evil, God's people just joined in with it. *The gods and demons of Canaan* demanded infant sacrifices (Deut. 12:31). So they cruelly joined in with that. Then they "worshipped" on the high places by means of fornicating with cultic prostitutes (see Hos. ch. 2). Thus worshipping *idols, utsub, becomes a snare to them,* or, vowelled differently, becomes an *etseb*, a pain or trouble.

Verses 40–46, *The judgment.* Six hundred years of apostasy followed! How amazing God is to keep on calling Israel "my people" throughout all that very long time! But at last came the inevitable crisis. This section of the psalm therefore speaks of the fall of Jerusalem to Nebuchadnezzar in 587 B.C. and of the subsequent exile in Babylonia. Self-will, it seems, was the basic sin of God's people, something that few people today even think of as a sin. Consequently this passage brings us up with a jerk, so to speak, since we recognize that it is speaking to us. Yet, even as we see at Hos. 11:9, God expresses his judgment, not as wrath, but as compassion and as an outpouring of his *hesed*; that is to say, he only punishes so as to express his steadfast love! This creative love of God actually creates love in the hearts of Israel's Assyrian and Babylonian captors (verse 46)! This is one of the most marvellous of the Magnalia Dei.

Verse 47. Quoting perhaps from Solomon's prayer at 1 Kings 8:50, where we read how Solomon tied God down, so to speak, to be faithful to himself, our poet now dares to rest his claim upon that same faithfulness of God. Perhaps he himself was amongst the worshippers in the Second Temple after it was restored, somewhere about 516 B.C. But there were many Israelites living scattered in many lands who did not return "home". We read of some of them in the book of Esther. The psalmist prays that they too may be gathered in to thank and praise their God.

Verse 48. The psalm ends with a common act of worship, a doxology to conclude appropriately both it and Book IV of the Psalter.

A SYNTHESIS IN SIX VIGNETTES (i)

Psalm 107:1–22

¹O give thanks to the Lord, for he is good;
  for his steadfast love endures for ever!
²Let the redeemed of the Lord say so,
  whom he has redeemed from trouble
³and gathered in from the lands,
  from the east and from the west,
  from the north and from the south.

⁴Some wandered in desert wastes,
  finding no way to a city to dwell in;
⁵hungry and thirsty,
  their soul fainted within them.
⁶Then they cried to the Lord in their trouble,
  and he delivered them from their distress;
⁷he led them by a straight way,
  till they reached a city to dwell in.
⁸Let them thank the Lord for his steadfast love,
  for his wonderful works to the sons of men!
⁹For he satisfies him who is thirsty,
  and the hungry he fills with good things.

¹⁰Some sat in darkness and in gloom,
  prisoners in affliction and in irons,
¹¹for they had rebelled against the words of God,
  and spurned the counsel of the Most High.
¹²Their hearts were bowed down with hard labour;
  they fell down, with none to help.
¹³Then they cried to the Lord in their trouble,
  and he delivered them from their distress;
¹⁴he brought them out of darkness and gloom,
  and broke their bonds asunder.
¹⁵Let them thank the Lord for his steadfast love,
  for his wonderful works to the sons of men!
¹⁶For he shatters the doors of bronze,
  and cuts in two the bars of iron.

¹⁷Some were sick through their sinful ways,
  and because of their iniquities suffered affliction;
¹⁸they loathed any kind of food,
  and they drew near to the gates of death.
¹⁹Then they cried to the Lord in their trouble,
  and he delivered them from their distress;
²⁰he sent forth his word, and healed them,
  and delivered them from destruction.
²¹Let them thank the Lord for his steadfast love,
  for his wonderful works to the sons of men!
²²And let them offer sacrifices of thanksgiving,
  and tell of his deeds in songs of joy!

This psalm is a synthesis of the themes of Psalms 105 and 106 made to remind worshippers how wonderfully Book IV of the Psalter had concluded. It sets the scene for what could almost be called a new chapter of revelation. Ps. 106:26 had contained the words *in the wilderness,* which is the Hebrew name for our book of Numbers, the Fourth Book of the *Torah.* If we had been present in an ancient synagogue we would now be about to hear psalms read that accompanied the reading in public of the Fifth Book of the *Torah,* viz. Deuteronomy. The latter was written after the settlement in Canaan was complete. In the same way, and parallel with it, Book V of the Psalter refers to the life of

Israel after its re-settlement on returning home to "Canaan" from its experience of the Exile. See Jer. 33:11 in connection with Ps. 107:8.

Verses 1-3. The Exile is now over. The lost sheep for whom Ps. 106:47 had prayed are now in the fold, gathered in from the four points of the compass. Had the journey home been an easy one? The psalmist answers this question by presenting us with a series of vignettes. Each of them is a word-picture. In them we see different groups of sheep, all of them in great trouble. Yet we are to remember that, in the providence of God, these vignettes illustrate the journey we all face as we seek our home in the heavenly Jerusalem. This psalm, therefore, is to be read much in the same way as we read *The Pilgrim's Progress*, that is, as an analogy that applies to all people everywhere.

Verses 4-9, *Vignette I.* The first picture is of weary returnees crossing the desert of northern Syria as they struggle, hungry and thirsty, to reach their ancient home. We are shown them in deep need. We are told that *they cried to the Lord in their trouble, and he delivered them from their distress.* That was God's first move. He *delivered* them *from* their distressful situation. His second step, however, was positive. He *led them by a straight way*—no getting lost among the sand dunes!—*till they reached a city to dwell in* (see Jer. 31:23-25). Jerusalem is, of course, the city in question, although *to dwell in* is the word *moshav* that means any hospitable place. This particular historical picture is then generalized to refer to anyone who is struggling through the deserts of life to reach the city of God. Nor only is it generalized, it is also spiritualized by the references to hunger and thirst. So verse 8 fits well at the end of the picture: *Let them thank the Lord for his hesed,* which does not fail when his people are hungry and thirsty and lost.

Verses 10-16, *Vignette II.* On this panel there is painted a picture of the exiles in Babylon. Isa. 42:22 portrays their plight in just one verse of poetry. But our psalmist declares that they were receiving in their *affliction* what was only their just judgment. For they had rebelled against the *words* (or perhaps "promises") *of God,* and had spurned the *counsel,* the plan, of the Most High

God which he had revealed for their lives through Moses. (Note how much of that was in the book of Deuteronomy that was read in parallel with this psalm.) Within that "plan" of God, as we can discover in the book of Deuteronomy, there is the reality which the NT sums up under the one word "the Cross". Despite this reality of history, however, many people today can see no meaning in events at all, preferring just to quote Henry Ford, who reportedly declared that "history is just one damn' thing after another." *Then they cried to the Lord in their trouble and he delivered them from their distress*—the same words as at verse 6. God's positive act in this case is to *break their bonds in sunder* (whether these are made of iron or of binding intellectual concepts does not affect the issue). Thus verse 15 is a repeat of verse 8, and verse 16 shows what God does when he delivers his people at any time.

The fact that we have produced hymns on the themes of this vignette shows how a particular Biblical historical situation can become available for all people to use throughout the centuries. A hymn such as "Come we that love the Lord, and let our joys be known", by Isaac Watts, is built upon the refrain that occurs in verses 8, 15, 21, and 31 of this psalm, while a hymn such as "Lift up your heads, ye gates of brass, Ye bars of iron yield", by James Montgomery, has been inspired by verse 16 (as well as by Psalm 24).

Verses 17–22, *Vignette III*. This time we see a picture of some stay-at-homes, especially if they are at home because they are sick. And this could apply of course to anyone anywhere. We note that our word-picture joins sickness with sin. *Some were fools* (RSV verse 17 ftn) *through their sinful ways*. They may have taken drugs, or alcohol, or have merely overeaten, or have developed a venereal disease. Yet even such fools are not beyond God's love and care. This time *he sent forth his word and healed them* (compare Ps. 105:19). Ps. 33:6 (like Gen. ch. 1) has told us of the Word controlling Nature. Here the Word heals people. It *delivered them from destruction*, that is, from the pit of Sheol into which they had nearly toppled. They at least were grateful. But we are glad to discover that the poet recognizes how gratitude ought to be costly.

A SYNTHESIS IN SIX VIGNETTES (ii)

Psalm 107:23–43

²³Some went down to the sea in ships,
  doing business on the great waters;
²⁴they saw the deeds of the Lord,
  his wondrous works in the deep.
²⁵For he commanded, and raised the stormy wind,
  which lifted up the waves of the sea.
²⁶They mounted up to heaven, they went down to the depths;
  their courage melted away in their evil plight;
²⁷they reeled and staggered like drunken men,
  and were at their wits' end.
²⁸Then they cried to the Lord in their trouble,
  and he delivered them from their distress;
²⁹he made the storm be still,
  and the waves of the sea were hushed.
³⁰Then they were glad because they had quiet,
  and he brought them to their desired haven.
³¹Let them thank the Lord for his steadfast love,
  for his wonderful works to the sons of men!
³²Let them extol him in the congregation of the people,
  and praise him in the assembly of the elders.

³³He turns rivers into a desert,
  springs of water into thirsty ground,
³⁴a fruitful land into a salty waste,
  because of the wickedness of its inhabitants.
³⁵He turns a desert into pools of water,
  a parched land into springs of water.
³⁶And there he lets the hungry dwell,
  and they establish a city to live in;
³⁷they sow fields, and plant vineyards,
  and get a fruitful yield.
³⁸By his blessing they multiply greatly;
  and he does not let their cattle decrease.

³⁹When they are diminished and brought low
  through oppression, trouble, and sorrow,
⁴⁰he pours contempt upon princes

and makes them wander in trackless wastes;
41but he raises up the needy out of affliction,
   and makes their families like flocks.
42The upright see it and are glad;
   and all wickedness stops its mouth.
43Whoever is wise, let him give heed to these things;
   let men consider the steadfast love of the Lord.

Verses 23–32, *Vignette IV.* Some exiles had evidently become successful merchants. Perhaps they were now trading down the Red Sea or amongst the Isles of Greece. But here they are wending their way home to Jerusalem. The dangers they faced as they crossed the sea were different from those faced by the returning exiles who crossed the desert. In each of the first four vignettes we see pictured for us God's testing ways when he uses suffering and loss to that end. Here of course what we have is a vivid picture of a storm at sea. The order is: (1) *they were at their wits' end.* God waited till they had finally realized that they could not save themselves. (2) *Then they cried to the Lord in their trouble,* as at verses 6, 13, and 19. (3) *He delivered them from their distress,* God's first and negative act. (4) *He made the storm be still,* God's positive act that followed and which continued on after his act of deliverance. (5) *He brought them to their desired haven* (compare verses 7, 14, 20). The last part of the picture shows us the merchantmen arriving in Jerusalem, going up to the Temple to worship, and *extolling God before the congregation of the people.*

Let us note again: (a) It needed a storm before there could be a calm, as we see at Gen. 1:2 and at Mark 4:37. (b) Therefore the "stormy" nature of God's *mighty deeds* in chastening Israel were only a means to an end—*and he brought them to their desired haven.* (c) The OT draws no line between "church" and "state". Some of the elders mentioned at verse 32 were "democratically" elected representatives of the people. They regularly sat in council, probably in an outer court of the Temple. Some of these elders again seem to have represented the village communities from which they and their worshippers came up to Jerusalem three times a year for the great festivals. In his village the elder acted as a kind of "Justice of the Peace". Thus he could bring up with him to the capital the thoughts and ideas of his village. Before the Exile this council of elders met both to advise the king—if he was willing to accept their advice!— as well as to share in the decisions relating to the conduct of the Temple. After the Exile the council of elders became the governing body of the nation under the authority of the Persian Governor of the Province. In a real sense what we have is a "theocracy" rather than a "democracy in council". Yet this Israelite system is much more the ancestor of our western governmental system than is the so-called democracy of the Greeks. At Athens it was only free men (never women or workers or foreigners) who had the vote, and only free men who were citizens of the city, not of the country. Athenian democracy is rather the ancestor of the apartheid form of government that obtains in South Africa than it is of other western models.

We read in Gen. 1 that everything God made he saw to be good. Yet how could a storm at sea be "good"? It is good, just because God sees it to be so. He sees it as an occasion for exercising his loving care over a group of frightened sailors. The occasion has thus been enriched by his seeing it not as a moment of terror but as an opportunity to allow a group of scared people to experience the protection of his love.

Verses 33–38, *Vignette V.* Till now we have seen four parable pictures of what God can do for his Covenant people. The fifth picture is rather different. In it we see all Nature suffering. It does so, moreover, at God's command. This suffering results, horrible as it is to discover, from man's *wickedness,* and not from any wickedness of Nature's own. When will this world learn that erosion, for example, is not a misfortune but is a sin? That man, all down the centuries, has actually created the deserts of the world? But God can override the basically "evil" nature of man (this is the word *wickedness* at verse 34) and reverse the processes brought about by man's misuse of his free will. Thus God can make deserts fertile again so as to produce food to enable human being to resettle the land they have lost, and to live under his *blessing* once again. God's creation is not conceived of as dead matter. The scientist has revealed to us only recently that the smallest unit of matter conceivable never actually stays still, but keeps on coalescing with other units, propagating, creating ever new life in new forms and positions. *By his blessing they multiply greatly*, says this poet. Yet, man is not just part of Nature; he is no mere "naked ape". God has set man *over* nature, *under* himself (Gen. 1), so that man's rule must necessarily be analogous to God's rule; it must, therefore, inevitably be informed by love.

This is because God loves us human beings as his children. The mosquito can and does multiply and die. But God is concerned if this other creature of his, man, goes hungry. Professor J. Bronowski writes: "There must be something unique about man because otherwise, evidently, ducks would be lecturing about the behaviour of humanity, and rats would be writing papers about the professor who was experimenting upon them."

Verses 39–42, *Vignette VI*. In the same way that God handles Nature and can produce new life out of the desert (a symbol, we remember, of the chaos of evil that was there "in the beginning"), so too he handles human nature. If people, even those at the top, important people, choose to walk the wrong path (compare this idea with turning arable land into desert), *he makes them wander in trackless wastes*, that is, he lets them go down the wrong road which they have freely chosen, and so go down into the "hellish" deserts of the world. *But he raises up the needy out of affliction*, parallel with how he feeds the hungry from land that once was dead (verse 36 above). So verse 41 notes that great affirmation made by the whole of the OT, that God deals, not so much with individual "souls", as with families as units. It is in this light, in fact, that we are to understand that the coming of Christ meant the forming first of the Holy Family.

This vignette concludes by showing us *the upright* as being *glad*, while *all wickedness*, personified as if it were a personal devil, *stops its mouth* in awe and shame.

Verse 43. Finally the poet says: If you are *wise*, think about the meaning of these word-pictures, and note how they all illustrate *the steadfast love of the Lord*.

UPDATING OLD PSALMS

Psalm 108:1–13

A Song. A Psalm of David.

[1]My heart is steadfast, O God,
　my heart is steadfast!
　I will sing and make melody!
　Awake my soul!
[2]Awake, O harp and lyre!
　I will awake the dawn!
[3]I will give thanks to thee, O Lord, among the peoples,
　I will sing praises to thee among the nations.
[4]For thy steadfast love is great above the heavens,
　thy faithfulness reaches to the clouds.

[5]Be exalted, O God, above the heavens!
　Let thy glory be over all the earth!
[6]That thy beloved may be delivered,
　give help to thy right hand, and answer me!

[7]God has promised in his sanctuary:
　"With exultation I will divide up Shechem,
　and portion out the Vale of Succoth.
[8]Gilead is mine; Manasseh is mine;
　Ephraim is my helmet;
　Judah my sceptre.
[9]Moad is my washbasin;
　upon Edom I cast my shoe;
　over Philistia I shout in triumph."

[10]Who will bring me to the fortified city?
　Who will lead me to Edom?
[11]Hast thou not rejected us, O God?
　Thou dost not go forth, O God, with our armies.
[12]O grant us help against the foe,
　for vain is the help of man!
[13]With God we shall do valiantly;
　it is he who will tread down our foes.

This psalm is a mosaic of other psalms, especially of Ps. 57 and Ps. 60. The heading is: *A Song. A Psalm of David*. The song-writer, who flourished in the period of the Second Temple, and who was perhaps one of the editors of Book V, wants his fellow-worshippers to be able to make use of psalms going back to the time of David and to sing them as their contemporary songs of praise. It is for just such a reason of course that modern hymn books include hymns from all centuries in the past.

Verses 1–4. Compare Ps. 57:7–10. The song-writer invites his friends to join him in *singing* God's praises out of a *steadfast heart*, that is, one unshaken by circumstances, and to do so first thing in the morning. For doing so helps him to recall the two things about God that Ps. 107 has emphasized—God's *steadfast love,* and God's *faithfulness*. These two great realities belong not just here on earth where we must live out our lives but in eternity (*above the heavens, reaches to the clouds*). Nor is the psalmist selfishly grasping merely at a faith for himself. He wants *all the nations* to know about this love of God. If he were alive today he would be shocked to hear anyone singing God's praises with one breath, and with another declaring: "I don't believe in foreign missions." This first paragraph is written in Hebrew in short, staccato lines— but what poetry it is in the original!

Verses 5–6. Compare Ps. 57:11 and Ps. 60:5. This short, neat little prayer is rather extraordinary. It is aimed at telling God to be himself! For although God is *exalted above the heavens,* he is to remember that he is also "my" Saviour! "Stoop down to *thy beloved,* help me and answer me," the psalmist pleads, knowing that he dare address God in such terms just because God loves him with a steadfast love and utter faithfulness.

Verses 7–13. Compare Ps. 60:6–12. See the Commentary on this psalm in Vol. I. "This is how God acted in the past", our song-writer wants the congregation to sing; and then proceeds to give instances out of history. *Moab* and *Edom,* he reminds us, had to do what they were told by God. The *Philistines* nearly wrecked the origins of the kingdom in David's day—but God "put them in their place in his plan".

Now that we are in trouble again with Edom, he says, won't *God grant us help against the foe*? (It is interesting to realize that long after even this late psalm was written, Herod who gave orders to have John the Baptist beheaded was in origin an Edomite.) The capital city of Edom was Petra, the rock-city, here called *the fortified city*. But evidently not fortified against the power of God.

A psalm such as this, then, invites us to make the whole Book of Psalms contemporary with ourselves, and to use it whenever in our day and in our turn we discover that *vain is the help of man*; yet that *with God we shall do valiantly*. For it is he, and not we, *who will tread down our enemies*.

REVENGE

Psalm 109:1–31

To the choirmaster. A Psalm of David.

¹Be not silent, O God of my praise!
²For wicked and deceitful mouths are opened against me,
  speaking against me with lying tongues.
³They beset me with words of hate,
  and attack me without cause.
⁴In return for my love they accuse me,
  even as I make prayer for them.
⁵So they reward me evil for good,
  and hatred for my love.

⁶Appoint a wicked man against him;
  let an accuser bring him to trial.
⁷When he is tried, let him come forth guilty;
  let his prayer be counted as sin!
⁸May his days be few;
  may another seize his goods!
⁹May his children be fatherless,
  and his wife a widow!
¹⁰May his children wander about and beg;
  may they be driven out of the ruins they inhabit!
¹¹May the creditor seize all that he has;
  may strangers plunder the fruits of his toil!

¹²Let there be none to extend kindness to him,
  nor any to pity his fatherless children!
¹³May his posterity be cut off;
  may his name be blotted out in the second generation!
¹⁴May the iniquity of his fathers be remembered before the Lord,
  and let not the sin of his mother be blotted out!
¹⁵Let them be before the Lord continually;
  and may his memory be cut off from the earth!
¹⁶For he did not remember to show kindness,
  but pursued the poor and needy
  and the brokenhearted to their death.
¹⁷He loved to curse; let curses come on him!
  He did not like blessing; may it be far from him!
¹⁸He clothed himself with cursing as his coat,
  may it soak into his body like water,
  like oil into his bones!
¹⁹May it be like a garment which he wraps round him,
  like a belt with which he daily girds himself!

²⁰May this be the reward of my accusers from the Lord,
  of those who speak evil against my life!
²¹But thou, O God my Lord,
  deal on my behalf for thy name's sake;
  because thy steadfast love is good, deliver me!
²²For I am poor and needy,
  and my heart is stricken within me.
²³I am gone, like a shadow at evening;
  I am shaken off like a locust.
²⁴My knees are weak through fasting;
  my body has become gaunt.
²⁵I am an object of scorn to my accusers;
  when they see me, they wag their heads.

²⁶Help me, O Lord my God!
  Save me according to thy steadfast love!
²⁷Let them know that this is thy hand;
  thou, O Lord, hast done it!
²⁸Let them curse, but do thou bless!
  Let my assailants be put to shame; may thy servant be glad!
²⁹May my accusers be clothed with dishonour;
  may they be wrapped in their own shame as in a mantle!

³⁰With my mouth I will give great thanks to the Lord;
  I will praise him in the midst of the throng.
³¹For he stands at the right hand of the needy,
  to save him from those who condemn him to death.

From very early on in Israel's history people used imprecatory psalms (copying their pagan neighbours in doing so), for by means of these they hoped God would take vengeance upon their enemies on their behalf. Such psalms used ancient stereotyped formulas. They represented a deeply felt desire for God to "put things right"; they asked God especially for retribution against gratuitous malice. See Lev. 24:19 for an instance to be found in "the Law", Jer. 11:20 for one in "the Prophets", and Prov. 17:13 as a case in "the Wisdom schools". "I am innocent," says the complainant. "He is guilty. So what he wants done to me, let it be done to him."

But there is more to it than mere malevolence. The psalmist is the Lord's *servant* (verse 28). Consequently he is jealous for God and for God's cause, the cause of righteousness and justice. He knows that God is love. He wants to be loving too, even as God is loving. But which is it to be—love or justice?

We react strongly against the indignation and vindictiveness displayed in this psalm, more strongly still when we recall that to the ancients cursing was not a mere matter of words, it was an action, and this action was potent, powerful, effective. We have to remember, however, that this psalm was written by a sinner like ourselves, yet one who desperately wanted to be loyal to God. Yet the Bible is about God, and not about man's thoughts of God. Therefore this psalm is ultimately a revelation of God's love triumphant. In Numbers chs. 22–24 we find a good instance of the ancient, ritualized, formularized cursing of one's enemies; but we read on to discover how God turned this very human desire to hurt one's enemies into a blessing. But then, of course, a blessing is also much more than words. It is an action that, like a curse, is potent, powerful, effective. It is an instance of active, creative love. (See the Commentary to Lev. 19:17–18 in this series.) We would do well to see this psalm in the light of that fascinating story in Numbers.

Verses 1–15. As we have said, the writer is not a bad man. He begins: "O God who helps me to praise", as line 1 means. Then straight away at verse 4 he tells God that he has even been praying for his enemies, and so it means that God has in fact been helping him to pray aright. It is a pity that after that he began to lose his temper.

Yet who were these enemies of his? Were they real persons, or were they evil ideas springing up out of his own heart? Some prefer the latter interpretation, some the former. *Let an accuser,* a *satan* (the Hebrew word) *bring him to trial* (verse 6). This, by the way, was the task of "the Satan" in all references to him elsewhere in the OT. *Let his prayer be counted as sin!* (verse 7). What a vindictive thing to say—to the God of love; and then to include his enemy's children in his curse, to the extent of calling upon God to render his line extinct! Sir George Adam Smith a century ago said of this passage: "This is the delirium of the conscience produced by a famine of justice." We can understand, but we dare not approve.

Verses 16–19. Yet we notice that the basis of this enemy's wickedness is to forget that God is love. In fact he tried to reverse the ways of God. God blesses, he prefers cursing. *He clothed himself with cursing as his coat.* This picture is taken from the commonly used description of the glory of God, where he wears "glory" like an outer garment, one that is visible to human eyes—but the sinner is turning it upside down. He is in effect turning total good into total evil. Vindictive he may be, but the psalmist is here pointing to a terrible truth of the gospel. Deut. 27:14–26 gives us a list of curses, a ritual of very old laws, uttered upon those who reverse the revealed Word, or *Torah,* of God, that is to say, who turn creative love into destructive evil. Nor did Jesus mince his words about what would happen to such people; see Matt. 18:6.

Verses 20–31. Verse 20 completes the curse by saying, "This is its effect on me". Yet verses 21–22 continue by saying, "But God is not like that". God will not necessarily act in the way you want him to, just because, as you say, "*I am poor and needy*". It is as if the psalmist is confessing: "I have got myself into a hopeless mess in my thinking." *O Lord my God, save me by thy steadfast love*, not by letting me curse my enemies. *Let them do the cursing*, but—*do thou bless! My assailants* must, naturally, be punished, and *be clothed with dishonour. Then I will give great thanks to the Lord.* For God will (a) have acted justly, (b) have rejected all vindictiveness, (c) have let people see me being vindicated, (d) and as in the days of Balaam, have turned a curse into a blessing. Is the psalmist beginning to understand that the God who says "Vengeance is mine, I will repay" is he who repays vindictiveness by love? We would like to think so.

There are those today who declare that they "don't believe in sin". We should note that in this psalm sin is *he did not remember to show kindness* (verse 16). All the evil actions of this "enemy" spring from just "not remembering". The nature of God, however, is the reverse of this. God is always mindful of his *faithfulness* (Ps. 108:4) and always acts in accordance with his *steadfast love*.

From Zech. 3:1 we learn that the *accuser,* the *satan,* stood at the right hand of the accused in court. That is what the Hebrew literally says at verse 6 (see RSV *ftn*). But at verse 31 we find that it is God who is there, *standing at the right hand of the needy!* Evidently God's task is very different from that of the *satan.* His task is to *save,* not to *condemn.*

In this psalm the evil man is quite unaware that life is an onward progression. He grabs what he can of money, possessions, fame, glory, saying, "I'll hold on to these till I die". But things may well turn out otherwise than what he expected. As Paul put it in 1 Cor. 7:31: "The fashion of this world passes away". Things change. You cannot step into the same river twice, a phrase attributed to Heraclitus the Greek philosopher. These "things" we hold on to can perish in earthquake, tornado, fire or war; but if they do, then the justice of God is revealed. And that justice turns out to be love! The psalmist, one feels, sees this, though unfortunately, being human, he cannot himself match that love.

SIT AT MY RIGHT HAND

Psalm 110:1–3

A Psalm of David.

¹The Lord says to my lord:
  "Sit at my right hand,
till I make your enemies your footstool."

²The Lord sends forth from Zion
  your mighty sceptre.
  Rule in the midst of your foes!
³Your people will offer themselves freely
  on the day you lead your host
  upon the holy mountains.
From the womb of the morning
  like dew your youth will come to you.

This psalm is very different in nature from most we have looked at. We have seen psalms that brought the past up to date at the time of writing. This psalm takes the distant time of David and makes it speak for a future yet to come. In a word, Ps. 110 is "Messianic" in its whole emphasis. Let us note these points about it:

(1) The Hebrew of it is unusually difficult. So it is wrong to be completely dogmatic about what it is saying. (2) On the other hand, verses 1 and 4 particularly were dogmatically used by the early Christian Church. (3) The verb in the phrase *The Lord says* occurs in only one other place in the psalms, at Ps. 36:1. It is a strange word, used much by the great prophets in the familiar phrase in English: "Thus saith the Lord". But modern translations seek to show the strange quality of the word by rendering it as "Oracle of the Lord". The word is found at Gen. 22:16 where the solemnity of God's oath is emphasized. Evidently the author of the psalm believed he had been given a revelation from God; consequently he speaks as if he were a prophet himself, like Amos.

The psalm is in three sections.

Verses 1–3, *Oracle I.* God addresses the king through the mouth of a cultic prophet at the great enthronement festival. He says: "Yahweh reveals his Word to my master", meaning the king. The phrase *Sit at my right hand* goes right back in time to ancient Egyptian usage where the reigning Pharaoh honours his own son with these very words. The son is placed where he can be the Pharaoh's right arm, that is, where he can be his father's executive. So here God calls David (1) to the place of honour, and (2) to be his viceroy on earth. (See 1 Chron. 29:23; at 1 Kings 2:19 King Solomon interestingly places his mother in this position of honour.)

Then God adds: *till I* "annihilate all evil", the meaning of *till I make your enemies your footstool.* But how is this to take place? *The Lord* (Yahweh) will *send forth*, or "stretch out", *from Zion* (which God has already made into his own footstool—Ps. 99:5) *your mighty sceptre.* David then raises his sceptre, his symbol of office, in his right hand, though of course it is God who empowers his arm to move (1 Sam. 2:10). Thus it is God who gives the command: *Rule in the midst of your foes*, not "over" them, let us note, but despite the fact that your foes are all around you. Rule in confidence, for I am the strength of your arm.

The Hebrew of verse 3 is almost impossible. But following upon the command of verse 2 it seems to mean: "Go forth to battle; your people will volunteer freely under your leadership *in holy array*" (RSV *ftn*). This is to be a Messianic war against the powers of evil. The "holy array" is David's army of ordinary folk, but now seen in the light of God's transcendent purpose for them, and doing God's holy will. (If the reading is *upon the holy mountains*, with RSV, then the reference is to the hills around the Holy City where the army will assemble.) So we have a beautiful poetic picture of the young men of Judah leaving their homes, with the *dew* of the dawn upon their brows, all flocking to follow their king. We are reminded of the Children's Crusade in Europe in the 13th century, for it too was composed of idealistic young folk. Clearly this psalm was not written for a David who was weak-kneed. It was written for strong young men who were to follow their strong young leader into action in his great divine crusade.

The quotation of the first verse of this psalm in Mark 12:36 shows that is was understood by Jesus as describing his own life and mission. We should not take too seriously the typically "rabbinic" way in which Jesus argues that since David is the author, someone other than David (himself of course!) must be meant by "my lord". The people listening would as good Jews get his point right away, which is that he, Jesus, was the new Messianic "king" of Israel. And if they knew the psalm well, they would realize that they were meant to respond to Jesus' invitation to them to "offer themselves freely" as soldiers in his army.

A PRIEST FOR EVER

Psalm 110:4–7

⁴The Lord has sworn
  and will not change his mind,
"You are a priest for ever
  after the order of Melchizedek."

⁵The Lord is at your right hand;
  he will shatter kings on the day of his wrath.
⁶He will execute judgment among the nations,
  filling them with corpses;
 he will shatter chiefs
  over the wide earth.
⁷He will drink from the brook by the way;
  therefore he will lift up his head.

Verse 4, *Oracle II*. Before the Exile the king sometimes acted as "chief priest". This psalm, then, is historically accurate in giving the title of *priest* to the reigning monarch (see also 2 Sam. 6:14). But God hails him as *priest for ever*. To understand this title we must go back to the giving of the Covenant as it is described in Exod. 19:6, when God's people as a whole were called by God to be a kingdom of priests. We can therefore now put the two oracles together, and find that the king, *with* his host of warriors, is to be God's intermediary to the nations of the earth. We recall the words of Dan. 7:27: "The kingdom (of priests)... shall be given to the people of the saints of the Most High; their kingdom shall be an everlasting kingdom." So we note next that Oracle II is just as absolute a divine oracle as is Oracle I. *The Lord has sworn and will not change his mind, "You are a priest for ever".* It would be foolish to think of the one addressed going on and on being a priest. Rather the meaning is that, since God himself is for ever, then this king-priest and his successors will be priest to the eternal God, uniquely, mediating God's eternal plan.

After the order of Melchizedek, or rather, "as we see in the case of Melchizedek". This strange man appears only in Gen. 14:17–20. There we read that (a) he was *priest of the Most High God*, a title later given to Israel's God (e.g. Ps. 46:4). (b) He was *king of Salem*, the name then given to Jerusalem. (c) Although not a member of the people of God himself, this unique priest-king blessed the "father" of that people, viz. Abraham, and so acted as an intermediary between God and all Israel who were descended from Abraham. (d) His name Melchizedek, meaning literally "The righteous One is my king", was later understood to mean "King of righteousness".

It is not surprising that a man with such titles was linked, as in this psalm, with the Davidic king ruling from Jerusalem, or that later on he was seen by the early Christians as a "type" or prefiguration of Jesus Christ. See Hebrews ch. 7 where he is also called "King of peace" (for *salem/shalom*). In that chapter it is emphasized that he preceded the Levitical priesthood of the OT, and that even Abraham, the first of the chosen people, bowed down before him and paid tithes to him and received his blessing. The chapter then goes on to picture Jesus as the only ideal and eternal High Priest, offering the perfect sacrifice for all mankind.

Verses 5–7, *The Holy War.* The Day of the Lord was a commonly held idea in OT times. "Day", we recall, signified God's special "moment" when he would act—to save, as the ordinary man supposed; and so it was something like the D-Day to which the Allies looked forward during World War II. "No," declared Amos, however. *The Day of the Lord is darkness and not light* (Amos 5:18). In fact it is to be a Day of Judgment. Salvation can come to this world only through judgment, which we can think of in terms of darkness. This way of thinking carried right on into the NT. For example, when God pronounced judgment on the world before its salvation, and so before the Resurrection, the by-standers at the Cross discovered they were overcome by a mysterious darkness (Mark 15:33). In Amos again, note how the "resurrection" of the booth of David also takes place only following the coming judgment (Amos 9:11). Then again, the "resurrection" of Israel from Babylon's "grave" (Ezek. 37:1–14) could take place only after the judgment had fallen upon God's people when Nebuchadnezzar destroyed both the city and the people.

The Day of Judgment in this psalm is a Day of Battle, the day when God the Warrior, the Lord of hosts will overwhelm the powers of evil and only then bring forth from the debacle a whole newness of life and of universal salvation. At Acts 4:24–28 both Peter and John announce the meaning of God's act of judgment in the Cross to the Jewish authorities, and they use words from a similar "royal psalm" (Ps. 2). John the Baptist, however, because he flourished before the crucifixion took place, had to recognize that all this was yet to happen in the person of Jesus if the OT was in any way to be fulfilled (Matt. 3:10).

The Lord is at your right hand. There is a nice contrast with verse 1, where it was the priest-king who was to be seated at the Lord's right hand. Clearly we are meant to see that any action of the Messianic king is an action of God. This action is to meet the opposing powers of evil head on, and to make them serve his plan. In Rev. 6 power *was given* (that is, by God) to the enemy. Nowhere in either the OT or the NT is the initiative in the war ever taken away from God (and the Lamb); so that in the Book of Revelation even chaos can be understood to be the result of the wrath of the Lamb. No wonder these events that our psalm deals with, and which are shown forth in similar "picture theology" in the Book of Revelation, should be accompanied by songs of praise in heaven. That is why Ps. 110 is part of the songs of praise of the Second Temple.

The reference in verse 7 may be to Gideon's supreme confidence that it was God who would win the battle he had to face, not his puny little army of three hundred men (Judg. 7:19–22). For it happened that because of his complete trust, not in himself but in God, God *lifted up his head*. The suppliant in those days was expected to lie on his face before an eastern monarch, in fear and trembling. But if the monarch saw fit to accept the suppliant's plea, he bent down, placed his hand under the poor man's chin, and lifted up his head. So too will God, says this psalm, completely justify the faith of his priestly king (see for its ultimate meaning 1 Cor. 15:25–27).

HALLELUJAH!

Psalm 111:1–10

¹Praise the Lord.
  I will give thanks to the Lord with all my heart,
    in the company of the upright, in the congregation.
²Great are the works of the Lord,
    studied by all who have pleasure in them.
³Full of honour and majesty is his work,
    and his righteousness endures for ever.
⁴He has caused his wonderful works to be remembered;
    the Lord is gracious and merciful.
⁵He provides food for those who fear him;
    he is ever mindful of his covenant.
⁶He has shown his people the power of his works,
    in giving them the heritage of the nations.
⁷The works of his hands are faithful and just;
    all his precepts are trustworthy,
⁸they are established for ever and ever,
    to be performed with faithfulness and uprightness.
⁹He sent redemption to his people;
    he has commanded his covenant for ever.
  Holy and terrible is his name!
¹⁰The fear of the Lord is the beginning of wisdom;
    a good understanding have all those who practise it.
  His praise endures for ever!

This is an acrostic psalm. There are twenty-two letters in the Hebrew alphabet. Each line of the twenty-two verses begins with its appropriate letter, line one beginning with *aleph* (or A to us), line two with *beth* (our B) and so on. Therefore the poem has been carefully created for use in public worship.

One can praise God in solitude. But can one do so with *a whole heart*? It is far better to praise him *in the congregation, in the company of the upright*. Moreover, it is only when we *study* God's great works (note the title of this series of commentaries!) that we are most moved to praise. J. B. Priestley, the author, once gazed at the Grand Canyon. Then he wrote: "I felt God had set it there as a sign. I felt wonder and awe, but at the heart of them a deep rich happiness. I had seen his handiwork and rejoiced." We praise God, moreover, because *his righteousness endures for ever*. Righteousness here in its feminine form means the power to love and recreate the lives of other people which God gives to those whom he has redeemed.

His wonderful works (verse 4) are therefore not only marvels like the Grand Canyon, they are the working out in the lives of his Covenant people of the effects of his grace and compassion. God has given *his people* proof of *the power of his works*—in fact, there it is! There is the Holy Land! There it sits on its hills, the land that formerly had been *the heritage of the nations* (the Canaanites). The fact of the Land is thus a proof that the works of God are *faithful*, that is, that God keeps his promises; and that these promises are *just* (*mishpat*), that is to say, they indubitably reveal God's plan for a whole new way of life for his people. We ought then to stop, and to realize what a marvel it is to see lives changed from self-centredness that is both mean and ugly to lives of self-emptying love and compassion for others.

A passage like this, then, shows us that the Bible is not primarily dealing with religion, or with what we think of as religion. It is concerned with revelation, yet revelation that makes sense only within the fellowship of God's Covenant people, or, as we would say today, within the community of God's baptized people. Outsiders can read this psalm, for example, and find nothing in it. "Faith," said Goethe the philosopher, "is not the beginning, but the end of all knowledge"—the knowledge of himself that God grants us through *his covenant* (verse 9).

Redemption (verse 9) is better translated as "ransom", as in the words of the favourite hymn, "Ransomed, healed, restored, forgiven, Who like me his praise should sing?". Note, moreover, that God *sent* this redemption, the verb used in the NT of God's action in Christ. Yet, even in this very verse, we are reminded of the theme of Ps. 110: *Holy and terrible is his name.* God's act in ransoming us comes about through the terrible judgment that his Messianic king must execute (Ps. 110:6). For a ransom has of course to be paid for. So God's greatest "work" is the forgiveness and the renewal of his people which he has "worked" at great cost to himself!

The last verse occurs also in the Wisdom books, for example at Job 28:28 and Prov. 1:7; 9:10. *Fear* means reverence and awe. *Wisdom* means to accept the guidance given us by the all-wise God with grace and gratitude—and then not to talk about it, but to *practise* it! Biblical wisdom is a practical thing. It means understanding how to live, that is, finding out what God's *mishpat* or "justice" means (see above) and putting it into practice. It means making this world here and now the real world in which God's love and compassion are at work. It means, in brief, learning how to be an artisan of life by the gift of God's Holy Spirit (compare Exod. 35:30–31).

ENJOYING GOD'S COMMANDMENTS

Psalm 112:1–10

[1]Praise the Lord.
  Blessed is the man who fears the Lord,
  who greatly delights in his commandments!
[2]His descendants will be mighty in the land;
  the generation of the upright will be blessed.
[3]Wealth and riches are in his house;
  and his righteousness endures for ever.
[4]Light rises in the darkness for the upright;

the Lord is gracious, merciful, and righteous.
⁵It is well with the man who deals generously and lends,
who conducts his affairs with justice.
⁶For the righteous will never be moved;
he will be remembered for ever.
⁷He is not afraid of evil tidings;
his heart is firm, trusting in the Lord.
⁸His heart is steady, he will not be afraid,
until he sees his desire on his adversaries.
⁹He has distributed freely, he has given to the poor;
his righteousness endures for ever;
his horn is exalted in honour.
¹⁰The wicked man sees it and is angry;
he gnashes his teeth and melts away;
the desire of the wicked man comes to naught.

This is another acrostic psalm, similar to Ps. 111, also written in twenty-two lines of verse. It might be a good idea for us in reading it to ask ourselves how much we would like to modify or add to this psalm in the light of Christ and the NT. The fact that we feel the need to do so shows that it was written for men and women who were still "on the way", so to speak, just as many of us are, despite the coming of Christ, for many of us too have not yet arrived.

Blessed is the man who fears the Lord, who greatly delights in his commandments. Yes, but what do these two lines mean for those who are still "on the way"? Does this blessedness mean to "feel oneself enjoying one's salvation Sunday by Sunday", as some people suppose to be the "goal" of the way? Or does it mean putting God's gift of *tsedaqah*, "righteousness" (Ps 111:3), into practice? The Greek word for "fear", *phobia*, is found in over seventy-five compound words in English. Most of these terms have been coined by psychologists and moral philosophers to cover the many aspects of modern man's basic fear of life. The fact is that fear is the great threat to mental health today. "Our children are living in a folklore of bombs," as one child educator has put it. Does fearing the Lord mean something like one of those phobias? Is it in fact that fear of hell-fire that was often instilled into children in earlier centuries?

Hebrew verse very often employs two lines in parallel, the one line to some degree either interpreting or else adding to the thought in the other line. So here, if this man *delighted in his commandments*, then his *fear of the Lord* must have been a glad awareness of the awe-ful mystery of God's holy love.

Unfortunately our poet is somewhat selfish in his rejoicing. He uses in verse 3 the word *tsedaqah* which Psalm 111 had also mentioned in verse 3. He knows that the urge to love his neighbour is a gift of God from on high, because God has first loved him, but he has a bit of "the lady bountiful" in him in his approach to the poor around him. He is an example of what has (very wrongly) been called "the Protestant ethic". This is, to many people, the command: "Be good, and you will prosper in your business." So he believes that *the light that rises in the darkness for the upright* will shine on him. He knows that he is to pass it on to others, but for him it is only by means of writing handsome cheques for good causes. By doing so, he will ensure that *it is well with the man who deals generously* (verse 5).

Yet the Hebrew of that phrase can mean something quite different. It can mean: "A man is good for, is meant to, lend graciously", even as God himself is *gracious, merciful and righteous* (verse 4). Surely this is a new kind of alms-giving, one that comes straight from the heart of God himself. Before *God's commandments* (verse 1) were given to Moses, who on earth had ever, out of all the world's cultures and civilizations, thought of such a thing? "Alms-giving" is still today in the Muslim faith the meaning of the Arabic equivalent of this very word *tsedaqah*.

But the psalmist has learned something from the thoughts he has expressed up to this point. At verse 9 he says: *He has distributed freely*, not merely given alms to the poor. The word is really "scattered", like the act of throwing coins in amongst a crowd of children, without looking to see who benefits from picking them up. This is something the *wicked see* happening, and which makes them incensed. But God honours the act of the righteous man. God has *exalted his horn in honour*. We wonder if the poet has learned why God has done this to such a man. For he had newly said (verse 8) that *his heart was steady, until he sees his desire on his adversaries*. These presumably are "the wicked". God has done it because God is (and we go back to verse 4) *gracious, merciful, and righteous*, even when such a man as our poet does not grasp what this means. The result is, as the poem ends by saying, *the desire of the wicked man comes to naught*. What happens to him is that he just melts away. He does so because he has lost face before such marvellous grace. So, then, the poem concludes, do not waste your pity on evil, for evil in the end is actually impotent.

WHO IS LIKE THE LORD?

Psalm 113:1–9

> [1]Praise the Lord!
>> Praise, O servants of the Lord,
>> praise the name of the Lord!
>
> [2]Blessed be the name of the Lord
>> from this time forth and for evermore!
> [3]From the rising of the sun to its setting
>> the name of the Lord is to be praised!
> [4]The Lord is high above all nations,
>> and his glory above the heavens!
>
> [5]Who is like the Lord our God,
>> who is seated on high,
> [6]who looks far down
>> upon the heavens and the earth?
> [7]He raises the poor from the dust,
>> and lifts the needy from the ash heap,
> [8]to make them sit with princes,
>> with the princes of his people.
> [9]He gives the barren woman a home,
>> making her the joyous mother of children.
>> Praise the Lord!

Pss. 113–118 form a section of Book V known in Jewish tradition as the *Hallel*. This is because most of them contain the word

Hallelujah. Hallel means "to praise". In NT times and right up to today the Synagogue has sung these psalms at the great festivals. Passover is of course one of these. Thus when Jesus led his disciples out of the Upper Room and down the hill to the Garden of Gethsemane after the Last Supper, he said to them: "Let us sing a hymn" (Mark 14:26). It could well have been the present psalm which they sang. Note that it is one with a universal vision.

Verses 1–4, *O servants of the Lord.* A servant obeys his master. To sing God's praise is thus our duty as his subjects. (See Luke 2:29 for the Greek translation of this word, and Luke 1:48 for its feminine equivalent). God's *name* is what tells us what God is like as he reveals himself by doing his mighty acts of love. *Praise* is to be made to him, then, always and everywhere.

Verses 5–8, *God is transcendent.* In the pictorial way of expressing truths that the OT uses (where we would use an abstract term) God is *seated on high* above all Creation, so that he has even to *look far down upon the heavens*! But that reality does not make him remote. We think of these words as describing space. But that idea is not Biblical. When Jesus "looked" at blind Bartimaeus, he looked far down from the heights of his oneness with the Father into the depths of a lost soul. "Looking" is the first step towards doing something about it. Unfortunately too many of us look at other people without either seeing them or their need. Israel is always astonished that God not only looks right down into human suffering, but even "comes down" into people's stricken lives. The psalmist thus reveals to us the true meaning of the word "exalted" when used of God. When man is exalted he is too proud to step down. But God "looks into the depths" below the surface of our minds. Then he empties himself of the *glory* he has *above the heavens,* and becomes the Brother of *the poor and needy,* and the Doctor of *the barren woman,* with the result that she becomes the *joyous mother* of a baby boy and girl. Just because he is "exalted", we learn, he is able to "bridge the gap" from the highest to the lowest.

How often, by the way, do the psalms "exalt" the family, because of God's paradoxical exaltation. Hannah sings a psalm

(1 Sam. 2:1): *My heart exults in the Lord, my strength is exalted in the Lord*—because God has just given her a baby.

What does God do all this for? For his own self-glorification? No, only because he loves us. God saves us by choosing to identify himself with us, by becoming one with us, by learning to "speak our language". To do so God does worldly things, not religious things. If we in our turn talk about God in religious language we are thereby making false statements about him. For God is here *with* us, on this side of eternity, in space and time (compare Exod. 3:12; and the meaning of the word *Immanuel*—Isa. 7:14; 8:8). We note too how we are to understand the Magnificat in the NT from this psalm which it quotes. Consequently we should never speak about God either in merely philosophical, or on the other hand in pietistic language, but always in human and responsible terms.

Sir Thomas Browne wrote: " 'Charity begins at home' is the voice of the world, not of the Bible." How many writers of letters to the newspapers quote the first four words only of his statement, and suppose that thereby they have said the last word about the meaning of love. But here we see how God does not "stay at home", but "comes down from heaven, and *lifts the needy from the ash heap*".

We are to praise the *name of the Lord* (verse 2), that is, his revealed nature. *Who is like the Lord,* indeed? Surely, then, we are not to praise him with our lips only, but with our lives, by doing to our brother in love what the God of love has done to us.

THE WORLD TAKEN BY SURPRISE

Psalm 114:1–8

¹When Israel went forth from Egypt,
  the house of Jacob from a people of strange language,
²Judah became his sanctuary,
  Israel his dominion.

³The sea looked and fled,
  Jordan turned back.

⁴The mountains skipped like rams,
   the hills like lambs.

⁵What ails you, O sea, that you flee?
   O Jordan, that you turn back?
⁶O mountains, that you skip like rams?
   O hills, like lambs?

⁷Tremble, O earth, at the presence of the Lord,
   at the presence of the God of Jacob,
⁸who turns the rock into a pool of water,
   the flint into a spring of water.

We can divide this psalm into four cantos.

I. Verses 1–2. The birth of Israel saw the beginning of the history of God on earth. For, at the Exodus from Egypt, God "came down" (Exod. 3:8; compare Ps. 113:6) and made *Judah his sanctuary and Israel his dominion,* by which is meant that place where he rules the affairs of men.

II. Verses 3–4. The whole forty years of the Wilderness wanderings are alluded to in this marvellous little canto. What it is saying is that God's action was much more than the mere history of Israel; it was in fact a miracle, for it was the history of God, who had chosen to dwell within Israel! So we read: (a) *The* (Reed) *Sea looked and fled.* At Ps. 78:13 we noticed how the crossing of the Red (or Reed, as the Hebrew has it) Sea, being a divine activity, cannot be described in scientific terms (see the Commentary). (b) *The Jordan turned back* when Joshua led his people into the Promised Land. That was a lyrical moment in their experience, so it could be referred to only in lyrical language. (c) According to mere man's historical memory, Mount Sinai was shaken by a volcanic eruption and an earthquake (Exod. 19:18). But in God's history of it *the mountains skipped like rams.*

III. Verses 5–6. In the same fascinating poetic language the psalmist then asks the Reed Sea, the Jordan River, and Mount Sinai, why they did all this.

IV. Verses 7–8. They do not answer, nor do they need to answer. Rather, the psalmist himself in imagination leaps out of the distant past into his own day. *Tremble, O earth,* he says, not just

Jordan and Sinai, but now the whole of this natural world. The word, indeed, is stronger than *tremble*. It is really "twist", "squirm", as if nature must needs wriggle away backwards from *the presence of the Lord* in awe and wonder, from *the God* who has covenated together with his people, *Jacob*.

The point the poet is making is this—all these events are moments in the history of God, and not just in the history of Israel. This is because God is *present* in all that happens! He was present in all that happened to Israel in the days of the Exodus; he is present to us now in all the events that we have to live through. We know that the poet means this, because in these verses he uses the present tense in all his verbs. And the corollary is—what happens to us happens to God!

God is the one who *turns the rock into the pool of water* (Exod. 17:6; Num. 20:11), *the flint into a spring of water*—both then and now. That is to say, he is the God who brings a pool of water out of dead rock, and gives his people the water of life to drink.

The world has indeed been taken by surprise by this psalm. "If I had only known that God is like that!" we say. Yes, replies the poet, we all feel that way, the whole earth does. Therefore all we can do is just adore *at the presence of the Lord* in our here and now. Jesus interpreted our psalm in this way, and Jesus was certainly present with us in the here and now: "The water that I shall give him will become in him *a spring of water* welling up to eternal life", that is, from now into eternity (John 4:14). And Paul was able, because of it and others like it (c.g. Ps. 113), to stress the reality that the utterly transcendent God, who has to look far down even to see the heavens beneath him, was "in Christ".

Traditionally the Synagogue has read this psalm at the Passover; traditionally the Church has read it at Easter. We can well understand why.

TRUST IN GOD

Psalm 115:1–11

> ¹Not to us, O Lord, not to us,
>   but to thy name give glory,

for the sake of thy steadfast love
and thy faithfulness!
²Why should the nations say,
"Where is their God?"

³Our God is in the heavens;
he does whatever he pleases.
⁴Their idols are silver and gold,
the work of men's hands.
⁵They have mouths, but do not speak;
eyes, but do not see.
⁶They have ears, but they do not hear;
noses, but do not smell.
⁷They have hands, but do not feel;
feet, but do not walk;
and they do not make a sound in their throat.
⁸Those who make them are like them;
so are all who trust in them.

⁹O Israel, trust in the Lord!
He is their help and their shield.
¹⁰O house of Aaron, put your trust in the Lord!
He is their help and their shield.
¹¹You who fear the Lord, trust in the Lord!
He is their help and their shield.

It has long been supposed that verses 1–11 of this psalm were sung in the rebuilt Second Temple while a sacrifice was actually being performed. For at verse 12 the priest virtually says: "The Lord has accepted it." Thereupon the remainder of the psalm becomes a blessing to follow after the sacrifice.

Verses 1–11. A priest speaks first: *Non nobis, Domine.* How often have these Latin words from the first line of this psalm been uttered down the centuries on occasions of great thanksgiving. Shakespeare makes Henry V exclaim after the battle of Agincourt, "Let there be sung 'Non nobis' and 'Te Deum'." How could the glory be to us?, declares the psalmist. *Thy steadfast love and thy faithfulness* turned our hearts to you before we could think of making any response. Consequently we must *give the glory* to God's *name* only, that is to the revelation of his love given us in the form of the steadfast love he has showered upon us within the bonds of his Covenant. So we do not need to pay any attention to *the nations* when they *say*: "Where is their God?" Their gods you can see; they are made of *silver and gold*. They are *the work of man's hands*, or, as we could add today, the produce of men's minds, ideologies, speculative philosophies, religious ideas, and the rest. The terrible thing, however, is that, once made, man cannot control his handiwork or his ideologies, simply because he cannot control himself. The dead image he thought he had made turns out to be a Frankenstein monster. For example, man makes a war, but it is soon out of control, and escalates beyond the intentions of either side in the quarrel. The result is that we fear (a word we should use of God alone) the creations of our own hands and brains (compare Rom. 1:25) and become their slaves.

But our God is not like that. He can do exactly what he plans to do. Men may become like their idols. They can become greedy if their idol is labelled "success"; they can become lascivious if their idol is labelled "sex". That is, *so are all who trust in them*—like god, like worshipper.

Our God, on the other hand, is *in the heavens*. That is, he is transcendent over all the powers of evil, and has not been made by the thoughts of humanity. Our God is therefore free.

(1) He is beyond Fate. Fate rules the plans even of Zeus, the king of all the ancient gods of Greece.

(2) He is beyond Karma, "fate", a similar idea known to the Buddhist religion.

(3) He is not as Allah, as God is known in Islam, for Allah is virtually Fate himself.

The great prophet of the Exile had said all this kind of thing at Isa. 44:9–20. Now, says the poet, we can see that he was right, and we who have come back home from Exile, we know it to be so!

The moral is, of course: *O Israel, trust in the Lord*, and you will become like him, a trustworthy person! Who then are summoned to find him to be *their help and their shield*? (1) The whole people of God, that is, all *Israel*; (2) *The house of Aaron*, that is, all the priests who function at public worship. It is always a tragedy when a priest or minister does not show the way to his congregation by himself *trusting* in God. (3) The *God-fearers*, proselytes, enquirers, non-Israelites who are learning to say, with Israel herself as in Ps. 118:2–4, "We have found that his steadfast love endures for ever". In this way, then, the Church must always hold out the answer to those who come knocking at its door.

THE BLESSING THAT FOLLOWS

Psalm 115:12–18

¹²The Lord has been mindful of us; he will bless us;
he will bless the house of Israel;
he will bless the house of Aaron;
¹³he will bless those who fear the Lord,
both small and great.

¹⁴May the Lord give you increase,
you and your children!
¹⁵May you be blessed by the Lord,
who made heaven and earth!

¹⁶The heavens are the Lord's heavens,
but the earth he has given to the sons of men.
¹⁷The dead do not praise the Lord,
nor do any that go down into silence.
¹⁸But we will bless the Lord
from this time forth and for evermore.
Praise the Lord!

The priest has performed the sacrifice. He then turns and blesses the people. It would seem therefore that God has accepted the sacrifice. We are to remember that in connection with the sacrifices, when the father of the family laid his hand on the head of the sacrificial beast, he did so representing not only himself, but also his wife and children. Thus, since the whole family belongs in God's Covenant of grace, the blessing of God is received by the whole family.

This is a case of the opposite of the Greek way of thinking that Paul had to contend with in Corinth, a way that had been learned from the East with its individualistic religions. We note how a "holy man" in India today will leave his family to fend for themselves and go and search for salvation up in the hills. The Greeks believed that (1) the deity, whoever he was, dealt only with intellectuals amongst humanity, only with adults capable of responding to the claim of the divine. They would have been amazed at the Christian's awareness of God's love for babies and for the intellectually handicapped. (2) Because to them this world here and now is not the real one, it meant that the real world was to be awaited beyond death.

These ideas were spreading throughout Palestine by the period of this psalm. So there were people whom the psalmist would know who declared that (a) whatever deities there were were certainly not present here with people on *the earth*, and that (b) it was only once they were beyond death that people would really encounter God. Here however, in the psalm's final little sermon of only two verses (16–17), we are told that *the earth he has given to the sons of men.* This meant of course that God must be here on this earth too, so that he is present with and cares for the children of men. In the year 1807 William Wilberforce carried his bill for the abolition of the Slave Trade; he was moved to do so from reading the psalms with an open and thoughtful mind. It was Jews and Christians who abolished the slave trade, not Hindus, or Buddhists, or Muslims. And it is Jews and Christians (to whose Scriptures the Marxists turned) who have sought to bring in a degree of social justice throughout the world.

May you be blessed by the Lord, adds the priest. The verb "to bless" demanded that the one blessed be present beside you; this is because, when you uttered the words, you laid your hands upon his head. And we are called upon to do this to others, what God does to us! And we are even to bless God! And we are able to do so just because he is close beside us here and is with us in all our daily life. *The dead do not praise the Lord*, he continues, for we know well that in the moment of blessing God we are not down in Sheol, in some hell of our own creation. God is here, and he is here with us *for evermore*. And of course, because he is *here* with us for *evermore*, we shall be *there* with him also *for evermore*. For "here" and "there" are all one in the Lord. So now the congregation responds at verse 18: "We give back to the Lord the blessing he has laid on our heads. We shall do so *from this time forth and* 'into all eternity'." It would be very instructive for us to read now, in the light of the above, what Paul was up against as he preached to the Greeks in the city of Corinth, as we find what he says in 1 Cor. 1.

This psalm, then, puts in very condensed form some great truths about God. (1) God is all in all. (2) God rules all, so his rule must include the Cross that Jesus faced that night when "they sang a hymn", as well as his death that followed. (3) Human beings cannot produce ideologies worth examination. (4) The sacrifice made here God graciously accepts (verse 12). St. Paul declares that God similarly accepts the sacrifice of Christ (see the Commentary on *Leviticus* in this series, pp. 93–96). (5) God permits us poor creatures, by grace alone, to bless him, the eternal God, even while we live here and now in this fallen world. (6) There is a resurrection hope expressed because of the power of God's blessing, a power that cannot be limited to the length of human life on earth.

THANK YOU, GOD

Psalm 116:1–11

[1]I love the Lord, because he has heard
my voice and my supplications.
[2]Because he inclined his ear to me,
therefore I will call on him as long as I live.
[3]The snares of death encompassed me;
the pangs of Sheol laid hold on me;
I suffered distress and anguish.
[4]Then I called on the name of the Lord:
"O Lord, I beseech thee, save my life!"

[5]Gracious is the Lord, and righteous;

our God is merciful.
⁶The Lord preserves the simple;
  when I was brought low, he saved me.
⁷Return, O my soul, to your rest;
  for the Lord has dealt bountifully with you.

⁸For thou hast delivered my soul from death
  my eyes from tears,
  my feet from stumbling;
⁹I walk before the Lord
  in the land of the living.
¹⁰I kept my faith, even when I said,
  "I am greatly afflicted";
¹¹I said in my consternation,
  "Men are all a vain hope."

Someone has suggested that this psalm begins like a love letter:
"Dear God, I love you; for you . . . *inclined your ear to me*. You
did so because you *heard my voice and my supplication*." This is
not so impossible, for all that the Hebrew actually says is, "I love,
for Yahweh hears . . ."

The poem is in several strophes or paragraphs, and is carefully
constructed by someone who has been either very ill physically,
or has suffered a nervous breakdown. In either case he or she is
immensely grateful for recovery. But this psalm can be ours too,
even if we have not been ill. For we all live on "Death Row", so to
speak, we all wait for the morning of execution. We might even
focus our general and inevitable expectation of death on the fear
that somewhere is a jittery underling who at this moment is about
to press that fatal button on the nuclear monstrosity we all loathe
and dread. In a word, no matter how we expound this psalm, it
emphasizes that there is no hope in man (verse 11). Notice that
death (Sheol) is actually shown to be aggressive. It has sent out its
octopus-like tentacles, the poet implies, to pull me under. No
wonder he "found" (AV) *distress and anguish*.

Verses 1–4. It was at that point of realization, that there is no
hope for man, that *I called on the name of the Lord*, that is to say, I
invoked his real presence as I knew it through all his goodness to

me within the Covenant. My cry was: *O Lord, I beseech thee, save my life!*

Verses 5–7. Notice (a) that the psalmist did try to pray; (b) that he expected to receive an answer; (c) that he believed that God was stronger than those tentacles of Sheol that had laid hold on him; and (d) that he looked for the healing of his whole personality. The word *life* at verse 4 is only one way of translating the Hebrew *nephesh*, which was usually translated in the old AV as "soul". It means "my whole being, my body, soul, mind and spirit". Finally (e) he found that God had answered him far beyond his asking.

So he goes on: *The Lord preserves the simple. Preserves* means protects, shepherds. *The simple* includes those with a low I.Q., the intellectually handicapped, the simple-minded, the very ordinary, uneducated person. The LXX even translates the word by "babies". Jesus seems to put the two ideas together at Matt. 11:25. The psalmist therefore is declaring here a reality to which we must ever hold fast, that we are not saved by a profession of our own faith. That would be what Paul calls a "work" on our part. For example, how could an intellectually handicapped child even know what the word "saved" means? What the psalmist is telling us is that we are saved by grace alone.

With such an assurance in his heart, then, the psalmist invited his own *nephesh*, his "life", to "come home", and to *rest* in the Lord, if we might borrow words from a well-known hymn. We should note however that the word *rest* can also mean, at the same time, "homes"—in the plural! For that is the way Hebrew expresses the idea of "many rooms in my Father's house", as Jesus puts it.

Verses 8–11. *For the Lord has dealt bountifully with you*, he says to his "life", to his "self". Literally this is: "The Lord has poured out his goodness over you". Sheol, the land of death, was supposed to be down below the ground, or, as we have noted in other psalms, down in the depths of humanity's evil *sub*conscious mind. But now, I am back up on this good earth again, he declares with joy; *I walk before the Lord in the land of the living*. He is quoting Ps. 56:13, just as we might quote a favourite hymn—but he adds to the quotation a very personal line about his *tears*!

We know that Paul was impressed with the psalmist's faith to which he held even in great *affliction*, for he quotes verse 10 at 2 Cor. 4:13. He spoke according to even the tiny degree of faith that was left to him in his misery, yet the smallness of his faith did not trouble God, for, as we see, God went on to honour his cry (verse 1).

TRUST MEANS OBEDIENCE

Psalm 116: 12–19

¹²What shall I render to the Lord
for all his bounty to me?
¹³I will lift up the cup of salvation
and call on the name of the Lord,
¹⁴I will pay my vows to the Lord
in the presence of all his people.
¹⁵Precious in the sight of the Lord
is the death of his saints.
¹⁶O Lord, I am thy servant;
I am thy servant, the son of thy handmaid
Thou hast loosed my bonds.
¹⁷I will offer to thee the sacrifice of thanksgiving
and call on the name of the Lord.
¹⁸I will pay my vows to the Lord
in the presence of all his people,
¹⁹in the courts of the house of the Lord,
in your midst, O Jerusalem.
Praise the Lord!

How then can I thank *him*, not thank *men*, who are but a vain hope? At this point, in all probability, the priest would show the psalmist, who would be an ordinary father of an ordinary family, exactly how he should perform the rites that acted out the words of his mouth, so as to say "Thank you, God" (see Lev. 7:11ff; Deut. 12:17–18). Even today in our liturgies we repeat the words that follow at verses 12–14, employing them as the invitation we need before we partake of Holy Communion.

What then can I give him? *What shall I render* (lit. "give back") to God? Nothing! So the priest helps me to declare. It is not a case of giving back at all, he says. It is a case of *taking the cup of salvation.* This last word is in the plural. So it hints at "full salvation", bountiful, the cup running over, the cup which God, acting in grace before I can make a move, has now handed to me to drink. (For the origin of this action see Num. 28:7.) We remember that, at the Last Supper, Jesus too acted first. He first handed the cup to his disciples, who only then took of it. In the *Torah* drink offerings were meant to be drunk by the priest only. In this psalm, and at the Last Supper, God offers the cup of salvation to all believers.

The action here is the opposite of that found at Jer. 25:15–29. It is our custom today in our modern world to touch glasses, and then to drink to each other's health. But in that passage God told Jeremiah to make all the nations of the earth drink to their own damnation. In this psalm, however, I am to drink to my own *salvation.* So we note: (a) the rejection of God's grace means damnation; (b) acceptance of it means life and joy; but (c) for many heroes of the Faith drinking this cup has meant both of these at once, for it meant the cup of martyrdom. This psalmist sees himself as having been almost in that category (verse 15). His cry to God was thus not "one-dimensional". Rather he was able to praise God only through the tension and pain he had suffered till the moment of his cry.

I will call on the name of the Lord, he continues. I will witness to those around me that it is the Lord who saves, and that I have not saved myself. And I will do it in public, at worship, *in the presence of all his people.*

In verses 15–19 the psalmist is "thinking aloud to God". He remembers how he has been at death's door; there is even the suggestion that he has been scorned, almost martyred (verses 10–11). But he now knows that God so loved him that he would never let him go. But the phrase in verse 15 means more than this. As the Jerusalem Bible renders it, "The death of the devout costs

Yahweh dear". That is to say, the Lord feels the death of his Covenant folk. He mourns with those who mourn, because he is actually present with them through the bonds of the Covenant. And so, when they suffer, he suffers too. We can see how this old psalmist points the way to a much later phrase: "The Cross at the heart of the universe".

The next words, *O Lord*, reflect a deep, heartfelt cry. The "O" is a very strong expression in Hebrew, for it is used of a cry that only comes out of pain. O Lord, I see now that that is what being a *saint* means. (For this word *hasid* describes one who is completely loyal to the *hesed* of Yahweh.) *Ki* (I swear that) I am your loyal *servant*, even unto death, *the son of thy handmaid*, meaning, "your adopted son, brought into the Covenant fellowship not by birth, but by grace" (see Gen. 16:1–11). How deeply then the psalmist feels he must make this cry and sincerely confess his love and faith! For what else can he do, now that, out of sheer grace, God has handed him the cup of salvation that he is to drink to the dregs, so that its wine may flow through all the veins of his body, and through his mind and soul as well? And then, along with that great thought, he is to be able also to cry: *Thou hast loosed my bonds*.

We have seen that Sheol, the powers of death and hell, had grasped him, octopus-like, with its terrible tentacles that no man can loosen (verses 3, 11). But God had done just that for him. The Lord had overcome the power of both death and evil.

There is nothing left for the psalmist to do, then, but to *offer to thee the sacrifice of thanksgiving*, and to do it in public, so that what he says and does becomes a witness to the city. The word "thanksgiving" (*todah*) means two things. It means thanksgiving (a) by the spoken word, and (b) by an action. These two cannot be separated—in fact there is only one word in Hebrew to cover the two! "I will not offer unto the Lord that which costs me nothing," said David in 2 Sam. 24:24. In David's case it is an expensive burnt offering that is meant. In our case, also, we should remember that no Christian congregation celebrates Holy Communion without at some point taking up an offering for the work of God. Contributing to it, for us, is pointed to by the words: *I will "pay" my vows to the Lord.*

GOD LOVES THE HEATHEN TOO

Psalm 117:1–2

> [1]Praise the Lord, all nations!
>   Extol him, all peoples!
> [2]For great is his steadfast love toward us;
>   and the faithfulness of the Lord endures for ever.
> Praise the Lord!

This psalm forms the shortest chapter in the Bible. But it is a little gem. Did Jesus and his disciples include it in the "hymn" they sang on the way to Gethsemane (Mark 14:26)? Small as it is, it deals with the most basic issue of the Bible, for it emphasizes that God's Covenant relationship of love with us, his people, is there *in order that* the heathen might praise him.

Martin Luther, the Reformer, wrote a very long commentary upon these two verses on the grounds that they were basic to our understanding of the love of God. He maintained that it needed Paul's questions at Rom. 10:14 before we could understand that Israel herself was called into being to be God's missionary to the heathen, as we see at Isa. 49:6. Then again he maintained that, since this psalm is "at war with all religions", the Word of God must indeed be a mighty power. For the Kingdom of God is more by far than all the heathen empires of the world (*nations* in verse 1 is *goyim*, that is, heathen peoples). "As I see it," Luther declared, "the whole book of Acts was written because of this psalm."

Verse 2 should read: (I declare that, *ki*) *his steadfast love* (his *hesed*) has been effective *over us*, victoriously, superabundantly, triumphantly covering us and enveloping us. So now we live in a new kingdom, God's Kingdom of grace, that is, one intended to be shared with sinners everywhere. So we must live out our lives by sharing our *hesed*, which God has showered on us, with the heathen nations of the world. This task will never end; for God's *hesed* to us, *the faithfulness*, or trustworthiness, *of the Lord endures for ever*. So, then, let us all shout, both the heathen and

ourselves together, *Hallelujah!* The love of God is on the war-
path, and he has invited us to share it with him and to do so by
being in the thick of the battle!

THE LORD RECEIVES A HEATHEN (i)

Psalm 118:1–14

¹O give thanks to the Lord, for he is good;
  his steadfast love endures for ever!

²Let Israel say,
  "His steadfast love endures for ever."
³Let the house of Aaron say,
  "His steadfast love endures for ever."
⁴Let those who fear the Lord say,
  "His steadfast love endures for ever."

⁵Out of my distress I called on the Lord;
  the Lord answered me and set me free.
⁶With the Lord on my side I do not fear.
  What can man do to me?
⁷The Lord is on my side to help me;
  I shall look in triumph on those who hate me.
⁸It is better to take refuge in the Lord
  than to put confidence in man.
⁹It is better to take refuge in the Lord
  than to put confidence in princes.

¹⁰All nations surrounded me;
  in the name of the Lord I cut them off!
¹¹They surrounded me, surrounded me on every side;
  in the name of the Lord I cut them off!
¹²They surrounded me like bees,
  they blazed like a fire of thorns;
  in the name of the Lord I cut them off!
¹³I was pushed hard, so that I was falling,
  but the Lord helped me.

¹⁴The Lord is my strength and my song;
  he has become my salvation.

This is one of the great missionary psalms. It follows directly from the command to love the heathen made clear in Ps. 117.

It covers an act of worship in which a pagan is received into the fellowship of the people of God. He is welcomed by the priest of the day as he invites the congregation, in the words of verse 1, to say with him the great liturgical statement that we find repeated so often in the Psalms (e.g. 107, 136).

Then in verses 2–4 three groups, standing as they are outside the gates of the Temple, are bidden to repeat this basic creed: "God's unshakeable Covenant love continues into eternity." The three groups are, first, Israel, the people of God as a whole; second, the "house of Aaron", that is, the priestly caste; and third, the proselytes, the converts, who have been invited to be present at this special service. We hear much about proselytes in the NT. These were Gentiles who had been greatly attracted to the faith of the synagogue, to the *mishpat* of God revealed through Moses, God's given way of life to be lived out in fellowship and in love for one's neighbour. This kind of life was so different from the welter of religions around the many heathen gods of the time, and the immoralities rampant in the pagan life of the Roman Empire. These people were known in Paul's day as "God-fearers", both men and women, just as they are here at verse 4. Yet, we must note, if God had not placed Israel (the Church of God) there first, had not called her into being in the first place, whither could a proselyte have turned to find the Living God?

Verses 5–9. The convert has probably been taught the required responses by his village Levite before coming up to Jerusalem. We are not to picture the Israelite people all living together as a homogeneous nation. What was said of Abraham a thousand years before was still true in the psalmist's day: "At that time the Canaanites were in the land" (Gen. 12:6; 2 Kings 17:24–40). The heathen inhabitants of Palestine continued to dwell there right up until Jesus' day, for Galilee in the first Christian century was known as "Galilee of the Gentiles". In other words, this proselyte had not come from a foreign country. He had been living next door to a member of the people of God.

Now that he has come up to Jerusalem, therefore, this particular enquirer has been invited to speak about his experience of *the steadfast love* of Israel's God. We see that he had been taught what Ps. 107 says in its several vignettes of God, that God's love *sets free* those who are *in distress* (from what had hemmed them in, squeezed them in, literally). But now he has Israel's God, *Yahweh*, on his side, and so he dares to declare: "What can man do to me?" (compare Rom. 8:31; Heb. 13:6). For now he has room to breathe, he is free of the horrible fears that overwhelm heathen people in every land of the world. An agnostic psychiatrist or social worker would not have been able to set him free. Instead of looking for secular help, what the enquirer did was to *call upon the Lord, and the Lord answered me and set me free*. And now, he adds, *the Lord is on my side to help me* (verse 7). The verb used in this verse is often associated with the coming of God's Spirit in power; so the convert proclaims that the Lord is now helping him to face the battle against those very powers of evil which he had seen manifested in the heathendom he had abandoned.

Verses 10–14, *Israel echoes his cry*. The congregation speaks as one "I", perhaps feeling themselves to be in the shoes of their first king, David, the warrior king. They could say so, because the phrase *cut them off* can mean "cut off their foreskins", just as David did with the Philistines (1 Sam. 18:25–27), *for the Lord was with David* (verse 28). The figure of speech is crude and the thought is triumphalist. But the significance of the imagery in that old story was that before David could be accounted worthy to marry King Saul's daughter he had to destroy (or, if he had been a North American Indian, scalp) two hundred enemy warriors. Israel, too, in seeking to fight the Lord's battles, found she could cut off her enemies, even though surrounded by them on every side as if by bees (Deut. 1:44).

Verse 14 sounds like a chorus that everyone sang together. It is on a worthier level than the verses preceding it. In it they declare that God is (a) *my strength*, that is, his Spirit moves upon my spirit; (b) *my song*, the one that God gave my forefathers at the Reed Sea (Hebrew never calls it the Red Sea, but *yam suph*,

which means Sea of Reeds). This song is now quoted as it was
sung by Moses and the people of Israel (Exod. 15:2) because it
allowed the worshippers to declare that (c) *my salvation* was God
himself when he rescued us from slavery and death.

THE LORD RECEIVES A HEATHEN (ii)

Psalm 118:15–25

> [15]Hark, glad songs of victory
>   in the tents of the righteous:
> "The right hand of the Lord does valiantly,
> [16]   the right hand of the Lord is exalted,
>   the right hand of the Lord does valiantly!"
> [17]I shall not die, but I shall live,
>   and recount the deeds of the Lord.
> [18]The Lord has chastened me sorely,
>   but he has not given me over to death.
>
> [19]Open to me the gates of righteousness,
>   that I may enter through them
>   and give thanks to the Lord.
>
> [20]This is the gate of the Lord;
>   the righteous shall enter through it.
>
> [21]I thank thee that thou hast answered me
>   and hast become my salvation.
> [22]The stone which the builders rejected
>   has become the head of the corner.
> [23]This is the Lord's doing;
>   it is marvellous in our eyes.
> [24]This is the day which the Lord has made;
>   let us rejoice and be glad in it.
> [25]Save us, we beseech thee, O Lord!
>   O Lord, we beseech thee, give us success!

Verses 15–20, *The proselyte arrives at the Temple gates.* Hark!
Listen!—cheers of victory *in the tents* (the people's homes in the
city, the word used to remind them that life is still a pilgrimage as

it used to be in the days of the Wilderness in the time of Moses). These were the cheers of *the righteous*. To us, that sounds rather like the "self-righteous". But in the Bible it means the believing community, whom God had long since "put right" with himself. Note that we find the same language used "above" as is here used "below" when, in Our Lord's words, the angels cheered for "one sinner that repents" (Luke 15:7). So the "battle" goes on above and below at the same time. Thus when a group of priests repeats very loudly, so that all can hear in the assembled crowd:

> The right hand of the Lord does valiantly,
> The right hand of the Lord is exalted,
> The right hand of the Lord does valiantly!

they are using the same language as that which described what God did when he overcame Pharaoh and brought Israel out of slavery into freedom. And here it is used of just one poor heathen enquirer!

But he has been saved out of death and destruction. He knows this, for in his excitement he now exclaims: "I am *not* to *die!*" (I believe that, *ki*) "I am going to *live,* so that I can tell others about the *mighty deeds of the Lord*. The Lord has 'educated' me (through suffering) very drastically, but what is so wonderful, *he has not given me over to death*."

Verses 19–20. A priest has evidently coached him on what to say next. He turns and looks at the huge outer gates of the Temple, and shouts aloud: *Open to me the gates of righteousness* (the realm of salvation, of the new life) *that I may enter through them, and give thanks to Yahweh*. Whereupon the priest opens the gates and, pointing, invites him in with the words: *This gate* belongs to Yahweh; the "saved" (those whom Yahweh has already "put right") *enter by it* (the emphasis being "and by it alone"). What this psalm is giving us, then, is a theology of God's saving love in an acted parable, one that later on was turned into a poem that was intended to be sung.

Verse 21, *He is in!* He is now one with all God's redeemed people. In entering the Temple he has entered into life. There have been no questions asked of him, whether he has lived a good life or anything else. He enters the Holy Place merely by responding to grace alone.

His heart is full. He simply must show his gratitude. So he thanks God for the experience of the journey he has travelled before reaching the Temple gates, when God had "disciplined" him, had "humbled" him, and had "made him get rid of his self-righteousness" (this rather than RSV's *answered*). And then, surprisingly, he adds, "Thou hast become the victory for me." He seems to have been witnessing to the fact that he has not saved himself from his own self-righteousness: it is God who has done it for him—and he a mere pagan foreigner! But now, wonder of wonders, he is a new creation!

Verses 22–25. Various voices now back up our new "member". Perhaps the issue of the corner-stone, which took the great weight of the Temple, was much debated when the Second Temple was being planned. A massive block had at first been rejected, but finally had been used to hold up the south-west corner of the outer wall to keep the whole edifice from sliding down into the Valley of Hinnom. This latter name becomes Gehenna in the LXX and so too in the Greek of the NT. It was used as a rubbish dump and was always burning, so it gradually became an alternative word for what we call hell-fire. The corner stone, then, was to keep God's people from sliding down to hell!

This use of the stone that the builders had rejected was God-inspired, it was not a sign of man's ingenuity. At Isa. 28:16 Isaiah had earlier used a similar metaphor when he spoke of the *tested, precious, cornerstone, a sure foundation* that God had set in Zion. No doubt that metaphor was in the psalmist's mind when he composed these verses, which are quoted no less than three times in the Gospels and Acts, as well as in Ephesians and 1 Peter, as a marvellously apt prophecy of what happened in the Cross of Jesus. It may even be that the keystone of the old Solomon's Temple had at first been lost in the rubble of the destruction in 587 B.C. but had been found and produced in Zerubbabel's day with great excitement (see Haggai 1:12–15). Be that as it may, the precious nature of this cornerstone was to reveal the continuity of God's *marvellous doings*. Each day as the people passed the

Temple walls a new revelation was offered them within the whole long series of miracles of revelation since the days of Moses.

The congregation next acclaim, with the thought of their new convert in mind, *This is the day in which the Lord* has acted (this rather then *made*). *Let us rejoice and be glad in it.* Each day that a heathen comes home to God is a miracle of God's grace, as Paul put it succinctly: "Now (today) is the day of salvation" (2 Cor. 6:2). See also Luke 19:9. They have all just beheld a miracle of grace when one sinner was brought home to God. So they add: *Save us too, O Lord!* Keep us always right with you. Make our lives *successful* in the battles still ahead of us. A century after the building of the Second Temple Nehemiah took this verse and applied it to himself (Neh. 1:11). Let us do so *this* very *day* in our turn.

THE LORD RECEIVES A HEATHEN (iii)

Psalm 118:26–29

> 26Blessed be he who enters in the name of the Lord!
>   We bless you from the house of the Lord.
> 27The Lord is God,
>   and he has given us light.
> Bind the festal procession with branches,
>   up to the horns of the altar!
>
> 28Thou art my God, and I will give thanks to thee;
>   thou art my God, I will extol thee.
>
> 29O give thanks to the Lord, for he is good;
>   for his steadfast love endures for ever!

We can understand how the Church throughout the centuries has chosen to sing this psalm particularly at Easter. At verse 17 we heard the assurance of God's gift of life. So the Church later coupled verse 24 with verse 17 and declared on Easter day: "This is the day when the Lord has acted" to bring life to man, life out of death, even death on a Cross. And the Church has continued to declare: Because of God's act on this day we shall be able to sing his praise to all eternity. The words of v. 25, *Save us, we beseech thee*, taken all together form the one Hebrew word *Hosanna*. This, we will remember, was the very word that was shouted by the crowd when Jesus entered into Jerusalem on Palm Sunday.

Verses 26–27. Next comes the festive procession. It had formed up inside the main gate that led into the great outer courtyard, but now it advances to enter through the inner gate to the Holy Place. A priest welcomes the procession there with the words of verse 26*a*. (Interestingly, this welcome is written today in Hebrew at the arrival platform of Jerusalem's railway station.) The people thereupon reply with the words of verse 26*b*, "We are in it!" Whereupon the priest proclaims: *The Lord is God, and he has given us light*—for of course God is light, and in him is no darkness at all.

Then the priest gives an order that greatly excites the worshippers. He invites ordinary "laymen" to come right through the barrier between them and the altar. (This is what Martin Luther did at the Reformation, when he invited the congregation to ignore the "fence" before the altar, in that all laymen are priests to God.) They were to bring branches in with them with which to decorate the four horns of the altar. These horns stuck out, one at each of its corners. They were intended to be grasped only when a man, fleeing from justice, could push his way right in and implore the justice of God, which is always mercy. Thus these horns actually preached the unspeakable love of God. At the Feast of Booths (according to the Jewish *Mishnah* or great Commentary on Scripture produced around A.D. 200) after the sacrifices had been offered, once a year *priests* in procession entered the holy place carrying willow branches and singing as they circled the altar: *Save now we beseech thee; send now prosperity* (compare verse 25). But this picture is different. Here God allows ordinary lay-folk, of course now including the proselyte to the faith, to come crowding into that one awesome spot on earth where he had caused his Name to dwell!

How did the crowd understand the entry of Jesus into Jerusalem on Palm Sunday when they strewed his way with palm branches and sang the words of verse 25? Was Jesus, in their eyes,

their chosen Priest who was on the way to enter the Holy of
Holies, not only on their behalf, but on behalf of all the heathen
nations of the earth?

Verses 28–29. The proselyte finally declares exultingly: *Thou
art my God* ... Whereupon all those good, ordinary folk who
have accompanied him in, answer him with the cultic cry with
which the psalm began, and which perfectly expresses the joy
God's people possess in believing in the living and everlasting
God.

Taken as a whole this psalm never loses sight of the fact that all
Israelites are one. In 932 B.C., at the death of Solomon, Israel
split into two kingdoms, but still they remained one Israel. Three
hundred and seventy years later Ezekiel saw that the "lost sheep
of the house of Israel", the northern kingdom destroyed in 722
B.C., were still one with the sheep of Judah that had remained in
the fold, for the latter too were "lost" in the Exile (Ezek.
37:15–23). Then again, after another six hundred years, when
Israel had once more been split in two in schism, into Jews and
Christians, Paul assures us that God (using the language that we
get in the psalms) cannot go back on his Covenant world, his
promise of love, so that in Christ both Jews and Christians are
still, *together*, the one Israel of God (Rom. 9:4–5; 11:29; Gal.
3:28–29; Eph. 2:14–22). We see in this psalm that that unity is to
be preserved even when the heathen Gentile world enters into it,
there to find their rest and their home. Paul says the same in Col.
3:11. One thing is sure, the Church is not "the new Israel", as
some thoughtless people declare. Nowhere in the NT is such a
thing ever suggested. The Church is the people of the New
Covenant that God has made with Israel (Jer. 31:31), and so with
the whole people of God. We must never forget that the word
"Israel" has no plural.

We have noted before Martin Luther's fascination with the
Hallel psalms. He observes that the whole action in this Ps. 118 is
sacramental, meaning that it shows us what God is like. Luther
recalls that Christ alone has entered the Holy Place as our High
Priest, so that, as a result, we dare to grasp the horns of the altar,
but only through his doing so first by ascending the Cross. He

recalls that Christ said, "I am the light of the world" (compare verse 17), and that Christ alone has opened the kingdom of heaven to all believers. He reminds us that in Isa. 56, a chapter which deals with the period to which this psalm alludes when the cornerstone of the Temple was being relaid, the question of proselytes being allowed to worship in the Temple was being warmly debated. Finally, Luther lists all the issues arising from this psalm which illuminate the work of Christ who, on the evening when, with his disciples, he "sang a hymn", knew that his death was for the redemption of even the heathen of the world.

THE GREAT PSALM (i)

Psalm 119:1

Aleph

[1]Blessed are those whose way is blameless.
   who walk in the law of the Lord!

Every schoolboy knows that this is the longest psalm in the Bible. Because it is so, perhaps we imagine it to be repetitive and in consequence rather boring. Yet a careful reading of it reveals that such is not the case, but that our title for it, *The Great Psalm*, is in fact well chosen.

First, of course, it is "great" in the sense that it is lengthy. We have met acrostic psalms before (e.g. Pss. 9; 10; 34; 37; 111; 112). But in each of those cases the twenty-two letters of the Hebrew alphabet produced a poem of twenty-two lines in length, or of twenty-two verses, each line or verse beginning with a letter of the alphabet. But Ps. 119 is composed of twenty-two strophes (the poetic name for paragraphs), each strophe comprising eight verses, which normally appear as sixteen lines in English, while each of these verses begins with the same letter of the alphabet. Obviously so carefully created a poem was meant to be learned off by heart, the lines of each strophe producing mnemonics that could easily be memorized.

The Arab world continued this type of writing throughout the centuries into the Middle Ages. For the shape of our psalm is no mere gimmick, but an instance of the highest literary art of the ancient world. The Arabs often produced poems very much longer than this, but all developed the one theme. They called their work a *diwan*. This particular Hebrew *diwan* tells a story. It is a story not dissimilar to the one that John Bunyan wrote behind prison bars. Its writer too has obviously been in deep trouble, but he is able to pen his *diwan* in the spirit of profound faith and hope that Bunyan displays.

The very first verse of his long poem strikes the keynote to the psalm, which is that of praise to God for *the law*. Clearly the law was regarded as being basic to Israel's faith. But then, as verse 1 says, this key-word is actually *the law of the Lord*! So we have reached the second reason for calling this psalm "great". This is that it concerns itself with a great theme.

We must be clear however what the word *law* means in the original Hebrew. We have met it in earlier psalms where we found that it is the word *Torah*. We found that this word does not mean "law" in the classical Roman sense of *lex* which has formed the basis of our western legal system. *Torah* actually means "teaching", so that it means teaching that has come out of the mouth of the Living God. When the disciple hears the words of his master's teaching, he receives through it a revelation of what is in the mind of his teacher, and so here, of what is in the mind of God. *Torah* then means both teaching and revelation, in fact, both these at once—from God!

By the time of the Second Temple (after 516 B.C.) *Torah* had become the name given to the first five books of the OT. In this "Pentateuch", as the scholar calls it (for *pente* is Greek for five), we have a very varied bag. There are the Genesis stories of God as Creator, and of the Garden of Eden and the fall of man. Then follow stories of God's judgment upon sin, and following that of his Covenant-making, first with Noah, and then with the Patriarchs. Exodus next gives us the story of God as Redeemer, that is of how God rescued his first-born son (Exod. 4:22) out of slavery, and gave him his "law" at the foot of Mount Sinai.

Thereafter the rest of the Pentateuch describes how God led Israel to the Promised Land. But on the way to it God "revealed" himself to them, and in this "instruction" he mapped out for them the kind of life he wanted them to live together as the people of God, within the Covenant relationship he had imposed on them when he said "I will be your God and you will be my people".

Ps. 119 expresses the joy of an individual Israelite as he studies this amazing *Torah*, this story of God's redeeming love and creative purpose. The poet is evidently a well-educated man, knowledgeable not only in the lore of his people, but also in the Greek view of life which was now beginning to invade his homeland (say, from about 300 B.C. onwards), and which was at total odds with the "revelation" given to Israel through the *Torah*.

The Greek philosopher Plato's interpretation of Socrates' teaching was then and still is one of the greatest contributions toward the meaning of life and the living of it that the world has seen. Socrates' thought centred round the two deep questions: (1) "What is the Good?" and (2) "How should a man live?" And thoughtful people have ruminated on his answers to these fundamental questions right till today. The poet will have known a good deal about Plato's writings, being an educated man, probably a government official, and living in the capital city of Jerusalem which was in touch with the thought of the nations of the earth. Plato offered mankind reasoned and intellectual propositions on these two issues raised by Socrates, yet reached, of course, only by the power of human thought. The poet, on the other hand, declares dogmatically that God, a thousand years before his day (long before Plato, long even before Homer offered a philosophy of the heroic life in his grand poems, *The Odyssey* and *The Iliad*), had taught man by means of his Word, and so had actually *revealed* to mankind the ways and means by which men may live together in society and in fellowship with each other—in short, both what is the Good (or, as Plato usually termed it, what is Justice) and what is the basic meaning of human life. As he began his poem the psalmist could well have had in mind the prophet Micah who had lived midway between his and Moses' day, when he declared (Mic. 6:8):

He has *showed* (told) you, O humanity, what is (the) Good and what
the Lord requires of you.
It is to do *justice*, and to love "steadfast love", and to walk (each as an
individual) humbly with your God.

THE GREAT PSALM (ii)

Psalm 119:2

[2]Blessed are those who keep his testimonies,
who seek him with their whole heart.

The issue before us here is an issue that has continued to be
debated to this day in western culture. This culture has been
motivated and continually formed by the interaction of two com-
peting, yet complementary strands within it, one Hellenic, one
Hebraic. The Hellenic has been that "man is the measure of all
things" and that, by means of the reason which is innate in him,
man is able to create the good life and the perfect society. Our
Hebraic heritage, on the contrary, has asserted that God has
already revealed the nature of the good life and the structure of
the perfect society. All that man has to do is to accept it in
gratitude and to ask God to give him the humility and the strength
to put it into practice.

Once Alexander the Great had unified the whole of the
known world from Greece to what is now Pakistan (in about
340 B.C.), he created the possibility of the free flow of ideas,
philosophies and religions over that vast area. And since many
thousands of Jews were by this time living scattered over this
great empire, they would necessarily meet up with the various
"mystery" religions to be found everywhere which offered salvation to the souls of individuals and promised them escape from a
wicked world. The psalmist would know about these. He would
also have come across several understandings of the word "law".
To the Greeks it meant "custom", to the Romans it meant
unchangeable rules. The "law" or *Torah*, however, which he
desperately wanted to show to his contemporary Jews, reveals a

God who, while indeed offering to be Shield and Shepherd to individual souls into all eternity, had a mighty plan in view for the whole world. Through the *Torah* God sought the co-operation of his Covenant people so that they together, God and man, might work for the salvation, not of individual souls out of this world of pain and sorrow, but in this world as it is, to the end that all people would come to know and trust in the Lord of all. In fact, it revealed God's purpose that the whole *cosmos* (John 3:16) should be saved.

The gospel as we hear it proclaimed in Ps. 119 therefore must be heard once again today in the face of the many individualistic quasi-Christian movements whose sole interest is in the selfish pursuit of "salvation" by single souls. It is tragic to learn of young people who have been brought up within the influence of Church or Synagogue going off to India to sit at the feet of a guru who promises to lead them to a private salvation.

The *Torah* has always shocked the world, for it asks so much of mankind. Whilst it offers many detailed regulations for the conduct of life in the redeemed community, it does not produce merely a kind of humanistic programme for social betterment (as some today search for in it), or a scheme of moral rearmament (as again some suppose is all that matters in the Biblical revelation), or a means whereby the individual can find satisfaction of soul (as not a few think is the only reason for reading the Bible). It offers all these things and more. But it puts them in perspective over against the amazing love and prevenient grace of God and of his plan and purpose as he works to make all things new both in heaven and on earth. For this reason the true disciple of *Torah*, the Word of God, cannot ever be given a label, such as "conservative", "evangelical", "progressive", or anything else. God is too big for his world. Consequently his Word, the *Torah* is too big also.

Another consequence of the unifying of the cultural world of the poet's day was the gradual rise within Jewish thought, possibly under the influence of Persian or Iranian doctrines, of a sharp dichotomy between the present age and the age to come. The latter has now begun to be called "God's Age". The present age, on the other hand, is under the dominion of Satan. This great psalm shows absolutely no influence from this quarter. It remains loyal to the *Torah*, to the only "Bible" that our writer possessed, for the OT prophets were not yet put on a level with it. God is Lord, declares the *Torah*, even of this present age, fallen as it undoubtedly is, but not fallen beyond the reach of the everlasting arms.

The faith of Ps. 119 leads directly to the words of Jesus. When Jesus declared: "My kingdom is not of this world" he was claiming neither the present age nor the world to come as his. Jesus bases the meaning of "his kingdom" upon the first three verses of Genesis. His kingdom does not develop by a natural progression, by evolution, by advances in technology, by the education of the masses. It advances through crises, by bringing light out of darkness (Gen. 1:3), health out of sickness, good out of evil, Resurrection out of the Cross. The revelation of God's purposes that we are given in Christ is already there in embryo in "the Great Psalm", and is God's gift to those who seek him with their whole heart (verse 2).

THE BLESSEDNESS OF OBEDIENCE

Psalm 119:3–8

Blessed are those . . .

³who also do no wrong,
   but walk in his ways!
⁴Thou hast commanded thy precepts
   to be kept diligently.
⁵O that my ways may be steadfast
   in keeping thy statutes!
⁶Then I shall not be put to shame,
   having my eyes fixed on all thy commandments.
⁷I will praise thee with an upright heart,
   when I learn thy righteous ordinances.
⁸I will observe thy statutes;
   O forsake me not utterly!

Since God has already revealed the Good to man, and shown him how to *walk in his ways* (verse 3), man has now no need to fight with his neighbour in order to obtain what is good, or imagine that what is good can be obtained only by what money can buy. Man can live his life in a state of *blessedness* if he but *walks in the law of the Lord.* Here we have the same word as Jesus uses in the Beatitudes when he says, "Blessed are those..." (Matt. 5:3ff).

It has been suggested that the poet was a young man, probably quite wealthy, educated in the best of Jerusalem's schools, in contact with the high officials of the capital city, and acquainted with the power invested in silver and gold. Yet, living in daily contact with both philosophically-minded men and rich and powerful politicians and officials, he is able to make *blessed* the first word of his poem, and to declare that it is possible to walk blamelessly through the quicksands of such a society. But, he states firmly, this is possible only by not having one foot in each camp. It comes about through *walking* only *in the law of the Lord.* Yet, as we saw from Micah, walking with God means to want to keep the Law as your own personal response to the wonder of the Presence of God to be obtained through his spoken Word.

In the seat of power in Jerusalem he had met with many a hedonist, another philosophy of life to which not only many Greeks had succumbed but also representatives of the whole international diplomatic community in the "City of God". We might call it today the "playboy" view of life. Robert Burns the poet had tasted the folly of such a philosophy. He wrote:

> But pleasures are like poppies spread;
> You seize the flower, its bloom is dead.

This poet, like Burns, knew the difference between pleasure and blessedness.

He uses a number of technical terms which we must now examine. These he has taken from the *Torah.*

(a) In verse 2 he mentions *testimonies.* The best modern English for this is "injunctions". The root meaning is "to bear witness". If you bear witness to the Word of God, then you are reflecting to your fellows the image of God. If you *keep his testimonies*, then you find happiness in obedience. You are witnessing to the reality that God has a plan for your life; thus you now have no worries, because it is God who does all the worrying for you. Because of that, and being without care, it is possible to *seek him with your whole heart*—not to seek a mere book, but to seek *him*, the eternal presence of the Living God.

(b) "Who have never done a twisted thing" (verse 3; the RSV has *wrong*). Instead they walk "straight" in their ways. They do not need to run, either from fear or from greed. They now live in obedience, so that their life is calm and natural. All they need to do is *walk*.

(c) This is because, unlike that good man, Plato, they do not need to construct a philosophical system or a code of morals to live by. For *thou hast commanded thy precepts*. They are there, all ready made by the Living God. He has not just suggested that man should try them as one possible alternative. He has *commanded* us to keep them, and very *diligently* too.

(d) *Statutes* (verse 5) (Hebrew *hoq*) is a noun derived from the trade of the stone-mason. The latter chisels his words upon everlasting stone. Such then are God's statutes. Such, for example, are the Ten Commandments, chiselled as they were onto stone tablets. They are thus the unchangeable words of the eternal God.

(e) Consequently, if *my eyes are fixed on all thy commandments* (such as the Decalogue, the Ten Commandments), there will be no room for me to feel *ashamed* of myself.

(f) God's *ordinances* (verse 7) are the decisions of the divine Judge. They have to do with the everyday duties I shall be glad to perform. The word *righteous*, as we have seen in previous psalms, can also mean "victorious". God's ordinances, if obeyed in a person's life, let him be effective in his relationship with other people, and thus live victoriously. One does not live a moral life just in order to be moral. One lives it in order to win other people into friendship with God. But "keep a grip on me, Lord" (verse 8), he asks, "till I have learned how to obey you in this world with its many temptations."

George Washington, like Moses in the *Torah*, knew how to seize courageously the golden moment to set free his nation from the incubus of slavery, and then to *create* faithful adherence to the law, which meant conscientious moderation in the use of power. He showed a shining personal example of modesty, honesty and purity, and finally that subtle and indefinable magnetism by which he brought people of all kinds to follow him to the victory—that of the gift of liberty to four million human beings. George Washington was one who had read the 119th Psalm and had made its message his own.

TEACH ME STILL MORE!

Psalm 119:9–16

Beth

⁹How can a young man keep his way pure?
    By guarding it according to thy word.
¹⁰With my whole heart I seek thee;
    let me not wander from thy commandments!
¹¹I have laid up thy word in my heart,
    that I might not sin against thee.
¹²Blessed be thou, O Lord;
    teach me thy statutes!
¹³With my lips I declare
    all the ordinances of thy mouth.
¹⁴In the way of thy testimonies I delight
    as much as in all riches.
¹⁵I will meditate on thy precepts,
    and fix my eyes on thy ways.
¹⁶I will delight in thy statutes;
    I will not forget thy word.

Verse 9, which begins the second strophe, virtually repeats the young man's plea that he made in verse 8. The purity he speaks of Jesus also mentions at Matt. 5:8. And the word *way* we shall find very commonly used in our long psalm. It too is taken up by Jesus when he declares: "I am the way".

Another term that explains God's *Torah* is *word* (verse 9); in fact this term covers all the other expressions we have now looked at. This is because in OT times the word was regarded as being alive, and so was portrayed as being sent out of the heart (mind/brain/mouth) of a living person, to leap to the goal at which it was directed. Then, when it arrived, it did the work of the speaker who had sent it forth, for it conveyed the power of the speaker to change the heart or the mind of the hearer of the word. We are well aware today that a child's soul can be scarred for life if its parent should even once declare, "I hate you." That is the power of the word. On the other hand, when the young man says to his girl in complete sincerity, "I love you", then his word has the power to change her heart, and to keep it changed "till death us do part". So it is with the Word of God. See Gen. 1:3; Ps. 33:6; Isa. 55:10–11; John 1:1–4, 14.

In Ps. 119:9 *Torah* is equated with Word! The living nature of the Word arises from the fact that God is living and always active. In the Hellenistic (Greek) civilization of our author's day the Word *(logos)* was commonly thought of as an "emanation" (the technical term) that proceeded out of the divine essence. Thus, if the Word of God is indeed alive and God is actually creating continuously in and by his Word, then such a thing as a Black Hole in outer space would not be empty after all. God's Word had created it, and so God himself would be in the Black Hole! Modern science has been saying that the universe is a closed system, simple, fundamentally unmysterious, a rigidly programmed machine. But we are now in the post-modern era, which finds that the universe is not like that at all, but is unbounded, incomplete, truly mysterious. The modern scientist, in consequence, humbly leaves room for the ever-creative Word (or activity) of the Living God. The Word is not independent of God. Rather, the Word is God doing the will of God. Remember that, in the Hebrew, "word" *(davar)* means also "thing" or "act". The title of the Books of Chronicles in Hebrew is "The words (or acts) of the days", in other words, "History". As we shall see, in this psalm the Word is actually regarded as Life and Love, lived out in the "history" of God's people Israel.

Jesus tells the parable of the demon who leaves a man, but leaves him empty. As we say today: "Nature abhors a vacuum". So seven other demons come to take possession of the empty heart (Matt. 12:43–45). In like manner, then, our young man here declares that *I have hidden thy word in my heart.* This is in order that there shall be no room left for *sin* to enter in (verse 11).

Let us now examine a few more of the words he uses. There are several terms for "word" in Hebrew. The one used at verse 11 can also mean "promise"—and it may well mean that here. Then the word for "sin"—how many there are in Hebrew! It is not good enough to use only this little English word every time we want to speak of "sin". We should realize that the word "sin" cuts little ice with many people in the modern world.

The idea in the Hebrew word in verse 11 appears in the General Confession we know so well: "We have left undone those things which we ought to have done, and we have done those things which we ought not to have done". It does not refer to deliberate wickedness (Hebrew has plenty of words for that!) but to aiming at the wrong things in life. Yet doing that, the poet says here, is actually to sin *against thee*! This is because God has a plan for the life of each one of us; consequently, to do something else with our time, energy, thoughts and money is to sin against God.

From verse 12 to verse 16, then, he uses once again those special terms that all interpret the reality of God's *Torah*, God's revelation of his will for us. I know all this, he says to God, but please go on teaching me more; or, as the man in the NT said to Jesus: "Lord, I believe, help my unbelief." So, he says, I repeat your *ordinances* "over and over one by one" (NEB). I *enjoy* reading the Bible, *the way of thy testimonies*, more indeed than anything money can buy! So I meditate quietly when I find myself all alone. This is something, we might add, which western man could well learn from the east (and our poet was an easterner, not a European). Western man is an activist to the extent that he has little time or desire to *meditate on thy precepts*. We too often suppose that Christianity is a European religion as against "the eastern religions". But Jerusalem and Galilee both lie in Asia, not in Europe. This young intellectual thus concludes his second strophe with: "I will get delightfully involved in your *statutes*, your unchangeable words of revelation; I will never forget your *Word*, now that it has been uttered, for it has become 'flesh' as part of my human life."

We notice that there is virtually no reference in Ps. 119 to the sacrifices that were constantly and continually being offered in the Temple in the poet's day, in fact every morning and every evening. There are two things to say about this. (1) By now tens of thousands of the people of God were living scattered over the whole Near East, and most of them had never seen, nor were they ever likely to see the Temple. For them, the Word had taken the place of the Temple as the centre of their faith. This poem therefore interpreted to such good believers their necessary shift in focus. (2) The philosophical treatises of the Greek philosophers which were now becoming known in Palestine argued on religious and social themes without aid of either temple or sacrifice. It would seem that this young scholar felt challenged to answer these great thinkers on their own ground.

OPEN MY EYES

Psalm 119:17–24

Gimel

[17]Deal bountifully with thy servant,
  that I may live and observe thy word.
[18]Open my eyes, that I may behold
  wondrous things out of thy law.
[19]I am a sojourner on earth;
  hide not thy commandments from me!
[20]My soul is consumed with longing
  for thy ordinances at all times.

[21]Thou dost rebuke the insolent, accursed ones,
  who wander from thy commandments;
[22]take away from me their scorn and contempt,
  for I have kept thy testimonies.
[23]Even though princes sit plotting against me,

thy servant will meditate on thy statutes.
²⁴Thy testimonies are my delight,
    they are my counsellors.

Now we reach the key-word of the whole long psalm. It is the word *live*. Our biological life is a gift from God. We do not create it ourselves. The *Torah*, however, uses this word quite differently from Plato and the Greeks. For the *Torah*, God is the Living God. This Living God offers his children *his* life, and that is not mere biological life. It is life in the Spirit, to which physical death has nothing to say. The five books of the Pentateuch culminate at Deut. 30:15, 19 with God's "Word": "See, I have set before you this day life and good, death and evil." The passage then goes on to declare that "life" is bound up with love and with obedience to God's revealed *commandments, statutes* and *ordinances*. The Greek view of the world was that life and death were in fact biologically different from each other. No, said the *Torah* a thousand years before Plato was born, the difference between life and death is a moral difference, not a biological one. Both that passage in Deut. and Amos 5:4, 6, 14 put it thus: "I am offering you the full life, the blessed life, the life of eternity. It is sin against my holy love for you that separates you from me, not physical death. Therefore choose life!"

A journalist was once imprisoned and placed in solitary confinement. But he was given a Bible to read. He had never opened one before. He read it right through three times. Upon release someone asked him what he had made of it. He replied: "Nothing." It is only when God *opens my eyes that I may behold wondrous things out of thy Torah* that I find it speaks of LIFE! That was the different experience of the psalmist. Then he goes on: My life on this earth is short, yet the longer I live, and the oftener I read the Torah, the more I get out of it. So please, God, don't *hide* the meaning of your *commandments* from me. For "my whole being" *is consumed with longing* to discover in it those guide posts to real, full, eternal life which are, I know, to be found there. It is interesting that Dr. Thomas Chalmers, the great Scottish ecclesiastic of the nineteenth century, in a period of deep depression, was able to come back to joy by repeating verse 20 of this psalm over and over again.

It seems that some of the poet's fellow government officials sneered at our young bureaucrat. Some *princes*, that is heads of departments, demanded his obedience to the secular rules for government only, and told him to give up insisting that God had already revealed the true way of life (*mishpat*) for his people. Its "cement" at all levels was love. He replies: "I prefer to obey God's *testimonies* rather than man's, for they are my true *counsellors*" (verse 24).

If one says, "I know best", one is committing the basic sin that humanity committed in the Garden. Adam and Eve did not commit murder, or larceny, they just *wandered from thy commandments* (verse 21). Yet such is the basic attitude of life of countless people in our western so-called Christian society. But their *scorn and contempt* mean nothing, after all, to one who *has kept thy testimonies*. We see, then, that our young man's state of blessedness continues *despite* contempt and ridicule, in fact, that God's Word comes to him *through* the *scorn* of those who, like lost sheep, have already *wandered* away. On the other hand, he is sure that the Hebraic form of democracy, based upon the revealed will of God in the *Torah*, with its representative government through elders elected by the people, is quite other than the Athenian form where only free men had a vote, while the working class had no say in the government at all.

MAKE ME REALLY ALIVE AGAIN

Psalm 119:25–32

Daleth

> 25My soul cleaves to the dust;
>   revive me according to thy word!
> 26When I told of my ways, thou didst answer me;
>   teach me thy statutes!
> 27Make me understand the way of thy precepts,
>   and I will meditate on thy wondrous works.

²⁸My soul melts away for sorrow;
    strengthen me according to thy word!
²⁹Put false ways far from me;
    and graciously teach me thy law!
³⁰I have chosen the way of faithfulness,
    I set thy ordinances before me.
³¹I cleave to thy testimonies, O Lord;
    let me not be put to shame!
³²I will run in the way of thy commandments
    when thou enlargest my understanding!

Even a healthy, believing young man can have his moods of despondency. As an easterner in the tradition of Job would express himself, he knows God well enough to say directly to him, *My soul cleaves to the dust*, and then to add: yet in the *Torah* you promised to give me life. Then he goes on to say how he has learned to chat with God about his own life and its problems; "and you were kind enough to answer me," he adds. Now, please go on further, and teach me more about your plan for our life as a nation.

Moods, of course, come and go. Naturally he has his ups and downs in his faith and obedience. As one scholar translates verse 28: "I am sleepless from worry—put me on my feet again." And so probably over a period he kept putting the same request to God in different words. One way was to say: "Let your revelation be your grace to me" (verse 29). Then the conversation continues: "I *have* obeyed you, and I *have* chosen the way you have pointed to—the way of *faithfulness*." Then he says to God: "It is good to have a good conscience, which happens when I make my will one with your will, O Lord." Finally he concludes by challenging God to see to it that he will be able to *run in the way of thy commandments*, if only God would first *enlarge my understanding*. So he really puts all the responsibility for his life and work upon God!

Throughout his conversation with God here he uses the word *way* four times. By so doing he is letting it be seen that his obedience to God requires him to be on the move, to be on an onward march, such as Israel had to undertake when "on the way" to the Promised Land. The revelation of *Torah* is all about such movement, for even *studying* is movement, and enlarging the *understanding* is movement. Life, in the Biblical sense, is not a static experience. It is an onward struggle towards a goal, through strife and war; but it offers a deep satisfaction to him who is on the way when he knows that, because of the faithfulness of God, eventually "we shall overcome".

But the study of the *Torah* also offers a developing understanding of the mind of God. It is in awe and wonder at the majesty of God that Moses first received the "Law", Exod. 20:1–23:19. This "Covenant Code" passage begins with the tremendous Ten Commandments. One would expect, as it advances, that the passage would reach a mighty climax. Yet it ends in the mere command "You shall not boil a kid in its mother's milk." What an extraordinary come down. What the Law is saying here, then, is that if you choose to live in the Covenant community, you must not only love God; you must also love your neighbour, especially the weak and the poor, and be concerned for the environment in which God has put you. And so we find the idea being expressed here that "keeping the law" actually is the life that God intends us to live.

There are interdenominational "para-church" movements that are widespread in their influence and that teach their adherents to believe that, in order to love God wholeheartedly, it is necessary to disengage oneself from those who do not love God, even though they be parents or friends. This is what happens to a "Christian" movement that does not accept *Torah* as the Word of God.

Our young friend's experience of *Torah* was that God is concerned with the whole of life and that, since it is alive with the life of God, it grows and develops in its power to rule the whole of human life, including man's relationship even with the animal world. The living Word of God has always kept on growing. In fact Jews and Christians now both recognize the importance of this command, even though they may interpret it differently. Yet, the strange reality is that they both may be right at the same time! This is because the *Torah*, in growing in its influence over the centuries, has developed from the "Law of Moses" in 1300 B.C. to meet ever new situations, such as those faced by the generation in the Wilderness and those who lived under the reign of David. The "Law of Moses" kept on adding new material to its corpus to bring it into focus for the years that followed. Thus we know of an extension of it made just before the fall of Jerusalem in 587 B.C., and then again faithful priests seem to have developed the original "Word" to meet the new but barren life of the Exile. The whole Pentateuch received its final form only after the Second Temple was built, just as did the Psalter we are studying, just in time, we would suggest, for the author of this psalm to have in his hands the same completed five books that were read in the synagogue in Jesus' day and which are in our hands now.

In the year 1620 the Pilgrim Fathers set sail for America from Plymouth. Great men and women of faith though they were, they were obstinately sure that they and they alone were right. In a farewell speech to them, therefore, the Rev. John Robinson, who was aware of their narrow views, encouraged them with the now famous statement: "The Lord hath yet more light and truth to break forth from his Word."

THE WAY

Psalm 119:33–40

He

33Teach me, O Lord, the way of thy statutes;
 and I will keep it to the end.
34Give me understanding, that I may keep thy law
 and observe it with my whole heart.
35Lead me in the path of thy commandments,
 for I delight in it.
36Incline my heart to thy testimonies,
 and not to gain!
37Turn my eyes from looking at vanities;
 and give me life in thy ways.
38Confirm to thy servant thy promise,

which is for those who fear thee.
³⁹Turn away the reproach which I dread;
for thy ordinances are good.
⁴⁰Behold, I long for thy precepts;
in thy righteousness give me life!

This stanza is about that *Way* the poet has now mentioned more than once. The NEB translates: "Teach me, O Lord, the way set out in thy statutes, and in keeping them I shall find my reward." So the Way is not identical with God's eternal statutes, cut in stone. This is because the Way is alive, it is the living Way, for God is the Living God, and it is his living Way that is taught to man in the *Torah*. Thus it is quite in character for one who says, "He who has seen me has seen the Father" to say also, "I am the Way". Had not God already said to Abraham, "I am your exceeding great reward" (Gen. 15:1, KJV), after he had first said, "Go on the way I will show you, and I will bless you"? God's Presence was thus his reward. How far this understanding of "the way" is from a set of legalistic commands preserved in a book of law!

In this strophe, then, our poet presents God with a series of requests much like the disciple Thomas who asked Jesus, "Lord, we do not know where you are going; so how can we know the way?" (John 14:5). Evidently he is saying, "It seems that I must first believe before I can understand" ("*Credo ut intelligam*", as St. Anselm summarized his conception of the relation between faith and knowledge). "In enjoying studying the various branches of learning, economics, physics... how much more then will I enjoy studying the meaning of life itself and how to live it!" Clearly one learns to live by enjoying being alive!

The opposite to this outward, forward-looking joy is self-centred search for *gain* (verse 36). This word means "filthy lucre" gained by extortion, robbery, deceit, wheeler-dealing, anything which hurts my neighbour, in fact and in general, covetousness. It is the basic attitude of life of the man who despises love. So it is also seen as the pursuit of *vanity*, of emptiness, of meaninglessness, of all that is negative, false, unreal, or merely frivolous. It was in face of such negation that Paul could write: "Whatsoever is true, honourable, just, pure, lovely, gracious . . . think about these things" (Phil. 4:8).

The way of life is dependent utterly upon the Presence of God with us on the road. We find it difficult at times to grasp this fact, since there is always a remnant of egotism even in the most committed amongst us. It is God who *confirms*, not we (verse 38). The rite of Confirmation does not signify that "I confirm (consciously) the Baptism I once underwent (unconsciously)." The rite means that "God confirms that what the Church did and undertook on my behalf was right." The Church was right, God wants me to know, because its act brought me into the Covenant fellowship wherein the steadfast love of the Lord is operative. So we may fill out the psalmist's final plea: *Turn away the reproach which I dread*, at being told that my parents were wrong to bring me into the Covenant by following your *good ordinance* of circumcision (Lev. 12:3). As we have just reminded ourselves, it is within the Covenant fellowship that a person does actually find the way of life. Because he knows this to be so, the young man concludes with the magnificent assertion: "I have longed to put your precepts into action, for it is when I live the life of love to my neighbour that you give me fullness of life in return." (For this meaning of the word *righteousness* see the Introduction to Vol. 1).

I LOVE THY COMMANDMENTS

Psalm 119:41–56

Waw: Zain

⁴¹Let thy steadfast love come to me, O Lord,
    thy salvation according to thy promise;
⁴²then shall I have an answer for those who taunt me,
    for I trust in thy word.
⁴³And take not the word of truth utterly out of my mouth,
    for my hope is in thy ordinances.
⁴⁴I will keep thy law continually,

for ever and ever;
45and I shall walk at liberty,
for I have sought thy precepts.
46I will also speak of thy testimonies before kings,
and shall not be put to shame;
47for I find my delight in thy commandments,
which I love.
48I revere thy commandments, which I love,
and I will meditate on thy statutes.

49Remember thy word to thy servant,
in which thou hast made me hope.
50This is my comfort in my affliction
that thy promise gives me life.
51Godless men utterly deride me,
but I do not turn away from thy law.
52When I think of thy ordinances from of old,
I take comfort, O Lord.
53Hot indignation seizes me because of the wicked,
who forsake thy law.
54Thy statutes have been my songs
in the house of my pilgrimage.
55I remember thy name in the night, O Lord,
and keep thy law.
56This blessing has fallen to me,
that I have kept thy precepts.

Verses 41–48 (*Waw*). Behind all that happens in our lives there is grace. Behind anything I can do or say is *the steadfast love* of God *to me*, his *hesed*, his Covenant love (compare verse 38). Even the creative love that I am now able to give to my neighbour (the word *salvation* here is in its feminine form, and so is parallel with the feminine noun *righteousness* of verse 40), is not mine to give, rather it has reached me *according to thy promise*. The love I show my scornful colleagues (see at verse 22) when I turn the other cheek, then becomes *the answer*, your answer, Lord, that has sprung out of your Word. I trust in it, and on it I depend. So never let me fail to speak out the right answer, for it is all there *in thy ordinances*.

Verse 44 may not be correctly rendered in the RSV. It may be:
"So let me keep thy *Torah*, O thou everlasting One"; with the
inference of course that the *Torah* too must be everlasting.
Knowing this, I shall be a free man. "In thy service is perfect
freedom," as the ancient prayer declares. "Liberation" always
means two things and not one. It means being set free *from*, and
being set free *to*. A country may be set free *from* colonialism, but
this avails nothing unless it is free to take its responsible place
in the family of nations. This young man feels himself free *from*
the innuendoes and abuse of his colleagues, *to* obedience to the
Word. So free does he feel himself to be that he is free to speak to
the imperial rulers of the day about God's *testimonies*. Such
freedom springs of course out of love. I actually *love thy commandments*, he says. Nehemiah was "free" in this sense to appeal
to King Artaxerxes that God's will might be done in Jerusalem
(Neh. 2:1–8). So the young man concludes this strophe by saying:
"I lift up my hands to your commandments", referring not just to
the Ten Commandments, but to the whole of the Covenant Code
in Exodus and much more besides in *Torah*; these he wholeheartedly *revered*, and he was ready to commit himself utterly to
them.

Verses 49–56 (*Zain*). It is a great task I have undertaken, to
witness to God's Word before my colleagues and superiors in
government. So, Lord, *remember thy word to thy servant, in
which thou hast made me hope*—thou hast, not me! It has been all
your doing, Lord; you have chosen me, I have not chosen you. So
please don't let me down. May I be comforted, when I am being
sneered at, by experiencing the LIFE you promised me as the real
thing. I keep recalling that the *Torah* is centuries *old*, and that
comforts me. I feel furiously angry when I see *godless* people
forsaking thy law, the very revelation of thy Word, thy Plan and
Purpose for humanity. It is intolerable that egotistical human
beings should so savage God's created world. It is not the heathen
I am angry at, of course; they have not had the opportunity to
hear the Word, and so they cannot be blamed for their ways. It is
my fellow "covenanters" who now sneer at all I love most dearly
(see Amos 3:2). Yet, as James 1:20 puts it: "The anger of man
does not work the righteousness of God."

Once again the psalmist goes on to describe obedience to God as going forward on the way that the purposes of God take, as a kind of pilgrimage, as a movement, and not just as a state of being, even of "being saved". It is a striving to bring in the Kingdom of God, with God, by *keeping* his revealed will for mankind. "This happened to me" (says the Hebrew, not as RSV, verse 56), *because I have kept thy precepts.*

THE LORD IS MY PORTION

Psalm 119:57–64

Heth

⁵⁷The Lord is my portion;
  I promise to keep thy words.
⁵⁸I entreat thy favour with all my heart;
  be gracious to me according to thy promise.
⁵⁹When I think of thy ways,
  I turn my feet to thy testimonies;
⁶⁰I hasten and do not delay
  to keep thy commandments.
⁶¹Though the cords of the wicked ensnare me,
  I do not forget thy law.
⁶²At midnight I rise to praise thee,
  because of thy righteous ordinances.
⁶³I am a companion of all who fear thee,
  of those who keep thy precepts.
⁶⁴The earth, O Lord, is full of thy steadfast love;
  teach me thy statutes!

"This happened to me," he has just said. What did happen? That which happened to Abraham, when he found that God was his reward (Gen. 15:1). Now the young man possessed an "allotment in paradise". The word *portion* suggests that he now possessed everything necccssary that leads to life. Some people have money as their portion, some have fame—but I have the Lord, he claims.

So I make a two-way plea: (1) *I promise to keep thy words.* (2) So please *be gracious to me according to thy promise.* When I think of *my* ways, then I despair. But *when I think of thy ways*, I repent in sorrow, and *turn my feet* to go back *to thy testimonies*, and I even *hasten* to do so. Even when I find myself in the dark night of the soul *I rise to praise thee.* In his great poem *Samson Agonistes*, Milton writes:

> O dark, dark, dark, amid the blaze of noon,
>   irrevocably dark, total eclipse,
>   without all hope of day.

Yet I can rise *because of thy ordinances* which bring about the victory over evil. I am no solitary believer. I am one of a happy band who march through the darkness together hand in hand. But *even the darkness is not dark to thee* (Ps. 139:12). The whole *earth*, both darkness and light, *is full of thy steadfast love.* So if I am to understand the meaning of that great fact, then, *teach me thy statutes*, Lord, that I may know how, walking along with you, I can share in making your loving plan known to all peoples.

It is deeply disappointing that within the Christian Church there are many who have never made the discovery that the Bible (in this case, the *Torah*) offers this kind of message. Many Christians today are obsessed with the issue of their own personal salvation. We recall that Jesus gave the warning that he who seeks to save his soul (or his life—the words are the same) will lose it, the same Jesus who "emptied out his soul" for men and women in conformity with the way that *Torah* speaks of God.

Let us notice the following points that this young poet fully appreciated about the *Torah*:

1. God's *Torah*, his Word, offers us freedom, and gives us power to maintain that freedom against man's own laws. This is because God's law is superimposed on *all* laws. "It is better to obey God rather than man."

2. God's *Torah* is not static, nor is it tyrannical, like "the laws of the Medes and Persians". We see in the Book of Daniel how even the great king could find no loophole through which he could wriggle out of having to put Daniel to death (see Daniel 6:5, and

contrast it with 6:14–15). *Torah* rather offers us a kind of strategy whereby really good relations between peoples may one day come into being.

3. Since it is "revelation" at the same time as it is "law", then it is not only law, it is also gospel.

4. The application of *Torah* turns man from being a slave to the laws of the nations, and to the all-demanding laws of his own egocentric human nature, into being a subject of the new realm of the freedom of God himself, where we can say with a deep sense of joy: "In thy service is perfect freedom."

GOD WAS RIGHT TO DISCIPLINE ME

Psalm 119:65–80

Teth: Yod

⁶⁵Thou hast dealt well with thy servant,
  O Lord, according to thy word.
⁶⁶Teach me good judgment and knowledge,
  for I believe in thy commandments.
⁶⁷Before I was afflicted I went astray;
  but now I keep thy word.
⁶⁸Thou art good and doest good;
  teach me thy statutes.
⁶⁹The godless besmear me with lies,
  but with my whole heart I keep thy precepts;
⁷⁰their heart is gross like fat,
  but I delight in thy law.
⁷¹It is good for me that I was afflicted,
  that I might learn thy statutes.
⁷²The law of thy mouth is better to me
  than thousands of gold and silver pieces.

⁷³Thy hands have made and fashioned me;
  give me understanding that I may learn thy commandments.
⁷⁴Those who fear thee shall see me and rejoice,
  because I have hoped in thy word.
⁷⁵I know, O Lord, that thy judgments are right,
  and that in faithfulness thou hast afflicted me.

⁷⁶Let thy steadfast love be ready to comfort me
	according to thy promise to thy servant.
⁷⁷Let thy mercy come to me, that I may live;
	for thy law is my delight.
⁷⁸Let the godless be put to shame,
	because they have subverted me with guile;
	as for me, I will meditate on thy precepts.
⁷⁹Let those who fear thee turn to me,
	that they may know thy testimonies.
⁸⁰May my heart be blameless in thy statutes,
	that I may not be put to shame!

Verses 65–72 *(Teth)*. The young writer continues: I have put in words my experience that the Lord is now my portion (verse 57). It was not always so, however. That he is now everything to me is the result of his keeping the promises he made in the *Torah*. So now I want him to do the next thing for me, and that is to teach me, first, *good judgment*, that is, the ability to know the difference between good and evil, and secondly, *knowledge*, which means being in close fellowship with God personally as I go along the way.

On their travels together Dr. Johnson once said to his faithful Boswell: "As a man advances in life he gets what is better than admiration, he gets judgment, the ability to estimate things and their true value." But Dr. Johnson omitted to note that such an ability comes in the first place from knowing God, in the same kind of way that a man "knows" his wife or his friend.

But before this, the psalmist goes on, I went astray like a prodigal son. I opted out of the Covenant fellowship. In your mercy therefore and for my own good you reprimanded me forcibly; you saw fit to afflict me. But *thou art good* and thou didst all this for my *good*.

My workmates saw this happen when I was in the far country of the soul and they smeared me with lies. "Your faith hasn't done you any good," they sneered. Actually their minds were as insensitive as butter; they couldn't even begin to understand what it means to enjoy God's *Torah*.

All this too has been for my good, to have been *afflicted* by so-called friends in a far country. Otherwise I wouldn't know the wonder of forgiveness and the depths of the love of God, or that he had all along been patiently waiting for me to return home.

The result is that the revelation (RSV *law*) that has come from your mouth means more to me than the glittering prizes that money can buy—not to mention the husks that the swine did eat, we might add!

There is the kind of Christian who wonders how the God of the OT could have been like this before the coming of Christ. But when Jesus told the story of the Prodigal Son (or rather, the story of the Loving Father) he was describing not only what God was like in the year A.D. 30 but also what he had always been like from the beginning of Creation. For God is the same, yesterday, today, and for ever. And *Torah* tells us so, firmly.

Verses 73–80 *(Yod).* The young man begins this strophe with a great statement of faith, confidence and assurance, one that is applicable for any one of us at any time; not just for the period when he or we have returned home to the Father. *Thy hands have made me,* he says, for a purpose. Please then give me *understanding* so that I may discover from your *commandments* what that means in my case; *because I have hoped in thy word.* I *know* that the Lord was right to *afflict me* and so to discipline me. But after doing so, he comforted me. I needed it, for I was a poor sinner come home. Moreover, you actually promised you would!

Let your "mother-love" (RSV *mercy*; the word is linked with the word for "womb") reach me *that I may live.* We recall that the last words of the story of the Prodigal Son (Luke 15:32) are: "For this your brother was dead, and is *alive*; he was lost and is found." Out of the "mother-love" of the Father in the story he does not say: "Your brother has been living an immoral life". Morals are not the mark of the Biblical gospel. That mark is *life*—and life more abundantly as Jesus says. To be lost, to stray away (verse 67) is to be "dead". To be found therefore is no less than "to come alive".

My so-called friends tried to seduce me, he adds now, by perversely arguing for what is false; but I countered their guileful arguments by *meditating on thy precepts.* So come, all you who fear the Lord, and I will tell you my story. I can do this because I have learned from God, first, and so must now teach others; yet even that I can do only with God's help. As Ernst Käsemann puts it: "Faith is living out the Word which bears witness to God's lordship, nothing more and nothing less." Then Käsemann adds a reference to Rom. 4:3 which speaks of how Abraham possessed this faith—and we find the story of that in the *Torah*.

WHY IS GOD SO SLOW?

Psalm 119:81-96

Kaph: Lamed

⁸¹My soul languishes for thy salvation;
    I hope in thy word.
⁸²My eyes fail with watching for thy promise;
    I ask, "When wilt thou comfort me?"
⁸³For I have become like a wineskin in the smoke,
    yet I have not forgotten thy statutes.
⁸⁴How long must thy servant endure?
    When wilt thou judge those who persecute me?
⁸⁵Godless men have dug pitfalls for me,
    men who do not conform to thy law.
⁸⁶All thy commandments are sure;
    they persecute me with falsehood; help me!
⁸⁷They have almost made an end of me on earth;
    but I have not forsaken thy precepts.
⁸⁸In thy steadfast love spare my life,
    that I may keep the testimonies of thy mouth.

⁸⁹For ever, O Lord, thy word
    is firmly fixed in the heavens.
⁹⁰Thy faithfulness endures to all generations;
    thou hast established the earth, and it stands fast.
⁹¹By thy appointment they stand this day;
    for all things are thy servants.
⁹²If thy law had not been my delight,
    I should have perished in my affliction.
⁹³I will never forget thy precepts;

for by them thou hast given me life.
⁹⁴I am thine, save me;
   for I have sought thy precepts.
⁹⁵The wicked lie in wait to destroy me;
   but I consider thy testimonies.
⁹⁶I have seen a limit to all perfection,
   but thy commandment is exceedingly broad.

Verses 81–88 *(Kaph)*. We move onwards in time, and in the experience of the poet. Remember, this is a kind of epic poem, like an Arab *diwan*. There comes the inevitable reaction—for life is like that—from the joy he had experienced in coming alive at the touch of God. "My whole being longs to possess thy saving power working in me", which I read about in the *Torah*. There you *promised* it to me; so please now complete your plan through me, which is, to make me love my neighbour creatively. We note that the verb *naham*, "to comfort", has this meaning of "completing a plan", as at Luke 2:25. But *my eyes*, he goes on, are "used up", "worn out", gazing for the fulfilment of your *promise*. It is as if I had been weeping from the effects of smoke (the smoke, perhaps, inside a sod cottage with no windows).

Ps. 119 began with the words, "Blessed are those whose way is blameless". But the young man is now going through an exceedingly *un*blessed time. Can this experience be the will of God? We see that he is discovering that, just because he is a member of the redeemed community of the Covenant, he is not meant to go about with a forced smile on his face, as if to tell the world, "I can take all the blows of fortune and still keep smiling; I am a believer, and I must show the world that a believer is always happy in the Lord." Surely not. It was to the Covenant people that Jesus enunciated another "Blessed", "Blessed are those who mourn", and this mourning extends far beyond mourning for the dead. "For they shall be comforted" does not mean that we should try to make the unhappy laugh. No, we are to weep with those who weep (Rom. 12:15), as Paul interprets the Beatitude. This, then, is what the young poet had found God himself was like and what God was actually doing with him. God, he was discovering, was now weeping along with him, since God was present with him in love and comfort.

What he had to learn—and we—is that God works in us at the pace which he sees fit, at the pace he sees we are able to walk. That is why God allowed him (verses 85–87) to go on suffering the scorn of his *persecutors*, even as he struggled to hold on to his faith and to remain sure of God's *steadfast love*. The lesson he was learning is that we have to keep on learning even after our "conversion", and not for a long time will we reach that point which Paul describes by the word "sanctification". For example, what a long time God took before he saw that Israel was ready for her "consolation" (Luke 2:25)! This is what this psalm calls God's *teshuah*, "salvation".

It is a prime rule on the mission field that you do not ordain a new convert in a hurry. Many young people in our churches who have undergone a genuine religious experience declare without hesitation, "I am a Christian—you are not", addressing an old saint. The latter, however, knows that *teshuah* is not so easily attained. Professor Hans Küng searches for words to express the meaning of this word: "Newly created insights; tendencies, intentions positive to others, commitment to people; identification with the poor, the handicapped; magnanimity, unselfishness, joy, kindness, pardon, service; readiness for complete self-sacrifice." The poet is beginning to realize this, and in so doing is beginning to find the answer to his question: "Why is God so slow?"

Verses 89–96 *(Lamed)*. The psalmist now tells us that part of his re-education has been to discover complete assurance in the *Torah*. "Right within eternity", Lord, *thy Word is firmly fixed in the heavens*. So too with *thy faithfulness*, thy utter reliability, thy dependability, thy loyalty. Now that he is back home he finds that God is just as faithful to him as he ever has been before. I can say this about myself, he concludes, because all Nature declares it to be so (and I am part of Nature), because the universe obeys the rules that God has made. I have learned that I live in an orderly universe.

In the same way, *thou hast given me life by thy precepts*. So I am meant to live an orderly life, a life obedient to the rules. Yet these "rules" are alive, and not dead matter, for they have come out of the mouth of the Living God.

From this point on, that is, from verse 94, his argument runs only in the words of the first half of each verse. The second half serves as a refrain, as in Ps. 136.

I am thine, save me. Though I am but a tiny creature in this vast universe, I belong to you in a special way. So *save me* from the reach of wicked men. The wicked man is he who believes he can create a perfect world, the ideal human being, the completely harmonious society, by means of scientific wizardry and by better education for all. I cannot accept that. It is *thy commandment* (in the singular, and thus meaning "thy Word"—see Deut. 11:22, which sums up God's basic command under the one word "love") that is unlimited, not scientific enquiry. The psalmist has found complete assurance of God's love from his devotion to the *Torah*, so that he can say firmly that the statement he made in the very first verse of this long psalm, made after a rich and varied experience of life, is true.

OH, HOW I LOVE THY LAW!

Psalm 119:97–104

Mem

⁹⁷Oh, how I love thy law!
    It is my meditation all the day.
⁹⁸Thy commandment makes me wiser than my enemies,
    for it is ever with me.
⁹⁹I have more understanding than all my teachers,
    for thy testimonies are my meditation.
¹⁰⁰I understand more than the aged,
    for I keep thy precepts.
¹⁰¹I hold back my feet from every evil way,
    in order to keep thy word.
¹⁰²I do not turn aside from thy ordinances,
    for thou hast taught me.
¹⁰³How sweet are thy words to my taste,
    sweeter than honey to my mouth!

104Through thy precepts I get understanding;
     therefore I hate every false way.

No wonder *I love* God's *Torah*, then, and want to keep on
meditating on it at all times; for, as I have said, I have found
complete assurance in it that God is working out a cosmic plan
and that he needs me to share in it. In fact, it is mine for *ever*. This
phrase in the Hebrew makes the *Torah* sound more like a person
than a book. In fact it is quite different from "law", as I have
come to see. For what citizen of any country would ever say: "Oh,
how I love the law!'"? Paul discussed the issue of being *wiser than
my enemies* (were they followers of Plato and Aristotle?) when he
wrote to the Corinthians in Greece (1 Cor. 1:18–31). Evidently
Paul agreed with this young government official that a simple
believer has *more understanding than the aged*, the wise old
philosophers; for he can meditate on the revealed mind of the
Living God.
     The great majority of ordinary people today do not know much
of history, and so could be excused for being surprised that the
psalmist discovers that love is the centre of all things and is the
basic meaning of life. For in the period B.C. in which he lived there
were many other views of the nature of man and many widely
varying cultures in which love played little or no part at all.
Merchants came and went, diplomats journeyed great distances.
Jerusalem was a staging post in those days for ideas from both
east and west. Hinduism, centuries old by now, would be well
discussed in Jerusalem by the upper classes; it is concerned with
spiritual self-realization, not love. In Buddhism, also several
centuries old at that time, a man aims, not at loving his neighbour, but at losing himself in Nirvana. Among the animist
peoples who then roamed Arabia's deserts, men were merely
"building blocks" (to use the term of a present-day theologian)
for the community: tribe, people or state. It is all so different
from *Torah*. There we read that (1) man is created free, free to
eat the fruit in the Garden or not to eat it; that (2) man is created
free to love; and that (3) man is created free to enjoy or to reject
the blessedness of freely chosen fellowship both with God and
with other men.

Clearly (a) the Law is not a perfect pattern laid up in heaven, as Plato would have put it, one that is meant to be taken literally and copied in every detail on earth. It is true that parts of it are (b) what scholars call "apodictic" declarations. To that group belong the Ten Commandments. These *are* absolutes "written in heaven" and are thus the unchangeable mind of God for man. But there are also (c) the many other regulations in the *Torah*, the legal sections as we call them,which are expressed as decisions made by the divine Judge to suit particular situations. These are evidently divinely given *guidelines* for the good life that this young administrator very much wants to put into practice in Judah.

Thus when he reads that the Covenant people are to care especially for the widow and orphan, that does not mean they are to neglect the widower or the intellectually handicapped child. it is as if God were saying: "For example . . . but when a new situation arises, then you are to branch out . . ." When the Law says, "You may stave off your hunger by helping yourself to your neighbour's standing grain (Deut. 23:25), but you are not to put a sickle to it", this is not just a rule for an agricultural community. You are meant to put the "spirit" of it into practice in all kinds of situations in sophisticated Jerusalem that were unknown in the simple life of a farm in the old days. The basic issue to be put into practice is, in fact, to love your neighbour in whatever situation you may find yourself. This, then, is why the poet can find that he is able to *love* the Law. In it he receives from God the challenge to found his social thinking upon the thinking of God, and then to work at it till it is turned into an aspect of practical living. To do this is indeed to know the blessedness of obedience, the words we put as a heading to 119:3–8.

How well I know, he continues, that the vision of the Word evaporates the moment I set my feet on any *evil way*, and try to put into practice alien ideas. But I don't do so, *for thou hast taught me* what to do; *thou* hast taught *me*! Like Ezekiel (3:1–3) I have found *thy words sweet to my taste*. So naturally *I hate every false way*, all those foreign social systems that are merely human ideas.

The strophe reveals to us the vital significance of the statement we find in the Prologue to John's Gospel at John 1:17—"For the Law was given through Moses; grace and truth came through Jesus Christ." The Greek word *nomos* means law that has been codified from ancient custom, as in ancient Greece. But God's *Torah* was given through Moses. The passive "was given", as used in the Gospels, usually means "God gave". But still grace and truth were needed to complete God's revelation. These two words in Greek are the commonly used terms in the LXX to translate the two Hebrew words we have met so often, *hesed* and *emeth*. God's steadfast love and his faithfulness are not attributes of God that he can give away at will. God does not possess attributes. These words represent what God always keeps on showing and what he is always doing, which is to "come" to his people in love and faithfulness at all times. Now, since the *Torah* has revealed that God "came" to his Covenant people in *hesed* and *emeth* in the days of Moses, it means that the God who be-*came* flesh in Jesus Christ is the God who had also *come* through the *Torah*. The Fourth Gospel goes on to express this reality in just one little simple phrase: "Before Abraham was, I am" (8:58).

THY WORD IS A LAMP

Psalm 119:105–112

Nun

105Thy word is a lamp to my feet
    and a light to my path.
106I have sworn an oath and confirmed it,
    to observe thy righteous ordinances.
107I am sorely afflicted;
    give me life, O Lord, according to thy word!
108Accept my offerings of praise, O Lord,
    and teach me thy ordinances.
109I hold my life in my hand continually,
    but I do not forget thy law.

110The wicked have laid a snare for me,
    but I do not stray from thy precepts.
111Thy testimonies are my heritage for ever;
    yea, they are the joy of my heart.
112I incline my heart to perform thy statutes
    for ever, to the end.

God's revealed will for our human life, made in grace and truth, in *hesed* and *emeth*, has again and again in this psalm been called a *way*—a route, a road, not a place where one sits down and examines his soul. The wayfarer has no time for that. His job on the way is to be obedient. A way is where one moves forward, where one travels along, where one wrestles against "the slings and arrows of outrageous fortune", ever looking to the goal ahead, ever aware that life is a journey and that those who walk the *way* are pilgrims.

Thy word is a lamp to my feet. We are not to picture a modern electric torch shining its light in a beam ahead into the darkness. The *lamp* in OT times looked like a flattened teapot; it carried one small wick which could only flutter in the breeze; and its *light* fell only one step ahead in the darkness. As the pilgrim took one step forward, so the light moved that much forward with him. Then again, the symbol of light is to remind us that God himself is the source of all light, to remind us, in fact, that he himself is with us on our journey along the way. God's light does not destroy the darkness. We cannot see into darkness, and so we cannot find a final answer to the problem of evil. But the figure here is sufficient for faith. God is *with* the pilgrim on his way (see Exod. 3:12), and is never more than one step ahead.

Such then is the light that comes to this psalmist in the *Torah*. He *has sworn* to *observe* it. Yet that does not mean the end of all fears. These, including the dark mystery of death, still lurk ahead beyond the flickering light of the lamp. So he cries to God for that one basic gift, not of what money can buy, not of scientific knowledge, not of morals, but of *life, according to the Torah* itself!

How then could anyone so misinterpret this psalm as to turn it into a song in praise of legalism? For, as *I hold my life in my hand continually*, I realize how precarious it is *if I forget thy Torah*—for it tells me of your steadfast love and faithfulness, *hesed* and *emeth*. In 1 Sam. 19:5; 28:21; and in Job 13:14 we find the idea which is presented in the above words to mean a readiness to give or risk one's life (or soul, for the two words are one in Hebrew). And that is what we learn from the *Torah*. How easily, however, the psalmist continues, I could lose my "life" through lack of faith; yet you have made it possible for me to hold on to it by keeping in mind your revelation. *Enemies of mine have laid a snare for me*; consequently the only answer to their action in this threat to my life is for me to say, *I do not stray from thy precepts which are the joy of my heart.* Not only so, they are my *heritage*, that is to say, they have been left to me by my parents "in their will", for they had me circumcised into the Covenant fellowship. Consequently, *thy testimonies are my heritage for ever.* Because of all this that they have let me inherit, *I incline my heart to perform thy statutes for ever, to the end* of the *way.*

YOU HAVE PROMISED ME LIFE

Psalm 119:113–128

Samek: Ayin

113I hate double-minded men,
  but I love thy law.
114Thou art my hiding place and my shield;
  I hope in thy word.
115Depart from me, you evildoers,
  that I may keep the commandments of my God.
116Uphold me according to thy promise, that I may live,
  and let me not be put to shame in my hope!
117Hold me up, that I may be safe
  and have regard for thy statutes continually!
118Thou dost spurn all who go astray from thy statutes;
  yea, their cunning is in vain.

119All the wicked of the earth thou dost count as dross;
  therefore I love thy testimonies.
120My flesh trembles for fear of thee,
  and I am afraid of thy judgments.

121I have done what is just and right;
  do not leave me to my oppressors.
122Be surety for thy servant for good;
  let not the godless oppress me.
123My eyes fail with watching for thy salvation,
  and for the fulfilment of thy righteous promise.
124Deal with thy servant according to thy steadfast love,
  and teach me thy statutes.
125I am thy servant; give me understanding,
  that I may know thy testimonies!
126It is time for the Lord to act,
  for thy law has been broken.
127Therefore I love thy commandments
  above gold, above fine gold.
128Therefore I direct my steps by all thy precepts;
  I hate every false way.

Verses 113–120 (*Samek*). Knowledge of *Torah* is basically simple. This is because *Torah* keeps saying one thing constantly and powerfully, and that is, "Blessed are the pure in heart". That describes one who is single-minded, a person of integrity. Duplicity is the mark of him who worships a double-minded god. Even the great Greek philosophers of our poet's day were *double-minded*, for they "doubled" the meaning of reality. They believed in body *and* soul, mind *and* spirit, heaven *and* earth, the world of ideals *and* the world of things. Elijah was the champion of the "pure in heart" when he challenged the priests of Baal: "How long will you go on limping with two different opinions?" (1 Kings 18:21). The worshippers of Baal, the Canaanite weather god, were tied to a nature religion with all its confusions. But, *I love thy law*, because, in thy Word, *thou art my hiding place* alone, where alone I can find the peace of integrity.

Once more, then, the psalmist distinguishes those who, with a private philosophy of life, one they have thought out on their own, sneer at the "single-minded", the "pure in heart". A newspaper reported the words of a university lecturer: "Professional philosophers now know many moral and ethical principles as absolute fact. For example, we know that God does not exist, that there is no life after death, that all sexual activity among consenting adults is morally permissible, and that the meaning and purpose of life is to have as much fun as possible." Shakespeare speaks of the man who can "smile and smile and be a villain". The poet is saying, in our modern language, "I won't fall for that one's smile, for I recognize his duplicity of mind." He is not concerned with religion, a word which does not occur in the OT. This is because the double-minded man may all the time be quite religious yet remain unloving and self-centred. The psalmist is concerned rather with *life*, with fullness, that is to say, with unity or integrity of life. And this is exactly what God has *promised*, as we learn at verse 116. Double-mindedness is a mark of those who *go astray from thy statutes, yea, their cunning is in vain* (that is, their self-deceit). It just leads to *vanity*, or, better, "duplicity", really another word for two-faced. Such the Lord *counts as* "scum" (NEB).

If God regards the two-faced in this way, then he is a terrible God. "The dread of thee makes my flesh creep" (NEB). How dare mere man declare to the living God: "I don't believe your Word; I stick to my own view of life"!

Verses 121–128 (*Ayin*). *Be surety*, therefore, *for thy servant—for good*. To stand surety for another is to stand in that other's place, and in one's own person to furnish a guarantee for his good behaviour. In other words, the daring young psalmist asks God to be a hostage for him (compare Job 17:3). He has done what he could to put the *Torah* into practice in his administrative capacity. Now, if it doesn't work, he dares God to take the blame for it. God is not simply to "go bail" for him and pay money to get him off; he is to take his place in the dock in the case brought against him by the *godless*. The words *oppressors* and *godless* are strong terms, the first meaning exploiters who extort money from innocent people, the second meaning arrogant atheists. Three times over, however, he calls himself *thy servant.* By that term he is declaring that he has been humbly trying to do God's will by obeying God's Word as he has found it in the *Torah. It is time for God to act* to get him off, *for thy law has been broken.*

He uses here what we would call covenantal language. A member of any covenant community could appeal to his master at any time to seek redress. But the Hebrew text tells us more than is obvious from the English of the RSV. The psalmist begs God to "get him off", since he is *watching for thy salvation* (verse 123), watching for God to do just that. This is the feminine of the word we have now met so often in the psalms. It carries the nuance that he is *watching* for a chance to show love and concern for those who are now oppressing him. In other words, he has learned the mighty truth of God, that God has put him right with himself only in order that he in turn might be able to put others right with God by doing what God does, that is, accepting the sinner, forgiving him, and loving him, and so bringing him home to God.

It is time the Covenant Lord did act, he says, for people have now actually "annulled" God's law. Is it possible for mere man to annul God's steadfast love? Such a thing is intolerable. There follow two *therefores*, showing surprisingly the "otherworldly" logic of God's *hesed*—(1) *Therefore I love . . .* and (2) *Therefore the precepts of Torah* "cover every aspect of life" (as we should probably render this doubtful line). False ways, on the contrary, can only lead to death.

"LOVE NEVER ENDS"

Psalm 119:129–144

Pe: Tsadde

129Thy testimonies are wonderful;
    therefore my soul keeps them.
130The unfolding of thy words gives light;
    it imparts understanding to the simple.
131With open mouth I pant,

because I long for thy commandments.
¹³²Turn to me and be gracious to me,
  as is thy wont toward those who love thy name.
¹³³Keep steady my steps according to thy promise,
  and let no iniquity get dominion over me.
¹³⁴Redeem me from man's oppression,
  that I may keep thy precepts.
¹³⁵Make thy face shine upon thy servant,
  and teach me thy statutes.
¹³⁶My eyes shed streams of tears,
  because men do not keep thy law.

¹³⁷Righteous art thou, O Lord,
  and right are thy judgments.
¹³⁸Thou hast appointed thy testimonies in righteousness
  and in all faithfulness.
¹³⁹My zeal consumes me,
  because my foes forget thy words.
¹⁴⁰Thy promise is well tried,
  and thy servant loves it.
¹⁴¹I am small and despised,
  yet I do not forget thy precepts.
¹⁴²Thy righteousness is righteous for ever,
  and thy law is true.
¹⁴³Trouble and anguish have come upon me,
  but thy commandments are my delight.
¹⁴⁴Thy testimonies are righteous for ever;
  give me understanding that I may live.

Verses 129–136 (*Pe*). *Wonderful* is a very special word. It means miraculous, paradoxical, coming from God, not man. That then is why *I keep thy testimonies*, and use them. But how can we ever *unfold* them? It is dangerous for us human beings to be counsellors of other people. It is best only to help people to reach their own conclusions. So it is with "unfolding" the Scriptures. Yet we find as we seek to unfold them that *thy words give light*. A famous artist has said: "The unfolding of God's Word offers more than all the discoveries of modern science, literature, art, music, and all sensual pleasures." The word *unfolding* can be translated by our term "exegesis", the word that the scholar uses for bringing out the meaning of a Biblical text. But it occurs here as a pun on the word "simple". Is it the case, then, that Biblical exegesis just means making a passage simple and straightforward to help the ordinary reader to understand its message for him?

Robinson Crusoe was able to salvage a Bible from the wreckage he had dragged ashore. But he did not open it till he fell ill. Then he read from it, and it suddenly took on meaning. Or, could we say, the Holy Spirit "unfolded" its meaning to him? Whereupon, for the first time since he had put foot on the island he knelt down and prayed.

One form of exegesis is the use of picture language. The theological statement we have made is that only God's Spirit can interpret God's Word. Now, the study of theology is a form of loving God with the mind. For that reason it is never a secret matter, but is always one that must be shared with ordinary folk, and not be the property of those who live in ivory towers. The picture expression for exegesis by the Spirit in this psalm is most attractive. It is to hold open one's mouth for God to fill it! Then its author adds, again in language we can all understand, "I love you: you love me; lead me not into temptation; deliver me from all evil" (almost as if he were repeating the Lord's Prayer). Finally he caps his wonderful cry by quoting in part the Aaronic blessing (Num. 6:24–26).

His last statement in verse 136 invites us to ask ourselves whether we feel as keenly as he did that *men do not keep thy law.* We ought to, of course, if we are ever to understand why Jesus wept over the city of Jerusalem.

Verses 137–144 (*Tsadde*). Since God is good, so must also his judgments be. Because I have discovered this, the psalmist continues, *my zeal consumes me* at the way *my foes forget thy words.* This shows that his foes are neither foreigners nor heathen living in Palestine. They are people of the Covenant who had grown up to know God's *words* but who had now *forgotten* them.

We find the word *zeal* in the Second Commandment, where it is rendered by "jealous" in English (Exod. 20:5). It is a "Covenant" word. The prophet Hosea portrays the Covenant relationship between God and Israel as one between the divine Husband

and his erring wife. So passionate is his love for her (his *hesed*) that the Lord will not be cuckolded by any other god. In that way he is totally jealous for the integrity of the marriage. That jealousy is shown by his zeal to win his bride back home to live with him in marital love. When Jesus cleared the Temple of the money-changers we read that: "His disciples remembered that it was written (at Ps. 69:9), 'Zeal for thy house will consume me'" (John 2:17). The psalmist then has learned something of God's passion in his indictment of his forgetful Covenant people.

The phrase *thy promise is well tried* means that it has been through the furnace of affliction and come out pure metal. It had, for example, been smelted, refined, tested, and come through the "fire" of suffering in the Exile, for his people found (Isa. 43:2) that God was *with* them in the fires and in the floods. Thus it had been tested in the lives of many believing people, and it had been found to be pure, that is, to work. That kind of promise is surely "lovable". I am merely *thy servant, small and despised*, a nobody, a very ordinary person. To how many authors has the expression been attributed: "God must love ordinary people very much, for he has made so many of them!" Even an ordinary person, then, can grasp how *true* thy *Torah* is, in fact just as easily as (if not better than!) the clever and the well educated.

Verse 142 sounds in English highly condensed, but the ordinary Hebrew man would easily understand its thrust. "The loving concern for others which I have received from God will never cease, now that God has rescued me and put me in a right relationship with himself" is what it says (compare 1 Cor. 13:8); "for his *Torah* is trustworthy." This is a great statement of faith by one who, in the next verse, admits that his wonderful relationship to God does not exclude *trouble* and *anguish*. Yet, he is able to claim, *thy commandments are my delight*. They are equally real to me in trouble as when all goes well. *Thy testimonies* (e.g. the Ten Commandments) will remain normative as the standard rule of my life, in trouble as in peace all my days, *for ever*. Help me then to understand them and to make them part of myself, so that I too may live for ever.

We can learn from verse 142, however, how easy it became for the great faith this psalmist had to deteriorate in a century or so into the legalism that gripped his descendants in Jesus' day. By then the word *tsedaqah* had come to mean for some merely "righteous deeds", "good works", even "almsgiving". For example, already by 180 B.C. Ben Sira could write: "Water extinguishes a blazing fire; so almsgiving atones for sin" (Ecclesiasticus 3:30). Then, in Islam, this great word "righteousness", which is the same in Arabic as in Hebrew, can even mean the tax for the poor which the authorities have the right to extract from believers. In his Letter to the Romans, however, Paul gives the Christian answer—the psalmist's answer—to such views. It is interesting that a contemporary theologian, Daniel Maguire, has been so bold as to assert of *tsedaqah* that it can mean "creative imagination"—but, as I would add, in forming a loving approach to one's fellows.

THE SUM OF THY WORD IS TRUTH

Psalm 119:145-160

Qoph: Resh

145With my whole heart I cry; answer me, O Lord,
  I will keep thy statutes.
146I cry to thee; save me,
  that I may observe thy testimonies.
147I rise before dawn and cry for help;
  I hope in thy words.
148My eyes are awake before the watches of the night,
  that I may meditate upon thy promise.
149Hear my voice in thy steadfast love;
  O Lord, in thy justice preserve my life.
150They draw near who persecute me with evil purpose;
  they are far from thy law.
151But thou art near, O Lord,
  and all thy commandments are true.
152Long have I known from thy testimonies
  that thou hast founded them for ever.

¹⁵³Look on my affliction and deliver me,
    for I do not forget thy law.
¹⁵⁴Plead my cause and redeem me;
    give me life according to thy promise!
¹⁵⁵Salvation is far from the wicked,
    for they do not seek thy statutes.
¹⁵⁶Great is thy mercy, O Lord;
    give me life according to thy justice.
¹⁵⁷Many are my persecutors and my adversaries,
    but I do not swerve from thy testimonies.
¹⁵⁸I look at the faithless with disgust,
    because they do not keep thy commands.
¹⁵⁹Consider how I love thy precepts!
    Preserve my life according to thy steadfast love.
¹⁶⁰The sum of thy word is truth;
    and every one of thy righteous ordinances endures for ever.

Verses 145–152 (*Qoph*). The psalmist continues to beg from God that fullness of life, which is the keynote of his long poem, and which will give him the strength to keep God's commandments. We should note the order of his thought. It is not: "Help me to keep the commandments so that I may be saved", that we find here. Rather it is the reverse. It is: "Give me fullness of life that I may have the strength to keep thy commandments." And how passionately he desires to keep them! Yet it is only because he is utterly sure of God's *hesed,* God's steadfast love which always comes first. It is *that* which gives him life, God's justice and love, not his own endeavours to keep God's law.

Note at verse 150: *They who persecute me draw near; but thou art* already *near*—that is to say, God got there first! *And all thy commandments are true*, that is, immutable, totally reliable, and effective. God is nearer to him in his reliable presence than are those who draw near *with evil purpose*. I have known for *long* now, from my own experience, that *thou hast founded thy testimonies* to last *for ever*.

St. Paul wrote his Letter to the Romans several hundred years after this anonymous young psalmist wrote this long Psalm 119. The Romans were West Europeans. Psalm 119, on the other hand, was aimed at easterners, Semites, Jews, who had known for centuries what it had meant to live in fellowship with God in the Covenant. The Romans didn't even know the word "covenant". Thus they had to learn that the content of the ancient Covenant was *grace and truth* (see verses 105–112). But in Palestine a hymn could be written on the theme to be sung at public services of worship. The new converts of the Church in Rome knew nothing of the roots of the faith that went back to Abraham until Paul was the first to tell them (see Rom. chs. 9–11). There he had to explain the faith to a rootless people, and to do so, he had to go to great lengths to open their eyes to the *grace and truth* of God that the Jews had known about all down the centuries. Again, those Romans were western individualists. Consequently they supposed that when one converts to a new religion one makes only a personal commitment. Paul had to show his converts the folly of trying to earn salvation either by obeying the law or by some kind of personal commitment. He had to show that God's love and grace had always been there and had always come first. Again, he taught them to discover that in becoming Christians they did not choose their God, it was God who chose them; indeed, he had chosen them since the foundation of the world. Because of that Paul necessarily had to go on to expound what John 14:15 says: "If you love me, you will keep my commandments."

Verses 153–160 (*Resh*). The last verse of this strophe is one of the climaxes of the poem. The psalmist leads up to it by pointing out that one can say such a thing about God's Word only because that is actually the truth! It is true not just as a philosophical proposition taken in isolation, such as Pilate hoped to hear from Jesus' lips (John 18:38). It is true also in the afflictions one meets in living one's life; or, to put it in another way, God's Word is true not just as Truth in itself, but is true *for* this world as we know it with all its dangers and problems and wickedness.

It is in this real world, therefore, that he now says: *Plead my cause and redeem me.* You must do so, Lord, because you have *promised* to do so! The great prophet of the Exile—and there was trouble enough when Israel was in Babylon—had declared to his people: "I, I am the Lord, and besides me there is no saviour. I declared and saved and proclaimed (equal to 'promised')—and you are my witnesses" (Isa. 43:11–12). Salvation can happen only through a personal relationship with God, one that can be seen by others to have taken place, such as happened at the Red Sea. The wicked avoid that, in *not seeking thy statutes.* Yet "the evidences of thy justice and mother-love" (as the Hebrew text of verse 156 has it) are many, Lord. So *give me life,* even in face of all manner of evil. *I look at the faithless with disgust.* I deplore the fact that they sneer at God's steadfast love, a love which I have come to love in return.

So then, what all the commandments, testimonies and statutes, in a word *thy precepts,* add up to—their sum, their essence—is that ultimate reality, that ground of our very being, which we call truth. Thus the whole lifestyle of those whom you have put right with yourself, and have founded in truth, belongs "into" eternity.

THE CRY OF A LOST SHEEP

Psalm 119:161–176

Shin: Tau

161Princes persecute me without cause,
   but my heart stands in awe of thy words.
162I rejoice at thy word
   like one who finds great spoil.
163I hate and abhor falsehood,
   but I love thy law.
164Seven times a day I praise thee
   for thy righteous ordinances.
165Great peace have those who love thy law;
   nothing can make them stumble.
166I hope for thy salvation, O Lord,
   and I do thy commandments.
167My soul keeps thy testimonies;
   I love them exceedingly.
168I keep thy precepts and testimonies,
   for all my ways are before thee.

¹⁶⁹Let my cry come before thee, O Lord;
  give me understanding according to thy word!
¹⁷⁰Let my supplication come before thee;
  deliver me according to thy word.
¹⁷¹My lips will pour forth praise
  that thou dost teach me thy statutes.
¹⁷²My tongue will sing of thy word,
  for all thy commandments are right.
¹⁷³Let thy hand be ready to help me,
  for I have chosen thy precepts.
¹⁷⁴I long for thy salvation, O Lord,
  and thy law is my delight.
¹⁷⁵Let me live, that I may praise thee,
  and let thy ordinances help me.
¹⁷⁶I have gone astray like a lost sheep; seek thy servant,
  for I do not forget thy commandments.

Verses 161–168 (*Shin*). The psalmist has called himself an ordinary man (verse 141). He speaks now in this section for countless ordinary people who live under oppressive regimes or a faceless bureaucracy, when he declares: "I am much more *in awe of thy words*—the ultimate reality that is rooted in eternity—than of 'the authorities' who *persecute me without cause.*" Whereupon he paints a vivid picture in just a couple of words (compare Isa. 9:3). It is a picture of simple peasant people who normally live close to the soil, probably from hand to mouth, and who have been robbed of the produce of their fields by a retreating army, rejoicing when that army leaves behind it more booty than it can carry away. For the psalmist, the *Torah* is like that! Holy joy is clearly consistent with holy awe.

Falsehood, fraud, deceit—these things do not exist in themselves, they are all actions done by persons. So I hate and abhor such persons. *Torah* is not a mere thing either; it is the Word of a Person. That is why I love it. So *seven times a day* (see Lev. 26:18; Prov. 24:16), evidently the complete and perfect number, that is to say, while I work, and walk the street, eat and play, *I praise thee.* I possess *great peace* of heart and mind. This is because I know that God knows best. Of course he does, for God is truth!

And his presence is my reward (see verses 3–8). *All my ways* (the roads I travel as a pilgrim) *are before thee* (see verses 3–8 again). I would be disloyal if I were to *stumble* on them. Nothing I could ever do or say would ever scandalize you, Lord, for, in your steadfast love you know all already, and you love me still. What a grand end to this strophe!

Verses 169–176 (*Tau*). And so we reach the last strophe. It opens with the word *Let*, a word we use in public prayer. After he has repeated in other words what he has newly said at the end of the previous strophe, we learn finally of this very likeable young man's longing for a still deeper understanding of God's Word. He asks for that other gift of God, a still fuller understanding of him, and of knowing how to love others and thus not be selfish in his faith (verse 174). So we see how he concludes his long poem on a truly humble note.

His last thought, therefore, is that of himself he is nothing, so that he cannot live his life without God's love and care. *I have gone astray like a lost sheep*, he says, thus imputing to himself the very sin that earlier on in his *diwan* he had implied his enemies had fallen into. In consequence he is very much aware that he is under both the judgment and the mercy of God. This is something that Paul also says about himself. His very last line, therefore, *for I do not forget thy commandments*, makes it clear that he is not showing any *self*-righteousness in saying this, but rather is revealing his complete sincerity. God's *hand* has chosen me, forgiven me, redeemed me, he says, so in return *I have chosen* his *precepts*. This means that I can only be his totally obedient servant, and give myself completely for the redemption, not just of my fellow citizens, but also for that of the whole great cosmos that God so loves (compare John 3:16).

As we conclude our study of it, we can perhaps understand better why John Ruskin, the art critic and social reformer (1819–1900), declared that "Psalm 119 has now become of all the psalms the most precious to me in its overflowing and glorious passion of love for the law of God."

THE BOOK OF PILGRIM SONGS

Psalm 120:1–7

A Song of Ascents.

¹In my distress I cry to the Lord,
 that he may answer me:
²"Deliver me, O Lord,
 from lying lips,
 from a deceitful tongue."

³What shall be given to you?
 And what more shall be done to you,
 you deceitful tongue?
⁴A warrior's sharp arrows,
 with glowing coals of the broom tree!

⁵Woe is me, that I sojourn in Meshech,
 that I dwell among the tents of Kedar!
⁶Too long have I had my dwelling
 among those who hate peace.
⁷I am for peace;
 but when I speak,
 they are for war!

Psalm 119 has told us what it means to be a pilgrim of the Way. Psalms 120 to 134 (fifteen in all) are known as *Songs of Ascents*, that is, "songs for the way up" to Jerusalem. These songs were sung by members of the Covenant people who either wanted to make the "ascent" to Jerusalem, which lies about 2,300 feet above sea-level, in order to attend one of the Covenant festivals, or by pilgrims who were already on the way up or had even reached the great outer gate of the Temple (see Isa. 30:29).

This little collection of songs, therefore, is a book of devotions for those "on *aliyah*", as Ezra 2:1 calls it. The same word is used today for the ingathering, the "coming up", of Jews to the modern state of Israel. Psalm 134 consequently forms the climax to the worshipper's "ascent" towards God, for each of these psalms can be individualized and spiritualized and used as a guide by the believing pilgrim as he marches each day towards the heavenly city.

Peace and War. En route to his goal, the pilgrim in the first song feels he must *cry to the Lord* for help against nasty and *deceitful* people. He is a diffident person, this man or woman, the kind who feels keenly any objectionable behaviour. He is very aware that he is not worthy to come before God. His mind is in a jumble, a mixture of excitement, feelings of unworthiness, and distress. "What's to happen to you?"he asks his own tongue; or is he addressing the tongues of those who are laughing at him on the way? The Epistle of James reminds us what an unruly member the tongue is. Has the timid man turned and perhaps given a biting reply and then felt ashamed at having done so? Did he think of himself as a warrior for God *shooting arrows* out of his mouth at his tormentors, or showering his burning wrath upon their gibes? (The broom tree was used to produce very hot fires in the making of charcoal.) Or, more likely, was this not the way that his Gentile neighbours had behaved to him?

Where was *Meshech*? Traditionally it was very far off indeed, for it was the name of that area beyond the Black Sea known today as Georgia. Or was this word but a cover-up for Babylon, just as Babylon was a cover-up name for Rome in the book of Revelation? Then again, *Kedar* lay far away to the south-east of Jerusalem in quite the opposite direction. There the *tent*-dwellers lived a life of robbery and plunder, raiding the settled areas and dashing back into the safety of the desert. Probably, then, we are to understand the condensed language of this poetry to mean: "Whether I sojourn in . . . or among . . ." *too long have I had my dwelling among those who hate peace.*

How truly we can sympathize with the pilgrim, if we have read anything about life in a Siberian prison camp. *I am for peace*, he says. Yet I am all the time surrounded by hate. Jeru-*shalom* is my goal, the city of peace. In "Babylon" I have dared to say so, and have tried to explain what the word "peace" means. But they interrupt me with contempt, for *they are for war!* What he is saying is that the heathen hate *shalom*. They do not even know what *shalom* means, as Isa. 48:22 says. Their way of life is one round of violence, selfishness and greed. How then can I explain peace to them? Yet the point we are to notice is that the Hebrew text does not say *I am for peace* at all. Peace is not a thing that exists in its own right. Peace is something that must be lived out by a person, and exhibited in his lifestyle. What the psalmist actually says is *I am peace*. Would that the followers of all peace movements could say the same as they violently declare their views. This is what the NT says about Christ. There we learn that he is not a teacher or an example of what peace means; rather, as St. Paul says, "He *is* our peace" (Eph. 2:14).

THE LORD IS YOUR KEEPER

Psalm 121:1–8

A Song of Ascents.

¹I lift up my eyes to the hills.
 From whence does my help come?
²My help comes from the Lord,
 who made heaven and earth.

³He will not let your foot be moved,
 he who keeps you will not slumber.
⁴Behold, he who keeps Israel
 will neither slumber nor sleep.

⁵The Lord is your keeper;
 the Lord is your shade
 on your right hand.
⁶The sun shall not smite you by day,
 nor the moon by night.

⁷The Lord will keep you from all evil;
 he will keep your life.
⁸The Lord will keep
 your going out and your coming in
 from this time forth and for evermore.

If you went up to Jerusalem only three times a year to the great festivals you would not expect the service to be over in an hour. In fact, the old Israelites did not speak of a "service" on those occasions, they spoke of a "season" of worship—and a season lasted for several days. When God put the sun and moon in the sky, even before he created man, he did so, first, for "signs and seasons", and only second for "days and years" (Gen. 1:14). The most important "sign" he created, also before he made man, was the Sabbath (Exod. 31:13); while the "seasons" were those festivals that recorded God's saving love for his people, such as God's redemptive act at the Exodus, and so on. Thus, in Hebrew belief *God* regarded these festivals as being of "cosmic" significance if he created them before he created the earth and man. The mere cycle of the year, summer and winter, was secondary to them.

No wonder, then, that the group of pilgrims, singing this psalm as they made the ascent to the "City of God", were tremendously excited. It was in imitation of the OT people that the Reformed Churches (until recently) did not hold a mere "Communion Sunday", but a "Communion Season", with preparatory services, visitation by elders in people's homes and so on. Those old Israelites were going up, not just to sing hymns; they were going up to sacrifice, to share in an act that taught them that sacrifice is to be found in the very heart of God. So ought our approach to the supreme Sacrifice of Christ to be.

The pilgrims are met at the gate of the Temple by elders who welcome them in the Name of the Lord. They certainly do not go straight in to join the sacrifice of the beast they have brought up with them and which they have now handed over to the priests to look after. "Fools rush in where angels fear to tread" is a phrase those old worshippers knew all about. So, as a preliminary, one of the group is invited to say: *I lift up my eyes to the hills*, on one of which Jerusalem stood; then adds: Is this where *my help comes* from? For some of those hills were the "high places" on which idolatrous sacrifice was offered to Baal and the goddess Astarte. An elder then prompts the group to reply: No! *My help comes from the Lord*, who actually made these hills. So these simple country folk are being instructed in the mighty meaning of what they are shortly going to do.

There follows a little sermon. Perhaps the elder is one of the "cultic prophets" we have met before, and whom we call a minister today. The Lord, he says, looks after you as a shepherd looks after his sheep. Since the 23rd Psalm was many centuries old by now, everyone would know it, and so perhaps they recited it together. Baal, he says, falls asleep every hot summer and goes down below the ground (see 1 Kings 18:27). But the Lord does not sleep; he never lets you go, and never lets your foot slip. We can picture the old people in the group especially, having clambered up the donkey-path to the city, being glad to hear these words.

Another minister now comes out through the Temple gate and welcomes the pilgrims in. Yes, indeed, he says, *the Lord is your keeper.* He never rests, he never leaves his post, he never goes off duty, just as he never goes to sleep. Simple language such as simple folk could understand. It had been very hot as they toiled up the hill. God, says the preacher, is the true Gentleman. Today, in our western culture, the gentleman walks on the traffic side of the lady to protect her from all harm. The preacher says, God is the true Gentleman; he walks *with* all pilgrims on the hot sunny side of the road to keep them cool in his shade. More simple language. A modern writer speaks of "the crippled, hunchbacked moon that may have been primordial man's first symbol of evil." This is because its light could make you mad, as many ancients believed; and so we have the word "lunatic", built from the Latin name for the moon. Perhaps the pilgrims had the same superstition; they are told sharply to forget it.

A third speaker takes up the tale. He proclaims: *The Lord will keep you from all evil*, including the so-called power of a gibbous moon. For the Lord, as they have just been reminded, is the Creator of the whole cosmos (see verse 2 and compare Acts 2:20), and as such *will keep your life* (or, your whole being, body, soul and spirit), guarding you against all that can kill the soul. So you can forget your superstitious worries and fears, this minister is saying. He who gave you "journeying mercies" on your road here, and who *keeps your soul*, will surely never let any harm befall you in days to come.

The group has reached the gate, and they are welcomed by another minister or, since the words spoken are really a blessing, by a priest: *The Lord will keep your going in and out* (of "church") and he will do so from the present moment on, and on even into all eternity. Entering the holy place, the Temple, is a symbol of entering the Presence of the eternal God.

The fact that we today can continue to *live* on the edge of the volcano, in the midst of the secularism and the nihilism of the world, is a tremendous miracle in itself, one that we should thank God for. The Jew even today fixes a *mezuzah* on the portal of his house door, which he touches each time he goes in or comes out of his home (and to the Jew far more than to us his home is his temple). This is a small metal cylinder containing a piece of parchment on which are written the words of Deut. 6:4–9 and 11:13–21. As he touches it, he repeats the words of verse 8 of this Psalm.

In Scotland this psalm in its metrical version has always been a great favourite. It is sung to the tune "French", which links the Scottish Church with the Huguenots and the Continental Reformation. It is precious to Scotsmen for that reason; but as they sing it, are they also thinking of the Scottish mountains, the "hills of home"? If they are, are they right? It is *not* from the hills, whether of Palestine or Scotland, but from the Lord that help comes.

THE PEACE OF JERUSALEM

Psalm 122:1–9

A Song of Ascents. Of David.

[1] I was glad when they said to me,
   "Let us go to the house of the Lord!"
[2] Our feet have been standing
   within your gates, O Jerusalem!

[3] Jerusalem, built as a city
   which is bound firmly together,
[4] to which the tribes go up,
   the tribes of the Lord,

as was decreed for Israel,
  to give thanks to the name of the Lord.
⁵There thrones for judgment were set,
  the thrones of the house of David.

⁶Pray for the peace of Jerusalem!
  "May they prosper who love you!
⁷Peace be within your walls,
  and security within your towers!"
⁸For my brethren and companions' sake
  I will say, "Peace be within you!"
⁹For the sake of the house of the Lord our God,
  I will seek your good.

Psalm 120 spoke of a man who was longing for the "peace" of Jerusalem, Jeru-*shalom*. Here we meet with pilgrims who have actually arrived at that city with the meaning of its name fully in mind.

"*I was glad* among those who said", runs the Hebrew. The English inclines us to think that the psalmist showed a selfish pleasure. But these are a group of people who fit into Jesus' saying, "Where two or three are gathered together in my name, there am I in the midst of them." They had come to a common decision to make the *aliyah*. They had said to each other, *Let us go to the house of the Lord.* Now they have arrived. They look round them in excited astonishment: *Our feet,* they say, *have* actually *been standing within your gates, O Jerusalem*! What a memory they will have to take back home with them! What a privilege is theirs to carry all their sins and griefs to the place of sacrifice, the footstool of the Living God, Maker of heaven and earth. Their whole lives have now found meaning and purpose as they join in the festal processions that precede the sacrifice, and follow behind the priests and Levites as they shout and dance "before the Lord" on the way up to the altar of sacrifice.

The ritual of the Temple worship which followed the "Book of Church Order" which we call Leviticus does not apply to us today. Yet what it does reveal to us is that our faith must not be just a "spiritual" thing. Our human minds need some form of physical movement, action, in the shape perhaps of marching, music, poetry, in order to clothe the "spiritual" approach to God that we hope to make. And, of course, the basic reality of sacrifice, though now not of bulls and goats, is not a spiritual one at all, but is a very physical one. The sacrifice of Christ on the Cross is something that actually happened as an event in history. So when Jesus said: "This *do*, in remembrance of me", he was summoning us to *do* something in the realm of the physical.

But before he joins in the worship, our spokesman looks round him. What a marvellously beautiful city this is, "compact in itself". But more, its unity symbolizes for him the unity of "the Church". Israel might be composed of twelve tribes, but representatives of all twelve went up together to worship there as one, *as was decreed for Israel*. So too the Church of the New Covenant came to be composed of the "children" of the extended twelve tribes, symbolized by the twelve Apostles. To them Jesus said, "That all may be one", but a oneness that was the outcome of the *shalom* which I leave you (John 14:27). This, then, is what our group marvels at, a peace which men do not build, but one that has its source in God.

Divine, and therefore perfect justice, is an aspect of all-comprehensive *shalom*. And it was to be found in Jeru-*shalom*! So what we see is that the whole family finds its needs met in Jerusalem. The "season" of the festival covered: (1) a sitting of the court of law; (2) a market for the sale of one's local produce and for buying new stock for the farm; (3) for the children there was "all the fun of the fair"; and (4) there was the act of sacrificial worship. This four-square exhibition of "peace" had found its source and power in the peace of God.

The pilgrims are now attracted to the call of a priest who bids them *pray for the peace of Jerusalem*. How else could there be that four-square peace to distinguish Jerusalem from any other eastern city with its quarrels and feuds, its greed and its lust? So they all, with one voice, by way of greetings to each other, reply: "May they prosper (a Hebrew word that sounds as a pun on *shalom*) who love you"; or, as we might express it simply: "Good luck to you, my friend, lover of this city!" Then they turn and look again at its fine architecture: "Peace, *shalom*, be within your walls," they repeat, "and *security*" (*shalwah*, another pun on *shalom*) "within your towers."

The lesson of this old liturgical action is that we dare not be selfish in our prayers. We are to remember that what we are doing will be for the eternal good of *our brethren and companions* if Jerusalem prospers, for only then will our friends experience that fullness of life that God plans should be found within its walls. St. Paul spoke of a local congregation as being composed of ordinary people who yet had a wonderful citizenship. For a local congregation, a local "Zion", could be seen by God as "a colony of heaven" (Phil. 3:20 in Moffatt's translation).

Finally, as we have noted before, "good" can mean "good for". So our poet adds this sentence for the pilgrims to say together: *I will seek* what is *good* for you, O city of peace, *for the sake of the house of the Lord our God*. This house, this Church of God, is all of the following together: (1) It is a particular place on earth; (2) it is a fellowship of people; (3) it is a fellowship of action as decreed by God; (4) it is the abode of justice expressed in love and loyalty; (5) it is the sum of the families of a given area; (6) it stands at any one moment for the whole people of God; (7) it is the place of the Presence of God. Therefore the peace that we must pray for must be creative (for peace is something we create—see Matt. 5:9) of all that is good for our four-square human life, that is (1) our church life, (2) our political life, (3) our business life, and (4) our family life; for only in and through all these do we discover our own private and personal life and faith.

This great psalm is sung in its metrical version at the end of the General Assembly of the Church of Scotland, as the "fathers and brethren" prepare to leave Edinburgh for their parishes throughout the land. A more fitting note of parting could hardly be struck.

KYRIE ELEISON

Psalm 123:1–4

A Song of Ascents.

¹To thee I lift up my eyes,
    O thou who art enthroned in the heavens!

²Behold, as the eyes of servants
    look to the hand of their master,
  as the eyes of a maid
    to the hand of her mistress,
  so our eyes look to the Lord our God,
    till he have mercy upon us.

³Have mercy upon us, O Lord, have mercy upon us,
    for we have had more than enough of contempt.
⁴Too long our soul has been sated
    with the scorn of those who are at ease,
    the contempt of the proud.

As he ascends the great staircase to the outer gate of the Temple, the pilgrim keeps looking upwards. His eyes look beyond the Temple gates to the heavenly throne, and so in faith and in sanctified imagination, through the scudding clouds above, he looks *to the Lord*. Thus he experiences what Isaiah went through when he "saw the Lord sitting upon a throne high and lifted up" (Isa. 6:1).

The OT is not an esoteric book, to be understood only by an inner group of holy people. It reveals reality through ordinary human life. The poet speaks of the lady of the house who organizes the work of her servants out on the fields, in the garden, in the farm-workshop, in the kitchen—altogether quite a domain. The workers in all these areas stand in awe of her and of her husband. So too, in the worship (which means service, workship) of the Temple, in which he is about to join. Worship is to be conducted in reverential awe. The master of the house could, of course, find fault with his men, and so the workers keep their eye on him. But one can also sense the utter relief of the worker if he is expecting a rebuke, when his master instead speaks kindly, understandingly, and forgivingly to him.

This, then, is where a kind of *Kyrie Eleison* fits in. In verse 3 we hear it spoken at the end of a veritable crescendo, in a rising tide of passion, *Lord, have mercy*. To experience *contempt* is to experience the worst kind of human behaviour, for then you are treated, not as a person, nor even as a servant or worker, but as a dog that scours the city garbage heap. We watch the pilgrim bringing up to Jerusalem in his heart all the bitterness and degradation he has suffered under the Babylonians. Prisoners of war can be emotionally distraught and embittered for years after their release. One aspect of worship is just this release that God gives us from the exacerbating and cruel effects of such treatment. Accordingly, what our pilgrim hopes and longs for in the worship he will soon participate in is that the God of Jeru-*shalom* will grant him what he now wants more than anything else—*peace* of heart.

I WILL NEVER LEAVE YOU OR FORSAKE YOU

Psalm 124:1–8

A Song of Ascents. Of David.

¹If it had not been the Lord who was on our side,
    let Israel now say—
²if it had not been the Lord who was on our side,
    when men rose up against us,
³then they would have swallowed us up alive,
    when their anger was kindled against us;
⁴then the flood would have swept us away,
    the torrent would have gone over us;
⁵then over us would have gone
    the raging waters.

⁶Blessed be the Lord,
    who has not given us
    as prey to their teeth!
⁷We have escaped as a bird
    from the snare of the fowlers;
 the snare is broken,
    and we have escaped!

⁸Our help is in the name of the Lord,
    who made heaven and earth.

In this psalm we meet with praise of God made, not as we might think it should be, but in a series of exclamations. There is no introduction whatsoever. We are plunged into envisaging a group of pilgrims, newly back home from their forced labour (as we see the Exile is called at Isa. 40:2 RSV *ftn*) in Babylon, their hearts bursting with emotion, as they approach the Holy City. Their excited cry is one of gratitude to God that he is what he is, their loving Saviour. "Had *the Lord not been* for us", as the idiom here has it. It is in these words, then, that they answer the question of the elder who has come out to meet them and welcome them in, and whose task it is to ask the question, "Why are you here?" "We are here," is the answer, "because of the Lord." It was *men who rose up against us*, and they *would have swallowed us up alive*. Note that these good folk do not blame God for war and human wickedness, cruelty and slavery. Rather, and now they shout it in joy, God is he who takes sides, who comes down into the shoes of the weak and the poor and the suffering masses of the world who live in danger and constant degradation.

Jer. 51:34 speaks of Nebuchadnezzar the king of Babylon swallowing "me" (Israel) like a monster, and then of how later he vomited "me" out again, *alive* (see verse 3). This passage gives us at least one clue for understanding the Jonah story. Isa. 43:2 is another. It was uttered during the Exile. "When you pass through the waters (*the flood*; see verse 4) I will be with you." The "waters" are of course more than just the Exile that the people had so newly suffered, terrible as it had been. In Gen. 1:2 the "waters" represent all the powers of cosmic evil (see *The Daily Study Bible*, Genesis, Vol. 1, p. 33). So God is *in* the flood; God is *in* the belly of the monster; God is *in* the horrors of the Exile along *with* his people. Moreover, he is there as Saviour and Redeemer, as One who saves, not from "up on high", but from within the situation, even as he shares its pain and contempt along with us.

It is all the Lord's doing, the pilgrims cry in another exclamation of faith. *The snare was broken, and we? yes, we escaped!* (as the Hebrew is literally). What an excited outburst this is! So in a wild mixture of expressions the pilgrims simply shout their joy and gratitude to God. For he has redeemed them from being a *prey to their teeth* and (as the Scottish metrical version adds) to their bloody cruelty.

God then has done it all. And since that is what God is like, he will continue to act like that, again, and again, and again.

It has long been the custom in Scotland to sing this psalm in its metrical version on occasions when God has reversed some crisis in national or local history. Since *God* had done it, as people have now been shown, then God the Creator must also be God the Recreator, recreating, renewing, resurrecting again and again. As John Calvin the Reformer put it: "The story of the Church is the story of many resurrections." No wonder, then, that the psalm ends with these great words of affirmation:

> *Our help is in the name of the Lord,*
> *who made heaven and earth.*

It may be that in our private devotions we find it hard to know how to begin. This psalm can show us that we can always begin by gratefully acknowledging what God has *done*. In our personal case what God has done is to resurrect us from the grip of evil and recreate us in the likeness of Christ. F. D. Maurice and B. F. Westcott, Anglican divines of the nineteenth century, both used to affirm that theology should not start from man's fall and his sinfulness, but from his creation in God's likeness and image. Richard Hooker also laid great emphasis on the doctrine of creation. We would be justified then in including in our private prayers our own affirmation: *"My help is . . . who made . . . and remade me."*

SURE AND STEADFAST

Psalm 125:1–5

A Song of Ascents.

¹Those who trust in the Lord are like Mount Zion,
  which cannot be moved, but abides for ever.
²As the mountains are round about Jerusalem,
  so the Lord is round about his people,
  from this time forth and for evermore.

³For the sceptre of wickedness shall not rest
   upon the land allotted to the righteous,
 lest the righteous put forth
   their hands to do wrong.
⁴Do good, O Lord, to those who are good,
   and to those who are upright in their hearts!
⁵But those who turn aside upon their crooked ways
   the Lord will lead away with evildoers!
   Peace be in Israel!

How solid Mount Zion must have looked to ascending pilgrims, for it was an outcrop of the basic rock. David of old had even called God "my Rock" and "my Fortress" just from looking at it (Ps. 18:2; 2 Sam. 22:2). What he meant was that those who *trust in the Lord* possess an impregnable faith (see also Ps. 46:5). The phrase *abides for ever* does not, however, mean "till the end of the world". That would be a "Greek" philosophical notion. It means that Mount Zion has an anchor within the veil, in that it belongs in eternity.

Next, we are given two symbols to strengthen our human faith.

1. The Hebrew runs: *Jerusalem? The mountains surround her. The Lord? He surrounds his people;* or, as Zech. 2:5 (a contemporary passage) expresses the same symbol: "I will be to her a wall of fire round about, says the Lord, and I will be the glory within her." And we are to remember that, in Zechariah's day, there was nothing to see, no rebuilt Temple, no fortifications as yet, nothing but fallen masonry and bare rock!

2. I don't believe, the poet goes on with his second symbolic utterance, that God will allow *the sceptre of wickedness*, that is, the dominion of evil, to remain *upon the land* that God long ago *allotted to the righteous.* God's "righteous ones", however, do not know just what the right course of action should be.

What the poet realizes is that there are situations in our human life where there is no ideal way forward. That is the thesis of Hamlet's famous soliloquy: "To be or not to be, that is the question". Anything we poor mortals try to do is bound to be wrong, or at least only a second best, for we live in an evil situation. We do not know what to do *first,* for example, to cure inflation, or *first*, to rid ourselves of the threat of nuclear war. This situation is what Jesus calls "the unrighteous mammon" (Luke 16:9). Even the believer knows that he is trapped in the logic of life as it is; yet he retains his faith. How much worse it is for the non-believer who can face only despair and total pessimism. The psalmist, however, assures us that if we accept the fact that we are in a trap from which there is no exit, then we can trust God absolutely to go forward where we cannot see, and establish his kingdom on earth, "even as it is in heaven". That is why he can conclude his psalm with the words: *Peace be* "upon" *Israel*; for he is asking God for that peace which comes, not from man, but down, "upon" God's people, from above, so to speak, that is, from God himself. (See Gal. 6:16)

OUR MOUTH WAS FILLED WITH LAUGHTER

Psalm 126:1–6

A Song of Ascents.

¹When the Lord restored the fortunes of Zion,
  we were like those who dream.
²Then our mouth was filled with laughter,
  and our tongue with shouts of joy;
 then they said among the nations,
  "The Lord has done great things for them."
³The Lord has done great things for us;
  we are glad.

⁴Restore our fortunes, O Lord,
  like the watercourses in the Negeb!
⁵May those who sow in tears
  reap with shouts of joy!
⁶He that goes forth weeping,
  bearing the seed for sowing,
 shall come home with shouts of joy,
  bringing his sheaves with him.

We today hold memorial services on anniversaries of important occasions. Here the believing community are remembering with joy and gratitude that God, in the year 538 B.C. (the year when

King Cyrus conquered Babylon and set the exiles free) had, through Cyrus' victory, *restored the fortunes of Zion*, or, perhaps better, "rehabilitated" his people. This event was by now a number of years back.

But not too long ago for them to recall the delirious joy they had experienced then. It had all been such a miracle. Who, even a week before the event, could have expected that the mighty Babylonian Empire would collapse overnight, or that Cyrus the Persian could have captured its capital city "without firing a shot", as actually happened. (In the same way, why could God not save his world from the threat of nuclear war "without firing a shot"?) So it had all been like a *dream*; we simply shouted for joy. And then that infectious phrase the world has never forgotten: *our mouth was filled with laughter*. We should realize that very few people could still have been living who had seen Jerusalem in its former glory, for fifty years and more had passed. But then Jerusalem was more than a city—it was an idea, it was a promise, it was the symbol of a Presence. Accordingly, the younger generation of the exiles even in far away Babylonia, had been instructed in all the way that God had led his people from the days of Abraham right till the comimg of Cyrus, thus fulfilling the command of God himself in Deut. 6:7; 11:19. That is why we today lay the duty of education in the faith upon parents at the time when they present their child for baptism.

The heathen noticed! Perhaps not in reality, of course. But the Israelites were sure they must have seen what God had done; and here they even put the words of praise to Israel's God into their mouths! This belief is on a par with Second-Isaiah's belief that pagan King Cyrus could be hailed as God's Messiah, though he did not realize it (Isa. 45:4). The point is that the prophecies of that great theologian had now actually been fulfilled before their very eyes, and they had in reality arrived back home to their beloved city of Jerusalem. It is a pity that the RSV has missed the point when it translates what the heathen are saying by, *The Lord has done great things for them*, when the Hebrew has, not "for" them, but "along with" them. As we saw in Psalm 124, God had been *with* his people when they were swallowed up by the monster of Babylon. It was from within that situation that God had set his people free. One whole line of verse records their joy, in the simple phrase, *We are glad*!

At verse 4 we reach the anniversary service, so to speak. God's people are still in trouble. They are still trying to rebuild their lives in the ruins of the ancient city. So on this anniversary of the events of 538 B.C. we hear them cry: "O Lord, lead back our captive ones". It is clear that not by any means all Israelites had returned from Babylon. Those referred to had probably lost the vision; they had prospered financially in that big city, and now preferred it to sharing the joy of reconstruction with those who were "roughing it" in Zion.

Our group here prays for prosperity to happen yet. There had evidently been some disastrous set-back in their community life. Perhaps they needed rain, as we learn from Haggai 1:11 was the case around 520 B.C. Perhaps they now hoped to welcome "home" some stragglers who had changed their minds in Babylon, and were now wending their way to Jerusalem. But whatever the situation was, the psalmist is insisting that God is the God who brings good out of evil, so that the good becomes doubly good after all. God is the God of hope, for the whole future lies in his hands, and at any time he can resurrect what is past and can give renewal and new life to his faithful people (cf. John 12:24–25; 16:20; 1 Cor. 15:36–38).

We can put the thesis of this psalm into one sentence that speaks home to us today: "The Lord has done great things *with me*; I am glad." And we can recall that at the very end of the Bible we have the reassuring cry: "Behold, I make all things new" (Rev. 21:5).

BUILDING A FAMILY

Psalm 127:1–5

A Song of Ascents. Of Solomon.

[1]Unless the Lord builds the house,
those who build it labour in vain.

Unless the Lord watches over the city,
the watchman stays awake in vain.
²It is in vain that you rise up early and go late to rest,
eating the bread of anxious toil;
for he gives to his beloved sleep.

³Lo, sons are a heritage from the Lord,
the fruit of the womb a reward.
⁴Like arrows in the hand of a warrior
are the sons of one's youth.
⁵Happy is the man who has
his quiver full of them!
He shall not be put to shame
when he speaks with his enemies in the gate.

Though probably written only after the returnees had got down to rebuilding their city and the Temple about 520 B.C. (the date we get from Haggai 1), this psalm bears the heading *Of Solomon,* and he flourished about 950 B.C.! But as we saw in the Introduction to Vol I, "of" can also mean "à la", in the French sense of "in the style of". Nevertheless, why Solomon? (1) One reason is that in verse 2 we find the words "his beloved". In Hebrew that sounds very like the name given to Solomon, viz. *Jedidiah* (2 Sam. 12:25). (2) Again, verse 2 speaks of a man having many children. Solomon certainly did, because he had so many wives! (3) But the most likely reason is that the psalm is written in the style of the Wisdom literature, of which Solomon was the "patron saint" (see the heading to the book of Proverbs).

The writer, then, intends to give some wise advice to pilgrims to take up to Jerusalem with them. To begin with, verse 1 has been quoted in its Latin form as a proverb all down the centuries: *Nisi Dominus frustra.* It is the motto of the city of Edinburgh (has any city a better?), and we find it inscribed on many a foundation stone of a church building.

First, then, there is the word "house". Here of course it means the House of the Lord, the Temple now being rebuilt. Second, there is the city, the City of God, Jerusalem. But it comes only second. Haggai too had tried to get his dispirited fellow-citizens to get their priorities right (see ch. 1, verses 2 ff.). Otherwise they would build *in vain.*

At this point, however, we must look at the very important pun which the writer deliberately introduces, but which cannot be rendered in English. It is that the word "builders" uses the same letters as the word for "sons". What the writer is getting at through this pun rests upon God's words to David through Nathan the prophet in 2 Sam. 7:5, 11–12, 29. There God promises to *build a house* for David. But at once we discover that what is meant is not a house of bricks and mortar, but of children.

At verse 2 we notice that the writer advises the builders not to worry, certainly not to become "workaholics—to the glory of God!" God has intended that man should work by day and *sleep* peacefully by night. Since sleep is God's kindly gift to all mankind, how much more is it a mark of his steadfast love, his *hesed, to his beloved,* his own Covenant people. We may recall the old German proverb: "God bestows his gifts during the night."

Then, at verse 3, we suddenly meet with the word "sons". Before it is an emphatic "Lo", meaning, Look, Listen, Think— have you ever asked yourself where your children came from? The answer, of course is, *from the Lord.* We do not create our children, even their mother's womb does not create them, as Adam and Eve discovered in surprise at the birth of their first child (Gen. 4:1). With this in mind let us go back to verse 1.

Unless the Lord builds the house—with children, then it is no house at all. Without the Lord we are not able to produce a family, we only beget children, a group of individuals perhaps quarrelling and querulous and rebellious. But let it be seen that children are *the heritage of the Lord,* that they are actually what we *inherit* from the Lord! When a man within the Covenant people begets many children, they are *like arrows in the hand of a warrior.* Along with his wife and children he is able to share with God the Warrior in his battle against the powers of evil.

Happy is the man . . . (verse 5). The creation of the happy family is God's will for mankind. Solomon built the first Temple and greatly increased the size and magnificence of the city of

Jerusalem. Now that the second one was going up before the eyes of the people back from Exile, some "enemies" had turned up to argue with those good folk *"in the gate"*, that is, where the "Justice of the Peace" sat and dispensed justice daily. We have such enemies with us today. They are those who have rejected the significance of Christian marriage, who regard sex as merely a source of individual pleasure, and children as little nuisances to be got rid of as soon as possible to a day-care centre or nursery. At Zech. 8:5, however, we read a passage that was written just at the time of the composition of this psalm. It runs: "The streets of the city shall be full of boys and girls playing"—and that vision was meant to be one aspect of the renewed community, living together in *shalom.* Such a community would never *be put to shame*.

In verse 1, again, we have the phrase, to build *in vain*. This is a word that expresses the very opposite of *shalom,* and it actually sounds like it *(shau)*; so its alliteration is meant to draw our attention to the contrast. A family is built in vain if it contains only tension, fear, jealousy, greed and selfishness. But those who build a family *with the Lord* do so trusting their children, so that all can sleep calmly at night, not *eating the bread of anxious toil.* That family truly knows the meaning of "peace".

The real lesson of this clever little psalm is that the health of both Church and community depends in the final analysis on the family life practised within them.

THE HAPPY FAMILY

Psalm 128:1–6

A Song of Ascents.

¹Blessed is every one who fears the Lord,
    who walks in his ways!
²You shall eat the fruit of the labour of your hands;
    you shall be happy, and it shall be well with you.

³Your wife will be like a fruitful vine
    within your house;

your children will be like olive shoots
  around your table.
⁴Lo, thus shall the man be blessed
  who fears the Lord.

⁵The Lord bless you from Zion!
  May you see the prosperity of Jerusalem
  all the days of your life!
⁶May you see your children's children!
  Peace be upon Israel!

The message of this psalm follows straight from that of Ps. 127. It
begins with the language of the great Wisdom Psalm 119 and of
Jesus' Beatitudes, viz. *Blessed. He who fears the Lord* is one who
is totally committed in obedience to God and loyal to his Covenant. He is blessed because he has no other loyalties or worries or
desires, for these would distract him from knowing peace of
mind. He has been liberated, set free from all contending pres-
sures and so is now able to obey and to *walk in his ways*. For, as
John Donne has said, no man is an island, entire of itself. In OT
thinking particularly he is the father of a family, and so must
walk, not as a mere individual, but as one with a responsibility
towards other human beings.

One aspect of his blessedness is finding satisfaction in his
work—but he must of course really work and not be lazy! Another aspect is the pleasure he finds in feeding and sustaining his
wife and family. But we note that the psalm has in verse 2 left the
word "he" and gone over to the word "you", in fact "thou",
singular; for it is addressing each separate individual father of any
family, anywhere!

Your wife. Throughout the Bible the *Vine* is employed as a
symbol of fruitfulness. One vine plant can produce an enormous
number of tendrils, each of which can also provide a bunch of
dozens of grapes. There are vines that have been trained along
fences reaching for hundreds of yards. God's ideal, then, is that
this man's wife should be supremely happy in mothering lots of
children. A famous mediaeval Rabbi wrote: "I never call my wife
'my wife'; I call her 'my home', she who makes a home for my
children."

Your children. Olive shoots were regarded as tender growths to be carefully nurtured. They are both pretty to look at and they are very productive. And so we are given a picture of a loving and caring family.

Around your table is the symbol not only of love and care, but also of family fellowship. We see each of the children happily shouting the other down at supper time in the evening, as each retails his day's experiences. The happy family is the blessed family, the holy family. We recall that the NT begins by speaking of *the* Holy Family. The OT likewise, we should note. In Gen. 1 we read that God created Adam, humanity, in his image and likeness; but he had no "helpmeet", and in Gen. 2 God created Eve. God has placed mankind in families. We can even, daringly (as in the Christian doctrine of the Trinity), speak of God as a family within himself. Even in the OT, in Job 38:7, we hear God asking Job the question, "Where were you when I laid the foundation of the earth ... When the morning stars sang together, and all the sons of God shouted for joy?" Surely "shouting for joy" is the reverse of the selfishness, sourness, greed and sullenness characteristic of the unbelieving human family. Yet it is the hallmark of any "family of God", of any "holy family". It is such blessed joy that is part and parcel of what it is to *fear the Lord* (verse 4).

Graham Greene, the novelist, felt keenly the sacredness of the family on one occasion during the blitz on London. He wrote:

> A person's home had a kind of innocency. When a house-front gave way before an explosion and showed the iron bed, the chairs, the hideous picture and the chamber-pot, you had a sense of rape: intrusion into a stranger's home was an act of lust.

Yet verse 4 can mean more than appears in the RSV rendering. The latter does not translate the curious little word *ken*. Thus the line may possibly be rendered: "The Reliable One will bless him as a reliable man, since he fears the Lord." Moreover, the word used for "man" describes a man of strength either of body or of character in whatever position he holds in the world.

Verse 3*a* ends with the word "house"; then verse 3*b* begins with the word "children". We saw in Ps. 127 that to have children means to build a house. This house of yours, then, he says, is part of the Covenant family of God's people. The priest is entitled to say to you: *The Lord bless you from Zion!* Today, of course, we use these words, which belong in the Aaronic blessing (Num. 6:24–26) at the baptism of a child into the family of God. The writer then adds: "May you *see* into the meaning of why Jerusalem is 'good for' God's purposes *all the days of your life!*" That is admittedly a paraphrase of the Hebrew. But what is meant is that the family must not be an end in itself. We should not live only for our family. All families of believers should gladly share in God's plan for the redemption of the world. *Prosperity* does not refer to being well-off in the material sense. It means, as we might say today, "sharing in the mission of the Church to the world, and never giving up!" How different such a description of the family is compared with that held in our promiscuous and lost society today!

Finally the poet says: *May you see your children's children.* While of course this means: "May you live long enough to be a grandfather", it means more. T. S. Eliot has written: "When I speak of the family I have in mind a bond which embraces the living, a piety toward the dead, and a solicitude for the unborn, however remote." So it can mean for us: "Remember that John Donne would have us be joined as peninsulas to a continental mass that has its roots in heaven, and not remain mere separate islands." Or, we could say, "As you look at your baby of this generation, remember that the Aaronic blessing sung at his baptism has 'eschatological significance'; for it is meant to be effective to the third and the fourth (and all subsequent) generations."

This psalm is included in the Songs of Ascents. By this we can infer that whole families went up together to worship God in Zion. When the father laid his hand on the head of the sacrificial animal, his family stood behind him, knowing that he was representing them all as he identified himself with the animal in its death, and in its "rising" again in smoke to God. For us today this family solidarity has much meaning. (1) It speaks to us of God's blessing upon the family pew. (2) It speaks to us of the vital part in the family that father has to play (we too often leave the bringing up of the children to mother) as he seeks to obey God in teaching his children the meaning of life. (3) It speaks to us of the fact that eating together *around your table* becomes both the sign and the symbol of the perfection of loving and joyous fellowship that is the will of God, and which indeed reflects the family nature of God himself as Holy Trinity.

THE UPS AND DOWNS OF LIFE

Psalm 129:1–8

A Song of Ascents.

¹"Sorely have they afflicted me from my youth,"
   let Israel now say—
²"Sorely have they afflicted me from my youth,
   yet they have not prevailed against me.
³The ploughers ploughed upon my back;
   they made long their furrows."
⁴The Lord is righteous;
   he has cut the cords of the wicked.
⁵May all who hate Zion
   be put to shame and turned backward!
⁶Let them be like the grass on the housetops,
   which withers before it grows up,
⁷with which the reaper does not fill his hand
   or the binder of sheaves his bosom,
⁸while those who pass by do not say,
   "The blessing of the Lord be upon you!
   We bless you in the name of the Lord!"

It is all Israel, the people of God, who speak in this psalm with one voice, the one personality of God's son (Exod. 4:22). We can compare this with our modern way of inviting the figures of John Bull, or La Belle France, or Uncle Sam to represent a whole nation. So Israel declares:

I was born in Babylon, a second generation exile, and there I suffered terribly. But *they* did not get me down. They used me as a forced labourer. I had to work on the land. There they exploited me till I was exhausted. *The ploughers ploughed upon my back; they made long their furrows.* Perhaps it is only an easterner who could describe his aching muscles in such forceful language!

But, *the Lord is righteous: he has cut the cords of the wicked*, those cruel Babylonians. Consequently, I, Israel have not been exterminated after all. I recall that God brought me out of captivity in Egypt centuries ago in the days of Moses. Now he has done the same again. He *put* the Egyptian Pharaoh *to shame*; now he has *turned backward* the power of the king of Babylonia. May it always be so, that an oppressor should be as short-lived as weeds growing on a flat roof which no reaper would think of cutting down to make into flour for bread.

What had Israel felt like, we ask ourselves, as we read this psalm, when her former masters had to stand by and watch her as she marched forth, men, women and children together, with the express permission of King Cyrus to do so? What did those Babylonians feel at that moment—did they feel they were indeed *haters of Zion*?

I received, says Israel, no friendly greetings or goodbyes when I marched forth, words such as *Grüss Gott* or *The Lord bless you*. But all that suffering and humiliation is now a thing of the past, and just a horrid memory. Now at last I am home, and here I am ascending the hill of the Lord. I can look forward to the priest in Jerusalem welcoming me with God's greeting: *We bless you in the name of the Lord.*

DE PROFUNDIS (i)

Psalm 130:1–8

A Song of Ascents.

[1]Out of the depths I cry to thee, O Lord!
[2] Lord, hear my voice!
 Let thy ears be attentive
  to the voice of my supplications!

[3]If thou, O Lord, shouldst mark iniquities,
  Lord, who could stand?

4But there is forgiveness with thee,
that thou mayest be feared.

5I wait for the Lord, my soul waits,
and in his word I hope;
6My soul waits for the Lord
more than watchmen for the morning,
more than watchmen for the morning.

7O Israel, hope in the Lord!
For with the Lord there is steadfast love,
and with him is plenteous redemption.
8And he will redeem Israel
from all his iniquities.

The heading we have above for this psalm is the well-known quotation in Latin of the first four words of verse 1. What *depths* is the psalmist referring to here, however? Fortunately he leaves the question open. So open is it that Martin Luther could say that Paul might have written this psalm. Actually, from the Middle Ages onward, it was used as a penitential psalm within the Church's liturgy.

The real enemy of course is one's own self, and the "depths" are the depths of the self-centred subconscious. Popularly speaking, humanity has always thought in terms of up and down, of heaven as being "up there", and of hell as being "down there". Because our human personality is a little copy of the universe as a whole, a microcosm of the macrocosm, we have always tended to use similar language about our own emotions. Thus it is that one day we are "up in the clouds" while next day we are "down in the depths". In this psalm, then, we are with the poet in the *depths* from which he cries to his God who seems not to hear *the voice of my supplications*. He feels he is too deep down in his own misery for his voice ever to reach "up" to God.

It is worth emphasizing that the psalm is a song for "the way up", for the ascent to God. The geographical climb up to Jerusalem that the pilgrim must make is thus used to help interpret the pilgrim's spiritual as well as his physical approach to God. This approach, it seems, will have to develop into a long ascent indeed. For he is "in hell", he is in the depths, the primal chaos of "the waters under the earth" (of the Second Commandment); he is experiencing the terrible nature of what human life is all about in this extraordinary world. Thus any hope for his rescue can lie only in the unmerited grace of God, without which existence before God, the world being what it is, is impossible. This then is no superficial cry, such as is too often uttered by people of little faith when they suddenly face the reality of death, a cry such as, "O God, if you will only get me out of this mess, I will honour you all the rest of my life." No, it is a cry out of the ultimate horror that can attack the mind even of the most sane person who has faced up to the ultimate mystery of life.

It is the cry, "I have sinned. It was my own fault. It was my very own fault. I am my own worst enemy." Our reaction today, on reading this cry, is, "Yes, indeed. I have been there too. I know what it means to wallow in my own particular hell. I know what this psalmist means." In a nutshell he is describing that awful awareness that there is nothing, just nothing, I can do to put back the clock and so bypass those unforgivable acts of mine which haunt me now and ruin my whole life.

No one describes such hell better than Shakespeare. His Lady Macbeth looks at her murderer's hands in horror: "Out, damned spot! out, I say! . . . Hell is murky . . . Here's the smell of the blood still: all the perfumes of Arabia will not sweeten this little hand." What depths of insight this psalmist shows, then, when he asks the question, *If thou, O Lord, shouldst mark iniquities, Lord, who could stand?* He has to learn—and he does—that God does not "mark" iniquities at all *as* iniquities, he "marks" them only as occasions for the showing of his grace and forgiveness!

DE PROFUNDIS (ii)

Psalm 130:1–8 (*cont'd*)

There follows, then, the great, central, Biblical affirmation: *But there is forgiveness with thee.* Baal, Buddha, Marx, Zeus, Cupid, the star under which I was born—to none of these gods could this cry be made. For our God is not a God who *marks iniquities*, that is to say, who waits gleefully to catch people out and to pounce on sinners in the act, as the gods of Olympus loved to do.

St. Augustine wrote the words of verse 4 on the wall of the room in which he lay dying. John Wesley was converted on a Sunday afternoon. That evening he heard these words in the anthem *De Profundis* sung in St. Paul's Cathedral. To quote himself: "My heart was strangely warmed." Both St. Augustine and John Wesley knew more, of course, about the "ascent from hell" than ever the psalmist could know. That is because they knew the words of the Christian Creed: "He descended into hell". No man climbs out of hell by his own determination. God, in Christ, they knew, had descended to bring up the sinner and lead him right back home to fullness of life. It is almost beyond belief that some churches in the United States have cut this clause out of the Creed. They have thereby removed the very cutting edge of the gospel. For there is certainly such a thing as a self-made hell. And unless the Lord is Saviour enough to go down into my own private hell and raise me up out of it, then he is not the kind of Saviour who is of any use to me.

The psalmist, however, cries: This is what I am looking for: *I wait for the Lord, my soul* (my whole being) *waits; and in his word I hope*, that *Word* about which Ps. 119 had such great things to say. One's whole being can be at its lowest ebb at four in the morning after *watching* hour after hour at the bedside of a dying loved one, or after one has tossed and turned all night in a spirit of utter self-loathing and dejection. The earliest name used in the OT for a prophet was "seer", and of course a seer was a *watchman*, that is, one who waits, looks, listens in complete concentration. It would seem that this psalmist had taken his grief and self-loathing, and had confessed how he was "in the depths" to one of the Temple prophets; and surely then that minister had led him back to discover again real hope in God. He could do so by showing him that one of the great "marvels" that God had revealed in the *Torah* is that God cannot see evil simply as evil, and cannot merely feel angry at it. God's sense of outrage is not like ours. We on our part see only the evil of a situation. God on his sees that, but he also sees an opportunity to pour on more grace, to forgive, to bring good out of the evil in question. God does not merely resist evil, for evil is not a "thing" to be resisted. Evil is an activity that has gone wrong. And so God seeks to turn such an activity into a creative activity. He does so by loving the sinner, by forgiving him, and by offering him fellowship with himself.

Then again, the psalmist has now found that, in the Lord, there is (1) *steadfast love*, such as never changes towards you whether you are in heaven or in hell; and there is (2) *plenteous redemption*, literally "multiplied ransom", multiplied by as many times as there are people in hell. How then, he asks himself, dare he keep such marvellous knowledge to himself? And so he tells it abroad: *O Israel, hope in the Lord . . . and he* (emphatic in the Hebrew) *will* "ransom" (not *redeem*, as RSV) *Israel from all his iniquities.* What we must remember is that God had already "saved" Israel, the sign of which was his rescuing her from slavery in Egypt. But Israel had rebelled and so had slipped down into "hell" (compare Num. 16:31–33). To get her out would be a costly business. A ransom is always a costly business. But God must consider it all worth while.

The Bible never tries to tell us—sensibly!—who God is. But it does tell us—amazingly!—what God is *for*! Here the psalmist puts his finger on the answer. God, he says, is for us, ever ready and eager to hear our cry, and to ransom us from the many hells into which, in our folly, we sink and in which we wallow in despair.

To *hope in God* means to trust him about the future, not confining him to our ideas of what should happen to our lives. It means to allow God to shape the future, not like those Millenarians who suggest they know exactly what God is going to do and that he will do it soon. Such an affirmation is not the Biblical hope. To quote Graham Greene again:

If we lived in a world which guaranteed a happy ending, should we be as long discovering it? Perhaps that's what the saints were at with their incomprehensible happiness—they had seen the end of the story when they came in and couldn't take the agonies seriously.

So what of him who cries *in hope*? He has already entered into the freedom of the children of God which, through grace, God had bestowed upon his Covenant people. So he is now able to begin to reflect some of God's glory with God in the form of a dialogue. He has discovered the truth of the old saying, "To know God means to suffer with God", and this is because God does not speak *to* us so much as *with* us. The psalmist rejects the mysticism which was current in his contemporary world, and which is a mark of many of the religions of the world today. For then he would have been expected to reach out and finally to achieve union with God the Lover of his soul. Rather he learns through prayer to turn his mind off "self" and to look upon others with the eyes of forgiveness and love. As theologians point out, there is no picture here of the proud humanity that the Greeks valued so much; rather it is the true humanity of humility. Thus it is that, with the immense purposes of God that embrace even "hell", men and women are led through God's all-embracing Covenant love to "come of age", to become that new humanity which is like the God who, though living in joy, emptied himself, and became one of us in the weariness of our flesh.

Dag Hammarskjöld wrote in his diary:

Give me a pure heart—that I may see Thee
  A humble heart—that I may hear Thee
A heart of love—that I may serve Thee
  A heart of faith—that I may abide in Thee.

RESTING IN GOD

Psalm 131:1–3

A Song of Ascents. Of David.

¹O Lord, my heart is not lifted up,
  my eyes are not raised too high;

I do not occupy myself with things
  too great and too marvellous for me.
²But I have calmed and quieted my soul,
  like a child quieted at its mother's breast;
  like a child that is quieted is my soul.

³O Israel, hope in the Lord
  from this time forth and for evermore.

In this tiny psalm we have a beautiful short meditation going to the heart of a human being's reliance upon the God of love. It is so short that only too easily it can be passed over unnoticed. It was evidently repeated by someone "going up" to worship in Jerusalem. The author believes that what he is thinking aloud to God could have met the case of David, the man who was forgiven for his great sinfulness. But, of course, so are we today forgiven for our great sinfulness.

This is what passes through his mind: Lord, there have been times when I rebelled against the mystery of life. At those times the belief I found in the *Torah* that you are love just did not fit, it seemed, with the pain and sorrow that is everywhere in the world. I could not see how your suffering love overcomes the brutality of evil and turns its force into creative energy. I am not much of a theologian, so I do *not occupy myself with things too great and marvellous for me.* (We recall at this point that *marvellous* is a word meaning specifically what is beyond human understanding because it reveals the mystery of the divine love.) There is the, probably apocryphal, story of the man who asked John Calvin what God was doing before he created the heavens and the earth. To which Calvin is alleged to have replied, "He was hotting up hell for those who would ask such questions"!

Clearly our pilgrim has had his struggles, spiritual, moral, intellectual, as we all do. But now, he says to God, *I have calmed* (literally "levelled", as if preparing the ground to allow God to sow the seed) *and quieted* myself, by taking my storms of passion, doubt and insecurity and quietly gagging them. The result has been that I have found that kind of security and peace that a three-year-old child finds in his mother's arms. (In the ancient world a child was weaned only by the time he was three years old or so.) Finally, the editor who has prepared this little song of trust for public use—and so for our use!—adds at the end one more verse. By it he takes this individual expression of commitment and makes it meet the needs of a congregation of trusting people.

What particularly do we notice in this little poem? The Scottish Crown and the Scottish regiments have as their motto: *Nemo me impune lacessit,* "No one interferes with me with impunity". But here is a character who has come to discover that the other party is not an aggressor but one made in the image of God. If the latter happens to be one of the many people in trouble in this world, then he is one of God's "little ones" who need, not just God's but our love and care, and certainly not our enmity. In this way, through putting his trust in God, he has learned to reflect the very nature of God in this world of strife and pain; and then to exhibit "motherly love" to all those who are in need of comfort and care.

FINDING A PLACE FOR THE LORD

Psalm 132:1–7

A Song of Ascents.

¹Remember, O Lord, in David's favour,
　　all the hardships he endured;
²how he swore to the Lord
　　and vowed to the Mighty One of Jacob,
³"I will not enter my house
　　or get into my bed;
⁴I will not give sleep to my eyes
　　or slumber to my eyelids,
⁵until I find a place for the Lord,
　　a dwelling place for the Mighty One of Jacob."

⁶Lo, we heard of it in Ephrathah,
　　we found it in the fields of Jaar.
⁷"Let us go to his dwelling place;
　　let us worship at his footstool!"

Verses 1–5. Centuries after David's day some anonymous person declared that David in a real sense made his true "ascent to the Lord" when he said: *until I find a place for the Lord* at the heart of the nation's life. Now, about say 500 B.C. when the Second Temple had been built, there appear good members of the Covenant people who are deeply concerned that that new building should be the abode indeed of the Lord, just as truly as Solomon's Temple had been so long before. On a public occasion held in the new Temple buildings someone asks God to remember, by inviting the congregation to remember, what David had done half a millennium before. Before proceeding, we should read 2 Sam. 6 to remind ourselves about what happened when David brought the Ark of the Covenant up to Jerusalem once it had been recovered from the Philistines, Israel's long-standing enemy. We should also read Solomon's great prayer at the dedication of the first Temple as we find it in 1 Kings 8 and 2 Chron. 6. For this psalm conjoins within it two important traditions, one being that God covenanted with David to be his Father for ever, the other being that God covenanted to make Zion his *place* on earth. Then, having read these passages, we may remind ourselves that in the time of this psalm the line of David was extinct, and that the *place* that God had chosen had been obliterated by Nebuchadnezzar, and only newly cleared of rubble and built on.

Shakespeare once said: "Uneasy lies the head that wears a crown." The passage in 2 Sam. 6 about what it meant to be a son of God certainly does not idealize David. He was a very fallible and very human being. Just because he knew he was both of these, and because he knew his people were no better than himself, he recognized that nothing could go right in his kingdom until he had put God the Lord in the midst of the nation's life. That is what he did. The Ark that is mentioned in verse 8 of this psalm was a little box, about the size of a child's coffin, that traditionally had come down from the days of Moses (Exod. 25:10–22) and which had accompanied the travelling Israelites all their forty years in the Wilderness. The important things about it however were these: (1) It was that one place on earth where God met with his people in a special way. (2) The Ark contained the moral law that covered the whole life of Israel—the Ten Commandments. (3) Over it was stationed, on the wing tips of the cherubim, what we call in English "the mercy seat". There God met with his people in judgment, which turned out to be his mercy. And now David intended to find a permanent site for the Ark.

This very ordinary sinful man, then, made some kind of a vow when he restored it in Zion, as we read in verse 3. The record of his oath seems to have been preserved carefully. The people adored him for it. "Remember, O Lord, the hardships David brought upon himself" when he fought to regain the Ark from the Philistines. It took him years to do so. But it was worth it. For it marked the Presence of the God, not just of David, but of David's ancient ancestor, Jacob. It was the *Mighty One,* however, who had done it all, not David.

A place for Yahweh, a dwelling place for the Mighty One. How strange that would sound to the ears of a Hindu or a Buddhist today! One spot on earth for the Living God to be found in? Is God not to be found everywhere, in fact is he not in everything and in every human being? The faith of the writers of both the Old and the New Testaments is unique among the religions of the world in answering "yes" to both these questions. But it is the first that we are concerned with. Such an idea is what the theologian calls the "particularism" of the OT revelation. Nor is it restricted to the OT, but appears in the NT too, as John 1:14 claims, when the Word became flesh and dwelt among us (compare *a dwelling place* at verse 5 of our psalm), that is, in one particular man at one particular moment in one particular land.

Verses 6–7. If, as many of today's scholars believe, this psalm was not just declared but was actually acted, in much the same way as we act the Christmas stories today, then these two verses may well be the words of the chorus sung by one of the Temple choirs, as they speak for all the worshippers present. *Lo* (meaning "Look" at what we are performing)! *we heard of it in Ephrathah.* That was the ancient name of Bethlehem, the *place* of the donkeys and the swaddling clothes. It was also David's birthplace—but there was no son of David by this time left alive. It was also where Ruth lived, the foreign ancestress of David, whom God led home in order to become David's great-grandmother. *We found it*—what? The Ark? *In the fields of Jaar*. Since *jaar* means "forest", the reference may be to that forested hill, among whose trees Abinadab's house was built (2 Sam. 6:3), and out of which David and his men carried the Ark in triumph (1 Sam. 7:1–2; 2 Chron. 1:4). Are we witnessing a kind of liturgical play in which, over again each year, some object that represented the Ark of the Lord was carried up to the priests, who then *placed* it with joy and rejoicing in the *dwelling place* (verse 5) that God had chosen for it? Yet, as we have said, the Ark had been lost when Nebuchadnezzar destroyed Jerusalem in 587 B.C.

GOD'S RESTING PLACE

Psalm 132.8–18

⁸Arise, O Lord, and go to thy resting place,
  thou and the ark of thy might.
⁹Let thy priests be clothed with righteousness,
  and let thy saints shout for joy.
¹⁰For thy servant David's sake
  do not turn away the face of thy anointed one.

¹¹The Lord swore to David a sure oath
  from which he will not turn back:
 "One of the sons of your body
  I will set on your throne.
¹²If your sons keep my covenant
  and my testimonies which I shall teach them,
 their sons also for ever
  shall sit upon your throne."
¹³For the Lord has chosen Zion;
  he has desired it for his habitation:
¹⁴"This is my resting place for ever;
  here I will dwell, for I have desired it.
¹⁵I will abundantly bless her provisions;
  I will satisfy her poor with bread.
¹⁶Her priests I will clothe with salvation,
  and her saints will shout for joy.

¹⁷There I will make a horn to sprout for David;
   I have prepared a lamp for my anointed.
¹⁸His enemies I will clothe with shame,
   but upon himself his crown will shed its lustre."

Verses 8–10. These verses could be part of the "script" used at the ceremony as the priests bore in the "Ark" in triumph. The wording of the script reminded God's people present of the two-fold election they were celebrating, that of God's election of a *person* (and here they were acting in faith, and only with an eye to the future) and that of God's election of a *place*. The place was there all right, on top of Zion's hill. But they had to think through the theological significance of the way in which God had chosen to reveal himself at one spot only. Both the priests and the people were evidently wearing their "Sunday best" for the ceremony, as it were, their wedding garments as God's "Bride" (see Hosea chs. 1–3). These were the symbol of God's saving love now set free in the lives of his people, that righteousness or *saving love* with which God had clothed his priestly people. The most important point to note in the whole ceremony, however, is the wording of the shout that the people put up: "Up Yahweh to thy resting-place, Thou, even thy mighty Ark." In this shout they recognized that God had been in some sense *in* the Ark, as the localized Presence of the Mighty One of Jacob. But the Ark was no more.

Verses 11–12, *The Reply*. The officiating minister now makes an announcement. He quotes 2 Sam. 7, putting special emphasis upon God's *Covenant* with David. For, as we have noted before, the Covenant is the legal "shell" that holds within it that unique contribution to the world of religions, God's *hesed,* what the RSV translates as God's "steadfast love". Faith in that love moreover is open-ended. As the minister declares, God will *teach* each new generation even more about his love than the previous one could possibly absorb. Through his *testimonies* God will offer Israel ever new revelation as the years roll on. (See Acts 8:26–38.) And this must include revelation of what his promise to David must mean, now that the line of David was extinct!

Verses 13–18, *God's choice*. Verse 13 begins with *ki*. Probably we are to translate by such a phrase as: "(We believe) that *the Lord has chosen Zion* to make into his 'home' " (as verse 8). *Here I will dwell, for I have desired it,* that is, planned it since the foundation of the earth.

But then God goes on to speak of the end-purpose of this choice. It is that *I will satiate her poor with bread*. Just as the Lord's Prayer deals with both material and spiritual bread in one, so does God's promise here. For into this section of the "script" at verse 16 goes again the wording that we heard at verse 9 where God's Presence is the real food that we need. Zion and her Temple and its liturgy and priests were still there, even if the Ark was gone.

Finally we learn once again of God's choice of David. How important it seems to be. In the *Benedictus* in the NT (Luke 1:68–79) we find a reference to verse 17 of this psalm. Verse 69 runs: "He has raised up a deliverer of victorious power from the house of his servant David." For the *horn* spoken of was that of a bull, the bull being the strongest animal known to the people of Israel (for by this date there were virtually no lions and bears left in the country). The *lamp* (see 2 Sam. 21:17) was the person of David himself, for he gave light to his soldier people (compare Luke 1:79) in the same way that all Israel was meant to be a light to the nations of the world (Isa. 49:6; 55:3–4). The word *anointed* means, first, having had oil poured over the head; then it symbolized consecration to an office, whether it be that of king, prophet or priest. But it is of course the Hebrew term *Messiah*, given to the deliverer who would one day come in David's place. The Greek equivalent is *Christ*. Not surprisingly, then, the NT Church came to discover in this psalm a promise of God for them that went back to 2 Sam. 7 in which God declares that David would be his son "for ever".

Upon himself his crown will shed its lustre is a poetic way of saying that David's royal position will blossom, will grow and develop from bud to flower. The word *crown,* being *nezer* in Hebrew, easily induced some Christians to see in it the name of the town of Nazareth. Yet the *nezer* was also the name of the diadem worn by the High Priest (Exod. 29:6); while the verb *yatsits* (*shed its lustre,* RSV) may mean rather to sparkle or glitter like the golden plate which the High Priest wore on his turban and which bore the lettering "Holiness to the Lord" (Exod. 28:36). If we put the stress, then, on these latter meanings, we can see how the Letter to the Hebrews in the NT was able to make much of seeing Christ as the great High Priest, as well as being King.

Taken all in all, however, what the psalm is saying is that the hope of Israel rested, not on any particular pious acts of the sinner, King David, but on the double promise of God to choose within the Covenant both the *person* of David as God's "son" (in the psalmist's day transferred to the Messiah who was to come) and the *place* Zion, for his "footstool". Whereupon they acted out those promises "sacramentally" when priests and people together played out and prayed over the contents of this psalm.

Finally we are bound to recognize that the psalmist declares for God that all these things are to happen only *if your sons* (David's sons in the first place, but in a sense also the whole of Israel) *keep my covenant* (verse 12). This is because it is the Covenant alone which defines for us what God is like, reveals God's *hesed* to man, requires man's obedience to the revealed Word given us in the *Torah,* and marks a relationship between God and Israel that will always go on being renewed (compare Deut. 5:2 ff.), so that eventually it must have its outcome in eternity. This, then, is the basis of our claim to possess not a "New" Testament or Covenant, but a "Renewed" Testament. The Christian reader of this psalm should therefore keep this verse solemnly in mind.

FAMILY LOVE

Psalm 133:1–3

A Song of Ascents.

[1]Behold, how good and pleasant it is
   when brothers dwell in unity!
[2]It is like the precious oil upon the head,
   running down upon the beard,

upon the beard of Aaron,
  running down on the collar of his robes!
³It is like the dew of Hermon,
  which falls on the mountains of Zion!
For there the Lord has commanded the blessing,
  life for evermore.

This psalm is in praise of brotherly love. We have seen that the Covenant love of God is "particularistic", that is to say, God sets his love upon certain people in a certain place at a certain time in a special way and for a special purpose. Their task thereafter is to love others in that kind of special way, and not to declare, for example, "I love humanity" or "I love the Eskimos", for that is merely being silly. The Marxist is such a person in that he calls everyone whether he likes him or not "comrade". That is not an expression of love, it is mere sentimentality. The model which God uses on the other hand for us to copy is the happy family, as we saw at Pss. 127 and 128.

Brothers are all those people who are interrelated within the extended family, as we see to be the case today in the Third World, and as was understood in Gen. 13:8 and Deut. 25.5. But *brothers* are also "brethren", as we use the word today, that is, members of any "particularized" group, such as our fellow-workers on the shop floor, or those with whom we work in the office, or with whom we play a game as a team. It is when such a group co-operates *in unity* that it is pleasing to God. Unity means on the one hand the absence of gossip and back-biting and no nasty criticisms; on the other hand it means positive interest and care and concern for one another within the group. A stranger walking on to that shop-floor or into that office feels at once the friendly atmosphere of mutual interest and concern.

It is like the precious oil upon the head! Nowadays we would thoroughly object to having oil poured over us, running down our beard and neck, and going right down into our underclothing! But of course our social circumstances are very different from Israel's way of life in days of old. But the emphasis here is upon the word *precious*, as it was in the case of the alabaster box of "very precious ointment" which a woman, in an outpouring of love, emptied over the head of Jesus (Matt. 26:7). A cricket club, or a neighbourhood fellowship will never really know a happy "family" feeling without all of its members giving time and patience and love and even money to making it into a true fellowship. The result of working hard at creating such a fellowship is described once again in a "particular" way, one that would be evident to any who lived within sight of beautiful *Mount Hermon*. For these particular folk at that particular spot in Palestine experience during their long, hot dry summer the life-giving qualities of Hermon's morning *dew*. This quality, says the poem, is to be transferred in our thinking to the *mountains of Zion*!

Three times in the poem we meet with the word *down* (*falls on* in verse 3 is the same Hebrew word as *running down* in verse 2). It is as if we were being asked to visualize the descent of the divine blessing upon the happy family. So we note a few points: (1) The spirit of unity is costly. (2) Like dew, it is refreshing, life-giving, and it is gentle. (3) It offers us true *life*, for it is life together with others, not the half-life of a Robinson Crusoe. (4) It is to be found where there is harmony, for there we find the blessing of God's love; we are then reminded of the words of Jesus: "Where two or three are gathered together in my name (i.e. in my spirit of love) there I am in the midst of them." (5) It is on *Zion* that the Lord has actually *commanded the blessing* to descend, that is to say, in the life and fellowship of the Church; for it is there, in God's "resting place", that God has commanded us to live together as the true family of God. (6) Unless the community of believers is indeed a family in this sense, the praise of God does not possess any kind of sounding-board, so to speak. What happens then is that, without true praise, the community possesses no established order and no centre of being. The result is that, in human society in general, we observe communities breaking up and disintegrating, and falling into chaos and disorder.

Many centuries ago St. Basil of Russia declared: "The left hand does not need the right hand more than the Church needs concord among its theologians." As we too, then, "go up to

Jerusalem" to worship the living God we are reminded of Jesus'
warning given us at Matt. 5:23–24, about being first reconciled to
our brother before we even dare to enter the courts of the Lord.

WAITING FOR THE DAWN

Psalm 134:1–3

A Song of Ascents.

¹Come, bless the Lord, all you servants of the Lord,
 who stand by night in the house of the Lord!
²Lift up your hands to the holy place,
 and bless the Lord!

³May the Lord bless you from Zion,
 he who made heaven and earth!

We are awaiting the "ascent" of the sun, waiting for the ap-
pearance of the Lord. In this way this short psalm takes its place
as one of the *Songs of Ascents* to be used by those "going up" to
worship in Zion—or, as we would do well to claim, at our local
church today. This is the last one of the Pilgrim Songs.

We might try to "place" the use of this psalm. The villager has
come up to Jerusalem. It is the night before the close of the great
Autumn Festival. Excitement is in the air. The lights are blazing.
All present, men, women and children, are eagerly waiting, not
for the sun to rise as the god who gives light and life to the world,
but rather to bless God for his gift of the sun, which symbolizes his
healing and creative power. The song is in three parts.

Verse 1, *The call to worship.* There is no word *Come* in
Hebrew. What we have is the word *hinneh* which is usually
rendered by "behold". It is employed here to invite the people
present to use their imagination and to build up a mental picture
of what is about to take place, in this case the wonder and mystery
of the idea of *blessing the Lord.* Imagine what it means, says the
psalmist, that mere mortal man should be invited to lay his hands
on the head of the eternal God! For that is actually what the verb
to bless implies.

To *stand* is the customary word for the service of the priests and Levites. They are then in a position of being ready to respond instantly to the will of the Lord. It is not just the people, then, who are being called to worship, but the priests also. The priests dare not think of themselves as mere functionaries, but, like the people whom they are serving, they too are sinners called to share in this waiting for God.

At the time of the Second Temple, the chief of the gate-keepers went at midnight bearing with him the massive keys of the inner Temple, and taking along with him some of the priests; whereupon they all ducked through the little wicket gate of the large fire-gate. Beyond it they patrolled the courtyard in two companies to make all ready for worship once the sun came up. Their task was to clean up the mess in the abattoir; then, in readiness for the first sacrifice at dawn, they had to drive the necessary number of sheep into their holding pens. These priests then went on to clean up the bake-house where "the bread of the High Priest" was baked. Those who were still to go on duty were then aroused from sleep. These latter had now to bathe and put on their "ecclesiastical" garments and be ready before first light. These all then went to the stone-chamber where lots were drawn assigning each priest his duty for the day (see Luke 1:8–9).

Verse 2, *The "sermon"*. All the above divisions of priests and Temple attendants were now told to say a prayer (i.e. *lift up your hands*) in blessing of God. This is because they were not to go about their various tasks without remembering that "unless the Lord watches over the city, the watchman stays awake in vain" (Ps. 127:1). So it is that if we in our turn bless God before we set out on our day's work he returns our blessing many times upon our head.

Verse 3, *The Benediction*. This is said (1) because God's blessing has in it the amplitude of the whole universe. But (2) he *blesses you from Zion*, that is, out of the fellowship of the Church where you have learned to know and trust God, so that, before each day's work begins, you are enabled to turn to him quite naturally in prayer

We today wonder at all the noise and the smell and the multiplicity of regulations that had to be observed in the period of the Second Temple. But the answer to our question about why all these were required may well be that God saw it to be important that we in our turn should start the day with prayer, and should prepare for public worship thoughtfully and carefully. We have to learn to regard worship as the basic element in life.

WHATEVER THE LORD PLEASES HE DOES (i)

Psalm 135:1–21

> [1]Praise the Lord.
>> Praise the name of the Lord,
>> give praise, O servants of the Lord,
> [2]you that stand in the house of the Lord,
>> in the courts of the house of our God!
> [3]Praise the Lord, for the Lord is good;
>> sing to his name, for he is gracious!
> [4]For the Lord has chosen Jacob for himself,
>> Israel as his own possession.
>
> [5]For I know that the Lord is great,
>> and that our Lord is above all gods.
> [6]Whatever the Lord pleases he does,
>> in heaven and on earth,
>> in the seas and all deeps.
> [7]He it is who makes the clouds rise at the end of the earth,
>> who makes lightnings for the rain
>> and brings forth the wind from his storehouses.
>
> [8]He it was who smote the first-born of Egypt,
>> both of man and of beast;
> [9]who in thy midst, O Egypt,
>> sent signs and wonders
>> against Pharaoh and all his servants;
> [10]who smote many nations
>> and slew mighty kings,
> [11]Sihon, king of the Amorites,
>> and Og, king of Bashan,

and all the kingdoms of Canaan,
¹²and gave their land as a heritage,
a heritage to his people Israel.

¹³Thy name, O Lord, endures for ever,
thy renown, O Lord, throughout all ages.
¹⁴For the Lord will vindicate his people,
and have compassion on his servants.

¹⁵The idols of the nations are silver and gold,
the work of men's hands.
¹⁶They have mouths, but they speak not,
they have eyes, but they see not,
¹⁷they have ears, but they hear not,
nor is there any breath in their mouths.
¹⁸Like them be those who make them!—
yea, every one who trusts in them!

¹⁹O house of Israel, bless the Lord!
O house of Aaron, bless the Lord!
²⁰O house of Levi, bless the Lord!
You that fear the Lord, bless the Lord!
²¹Blessed be the Lord from Zion,
he who dwells in Jerusalem!
Praise the Lord!

Psalm 134 spoke of waiting for the hour of worship. This psalm tells us what to say when the hour comes!

Verses 1–2. If we realize that this call to praise, made three times over, begins virtually by saying: "Do what Miriam and her female friends did after the crossing of the Reed Sea" (see Exod. 15:20–21), then we discover that the worship spoken of here is not confined to the routine cycle of the Temple festivals. It has to do with the meaning of life itself. For these women *saw* what God had done. This seeing was not in the sense we noted at Ps. 134:1, where the word *hinneh* invited the worshipper to have a mental picture. Nor was what they saw a mere combination of a high wind, a tidal wave and a heap of corpses of drowned men. They actually *saw God act!*

Historians today take it for granted that God is to be excluded from history writing, just as many scientists similarly take it for granted that God has nothing to do with the workings of Nature. Consequently many ordinary folk have now been left with the choice of seeking God only through their personal religious experience. And as that can be very "dicey", as we say, since our personal experience can depend on the workings of our stomach or our liver, there is not much that the ordinary person can find left to him. But the psalmist is not like that. He keeps a sense of wonder and of the reality of miracle as the basis of the tradition which leads people to worship God and praise his name. Martin Buber, the Jewish theologian, pointed out that an event in history, as the OT understands it, is something transparent, something that offers a glimpse, to use his words, "of the sphere of the sole Power". It is in this way, then, that Miriam *saw* those great events.

Who has not hesitated when, within the context of divine worship, he has heard the words, "Let us now praise famous men"? But of course these words do not belong to the OT but come from an apocryphal book (Ecclesiasticus). You find nothing like that in the Psalms. What the psalmist here calls upon us to do is to *praise God*, not man, for he alone is *good*, he alone is *gracious* (verse 3).

WHATEVER THE LORD PLEASES HE DOES (ii)

Psalm 135:1–21 (*cont'd*)

Verses 3–4. God is good and gracious because of what he has done, in particular because of his *election of Jacob*. We recall that *Jacob* was a very unlikely choice for God to make, for he was a mean, self-seeking and deceiving man. But God went on to "change" him; and so Jacob became a "new man". The result was that he needed a new name to describe him, viz. *Israel* (Gen. 32:22–28). That act of election was therefore transparent of the purposeful, forgiving, creative love of God.

His own possession is a direct quotation from Exod. 19:5, repeated at Deut. 7:6 and 14:2. See also Mal. 3:17. There the elective love of God is described in the language used by the ancient great kings of Mesopotamia. Each of these regarded himself as King of kings and Lord of lords. As such he owned everything in his wide domains, every house, every street, every bullock and every plough. But that kind of owning did not give him any real satisfaction. In his palace, therefore, the Great King kept a box in which he placed his "jewels, all his jewels, precious jewels, his loved and his own" (to quote the old children's hymn, the words of which are taken from Mal. 3:17 in the AV). At intervals the Great King would open his box and finger his jewels, and say with a sigh of satisfaction, "Ah, these are really mine." This box of jewels, then, is the Hebrew word *segullah*, translated here as "*his own possession*". For the God of the Covenant had declared at Sinai, "All the earth is mine, but you shall be my *segullah*, my precious jewel, among all peoples."

So when the psalmist calls out: *Praise the "name" of the Lord* (verse 1) he is saying, "Praise him who has revealed himself to be that kind of God who loved Jacob and who acted as he did at the Reed Sea." *His servants* are the jewels in the box of the heavenly King of kings, not those in the box of the kings of Mesopotamia.

Verses 5–12. The customary sermon, after the call to worship, begins with a personal witness, *I know that the Lord is great.* It is not that God can do anything on the ground that he is Lord of all, *heaven and earth*, the oceans, as well as the *deeps* of chaos. We notice that the preacher turns quickly from Nature to history, and goes on to refer to the idea expressed at Exod. 18:11. It is only *whatever the Lord pleases he does*; it is not a case of "the Almighty must be able to do anything at all." Thus it *pleased* him to rescue Israel from slavery in Egypt and lead his people through all opposition into the land of Canaan. We are thus to understand the word *pleases* as meaning "what God sees to be good for his loving purposes", and that is basically his "plan" to save all mankind.

When a woman is first married, according to many cultures she brings a dowry with her. God acted otherwise, however. For he acted in grace. When God brought his Bride into Canaan (the theme of Hosea and his successors amongst the prophets), God himself supplied the dowry, the *heritage*, by giving the *land* to his Bride Israel as a wedding gift!

Verses 13–14. No wonder the sermon is interrupted by the chorus breaking in. Since the choristers naturally liked to sing in verse, they chose here the words of that ancient poem which everyone would know off by heart; so they quoted from Deut. 32:36.

Verses 15–21. The sermon continues. Here some of the wording, with its scorn of idol-worship, especially verse 18, seems to have been taken from the prophets, perhaps here from Isa. 44. What good reasons we have to praise the *Living* God, is the preacher's argument. And so he concludes by calling upon: (1) the people (*O house of Israel*), (2) the priests (*O house of Aaron*), (3) the Levites (*O house of Levi*), (4) Gentile converts, worshipping with them as enquirers or proselytes (*you that fear the Lord*), to bless the Lord whose nature and purpose he has revealed to us as wonderful beyond compare. Already the election of Israel is taking effect, we can sense, through this preacher, for Israel has been asking why she had been chosen at all. His reply is that she had not been chosen to be saved, though of course she had been chosen to be loved as God's *segullah*. Rather God's jewel, his loved one had been chosen to learn of him so that she might be a light to lighten the Gentiles (Isa. 49:6), and to be God's salvation to the end of the earth. Just that had already begun to take place in our preacher's day, with the presence at public worship of so many converts from amongst the nations of the earth.

THE GREAT LITANY

Psalm 136:1–26

¹O give thanks to the Lord, for he is good,
   for his steadfast love endures for ever.
²O give thanks to the God of gods,
   for his steadfast love endures for ever.

³O give thanks to the Lord of lords,
  for his steadfast love endures for ever;

⁴to him who alone does great wonders,
  for his steadfast love endures for ever;
⁵to him who by understanding made the heavens,
  for his steadfast love endures for ever;
⁶to him who spread out the earth upon the waters,
  for his steadfast love endures for ever;
⁷to him who made the great lights,
  for his steadfast love endures for ever;
⁸the sun to rule over the day,
  for his steadfast love endures for ever;
⁹the moon and stars to rule over the night,
  for his steadfast love endures for ever;

¹⁰to him who smote the first-born of Egypt,
  for his steadfast love endures for ever;
¹¹and brought Israel out from among them,
  for his steadfast love endures for ever;
¹²with a strong hand and an outstretched arm,
  for his steadfast love endures for ever;
¹³to him who divided the Red Sea in sunder,
  for his steadfast love endures for ever;
¹⁴and made Israel pass through the midst of it,
  for his steadfast love endures for ever;
¹⁵but overthrew Pharaoh and his host in the Red Sea,
  for his steadfast love endures for ever;
¹⁶to him who led his people through the wilderness,
  for his steadfast love endures for ever;
¹⁷to him who smote great kings,
  for his steadfast love endures for ever;
¹⁸and slew famous kings,
  for his steadfast love endures for ever;
¹⁹Sihon, king of the Amorites,
  for his steadfast love endures for ever;
²⁰and Og, king of Bashan,
  for his steadfast love endures for ever;
²¹and gave their land as a heritage,
  for his steadfast love endures for ever;
²²a heritage to Israel his servant,
  for his steadfast love endures for ever;

²³It is he who remembered us in our low estate,
      for his steadfast love endures for ever;
²⁴and rescued us from our foes,
      for his steadfast love endures for ever;
²⁵he who gives food to all flesh,
      for his steadfast love endures for ever.
²⁶O give thanks to the God of heaven,
      for his steadfast love endures for ever.

As we would expect, this Litany, prepared for use in public worship, incorporates in it many quotations from and fragments of other psalms. Most congregations enjoy singing words they already know. Probably a priest or minister sang the first line, and then the congregation responded with the same three words in every case—*ki le-olam hasdo* (see Ezra 3:11), no fewer than twenty-six times! It was from this Litany that John Milton produced his much-loved hymn: "Let us with a gladsome mind, praise the Lord for he is kind".

The Litany is in the form of a dialogue. To the folk of OT days "reality" was inconceivable without God acting in history, for God's Word and God's actions are one. So it is really God here who is in dialogue with his people, and in this way he draws out of them a response of faith.

Steadfast love is the word *hesed* we have met so frequently, as these two English words valiantly attempt to express the nature of the Covenant love of God with which he has bound himself to his people; while the word *ki*, here translated *for*, is actually the word "that". Its use in such a sentence, as we recall, indicates that the congregation regards their response to be a statement of faith, beginning each time with the words "We believe . . ."

Each of the first three verses opens with *O give thanks*, so that all three together form a call to worship. Verses 4–9 then deal with Creation as we read of it in Gen. 1. Yet the language of the passage is also drawn from the Wisdom literature. For at Prov. 3:19; 8:22ff; Jer. 10:12 and elsewhere God's work in Nature is performed by his "daughter" Wisdom. Here the parallel noun *understanding* is employed (verse 5). Thereafter from verse 10 on the congregation is called upon to give thanks to God for what God did for them in the days of the Exodus from Egypt, and so on throughout the Wilderness wanderings. It would seem that, no matter what set-backs they had to endure, God's *steadfast love* had never let them go.

Then verses 23–25 seem to cover the experience of the Exile in Babylonia (*our low estate*), of the return to Jerusalem (*rescued us from our foes*), and then of the period up to the poet's own day (*who gives food to all flesh*). But in this last verse we move from the particular to the general, so to speak. For the verse covers God's care not only for Israel, but for all his creatures, including even the animal kingdom. The poem ends finally with a repetition of verse 1.

It would be too easy to make no further comment. The congregation, however, was well aware what God had given them the Covenant for. God had cared for his people with all these expressions of his *hesed*, with a purpose. He had hidden his servant people in the shadow of his hand, had made them like a polished arrow hidden away in his quiver (Isa. 49:2–3). And why? "For you are my servant Israel in whom I will be glorified . . . I will give you as a light to the nations, that my salvation may reach to the end of the earth" (Isa. 49:6).

That, then, is why Israel sings here with exultation and joy, and with a sense of unlimited wonder at the depth and all-pervading purpose of the love of God.

BY THE WATERS OF BABYLON

Psalm 137:1–7

¹By the waters of Babylon,
   there we sat down and wept,
   when we remembered Zion
²On the willows there
   we hung up our lyres.
³For there our captors
   required of us songs,

and our tormentors, mirth, saying,
"Sing us one of the songs of Zion!"

⁴How shall we sing the Lord's song
in a foreign land?
⁵If I forget you, O Jerusalem,
let my right hand wither!
⁶Let my tongue cleave to the roof of my mouth,
if I do not remember you,
if I do not set Jerusalem
above my highest joy!

⁷Remember, O Lord, against the Edomites
the day of Jerusalem,
how they said, "Rase it, rase it!
Down to its foundations!"

The strangeness of this psalm, the marvel of it, is that, despite the shock we feel when we reach verse 9, every branch of the Christian Church cherishes it. In this regard we dare not gloss over the fact that Jesus himself made use of the imprecatory or cursing psalms. He was not one to think of love as mere sentiment. He accepted as his own the consuming passion of love that characterizes the God of the OT. No psalm, then, demands more careful study than this one. In fact, to have it sung *at* us by a choir can even do us harm as a worshipping congregation in our expectation of hearing the Word of God spoken to us through it. No psalm deserves to be read with the idea in mind of "Go slow!" more than this one.

The waters of Babylon were man-made canals running between the Tigris and the Euphrates rivers. The Tigris flows along the foot of the mountains on the northern side of the Mesopotamian plain at a somewhat higher level than the Euphrates. So there was a natural fall that produced a current in the connecting canals. We meet with one of these canals at Ezek. 1:3, where it is called the River Chebar. We can picture the scene—the slow-moving waters lined with *willows* (or perhaps poplars; see RSV *ftn*), the evening of a stiflingly hot day, a day of heavy work in the fields, the Israelite forced labourers (see Isa. 40:2 RSV *ftn*), weary and exhausted, meeting for the short period before retiring to sleep to chat together. But all we could do, they reported, was to *hang up our lyres on the willows, and sit down and weep when we remembered Zion.*

The Babylonian gang leaders, however, did not even allow them to have their time of mourning in private. They "ordered" mirth! What does that remind us of today? Of a Nazi extermination camp? Of a gang of labourers in a mosquito-infested correction camp in central Siberia? Two of the songs of Zion that we possess are Ps. 46 and Ps. 48. As we read them now, we are struck by the incongruity of their language compared with the situation of the exiles. Here in this psalm we discern a band of brave, thoughtful, believing people, thinking back to their beloved Jerusalem, now in ruins, who were being taunted and tormented by their cruel guards and made to sing: "God is in the midst of her, she shall not be moved" (Ps. 46:5), or, "His holy mountain, beautiful in elevation, is the joy of all the earth . . . within her citadels God has shown himself a sure defence" (Ps. 48:2–3). Or, with the emphasis on David, "I have set my king on Zion, my holy hill" (Ps. 2:6). No wonder they ask each other: *How shall we sing the Lord's song in a foreign land?*

What is so remarkable is that these exiles were able to keep their faith at all; for the obvious thing to conclude was that God had broken all his promises, and was no better than the gods of Babylon. Jerusalem was now in ruins, the Temple a heap of stones, and the line of David virtually extinct. *If I forget you, O Jerusalem . . .* is thus an extraordinary statement. It means that the exiles fully understood the depth of the Covenant promise despite all appearances. Basically it was just this: "I love you, and I will never let you go." In the "Easter Saturday" of their experience these brave folk remained utterly sure that an "Easter Sunday" would surely follow. They held stoutly to the faith that, if the Living God had declared, "I shall be found and met with in Zion", then it was irrelevant if Zion should now happen to be in ruins. We see how their faith was justified in a psalm we have just looked at, written after the return to Zion: *It is he who "remembered" us in our low estate* (Ps. 136:23).

The exiles apparently had some knowledge of what was happening at home. Jerusalem had fallen to the Babylonians in 587 B.C. and since then nomads, warriors all, had kept coming into Palestine crossing the Jordan from the east and plundering the ruins of the city. They created havoc amongst those (mainly the peasant groups) who had been permitted to remain there to eke out a living as best as they could. Among these nomads were the Edomites. Their arrival was what is called here "the day of Jerusalem". Amos and others had already spoken of *the Day* as that of judgment, of war, of the "end" of Jerusalem.

The Edomites were Israel's cousins. Tradition has it that they were descended from Esau; Israel was of course descended from Esau's brother Jacob. Esau was a wild and hairy man. But more. Easu was the elder brother who had so scorned God's choice of him to be his agent in the world that he sold it for "a mess of pottage" (see Gen. 25:30–34). Along with the birthright there ought to have gone the father's blessing. Esau therefore had now lost that too. Instead, Isaac had given another and more meaningful blessing to Jacob. *Esau* consequently *hated Jacob* because of the blessing with which his father had blessed him (Gen. 27:41). "And Esau said to himself . . . I will surely kill my brother Jacob."

Such was the tradition that Israel could not forget. Esau had committed the ultimate sin of scorning God's loving plan for the world and had then compounded it by promising to prevent its fulfilment through Jacob's descendants by murdering him. He nearly succeeded. The heinousness of Edom's assault, therefore, was that it was not aimed at man, but against God himself. That is why the exiles could call upon God to *"remember" against the Edomites the day of Jerusalem*, that is, the day when they "kicked their man when he was down", as we might describe their action; how they said, *Rase it, rase it! down to its foundations!* Its foundations, however, were God's foundations. Even in her all too human bitterness Israel knew that.

THE TERRIBLE CRY

Psalm 137:8–9

> 8O daughter of Babylon, you devastator!
>   Happy shall he be who requites you
>   with what you have done to us!
> 9Happy shall he be who takes your little ones
>   and dashes them against the rock!

As to the Babylonians, they had set out with total deliberation to *devastate* all the surrounding nations. Isaiah had foretold that, in consequence, "their infants will be dashed in pieces before their eyes" (Isa. 13:16–18; 14:21). The reason for doing this was to prevent a new generation of Babylonians arising whose aim also would be to *devastate* the earth. The phrase *daughter of Babylon* personalizes the reality of the judgment to come. "She", the people themselves, not an abstraction like "the nation", was to receive what she had done to others. We must keep in mind that there is no such thing as cruelty; there are only cruel people acting cruelly. Consequently, to rid the earth of "cruelty", one has to rid it of cruel persons. Isaiah's prediction, we should realize, was made in the form of a curse. A blessing and a curse were composed of no mere idle chatter. Their sombre words actually conveyed the contents of the curse or blessing to the recipient. There might be a time-span between the uttering of the curse and the moment when the curse, like an arrow that has sped through the air a long distance, finally reaches its target. God's blessing, made through the lips of Isaac, *must* eventually hit its target. God's curse, made through the lips of Isaiah, must also eventually meet its target too. (We should note the similar effect of the curse uttered by Jesus on the fig tree at Matt. 21:18–22.)

Dashing little ones against the rock was (sadly) normal practice in the warfare of those days (see 2 Kings 8:12; Hos. 13:16; Nah. 3:10). Was it any more horrible than the practices of modern warfare, of throwing napalm on the naked bodies of little children in Vietnam, of saturation bombing of built up areas of modern cities, of chemical warfare over wide areas, of the creation of hell on earth for the children of Hiroshima? This last historical event was not an action of purposeful cruelty made deliberately against little babies. It was part of the total policy "vowed" against the people of Japan. Isaiah, on another occasion, accused the good-living citizens of Jerusalem of having their hands filled with blood (Isa. 1:15). He might well say the same to us as we watch on television, and do nothing about it, the emaciated bodies of little children who are the sufferers from war and famine. Let us remember that as we study these terrible verses.

The exiles we meet here, then, as they hung their harps on the willow trees, were not showing deliberate hatred against the Babylonians, far less their babies. They were asking that they should suffer total war as they had so often waged it. The prayer is cruel, but they were acting upon a moral code that was not unenlightened for its day, the code of "an eye for an eye" (Exod. 21:24). Can we say the same of the spraying of a whole village with napalm? Is that not rather the re-enactment of the exaggerated sin of Lamech (Gen. 4:23–24)—"If Cain is avenged sevenfold, truly Lamech seventy-sevenfold." Gen. 4 shows us in its theological picture language the reality that, once outside of Eden, man's egotistical lust for domination grows, snowball-like, until it reaches its ultimate expression in the type of Lamech. When Moses regulated that lust to merely "one eye for one eye" he gave the world a great ideal, one indeed which it has not yet reached or even attempted to practise. Peter asked Jesus if he ought to call down fire from heaven and consume his traditional enemies. The spirit of Jesus however was quite other. He represented a new kind of nature, a new breed of Adam. With direct reference to Lamech, he reversed that characteristic heathen's boast, and spoke of forgiving one's enemy seventy times seven (Matt. 18:21–22). We, every bit as much as the Israel of Ps. 137, stand condemned by his standard.

Finally, we are to note that God seems to deal with nations, peoples, cities, before he deals with individuals. This sounds strange to those modern Christians who suppose that salvation in Christ means individual exemption from the penalties due to a whole city or nation, with the expectation that "my" individual soul will be saved out of a wicked world, leaving behind scores of babies to sink or swim. Jesus wept over the whole city of Jerusalem, upon which the judgment was coming, babies and all. Isaiah had uttered God's judgment of damnation upon Babylon —God's opposite—babies and all; and this psalm repeats it. Edom had cried *Rase it, rase it, down to its foundations*, babies and all. On the other hand, God who is himself the foundation of the Holy City, offers his salvation to the city, to the nation, to the world—babies and all.

THE LORD WORKS IN ME

Psalm 138:1–8

A Psalm of David.

¹I give thee thanks, O Lord, with my whole heart;
  before the gods I sing thy praise;
²I bow down toward thy holy temple
  and give thanks to thy name for thy steadfast love and thy faithfulness;
 for thou hast exalted above everything
  thy name and thy word.
³On the day I called, thou didst answer me,
  my strength of soul thou didst increase.

⁴All the kings of the earth shall praise thee, O Lord,
  for they have heard the words of thy mouth;
⁵and they shall sing of the ways of the Lord,
  for great is the glory of the Lord.
⁶For though the Lord is high, he regards the lowly;
  but the haughty he knows from afar.

⁷Though I walk in the midst of trouble,
  thou dost preserve my life;
 thou dost stretch out thy hand against the wrath of my enemies,
  and thy right hand delivers me.
⁸The Lord will fulfil his purpose for me;
  thy steadfast love, O Lord, endures for ever.
  Do not forsake the work of thy hands.

Verses 1–3. Through the heart of the city of Babylon there ran a spacious boulevard. At one end of it there stood the temple of the god Bel (known often as Baal in the OT), and at the other end was the temple of Nebo. Once a year in a great ceremony the position of these gods was interchanged. Their big statues were put onto waggons; these then bore them, bump, bump, bump, over the long cobbled street to their new site. The prophet whom we call Second Isaiah was among the exiles who would be given a holiday that day. He must have stood on a sidewalk, watching the proceedings, and listening to the ribald comments of his fellow-exiles.

"Bel's knees are giving way!" "Look, Nebo's toppling over!" "They've actually put the graven images on carts pulled by bullocks!" "What loads your cargoes are!" "They are only freight for weary beasts of burden!" "Look, the men have stumbled; their knees are giving way!" "They can't rescue their freight!" "So the gods themselves are going off into exile!" (Isa. 46:1–2, in free translation).

Now, however, these exiles were back home in Jerusalem and the new Temple was up and dedicated. Accordingly the psalmist thanks God *with my whole heart* (that is with my mind and intelligence) that he is what he is, that he is not like those gilded Babylonian gods. They couldn't even save themselves from falling off a waggon! So he thanks God for revealing his *self* (Name) as *steadfast love and faithfulness*. In fact, he says, *You have shown yourself to be kinder than we could ever have known* (see RSV verse *2b ftn*, and compare Eph. 3:20). Unlike Bel and Nebo who could only fall off freight-cars, God had revealed himself by *doing* things, by carrying his people (Isa. 46:3–4), by rescuing them as Bel could not rescue the Babylonians. And he had revealed himself by *speaking* his Word. Speaking as an individual in my turn (the psalmist says to God), I have now experienced your *hesed* for myself, and as a result you have put in my heart a new power to love others.

Verses 4–6. The day is coming, he continues, when *all the kings of the earth shall praise thee, O Yahweh*, for they will have abandoned the worship of Bel and Nebo, and Zeus and Minerva,

and Cupid and their lucky stars, regarding these as all mere
superstitious nonsense, *for they* will *have heard the words of thy
mouth.* This will have come about, of course, only because God's
people will have remembered the reason for their election. God
had not chosen them to be saved out of this wicked world. He had
chosen them to be God's mission to the world, to be a light to
lighten the Gentiles, to express to the heathen the love God had
now put in their heart. For they will have told the nations what
God is like, that *though the Lord is high*, the transcendent
Creator of all things, yet *he regards the lowly*, the simple folk of
the world, by coming down and sharing their life with them. This
also is what he has chosen Israel to do in his strength, to identify
themselves with the underprivileged. At the same time *he knows*,
that is, he sees right into the heart and mind of, *the haughty*, those
who despise the "submerged nine-tenths" and who attempt to
"play God" with the lives of the poor.

Verses 7–8, *My own confession.* Verse 7 contains a realistic
Biblical statement of faith. It echoes the words of Isa. 43:1–4,
which the psalmist may well have heard Second Isaiah preach
when still in Exile. Yet, in verse 8, he makes another very basic
affirmation: *The Lord will fulfil his purpose for me.* What he
means is that, though he is a poor, simple member of the Covenant community—we know he is making this emphasis, for he
goes on to use the Covenant term *hesed*—yet God has a plan for
his individual life. This plan is now actually in operation. By
humbly accepting the guidance of God's Word in his life (as Ps.
119 explains in full), he finds that his life has developed meaning
and purpose. The awareness of this purpose will continue on,
both now and "into" eternity (not just *for ever*, as RSV). And so
he concludes with this great personal cry to God: "You have
begun your great work in me—so *do not forsake the work of thy
hands.* I know that without any doubt I shall have to meet with the
accident of death; but don't let that make any difference. Keep on
with your *steadfast love* working in and through me into all
eternity."

OUR UNSPEAKABLY WONDERFUL GOD

Psalm 139:1–6

To the choirmaster. A Psalm of David.

¹O Lord, thou hast searched me and known me!
²Thou knowest when I sit down and when I rise up;
    thou discernest my thoughts from afar.
³Thou searchest out my path and my lying down,
    and art acquainted with all my ways.
⁴Even before a word is on my tongue,
    lo, O Lord, thou knowest it altogether.
⁵Thou dost beset me behind and before,
    and layest thy hand upon me.
⁶Such knowledge is too wonderful for me;
    it is high, I cannot attain it.

With this psalm we are entering some of the deepest levels of human experience. It comes from the hand of a man or woman who knows that God is the Saviour God, for he had recently brought his people home from Exile, and had re-established them in Zion. In fact the Hebrew of this psalm is full of Aramaisms, picked up from the speech of Babylon. What, then, does God's saving love mean for him or for her as an individual person?

First, God is always doing things. *Thou hast seached me*, says this psalmist, or, to be more precise, "Thou hast dug deep into me". We speak today of our "deep" subconscious. Our psalmist too was aware how deep human beings are. We are naïve if we think that people who lived about 500 B.C. knew nothing about psychology—though of course they did not know that term! He continues: *and known me*. Of course God knew who he was. This verb, however, does not mean that. It is used in a very personal manner. It refers to that kind of total knowledge that a husband and wife have of each other. It is knowledge that leaves us completely naked in God's sight and therefore no longer belonging only to ourselves, no longer wanting or able to declare that "I am the master of my fate, the captain of my soul". This awareness reminds us that, if we should try to talk about God to a man who says, "But I don't believe in God", it is possible to declare (and so to help him to faith): "But that is not the first issue. The first issue is that God believes in you." Since that is what God is like, God must be known as a real "Person".

On some children's bedroom walls in the Victorian era there hung a framed picture of a huge eye, enough to scare the wits out of a sensitive child; for underneath the frame were the words: "Thou Lord seest me" (from Gen. 16:13, AV). Today, an unfeeling parent might hang a picture of an "almighty" Data Bank in place of the eye. But as we proceed to read this powerful psalm, we find that the almighty Eye does not create fear in mankind, far less in little children. It creates an outspilling of love beyond all that the human mind can conceive.

The psalmist continues: You "know" when I get out of bed in the morning, and when I go to bed at night—all intimate, personal, private affairs. You have known my thoughts centuries before they entered my mind. You sift all my actions, putting them through a sieve, as it were, so as to discover every detail about them, what has motivated them, what effect they have upon me and upon others, in fact, everything conceivable about them (verse 3). In a word, God's action in his search for the real "me" is like winnowing through a whole load of wheat in search of, say, just one pin.

For my part, I don't know what I am going to say till I say it; but you know what I am going to say before I open my mouth. You know every detail about the flow of my sentences, their superficial sound, their real meaning, their connection with my attitude to life, my faith, or even my lack of it. There you are, Lord, in front of me and behind me in space, as well as before me in time, and after me also, after I experience this moment and then can look back upon it. I cannot put back the clock to escape you, or put it forward to an unthinkable future. But apart from "before" and "after", at this very moment your hand lies on my head in blessing (verse 5). I have discovered that I am fenced in by you, fenced in by your love. Verse 6 then gives us an exclamation, not of fear and horror, but of reverent awe at the mystery of such a wonderful God. The psalmist uses here a new word for *knowl-*

edge, one he had evidently picked up in Babylon; for the poor man was desperately trying with mere human language to point to what can be described only as miraculous, to "a reality which at once includes and transcends intellectual disquisition, for it involves a man's total personality in the presence of God", as a modern commentator puts it. He is learning from day to day always more about what total commitment to God must mean for him and for his people.

GOD'S OMNIPRESENCE

Psalm 139:7–12

> 7Whither shall I go from thy Spirit?
>   Or whither shall I flee from thy presence?
> 8If I ascend to heaven, thou art there!
>   If I make my bed in Sheol, thou art there!
> 9If I take the wings of the morning
>   and dwell in the uttermost parts of the sea,
> 10even there thy hand shall lead me,
>   and thy right hand shall hold me.
> 11If I say, "Let only darkness cover me,
>   and the light about me be night,"
> 12even the darkness is not dark to thee,
>   the night is bright as the day;
>   for darkness is as light with thee.

We should not claim for the Bible what it does not claim for itself. Most religions of man take for granted both that God is to be found everywhere and that he is at the same time all-knowing. So it was with the thinking of the ancient Greeks and with the Hindu Vedas of India. But such a belief borders only too easily on pantheism, which conceives of God as almost identical with his own Creation. And since God made me as part of his Creation, then God is obviously to be found also in me. Or, as an eastern Guru put it to me, each of us is in fact God himself.

But there is a reality here in our psalmist's statement of faith that is not to be found in any of the other religions of the world. This is that God maintains his Personhood, and remains other than his Creation; and that is shown in that he is able to be present anywhere that he chooses, and so to be present with me anywhere that I, in my folly, may choose to be. This reality produces in me, in return, my personal awareness of God, so that I can address him as Thou, and never think of speaking to him as It. As in Francis Thompson's poem, *The Hound of Heaven*, the psalmist can say: "I fled Him down the nights and down the days, I fled Him down the arches of the years". Like Judas Iscariot, we might add, "I fled him down the road to hell". Verse 8, then, is one of the few passages in the OT where God's power is seen to extend down even into Sheol. However, the Church has always been aware that God is like that, even when it has been in contact with the religions of the East; and it has never failed to include in its Creed, "He descended into hell".

If I try *to go from thy Spirit*, then I am an egotist and want to escape from the Spirit's leading. If *I flee from thy presence*, then I have turned my back on the Face of God (for that is the meaning of the word "presence"). Thus there is absolutely nowhere I can go to escape him. *If I ascend to heaven* (perhaps that means to scale the heights of philosophy, seeking to be "up in the clouds" of individual satisfaction, or, like the Greeks, to believe in a power beyond even that of the gods, viz. Fate) . . . *If I make my bed in Sheol* (perhaps that means "If I let myself sink down into the depths to which drink, drugs, and sex can depress a man, or if I choose a secularist philosophy of nihilism that prevents any of the higher regions of the spirit from finding room in my mind) . . . in fact, we could go on and on. But why should I thus flee from God who is both Love and Light? I have now proved to myself that God can descend into Sheol if he wills, for the life of exile I underwent was no less than hell on earth: and I found that God was there.

Even in *the uttermost parts of the sea*, in places no one knew of in those days, in far-off China and Japan and in the Isles of the Sea, there *thy right hand* would "keep a grip on me." Even in the realms of darkness (and in the Bible darkness can be used as the symbol of evil), even there *the night is bright as the day; for darkness is as light with thee*. How can this be so? The answer is, of course, that God *is light*, and in him is no *darkness* at all (see 1 John 1:5). That is to say, God can make use of evil as his tool, and bring forth good even out of chaos. Consequently, I who know now all about the hellishness of life as I had to live it in Babylon, am completely assured that God can make use of my own private hell at any time to lead me out into his marvellous *light*.

WHAT A MARVELLOUS CREATURE I AM!

Psalm 139:13–18

> 13For thou didst form my inward parts,
>   thou didst knit me together in my mother's womb.
> 14I praise thee, for thou art fearful and wonderful.
>   Wonderful are thy works!
>   Thou knowest me right well;
> 15   my frame was not hidden from thee,
>   when I was being made in secret,
>   intricately wrought in the depths of the earth.
> 16Thy eyes beheld my unformed substance;
>   in thy book were written, every one of them,
>   the days that were formed for me,
>   when as yet there was none of them.
> 17How precious to me are thy thoughts, O God!
>   How vast is the sum of them!
> 18If I would count them, they are more than the sand.
>   When I awake, I am still with thee.

A thoughtful scientist may well burst out in praise when he discovers a new star. A medical researcher may do so when he discovers a new control of or cure for cancer. Even I can do so when I realize the mysterious intricacies of that brain of mine which is at this moment doing the thinking for me that I need as I read this psalm. The psalmist likewise refers in awe to the mysterious complexity of his liver, kidneys, blood circulation, and the rest, all of which God had *knit together* while he was still an embryo in his mother's womb, seen by God but not by man. This fact alone is sufficient to make any human being, either then or now, burst out with the words *Wonderful are thy works!*

The phrase *intricately wrought in the depths of the earth* may puzzle today's reader. It points, however, to what all parts of the Bible take for granted, that mankind is of the earth, earthy; that dust we are, and that to dust we shall return; that when God created *adam*, man and woman, according to the ancient theological picture to be found in Gen. 2:7, he took soil and with it, like a potter at his wheel, built up a human body into which he had then only to breathe life for this *adam* to become a "living person". But that living being was of the earth, one with the womb of Mother Earth who herself had been formed in the womb of time. We are always to remember that poetic imagery can reach the truth sooner than science can ever hope to do. The phrase that our psalmist uses, then, is one that declares in a telling pictorial manner that man is not God, he is but part of created matter—and yet! every ligament, every tissue, every blood-vessel in his body, the hundred billion neurons or nerve cells inside his skull, its chemical reactions that take as little time as one-millionth of a second to act, all these marvels are listed in the master plan or diagram or on the drawing board that God had before him, and on which he designed the various components he needed to create *me*.

In Gen. 1:1–3 we find that God does not create anything at all, me included, *ex nihilo*, out of nothing. That particular idea is not to be found in the Bible. God creates out of chaos, or in face of chaos; so here, then, he created me out of *unformed substance*. In the same vein the Qoran calls the place where the foetus is formed "a threefold darkness". So even unimportant little "me" is part and parcel of the Creation as a whole that God saw to be good, and which God never ceases to work at until finally he will create the new heavens and the new earth—again not out of nothing, but out of this imperfect world that we know, imperfect because we have made it so. So the psalmist praises God for his *hidden* activities, particularly for his own creation in the womb. God's creative ideas are utterly vast in number (verse 17). Today's scientist humbly declares that the more we learn about this mysterious universe and about our human body the more we are aware of what we do not know. In fact, when we talk of an expanding universe we are really only saying that God's Creation is open-ended, and will always continue to expand at least at the pace of a step ahead of the speed that the intellect of man can follow.

In referring these ideas to the individual person, a modern philosopher puts it thus: "Clearly this electronic wonder inside my skull is far cleverer than I am. Most of the time it teaches me, I don't teach it. I still insist, however, that this is *my brain*, it *isn't me*. For one thing I use clock time; my brain uses millionths of our seconds."

The poet's response to this great mystery cannot be one of intellectual satisfaction, but can only be one of gratitude and faith—*when I awake*, that is, from ruminating on these vast mysteries, *I am still with thee* (compare Ps. 73:23). Joachim Neander read this psalm, and put the mystery into our modern words in his great hymn:

God's great goodness aye endureth
Deep his wisdom passing thought.

THE FACT OF SIN

Psalm 139:19–24

19O that thou wouldst slay the wicked, O God,
    and that men of blood would depart from me,
20men who maliciously defy thee,
    who lift themselves up against thee for evil!
21Do I not hate them that hate thee, O Lord?
    And do I not loathe them that rise up against thee?
22I hate them with perfect hatred;
    I count them my enemies.
23Search me, O God, and know my heart!
    Try me and know my thoughts!
24And see if there be any wicked way in me,
    and lead me in the way everlasting!

But now the psalmist receives a shock. When he comes out of his reverie he finds himself facing reality in the here and now. And that reality is what spoils everything in God's Creation, the fact of sin. "O God, get rid of it," he cries; in fact he says, "Get rid of those people who incarnate sin", that is to say, "Get rid of all the sinners of the earth". "I hate them for 'throwing a spanner into the works' of thy wonderful Creation."

He believes, then, that sinners are those people (1) who deny the mystery of God's creative activity, saying, "It is all just a natural process; it is all just a matter of evolution"; (2) who destroy God's Creation and hinder his creative activities; and particularly (3) they are those who disrupt the harmony of mankind's social life, for it was God's plan for humanity that they should live together in harmony and peace. So the psalmist hates them for God's sake, *hates them with a perfect hatred*; because, of course, he had just been contemplating the *perfect* plan of God for the universe made visible in God's *perfect* plan for each individual unborn child. Note that he doesn't say, "Let me destroy them, Lord". Rather, he leaves all judgment upon them to the justice of the God of all.

Yet there is more to this issue still for us to recognize. The words that end verse 20, "for evil", mean more than just the idea of sin. The word in Hebrew is *shau*, which refers, not to moral offences, but to that total emptiness and vacuity which can lie behind human life, loneliness, meaninglessness, numbness, purposelessness, sterility, aridity. This reality was known to the mediaeval Church as "accidie". Against such the creative and life-giving love of God must be implacably at war. That state of negation to which some people have actually sold themselves is of the very devil himself. So that is why a believer must necessarily say with our poet: *Do not I hate them that hate thee, O Lord?*

Suddenly, however, he remembers that since all men are sinners then he too is one. In shock and horror at what he has been saying about other people he recalls that he too is under the judgment of God. Yet it was really his zeal for God that had led him to make these violent statements. Consequently he now humbly asks God to *search me*. We have seen at verse 1 that that is exactly what God has already done, "dug deep into me", that is, dug right down into my dirty, egotistical subconscious mind. But there is one difference here in approach compared with verse 1. Now he does not address God as Yahweh, the Lord of the Covenant; he calls him *El*, the Mighty God, the King and Creator of all things. He does not waste time, so to speak, in repeating to God what God has now revealed to him about his sinfulness and his egotism; rather he goes straight to the point, and asks God for pardon. For he knows he may do so since God has pardoned him already. And so, by ending his poem as he began it, he rounds off a marvellous theological outpouring that all of us can echo when he asks God for something positive: *Lead me in the way everlasting*, or, probably, and more likely in the present context, the rendering which the RSV *ftn* offers us as an alternative plea: *Lead me in the ancient way*, that way which was revealed in ancient times by God to Israel through Moses, the way that is described and preserved for "me" in the words of the *Torah* of old (compare Jer. 6:16).

This ancient way is still of course the only way; for God does not change. It is the way that Christ points to when he says to a later generation, "I am the Way". For of course Christ who is the Way now was the Way even in the days of Moses.

IN THE FACE OF VIOLENCE GOD CARES

Psalm 140:1–13

To the choirmaster. A Psalm of David.

¹Deliver me, O Lord, from evil men;
    preserve me from violent men,
²who plan evil things in their heart,
    ˙and stir up wars continually.
³They make their tongue sharp as a serpent's,
    and under their lips is the poison of vipers.   *Selah*

⁴Guard me, O Lord, from the hands of the wicked;
    preserve me from violent men,
    who have planned to trip up my feet.

⁵Arrogant men have hidden a trap for me,
 and with cords they have spread a net,
 by the wayside they have set snares for me. *Selah*

⁶I say to the Lord, Thou art my God;
 give ear to the voice of my supplications, O Lord!
⁷O Lord, my Lord, my strong deliverer,
 thou hast covered my head in the day of battle.
⁸Grant not, O Lord, the desires of the wicked;
 do not further his evil plot! *Selah*

⁹Those who surround me lift up their head,
 let the mischief of their lips overwhelm them!
¹⁰Let burning coals fall upon them!
 Let them be cast into pits, no more to rise!
¹¹Let not the slanderer be established in the land;
 let evil hunt down the violent man speedily!

¹²I know that the Lord maintains the cause of the afflicted,
 and executes justice for the needy.
¹³Surely the righteous shall give thanks to thy name;
 the upright shall dwell in thy presence.

Verses 1–5. This psalm says what the author of Ps. 139:10–22 valiantly refrained from saying. Once again, and after a long interval, we have a psalm in the Davidic style. For David went through just such an experience as is recorded here. Even today our generation is plagued by *violent men*. Most human beings everywhere long to live in peace. We all hate the violence that stalks our streets on a dark night, or that holds public figures to ransom. Aldous Huxley once wrote: "Violence makes men worse; non-violence makes them better. The use of violence is accompanied by anger, hatred, and fear, or by exultant malice and conscious cruelty." Violent people, such as the psalmist refers to here, make war against society, and fight against, not just tanks and guns, but against families, and against even old and frail individuals or, in the case of rape, against helpless women and girls. Verse 3 alludes to the subtlety of the *serpent* in the Garden of Eden that called the God of peace and love a liar, yet in such a way that Eve did not notice the significance of what he was saying. A serpent has a forked tongue; it is "two-tongued", an attitude that in a human being might be called "two-faced". With his tongue the serpent can inject his victim with poison. That is the essential horror of the act of rape, for example. It poisons the psyche as well as the body. Yet, like Eve, countless people today seem to be unaware of the heinousness of violence.

Arrogance is the outer sign of the sin of egotism run rampant, and so actually of *self*-worship. It is thus the rejection of the First Commandment. The result is, says our psalmist, that violent men treat me, not as a human being, but as if I were a mere wild antelope to be hunted ruthlessly down (verse 5).

Verses 6–11. Let evil, then, Lord hunt them, he declares, just as they have hunted me. Thus our poet asks God to do for him what the ballot box, rather than force, should accomplish in a democratic society. *Thou art my God*, "so do what I want you to do for me!" One notices a rather modern tone in this command to God, for many today think of God as the Power in the sky that one turns to only in moments of emergency.

The Hebrew of verses 8–9 has suffered in transmission. But that is of little consequence, since we can easily grasp the general drift of the argument. It is one of appeal to God to crush the violence that is all about the psalmist; moreover, as an aspect of this prevailing violence he includes the sin of slander. Slander is a form of violence, just as is the modern zeal for "debunking" a public figure. It is violence done, not by the fist, but by the tongue or the pen, and so can be practised by the physically weak, in fact, even by the bed-ridden.

The phrase *let evil hunt down the violent man speedily* is interesting, for the psalmist shows that he believes he does not need to ask God to act for him against violence. For all God needs to do is to allow evil to work itself out upon *the violent man* himself.

Verses 12–13, *Yet God cares. I know that . . .* As we have seen in other psalms, here is a form of speech used in a profession of faith. So he is declaring: *I know that the Lord* cares for the one who suffers this violence and this slander. We should remember that this psalm was written for all ages of man, so that it now includes "me"! Then a very strong exclamation follows: *Surely the righteous*, the members of God's Covenant people, will always give thanks that that is what God is like (and not like the Greek gods whom the Israelites were now learning about, and who were always ready to hurl thunderbolts!), so that, as *the upright*, they will continue *to dwell in thy presence*. And they shall do so, come what may, slandered or not, whether they are sufferers from violence or not; for whatever happens in the world, nothing can make any difference to those who *dwell in thy presence*.

AN EVENING PRAYER

Psalm 141:1–10

A Psalm of David.

¹I call upon thee, O Lord; make haste to me!
  Give ear to my voice, when I call to thee!
²Let my prayer be counted as incense before thee,
  and the lifting up of my hands as an evening sacrifice!

³Set a guard over my mouth, O Lord,
  keep watch over the door of my lips!
⁴Incline not my heart to any evil,
  to busy myself with wicked deeds
 in company with men who work iniquity;
  and let me not eat of their dainties!

⁵Let a good man strike or rebuke me in kindness,
  but let the oil of the wicked never anoint my head;
  for my prayer is continually against their wicked deeds.
⁶When they are given over to those who shall condemn them,
  then they shall learn that the word of the Lord is true.
⁷As a rock which one cleaves and shatters on the land,
  so shall their bones be strewn at the mouth of Sheol.

⁸But my eyes are toward thee, O Lord God;
  in thee I seek refuge; leave me not defenceless!
⁹Keep me from the trap which they have laid for me,
  and from the snares of evildoers!
¹⁰Let the wicked together fall into their own nets,
  while I escape.

Verses 1–2. Our own small and unimportant life of faith can be put in perspective when we remember the countless thousands of men and women through century after century who have recited this psalm in the evening, in churches, in monasteries, in institutions, in private, perhaps oftenest of all in olden days in the Latin language.

Incense was used in the sanctuary in Jerusalem to serve as an acted *prayer.* The worshipper could see the column of smoke ascending as if going up to God, its sweet smell, they believed, being something that God appreciated in his nostrils. The psalmist, however, seems to be making this prayer at home. He asks God to let this prayer ascend to him because he is not able at the moment to be in the Temple, and to accept *the lifting up of my hands* (that was one of the attitudes of prayer in OT times) as being equivalent to the offering of a lamb (see Exod. 29:38–39). The *evening sacrifice* took time, it took care, it took preparation, it was extremely costly, every action in it was clearly thought out and performed in logical sequence. Our friend's evening prayer, therefore, was no mere two-minute, superficial saying of a collect or the Lord's Prayer, as we might do today, or the utterance of the first few thoughts that arose in his head.

Verses 3–4. He knows that we human beings need the Spirit of God acting on our spirits if we are even to pray aright. Only then do we have "clean hands and a pure heart". Man cannot worship God without God. One element in his prayer (verse 4) we find also in the Lord's Prayer, in the phrase "Lead us not into temptation". We should not just not pray wrongly; we should not act wrongly. One such wrongness is to company with people who put their stomachs first, or, more generally, to compromise with hedonists who put their personal pleasures before things of the spirit.

Verses 5–7. Three unusual requests follow: (1) "Let me accept meekly a rebuke that is meant kindly by a good man," he continues (compare Prov. 27:6). "It shall be as oil for my head; let not my head refuse it" (see Ps. 133:2). (2) "Let my prayer be continually against the deeds of wicked men." That is to say, most interestingly he prays continually for his enemies, as Jesus himself has asked us to do. We must admit that the Hebrew here is obscure. But at least this second clause of his prayer may mean that prayer should be the only weapon a believing person should wield; certainly he should never use violence. (3) For then (the Hebrew is again obscure) *the wicked shall learn* (from my response of love?) *that the Word of the Lord is true.* The problem of understanding this verse strikes us still more if we care to look up the AV rendering of it: "When their judges have been thrown down by the sides of the cliff, they will hear my words, that they are sweet." Verse 7 is also obscure. Professor Dahood, whose commentary on the Psalms makes full use of the relationship between Biblical Hebrew and the Canaanite language, renders verse 6: "Their judges have fallen into the hands of the Rock; then they shall hear how sweet my words are." His rendering of verse 7 is close to that of the RSV. The first part of it may refer to the breaking up of virgin soil before the sowing of seed. Thus verse 7 *may* refer to God's shattering but creative handling of the bones or bodies of wicked men, declaring that he will go on doing so right until they'reach the end of their lives and go down into *Sheol*, and so to death. For God acts this way with their stony hearts in the hope that at least some seed will grow in such unresponsive soil.

Verses 8–10. "However," continues the psalmist, "don't break up and shatter my life in this way. *My eyes*, unlike those of the wicked, *are toward thee, O Lord God; so keep me from the trap they have laid for me.*"

We should note two points about these last verses: (1) Just as other psalmists have said before him, the worshipper recognizes that since evil is self-defeating, God does not need to punish evil-doers. They make their own choice, and in consequence they rush to meet their doom. (2) He ends his evening prayer, after the rather obscure argument and discussion he has had with God, by uttering a vivid and daringly personal challenge which he actually addresses to Almighty God!

IN A CAVE

Psalm 142:1–7

> *A Maskil of David, when he was in the cave. A Prayer.*

¹I cry with my voice to the Lord,
   with my voice I make supplication to the Lord,
²I pour out my complaint before him,
   I tell my trouble before him.
³When my spirit is faint,
   thou knowest my way!

  In the path where I walk
   they have hidden a trap for me.
⁴I look to the right and watch,
   but there is none who takes notice of me;
  no refuge remains to me,
   no man cares for me.

⁵I cry to thee, O Lord;
   I say, Thou art my refuge,
   my portion in the land of the living.
⁶Give heed to my cry;
   for I am brought very low!

  Deliver me from my persecutors;
   for they are too strong for me!
⁷Bring me out of prison,
   that I may give thanks to thy name!
  The righteous will surround me;
   for thou wilt deal bountifully with me.

Verses 1–4. It helps us to understand a psalm if we discover what it has meant to other people. Thus, when we learn that Ps. 142 was on the lips of one of the great saints of history, St. Francis of Assisi, when he died on 3rd October, 1226, we look to see if it could speak equally forcibly to us in our turn. St. Francis, like David of old, was not too shy to cry out loud to God, or pound on God's door, so to speak, and tell him, please to listen to his *complaint*. Two hundred years ago the philosopher Heinrich

Heine, in his turn, lay dying, and as he neared death he said: "It is a great blessing to know that there is someone in heaven to whom I can complain. It is a wonderful relief to whine the whole list of my sufferings." It seems, then, that God does not mind, but even expects such behaviour from us, as Jesus too implies at Luke 18:1-8.

If this psalm were originally from the hand of David, then his persecutors were real persons (see also the heading to Ps. 57). David hid from his enemies in a cave on two occasions, at Adullam (1 Sam. 22), and at Engedi (1 Sam. 24). However, the title *A Maskil of David* invites us to regard the psalm as being rather "religious instruction" based on David's experience in the cave, expressed here in the form of a prayer. In which case the psalm can roll off the tongue of a St. Francis, of a John Bunyan in prison, or of any ordinary person who is suffering in the prison house of the spirit.

I make supplication (verse 1) means "I plead for grace". *My complaint* means rather "my worries". Again, *when my spirit is faint* (verse 3) means literally "when things fall in on top of me". Yet the writer can add at once, "Yet you know my way—I don't, for I have got trapped. Moreover, you know all about that trap." What a relief it is that God is concerned about such small things as the traps into which little people like us can fall!

Now (verse 4) the author tells God to *look to the right* (see RSV *ftn*), for it is on a man's right that a patron, or a champion, or an advocate takes his stand; and then he asks God to see that *there is none who takes notice of me*, that there is no one standing there *for me*. This poor man thus represents the many who utter the typical cry: "No one loves me".

Verses 5-7, A second cry. *But you, O Lord*, are my champion and *my refuge*, when there is no human being to act for me. We note that in this second cry the speaker does not use the same word as he did in verse 4. Consequently he is offering us another facet on what an advocate is and what is expected of him. But more, he continues, *Thou art my portion*, that is, the very meaning of my life. Despite all this our psalmist is still depressed. As we noted above, this psalm can be used by anyone at all who is going through what nearly every human being faces at some time or other in his life, viz. "the dark night of the soul", pictured for us in this psalm as "the cave of Adullam".

When we read the *Torah* we discover that *prison* was never used for punishing an offender as it is in modern society. The idea of imprisonment implied for OT man an assault on the freedom and dignity of the human personality. Prison was only used for detaining a wrongdoer till his trial could come up (Lev. 24:12; Num. 15:34). Punishment, on the other hand, usually took the form of paying back exactly what damage one had done. The wrongdoer had thus to work hard to find the money to do so. But then, over and above the total sum he had to repay, he had to find another 20% as well!

What would happen, then, he wonders, if God fetched him out of prison to stand trial and he was found guilty—could he ever repay what he owed, plus 20%? Oh, but God is not like that, for he is both my Judge and my Advocate at my right hand! He would declare of me "Not guilty!" Then (1) I would *give thanks to thy name*. Next, (2) when my fellow-believers saw how good you were to me they would *surround me* with love and congratulations. Or, as this verb could mean, "they would appear (in the courtroom) with crowns". That is, they would rejoice along with me; they would crown me with their joy; for they would be rejoicing with me that I had been declared "Not guilty!"

GENUINE PENITENCE

Psalm 143:1–12

A Psalm of David.

[1]Hear my prayer, O Lord; give ear to my supplications!
  In thy faithfulness answer me, in thy righteousness!
[2]Enter not into judgment with thy servant;
  for no man living is righteous before thee.

[3]For the enemy has pursued me·
  he has crushed my life to the ground;

he has made me sit in darkness like those long dead.
⁴Therefore my spirit faints within me;
    my heart within me is appalled.

⁵I remember the days of old,
    I meditate on all that thou hast done;
    I muse on what thy hands have wrought.
⁶I stretch out my hands to thee;
    my soul thirsts for thee like a parched land.   *Selah*

⁷Make haste to answer me, O Lord!
    My spirit fails!
 Hide not thy face from me,
    lest I be like those who go down to the Pit.
⁸Let me hear in the morning of thy steadfast love,
    for in thee I put my trust.
Teach me the way I should go,
    for to thee I lift up my soul.

⁹Deliver me, O Lord, from my enemies!
    I have fled to thee for refuge!
¹⁰Teach me to do thy will,
    for thou art my God!
Let thy good spirit lead me
    on a level path!

¹¹For thy name's sake, O Lord, preserve my life!
    In thy righteousness bring me out of trouble!
¹²And in thy steadfast love cut off my enemies,
    and destroy all my adversaries,
    for I am thy servant.

Verses 1–2. We noted at Ps. 142:7 that the psalmist had been in prison awaiting trial. It is perhaps in detention that he prays to God not to *enter into judgment with thy servant.* "Don't bring me to trial," he begs God, "for I fear in advance that you will find me guilty." Clearly, then, this prison is now no longer limited to a building of wood or stone.

Answer me in thy faithfulness, he prays, meaning by that, "in your utter reliability and integrity". He asks that God will be totally fair to him in his judgment; and then he adds, *and in thy righteousness*. This last word is the feminine word we discussed in the Introduction to Volume 1. So it means here "God's gift to me of a love that will enable me to love my neighbour". For I am persuaded that God will never now deprive me of this power, and so go back on his gift to me, no matter how guilty I may be. So the psalmist is referring to one facet of the whole great gospel of God's love that is, of course, present in the NT, but which is difficult to isolate and point to without the help of this and similar passages in the OT.

He recognizes in short that *no man living* is in a right relationship to God. It is not surprising that St. Paul quotes this verse freely in Rom. 3:20 and Gal. 2:16, the difference in wording arising from the fact that he used the Greek Version of the OT and not the Hebrew that lies behind the RSV we are reading here. With the help of this psalm we see how Paul meant that no man dare exclaim to either God or man, "I am saved", and then continue to live in great self-satisfaction at the fact. God had loved him out of his state of rebellion by that love which had touched him only through the Cross. Therefore, Paul meant, we now possess God's own sacrificial love in our heart (the word *tsedaqah*, "righteousness" in verse 1), with the result that we are called upon in our turn to take up our cross and follow Christ. For the new Christian does what Christ does; he empties himself in compassionate love and concern for the lost sheep of the world. It is only when he does that, that he is "saved" at all! (see also Ps. 85).

There are scholars today who would translate Paul's phrase "the righteousness of God" that we find at Rom. 3:21 and 10:3 by some such phrase as "God's salvation-creating love". Paul knew that in the OT the word "righteousness" has both a masculine and a feminine form; but until we know that too, it is difficult to grasp some of his argument in Romans. If we did not know this fact before about the OT's interpretation of "righteousness", we learn now how we should never try to "master" the Bible, looking to find in it what we think ought to be there. Rather, we should "befriend" the Bible so as to become sufficiently intimate with it to be able to listen to what *it* has to say to us.

Verses 3–4. The words *long dead* are used to represent the opposite of that fullness of life which God gives. In fact, *the enemy* here could be death itself in the form, perhaps, of an incurable disease; and like that disease, and since the wages of sin is death, God's judgment can only be a foregone conclusion. So this poor man speaks as if he were already buried alive.

Verses 5–6. Wisely, however, he turns his mind off himself onto what God has done, not onto wondering whether God is there or not, but onto what he has seen. For having done that, he does not need to wonder if God exists! And so he goes over in his mind certain facts, not philosophical ideas about God. These facts are that God had brought his people out of Egypt, had given them their great king David, and had chosen for them the hill that God himself had named Zion. And right in the middle of the Temple on Zion hill was the Mercy Seat. So he can cry out with conviction: "You have saved before, Lord; *I stretch out my hands to thee* therefore with the agony of a *thirsty soul in a parched land.*"

Verses 7–8. Do answer me, please, Lord! Else I shall experience hell (*the Pit*) even in this life. Your *steadfast love* is the only answer to the impasse I have reached, that of knowing that, if I come up for judgment, I shall have to confess to the accusation of "Guilty".

Verses 9–12. What a strange discovery he now makes! It is that the only *way he can go* is to flee from God to God, and to discover when there at last that God's *good spirit* will lead him aright.

Thomas à Kempis wrote of this verse: "Teach me to do thy will, for thou art my wisdom. Thou didst know me before the world was made, and before I was born into the world."

After the usual plea to God that so many psalmists make, asking God to act against evil, this psalmist finally makes the firm statement *for I am thy servant.* There are two points to be noted. With hindsight we are aware that (1) God did finally act against evil in a manner beyond our psalmist's wildest thought—in the Cross of Christ. (2) The individual who is a member of the Covenant community learns that what is required of him is to be totally obedient, as a servant must be, to the revealed will of God.

Thus it is that today when we celebrate the sacrament of baptism, the officiating minister declares of either child or adult, that he is now "engaged to be Christ's faithful soldier and *servant* unto his life's end."

UPDATING THE PSALMS OF DAVID

Psalm 144:1–15

A Psalm of David.

¹Blessed be the Lord, my rock,
  who trains my hands for war,
    and my fingers for battle;
²my rock and my fortress,
    my stronghold and my deliverer,
  my shield and he in whom I take refuge,
    who subdues the peoples under him.

³O Lord, what is man that thou dost regard him,
    or the son of man that thou dost think of him?
⁴Man is like a breath,
    his days are like a passing shadow.

⁵Bow thy heavens, O Lord, and come down!
    Touch the mountains that they smoke!
⁶Flash forth the lightning and scatter them,
    send out thy arrows and rout them!
⁷Stretch forth thy hand from on high,
    rescue me and deliver me from the many waters,
    from the hand of aliens,
⁸whose mouths speak lies,
    and whose right hand is a right hand of falsehood.

⁹I will sing a new song to thee, O God;
    upon a ten-stringed harp I will play to thee,
¹⁰who givest victory to kings,
    who rescuest David thy servant.
¹¹Rescue me from the cruel sword,
    and deliver me from the hand of aliens,
  whose mouths speak lies,
    and whose right hand is a right hand of falsehood.

¹²May our sons in their youth
  be like plants full grown,
 our daughters like corner pillars
  cut for the structure of a palace;
¹³may our garners be full,
  providing all manner of store;
 may our sheep bring forth thousands
  and ten thousands in our fields;
¹⁴may our cattle be heavy with young,
  suffering no mischance or failure in bearing;
 may there be no cry of distress in our streets!
¹⁵Happy the people to whom such blessings fall!
 Happy the people whose God is the Lord!

Verses 1–11. The Psalter is a collection of hymns, songs, and prayers made over a period of perhaps eight hundred years. The last section of this psalm, i.e. verses 12–15, is written in "late" Hebrew, and so can be dated towards the end of the OT period. But verses 1–11 quote in a revised form quite a number of older psalms, notably 8, 18, 33, 39, and 69. The LXX even adds into the title, after "A Psalm of David", the words "against Goliath". Now, since the compiler of the psalm knew perfectly well that he was composing a hymn for worship out of several ancient psalms already to be found in the Temple collection, and binding them into one by setting over them the heading "A Psalm of David", he was clearly saying: "The ideas here could have been what David had in mind when he felled Goliath; so we too can use them in our day and generation many centuries later."

Verse 2 gives a good example of his "updating" technique. There is a footnote to the RSV telling us that the Hebrew has *my steadfast love*, while the RSV prefers to change this to *my rock*. The quotation comes from Ps. 18:2 and 2 Sam. 22:2, both of which passages contain David's original words, including "my rock". But could the psalmist not have known he was making a "mistake"? Could he not have been obliquely suggesting that God's *steadfast love* is as unchanging as a rock?

At verses 3–4 he puts together ideas from Ps. 8:4 and Ps. 39:5–6 (compare Ps. 90). We should turn to these psalms at this point and read them again. Man, he is suggesting, is not so exalted as a wrong reading of Ps. 8 might lead us to suppose, rather he is like a *breath*, a mere puff of wind, in comparison with the majesty of God.

In verse 5 he seems to be suggesting (on the basis of Ps. 18:9 and Ps. 33:13): "O Lord, spread open thy heavens and come down! Smite the mountains so that they may give forth smoke!", and in this way repeat the "descent" of the Word of God at Mount Sinai in the days of Moses. But he knows that God does not turn the clock back. Elijah had to learn this fact when he fled to Horeb to the exact spot where Moses had been before, expecting God to speak once again in earthquake, wind and fire (1 Kings 19:8–13). Instead he spoke in a whisper. The psalmist has updated old psalms; but as he does so he recognizes that God continues to reveal his will in ever new situations and in new ways.

Similarly in verse 7 *the many waters* and *the hand of aliens* make us think of the Exodus from Egypt, but also of the more recent deliverance from Exile in Babylon, and beyond that of God's ability to save us from the power of scoffers and sceptics, or of Sheol and death, or even of our own raging *subconscious*. Compare Pss. 69:1–4; 12:2; 18:16; 116:3–4, etc.

It is in that sense of expecting the unexpected that the psalmist invites us to join him in singing *a new song* (compare Pss. 33:2–3; 96:1; 98:1), one based on the experience of David and of God's people of old, but one fitted nevertheless to the changed circumstances of our own day. He is giving us, indeed, a lesson from within the Psalms on how to interpret the Psalms.

Verses 12–15. In these verses we have a little composition of the psalmist's own, not obviously connected with what has gone before except in so far as both it and the psalms he has just "updated" could well be summed up in its final line, *Happy the people whose God is the Lord!*

It is altogether made up of picture language once again, pictures of the prosperity of both country and town when people take God seriously to be their Rock. Archaeologists have turned up from the ruins of Tell Halaf in Upper Mesopotamia the statue of a girl adorning the sanctuary (verse 12), *like corner pillars*. It is true that angels are always pictured in both Testaments as young men. But Israel's religious thinking has left room for girl angels as well (for "angel" is just the word for "missionary"), to express the mind of God to man. In the city there is to be no more violent behaviour, *no cry of distress* (verse 14). For the Promised Land is now the land of peace, and all its people now know the *shalom* of God.

GOD'S OUTRAGEOUS LOVE (i)

Psalm 145:1–7

A Song of Praise. Of David.

¹I will extol thee, my God and King,
and bless thy name for ever and ever.
²Every day I will bless thee,
and praise thy name for ever and ever.
³Great is the Lord, and greatly to be praised,
and his greatness is unsearchable.

⁴One generation shall laud thy works to another,
and shall declare thy mighty acts.
⁵On the glorious splendour of thy majesty,
and on thy wondrous works, I will meditate.
⁶Men shall proclaim the might of thy terrible acts,
and I will declare thy greatness.
⁷They shall pour forth the fame of thy abundant goodness,
and shall sing aloud of thy righteousness.

This is a carefully composed psalm for use in public worship. It is an alphabetic-acrostic; but curiously the lines of verse beginning with the letter *nun* (our "n") are missing. But as we see from the RSV footnote at verse 13, its editors have been able to supply us with the missing lines from a single Hebrew manuscript—and surely these lines have been worth recovering!

H. M. Loewe, the English Jewish scholar, has written: "Psalm 145 is of permanent importance. So profound is it that it became a model of the *imitatio dei*, the imitation of God." In fact it is used three times in the Hebrew Daily Liturgy.

Again, we might quote John Calvin, the Reformer. He says: "All the griefs, sorrows, fears, misgivings, hopes, cares, anxieties, in short all the disquieting emotions with which the minds of men are wont to be agitated, the Holy Spirit has here pictured exactly."

Finally, since this psalm, like so many others, points to God's compassion for the depressed and underprivileged of the earth, we may quote a present-day theologian who declares that "the evangelistic message which deals with man as the sinner, but not the sinned against, is not remaining true to the Bible as the Word of God."

Since we begin (verse 2) with the words *Every day I will bless thee*, we are learning to remind ourselves daily, in fact over and over again, how great God is, *and his greatness is unsearchable*. It goes beyond all our theologies and our various doctrines even when we turn them into dogmas, and quite beyond what scientific enquiry can hope to reach, and certainly beyond what we can ever hope to know of God in our personal religious experience. In our daily worship we are made to remember the continuity of the praise of God that has gone on for three thousand years, with parents telling their children of God's *mighty acts* (verse 4). So now this individual worshipper, one of the congregation as a body, pauses to *meditate* in his turn on *thy wondrous works*, really "thy wondrous words"; for an act of God is first a word he has spoken into space and time. *Wondrous* is the adjective we have met before, meaning "miraculous". For example, it describes what happened when Israel came safely through the Red (Reed) Sea, when God "spoke" the Word and held back Pharaoh's army, or even when an incorrigible sinner is turned into a compassionate human being, again, *by the might of thy terrible acts*. We know that this is the kind of miracle he is referring to, for *thy righteousness* here is the feminine form of that word we have met before and which means just this. For it is a *terrible act* of God to redeem a sinner, terrible, not to the sinner, but to God himself.

What does all this mean? We are to remember that, in Christ, these terrible acts are finally made visible at a historical moment. What the OT has done is to offer us, *before the event*, the *theology* of Paul's basic assertion that "God was in Christ, reconciling the world to himself" (2 Cor. 5:19). There were at least two "moments" of revelation that helped the Israel of the disciples' day to think through and to grasp the meaning of the Cross of Christ One was at Exod. 4:22, "Israel is my son", and the other at Isa. 45:14–15, "God is *in* you only" (not "with", as RSV), "a God who hides himself"—*in* Israel (see Luke 24:27). Thus, without this psalm and others like it we could not have discovered that, when Christ the Son went through the experience of being forsaken by God while on the Cross and in his descent to meet the last enemy, death, God the Father, who was *in* Christ, also experienced that final and total forsakenness. For Christ did what Israel before him had done, and more than that, he did what Israel could not do. Thus it is that when the NT "fulfils" the OT, what it does is to fulfil its theology in the person and work of Christ, a theology that had been revealed in a continuous line of *terrible acts*, always made plain by God himself in pictorial terms and in historical incidents, beginning from God's *mighty acts* in the days of Moses, continued through the destruction and "death" of Jerusalem, as Ezekiel called it, on through the Exile and the "resurrection" from it, right to the day on which this poet was writing his great psalm.

Because they have glimpsed a little of all this, Israel will want to *pour forth* (the verb pictures an action like turning on a tap out of which the water gushes, unstoppable), *the fame*, or "the story" (NEB) or "the memory" of thy huge *goodness*—for them, as we must add. For *tov, goodness*, carries just that potent meaning. It does not describe an abstract idea of mere goodness, but refers to God's kindness and love that he never ceases to pour out upon his dear ones. And so it speaks in the last resort of that *terrible* love of God that we see in the Cross of Christ.

GOD'S OUTRAGEOUS LOVE (ii)

Psalm 145:8–21

⁸The Lord is gracious and merciful,
  slow to anger and abounding in steadfast love.
⁹The Lord is good to all,
  and his compassion is over all that he has made.

¹⁰All thy works shall give thanks to thee, O Lord,
  and all thy saints shall bless thee!
¹¹They shall speak of the glory of thy kingdom,
  and tell of thy power,
¹²to make known to the sons of men thy mighty deeds,
  and the glorious splendour of thy kingdom.
¹³Thy kingdom is an everlasting kingdom,
  and thy dominion endures throughout all generations.

The Lord is faithful in all his words,
  and gracious in all his deeds.
¹⁴The Lord upholds all who are falling,
  and raises up all who are bowed down.
¹⁵The eyes of all look to thee,
  and thou givest them their food in due season.
¹⁶Thou openest thy hand,
  thou satisfiest the desire of every living thing.
¹⁷The Lord is just in all his ways,
  and kind in all his doings.
¹⁸The Lord is near to all who call upon him,
  to all who call upon him in truth.
¹⁹He fulfils the desire of all who fear him,
  he also hears their cry, and saves them.
²⁰The Lord preserves all who love him;
  but all the wicked he will destroy.

²¹My mouth will speak the praise of the Lord,
  and let all flesh bless his holy name for ever and ever.

Verses 8–9. These two verses express the basic faith of the whole OT about what God is like. They come from Exod. 34:6, and are repeated again and again throughout the OT. What greater words are there than these to express the faith of mankind down the centuries about the miracle of the fact that God is love? We should note further that verse 9 could be rendered by "his mother-love (compassion) is over all that he has made", as if all things were God's own beloved offspring—not just people but animals as well.

Verses 10–13*a*. This is why *all his works* reciprocate God's love by *giving thanks to him*—we think of the dawn chorus of the birds that rejoice at God's good gift of life, of the hum of the bees, of the joyous excitement of the young calf or lion cub as he finds out how strong and beautiful he is. But as for man, it is only *his saints* that *bless* God, unlike the realm of Nature, all of which adores its God. What, then, do they do to bless his name? (1) *They speak of the glory of thy kingdom*. (2) They tell *the sons of men*, that is, all other human beings who do not normally praise the Lord, that there are two kinds of kingdom in the world. There are the kingdoms of men, and there is *the kingdom of God*. (3) They declare that God's kingdom is created by his *power* and by his *mighty deeds* of recreative love. Consequently this kingdom shall not pass away, for it belongs to the eternity of love. Writing about A.D. 400, when the Roman Empire was losing its grip, and licence was spreading over North Africa where he lived, St. Augustine had this to say: "What else are the great kingdoms but great robberies?"

Verse 13*a* is quoted most aptly at Dan. 4:3 and 4:34. The Book of Daniel goes on to reveal that the kingdom of God is not of this world. All the world's kingdoms, on the other hand, are in the grip of forces outside of themselves, so that they cannot save themselves.

Verses 13*b*–20. The *might* and *power* of God, however, is the strength of the gentle giant. His greatness is, in fact, his graciousness! (a) He stoops down and takes the arm of *all those who are falling* and holds them steady. (b) He raises up the chin of those who are overwhelmed by life's cares, and smiles into their eyes. (c) The whole animal creation, birds, beasts and fishes look longingly and trustingly to God for their food, just as cows come lowing home to be milked and fed, just as hens look for their supper of grain, and as the birds in the garden for crumbs on a

cold winter's morning—from us, mankind, who are God's care-
takers of the earth. We do all these things because God has first
shown us the way. *He* does all these things *justly* (with *tsedeq*) and
kindly (with *hesed*). Therefore so should we. Even as our dogs
and cats come running to us for their food, so is God near to all
who *call upon him in truth*, that is, in total sincerity.

There are several words for *love* in the OT. The word used in
verse 20 is the word for parents-and-child love; but the wicked,
says the psalmist, that is, those who reject the fellowship typified
by the happy family, God destroys, by letting them, as we might
phrase it, "stew in their own juice", that is to say, by leaving them
to their own devices, the while refusing to transgress on the
freedom of their will. For what else can God do with them but
wait for them to return home like the Prodigal Son? The true
lover will never force his loved one to return his love. Thus it is
that the fear of God and the love of God are inseparable. Fear
preserves love from degenerating into presumptuous familiarity;
love prevents fear from becoming a dread of God as only Judge
and Lord.

Verse 21. The Chorus understands this. It gladly proclaims the
praise of God for not forcing the rebellious to do his will, but
blessing him for the revelation he has always given them of his
very Self, his *Name*, a Name that shall remain to all time and on
into eternity. And that name is Love.

PRAISING GOD BY LOVING

Psalm 146:1–10

[1]Praise the Lord!
  Praise the Lord, O my soul!
[2]I will praise the Lord as long as I live;
  I will sing praises to my God while I have being.

[3]Put not your trust in princes,
  in a son of man, in whom there is no help.
[4]When his breath departs he returns to his earth;
  on that very day his plans perish.

[5]Happy is he whose help is the God of Jacob,
  whose hope is in the Lord his God,

⁶who made heaven and earth,
  the sea, and all that is in them;
who keeps faith for ever;
⁷   who executes justice for the oppressed;
  who gives food to the hungry.

The Lord sets the prisoners free;
⁸   the Lord opens the eyes of the blind.
The Lord lifts up those who are bowed down,
  the Lord loves the righteous.
⁹The Lord watches over the sojourners,
  he upholds the widow and the fatherless;
  but the way of the wicked he brings to ruin.

¹⁰The Lord will reign for ever,
  thy God, O Zion, to all generations.
Praise the Lord!

In this psalm, meant for congregational worship, we hear individuals each exhorting the other to do what each "I" am exhorting myself to do, that is, to praise the Lord *while I have being*. What we are to note, however, is that we are to praise God, not just for an hour a week in song, but with the whole of our being at all times and in all places. Just what that means the poet does not reveal until we come to the very last verse of his poem.

The Bible has been scrutinized and weighed up and examined from every possible angle. Those people who have counted its very verses and letters tell us that verse 3 is the mid-point of the whole (English) Bible. That verse certainly offers us wise advice; but it does so, not in order to disparage man, as being of no account, but in order to exalt God who is all in all. This truth is then emphasized in verses 5–7. For example, says the poet, a man or a woman may promise you the gift of a sum of money and may even agree to set down his kind offer in writing. But before he can put pen to paper he most unfortunately falls dead. Because of that the money never becomes yours after all. But God does not die. *He keeps faith for ever*, for of course he is the Living God. God even goes the second mile in his promise of love. Not only does he *execute justice* impartially, he "bends over backwards", as we say today, to give *justice* a human face, not only to the "just" but also even to *the oppressed*; and while he provides food for all humanity, he gives it primarily *to the hungry*.

Imagine a king, runs the second example, in the days and in the civilization in which our psalmist lived. This king rules as mighty lord over his wide dominions, seeking out from his splendid pillared palace the poor folk who are languishing in prison in the capital city, the blind and the beggars on its streets, the exhausted displaced persons and elderly forced labourers in detention camps, widows living in hovels, orphans stealing to get something to eat—but can you really imagine such a king? But our King, our God, is actually like that! *Therefore*, claims the psalmist, God is worthy of our trust. *Therefore*, he implies throughout this psalm, we are to learn to be like him and do the same. *The Lord loves the righteous*, he adds (verse 8), the people whom he has "put right" so that they can live in this way, and he will never let them down. But if people simply refuse to accept from him this new way of loving and instead oppress their workers and the under-privileged, then God *brings the way of* these *wicked to ruin*, literally "to perversion"!

This all means, then, that we are do as God does, and by living out a life of love, we are praising him all day and every day, not only with our lips but with our lives. It is only when we, like God, *uphold the widow and the fatherless* and care for *the prisoner* and *the blind* (and of course all the other victims of human tragedy as well) that we shall be able to understand Jesus' parable which he tells us at Matt. 25:31–46. But the point is, loving our neighbour is praising the Lord!

The last verse gives us the guarantee about all this. *The Lord reigns for ever*, that is, reigns in his love in this way. So don't forget, *Zion*, he is *thy God*—and we can be like him for ever.

GOD'S CARING LOVE (i)

Psalm 147:1–11

¹Praise the Lord!
    For it is good to sing praises to our God;

for he is gracious, and a song of praise is seemly.
²The Lord builds up Jerusalem;
  he gathers the outcasts of Israel.
³He heals the brokenhearted,
  and binds up their wounds.
⁴He determines the number of the stars,
  he gives to all of them their names.
⁵Great is our Lord, and abundant in power;
  his understanding is beyond measure.
⁶The Lord lifts up the downtrodden,
  he casts the wicked to the ground.

⁷Sing to the Lord with thanksgiving;
  make melody to our God upon the lyre!
⁸He covers the heavens with clouds,
  he prepares rain for the earth,
  he makes grass grow upon the hills.
⁹He gives to the beasts their food,
  and to the young ravens which cry.
¹⁰His delight is not in the strength of the horse,
  nor his pleasure in the legs of a man;
¹¹but the Lord takes pleasure in those who fear him,
  in those who hope in his steadfast love.

Verses 1–6. We have been made aware that our collection of psalms was put together in roughly chronological order (see the Introduction to this volume). Some of the first psalms in our Psalter are from the hand of David (about 1000 B.C.). Then follow others from the period of the kings of Israel and Judah (that is, up till 587 B.C. when Jerusalem was destroyed). Then came the Exile and with it a cry to God in despair and hopelessness. But there are other psalms in which men and women of faith reveal that they had found an answer to their distress by remembering God's Covenant with his *hesed* as its "cement". Then there follow songs of the Return, of the rebuilding of Jerusalem, of the rededication of the Temple, and thus finally of the life of praise and thanksgiving within the Covenant community. This psalm belongs in this last category. Ezra and Nehemiah were both Israelites who were born and brought up under the Persians in a

far away land and who only obtained their first view of Jerusalem
a century or more after Cyrus had permitted the first "returnees"
to go home from Babylon. We know little about life in Jerusalem
in those centuries, once Nehemiah had secured its walls (Neh. 4).
But there seems to have been a long period of comparative peace.
Psalm 147 may come from this period when descendants of those
who had stayed in Babylon or who had gone further from home
right into Persia were slowly trickling back, and being welcomed
home to Zion. There they were glad indeed to sing the praise of
their Redeemer God.

Like the Father who welcomed home the Prodigal Son, so God
gathers the outcasts of Israel. Even as these newcomers found
their true home physically in Zion, they also found it to be so
spiritually. This historical reality reminds us that, in our time,
once God's lost sheep return home to the local "Zion" at the
street corner, they ought to be finding an elder brother ready and
willing to *heal the brokenhearted and bind up their wounds.*

The God who gives his redeemed people the power to love the
lost is he who *determines* (or "counts") *the number of the stars.* He
does that, because he wants to learn how many of his sheep are
still lost. Today in our astronomy books we learn the names of the
well-known stars. The astrophysicist, however, cannot give
names to the many million more stars he knows there are, because they are beyond human reckoning. Yet God had promised
Abraham: "I will multiply your descendants as the stars of
heaven" (Gen. 22:17). In the light of this great expression of
God's overwhelming love, how the columns of the astrologers in
the daily papers appear as just so much hocus-pocus! They can
name a few of the visible "stars", Leo, Sagittarius, and the rest,
and declare that these particular stars can affect our lives. But the
poor empty-minded astrologer takes no account of the millions of
other stars he cannot see, just as he takes no account of the
unlimited grace of the Living God. But the psalmist exclaims with
exultation: *Great is our Lord, and abundant in power, his understanding is beyond measure.*

How does this great God show his power? There follows one of
the constant surprises of the Bible. He shows his *power by lifting*

up the downtrodden! This God, who is *beyond measure*, is actually in a personal relationship of love with all his creatures here below, with the wretched victims of human greed and selfishness—and he is in opposition to all those who cause their wretchedness!

This reality about God, that his power and his understanding *are* his love beyond measure, hit home powerfully one day to Martin Luther, the Reformer, at a time when he had exhausted himself and was in poor health. A Marshal of the Court accordingly invited him to come and rest in his castle. He arranged a hunting-party to let Luther breathe the fresh air, suggesting that he follow the hunt in a private carriage. But once safely tucked into his carriage Luther opened his Bible at this psalm. Quite forgetting where he was, he there and then penned an exposition of it that plumbs its depths as a great revelation of the love of God.

Verses 7–11. Each of the three sections of this psalm begins with a call to praise, and then explains why it does so. The first call, in verses 1–3, was on account of God's care for Zion. The second one here is because of his care for Nature. The third call will be because of God's gift of *shalom* to his people, as we shall see (verse 14).

The rain-clouds, without which nothing can grow, are God's good provision. He is concerned for all the animal creation, even for baby ravens (who will turn out to be what easterners detested, scavengers) raucously crying in the nest for their food. Or, as Jesus put it, in a later century, God is "moved" by the fall of even one sparrow—and there are billions of these little creatures on this earth.

The *horse* in Biblical times was not used as a farmyard animal. It was oxen that pulled the plough. The horse was stabled in the royal armoury, for the horse was an instrument of war. But God does not like war. The strong *legs* of the infantryman, too, *God takes no pleasure in*. What he does *take pleasure in*, on the other hand, is having a personal relationship with those *who fear him* ("reverence" him, that is to say, those who are not impertinently "pally" with him). These place their *hope*, not in their own ability to face the fiercest odds, but in God's *hesed*, his *steadfast love*.

GOD'S CARING LOVE (ii)

Psalm 147:12–20

12Praise the Lord, O Jerusalem!
  Praise your God, O Zion!
13For he strengthens the bars of your gates;
  he blesses your sons within you.
14He makes peace in your borders;
  he fills you with the finest of the wheat.
15He sends forth his command to the earth;
  his word runs swiftly.
16He gives snow like wool;
  he scatters hoarfrost like ashes.
17He casts forth his ice like morsels;
  who can stand before his cold?
18He sends forth his word, and melts them;
  he makes his wind blow, and the waters flow.
19He declares his word to Jacob,
  his statutes and ordinances to Israel.
20He has not dealt thus with any other nation;
  they do not know his ordinances.
  Praise the Lord!

We have now reached the third call to praise. What this time is the reason? *For he strengthens the bars of your gates.* These words refer in the first instance to such an activity as Nehemiah's when he built up Jerusalem's defences. Note though that it was not Nehemiah who did the strengthening of the gates, it was God (compare Ps. 127:1). Consequently the historical incident becomes at the same time a revelation of God's activities and of his love and care for the city. There is thus no reason why we should not make this verse apply to God's care for our own local church building, on the grounds that God's care never changes or ends. But our poet wants us to see more in this verse still. It is the people who live in the city for whom God cares, not just stone walls and iron gates. He increases the congregation by blessing the young people within it. Clearly this is rather different from some congregations today which are composed largely of old folk! *You* in verse 13 is feminine singular in form. Thus it refers to Zion, the people of God, whom God blesses by giving them the warmth of a true fellowship.

Verse 14 runs, *He makes peace in your borders. Shalom*, as we have seen before, covers such realities as peace of mind, tranquillity of heart, social welfare, even material prosperity. Such, then, is God's will and plan for his people as they settle in again to become the ideal Zion that is meant to be copied by the nations of the world. To this end God creates the right conditions for Nature to co-operate with his plan. These conditions are to enable *Jacob* (the people of God) to concentrate on the fact that he has revealed his *Word* already in the *Torah*, so that they (*Israel* this time, meaning the "forgiven people"; see Gen. 32:24–31) may be set free to turn their whole attention to *his statutes and ordinances*.

We cannot, however, limit the phrase *he makes his wind blow and the waters flow* (verse 18*b*) to the natural processes, because this verse is directly linked with what follows at verse 19. We have noted frequently that God's Spirit works in and through Nature for the redemption of mankind. "Wind" and "spirit" are the same word in both the Hebrew of the OT and the Greek of the NT, while "running water" in Hebrew is expressed as "living water". It is God's *wind that he makes to blow*, not just "Nature's" wind. It may well be that Jesus had these two verses in mind, among others, when he raised his voice *on the last day of the feast, the great day*, and applied these two terms (John 7:37–39), spirit and water, to himself.

We are not to envisage the little post-exilic city-state of Judah-Jerusalem as being isolated from the great big world. Around them throughout the pre-exilic period the Edomites, the Moabites and the Philistines and others had already been in touch with the people of Jerusalem. The Canaanites, meanwhile, lived alongside the Israelites even "in the same street", we might say. Moreover, in Nehemiah's day, the religions of the Persians, Arabs, Phoenicians and Greeks were all represented in Jerusalem's squares by visiting foreign merchants, diplomats and philosophers. Israel, however, was totally convinced that she possessed a unique revelation from God—not a unique "religion", let us note, but a unique revelation. For the other religions of mankind possessed no divinely given guidelines, no *ordinances*. All they had were code-books on legal and moral behaviour which they themselves had written.

In the present day the peoples of the world have become much more mixed up than they used to be, and Christians may have Muslims, Parsees, Hindus, Sikhs, Rosicrucians, Theosophists, Astrologers, Scientologists and many others living as their next-door neighbours. We can therefore understand Israel's situation better than our forefathers could. Despite it, the poet, at verse 20, can grandly say: *He has not dealt thus with any other nation*; *they do not know his ordinances*. How had God dealt with Israel? He had singled her out to make Covenant with her, had given her a revelation that covered the whole of life. He had educated her both through his *Torah* and, more than that, through the suffering he had brought her through in the Babylonian Exile. In all this he had one end in view, that *I will give you as a light to the nations*, *that my salvation may reach to the end of the earth* (Isa. 49:6). Or, since "salvation" is in its feminine form, "that you may become my saving love to the end of the earth"! The religions of man all offer salvation in some form or other for their adherents. Israel alone possessed a "religion" that was meant, not for her alone, but for all the men, women and children of the earth.

An old Alaskan Inuit woman, drink-sodden and *broken-hearted* (see verse 3) who possessed an "excellent" religion in the estimation of many North Americans, once declared: "No one gave a damn for us till the Church came." That is why the last words of the psalm are, simply, *Praise the Lord!*

COSMIC PRAISE (i)

Psalm 148:1–14

[1]Praise the Lord!
  Praise the Lord from the heavens,
    praise him in the heights!

²Praise him, all his angels,
   praise him, all his host!

³Praise him, sun and moon,
   praise him, all you shining stars!
⁴Praise him, you highest heavens,
   and you waters above the heavens!

⁵Let them praise the name of the Lord!
   For he commanded and they were created.
⁶And he established them for ever and ever;
   he fixed their bounds which cannot be passed.

⁷Praise the Lord from the earth,
   you sea monsters and all deeps,
⁸fire and hail, snow and frost,
   stormy wind fulfilling his command!

⁹Mountains and all hills,
   fruit trees and all cedars!
¹⁰Beasts and all cattle,
   creeping things and flying birds!

¹¹Kings of the earth and all peoples,
   princes and all rulers of the earth!
¹²Young men and maidens together,
   old men and children!

¹³Let them praise the name of the Lord,
   for his name alone is exalted;
   his glory is above earth and heaven.
¹⁴He has raised up a horn for his people,
   praise for all his saints,
   for the people of Israel who are near to him.
  Praise the Lord!

We begin with *Praise the Lord!* and we end at verse 14 with *Praise the Lord!* Enclosed, in between, we meet with the whole of God's Creation. God is not only the Creator of all things, he is also the Redeemer of all *things*, and not just of mankind. How else could we look forward to a "new heaven and a new earth"? That is why all *things* must praise him, again, not just mankind.

St. Francis of Assisi (A.D. 1182–1226) based his *Canticle of the Sun* upon this psalm. We should compare also the words of the *Benedicite*, the Apocryphal "Song of the Three Children" to be inserted after Daniel 3:23, and to be found also in the Book of Common Prayer. The hymn "All creatures of our God and King, lift up your voice and with us sing, Hallelujah, Hallelujah!" is but one of many modern hymns that take up the strain of Ps. 148.

Like not a few others, it contains no "search for God". Rather it is a dialogue of a man with God, a man who is completely sure of God's love and care for his universe. He is able, of course, to sing as he does, because he knows that he has been redeemed by God. For the post-exilic generation recognized that the physical redemption they had experienced in being released from bondage in Babylon was but one side of the coin. It was but the sacramental sign of God's total redemption of his loved ones from the power of all evil. It even included the cosmos. As John 3:16 later puts it in Christian terms, "God so loved the cosmos . . ." (not just mankind). So now in this psalm the cosmos makes reply in glorious praise.

The poet begins with the world of the spirit, with all the angelic host. They must be the first to say "Hallelujah". Then comes the sky above, with its sun by day and its moon and stars by night. They too are to join in the Hebrew word *Hallelujah*, "Praise the Lord". They are able to do so because in a sense beyond our materialistic notions today, they are "alive" in their response to the goodness of God. Our hearts hear it in what the mediaeval mystics called the music of the spheres.

During the Second World War the British Broadcasting Corporation sponsored a series of radio talks which they entitled "People Matter". That was in face of the war machine as it devoured men and women in uniform and in the armaments factories. When the series ended, that great man, Archbishop Temple, asked if he might give one further talk on the theme "Things Matter".

But the heavens above are not free of evil. *The waters above the heavens*, or rather "the skies" (Gen. 1:6–7), were not to the Hebrews only a physical or scientific phenomenon. Such language is what we would call "theology in pictures". For, along with "the waters under the earth" (Exod. 20:4) these are the waters of chaos, of the powers of evil, or, as the early Church called them, of the elemental spirits. In the beginning, however, God had conquered these forces when he uttered the words: *Let there be light.* Yet he permitted them to remain in their conquered condition. For otherwise man could not have become a moral creature with freedom to choose between good and evil.

In later centuries this two-fold evil, above and below the life of man, came to be personified in the Devil and all his angels above and in the principalities and powers resident in the heart of evil men below. In fact, it was present even in what is good, what is the revealed will of God. For man's interpretation of God's will cannot be fully understood. That is why Paul could sometimes regard the Law of Moses as an enemy; yet, even as an enemy it could point to Christ. Even these powers, then, both above and below, are to *praise the Lord*! For it was he who *commanded and they were created*, the forces of Nature, the powers of chaos, the lot; and to them all God gave freedom within bounds to pursue their various courses. Yet *their bounds are fixed, which cannot be passed.*

COSMIC PRAISE (ii)

Psalm 148:1–14 *(cont'd)*

Verses 7ff. The great paean of praise keeps pressing through in all ages and in all places into the consciousness of man, through *fire, hail, snow and frost*; through *stormy wind fulfilling*, not its own desires, but *his command*!; through *mountains*, without which there would be no rain, *fruit trees* useful to man, as indeed *cedars* are too, through the whole animal creation as listed in Genesis chapter one. And again we have a reminder of evil; for included in the list, and also to be found in Gen. 1, are *you sea-monsters and all deeps*. These too are his "ministers" (compare Ps. 103:21), powers that represent the evil latent in the universe, and that includes the serpent which God had himself created to live in the Garden with man (Gen. 3:1). And they too are *commanded* to sing "Hallelujah". But how can the Deep, the *tehom* of Gen. 1:2, with its resident monster, Leviathan, Tiamat, the Dragon, or whatever name you might like to give it, how could these sing the praise of God? Once again, as we have noted before, the OT is providing us with the theology (in pictures) that we need to interpret what happened when God, in Christ, was put to death on Calvary. For then the forces of evil, which God had permitted to exist within their strict bounds, were allowed actually to overcome the power of God himself. In doing so, they were indeed praising God. For they were showing forth the terrible and unspeakable love of God to which both the OT and the NT give never-ending witness.

The Word, then, that sounds behind, in and through the whole created world is Praise, and it is Good News. From time to time it keeps bursting through the veil. It was heard in the song of the angels at Bethlehem (Luke 2:10–14). But it has been there since the beginning, when "all the stars sang together and all the sons of God shouted for joy" (Job 38:7).

The Good News reaches the ears of kings and commoners alike (verse 11–12), both young and old. The OT never forgets that God's basic unit for mankind is the family, the community. J. B. Priestley, the novelist, writes, "Something I never knew in earlier years, the blessed feeling, coming through occasionally like some snatch of heavenly song, the blessed feeling of *conscious love*. What a prize for fumbling and bewildered old age!"

Nature with its massive forces locked up in atoms and in light may think that it rules and commands the life of the universe. Mankind, again, with his power of thought and invention, may believe so even more. But no—*his name alone is exalted, his glory is above earth and heaven*, above Nature, above mankind, and even above the world of the spirit.

But the psalm ends in a paradox. *He raised up a horn for his people*, the horn of a bull. The Biblical world saw the bull as the ultimate picture of the power of brute force. Israel's neighbours, the Canaanites, had for centuries worshipped their god Baal under the guise of a bull, mighty in war, powerful in sex, riding on the clouds of the sky. Israel's God, however, had *raised up a horn for his people*. God had given them, now that they were redeemed, a vital power denied to the forces of Nature and to the ability of the human intellect. This was the power to do God's will in the world by loving all peoples into the fellowship of the kingdom of God.

This statement is capped by one just as amazing: *He has raised up*, produced, *praise for all his saints*. Through the sheer grace of his unsearchable understanding (see 147:5), not only does God accept praise, *for his name is exalted* (148:13), he actually exalts Israel, his people, and gives *them* praise in return! *His saints* means, of course, his redeemed people, *who are near to him* within the bonds of the Covenant. For at Exod. 19:5 God had claimed Israel as *my own possession*, a claim to be followed at once however by the words, *a kingdom of priests*. They were a people called, chosen, reared, educated, and ordained to perform their priestly function to all the other nations of the earth. This function seemed to have been interrupted, even destroyed, by the events of the Exile. But now Israel was back home again in Jerusalem. The full meaning of "redemption", of "salvation", of "resurrection", of "re-creation" could not, however, stop there. Israel had to be re-equipped for her task of *yeshuah*, of exerting, of living out, rescuing and saving love, as we see it described in Ps. 147:1–6. That is, of course, first of all, God's task, but it is also Israel's task. No wonder the psalmist invites the congregation in return to respond to that great privilege by exclaiming just the one word: "Hallelujah!"

PRAISE IS A TWO-EDGED SWORD

Psalms 149:1–9

> [1]Praise the Lord!
>   Sing to the Lord a new song,
>   his praise in the assembly of the faithful!
> [2]Let Israel be glad in his Maker,
>   let the sons of Zion rejoice in their King!

³Let them praise his name with dancing,
    making melody to him with timbrel and lyre!
⁴For the Lord takes pleasure in his people;
    he adorns the humble with victory.
⁵Let the faithful exult in glory;
    let them sing for joy on their couches.
⁶Let the high praises of God be in their throats
    and two-edged swords in their hands,
⁷to wreak vengeance on the nations
    and chastisement on the peoples,
⁸to bind their kings with chains
    and their nobles with fetters of iron,
⁹to execute on them the judgment written!
    This is glory for all his faithful ones.
  Praise the Lord!

Our cultural life is very different from that of the people of Jerusalem in the late OT period. So we in our turn must find *a new song* by which to *praise the Lord*, one that has meaning for those called upon to sing "Hallelujah" in the twentieth century. Some of the old songs of David, by our poet's day, were no longer directly relevant to the people of the Second Temple. For Israel had experienced her "death" in the horrors of the Exile, and yet also her "resurrection" from it, followed by her "ascension" thereafter up to God's holy hill. Thus in this psalm no mention is made of David as Israel's king. Israel had now "ascended up on high" where only God is *King*, to apply the *theological* meaning of the "Songs of Ascents" (Pss. 120–134). But more, God alone, says the psalmist, is Israel's *Maker*.

But praise is a *two-edged sword* (verse 6), a sword that cuts both ways. First, it represents an expression of straightforward joy and gratitude to God in song and exultation of spirit, some-times even *with dancing*, as fitted into the culture of the period some centuries before Christ. Yet each new generation has to find *a new song* to fit God's never-ending revelation in always new social conditions. While present-day, westernized, urbanized and scientifically-minded congregations may employ quite a different "song" or liturgy from that which came naturally to ancient

Israel, yet it must be one that acknowledges with joy that *the Lord* still *takes pleasure in his people*, and still *adorns* (makes them appear glorious) *the humble*, not *with victory* (as the RSV), but with "the power (the 'horn' of 148:14) to love others *into* God's salvation". What a pity the RSV misleads us here by the barely possible translation it uses!

How warmly this power is now described! In the NT it would be called the Holy Spirit, the power to love being the greatest of all God's gifts, outshining all the rest (I Cor. 12:31; 13:13). God's *faithful*, in Hebrew *hasidim* (from the noun *hesed* which we have met so often), that is, those who belong to God's Covenant people, *exult in glory*. Yet glory belongs to God alone! Remembering this in bed at night they will naturally want to *sing* out loud (verse 5).

But then we come, second, to the other edge of the sword. The first has been this straightforward praise that bubbles up from the throats of the redeemed. The second, on the other hand, has a meaning that stems from the "horn of power" which God has put in the hands of his faithful ones. And it is that power which is now described as the power of the sword.

As a result of their experience of being born again out of the wrath of the Exile, of having been forgiven and renewed, God's people have now been equipped to fight the battles of the Lord. God's attack upon the evil in the world is here pictured, as so often in the OT, in terms of war, and because of that Israel is known as his *host* or army. For God is he who is "trampling out the vintage where the grapes of wrath are stored", to quote Julia Ward Howe's great hymn. At Isa. 63:1-6, where she found her inspiration, it is God himself who, all alone, saves the nations by the spilling of his own blood.

But now, in logical sequence, this psalm takes the next step. First, God had declared that the life-blood of the peoples is sprinkled upon his garments like one who treads out "the grapes of wrath" (Isa. 63:3). These words were spoken about 520 B.C. to the people whom God had newly redeemed from exile in Babylon. In other words, he had saved them at the cost of his own blood. For it had "broken God's heart", as we might say, to have

brought in the day of vengeance upon the cruelty of the Babylonians. Yet that "day" was needed, for it produced "my year" of
Israel's redemption. Israel had been redeemed only through the
pain and suffering of others, of both God and man.

Second, what God had done had been the great task laid upon
the Messianic king, as we saw in Pss. 2, 110 and others. The latter
would one day come to be God's instrument in bringing in his
Kingdom, by wielding this two-edged sword.

But third, as we also saw when studying the Messianic psalms,
the king is the head cornerstone of his people. This means that
what God calls him to do, the king's people are to do with him and
in him as one "sword" together in the hand of God. We may not
today care for such warlike metaphors; but let us carefully consider the following illustrations of their truth:

For the Word of God is living and active, sharper than any two-edged
sword, piercing to the division of soul and spirit . . . (Heb. 4:12).

I have not come to bring peace, but a sword (Matt. 10:34).

Bring me my bow of burning gold!
  Bring me my arrows of desire!
Bring me my spear! O clouds, unfold!
  Bring me my chariot of fire!

I will not cease from mental fight,
  Nor shall my sword sleep in my hand,
Till we have built Jerusalem
  In England's green and pleasant land.

(William Blake)

Tie in a living tether
  The prince and priest and thrall;
Bind all our lives together,
  Smite us and save us all;
In ire and exultation,
  Aflame with faith, and free,
Lift up a living nation,
  A single sword to thee.

(Gilbert Keith Chesterton)

There *is* a *judgment written*, written at the core of the Biblical revelation (see Deut. 30:15-19). The absolute and irrevocable judgment of God rests upon *all* nations, even including Israel, God's own special people (Amos 3:1-2; 8:2)! God cannot go back on his word of judgment, else he would not be true to himself. But God's understanding is beyond measure (Ps. 147:5). God alone therefore can do what no man can do, and that is to turn the necessary judgment into the means of redemption. And for this purpose Israel is his servant!

This, then, is to be the content of Israel's *new song*, one not just to be sung in the Temple, but one that is to be lived out in the market-place. And lived out not only in the city of Jerusalem, but also in the cities of Athens, Rome, London, New York, and Calcutta.

THE PRAISE OF ALL CREATION

Psalm 150:1-6

¹Praise the Lord!
　　Praise God in his sanctuary;
　　praise him in his mighty firmament!
²Praise him for his mighty deeds;
　　praise him according to his exceeding greatness!

³Praise him with trumpet sound;
　　praise him with lute and harp!
⁴Praise him with timbrel and dance;
　　praise him with strings and pipe!

⁵Praise him with sounding cymbals;
　　praise him with loud clashing cymbals!
⁶Let everything that breathes praise the Lord!
　Praise the Lord!

The last psalm of the whole wonderful Psalter is a kind of doxology, fittingly placed after the vision of God's total redemptive act that is the other edge of the two-edged sword of justice in the hand of the servants of God on earth. The last chapters of the New Testament offer us a glimpse, so to speak, into the eternal outcome of all God's terrible acts. These had begun with Abraham and Moses and had continued till Christ ascended to the Holy City of God. In these chapters which end the whole Bible we hear this great song of praise: "And he shall reign for ever and ever." Handel's "Hallelujah Chorus" would never stir us as it does without the many human voices sounding together in majesty and without the harmony of all the musical instruments that we can employ today. These sing forth on the strings of the violin, and resonate deeply on the heart-shattering bass of the great array of drums, enhancing the words of exultant praise. So, too, in this final psalm every voice in heaven and earth, and every musical instrument that human ingenuity has produced are called upon to join in the praise of the Living God.

More and more as we have studied the psalms in their fascinating order of thought which follows on the historical experience of Israel, we have been given an insight into the pattern of revelation which the Holy Spirit has led the compilers of the Psalter to grasp. And more and more climactic have we found the theology of the Psalter to be. For we have learned, through the interpretation the psalm writers have made of their own history as the "place" of God's revelation of himself and of his loving plan for the world, that what took place in Israel's history were indeed God's "mighty acts", but that they were at the same time God's "terrible" acts arising from the pain in his own heart.

So this psalm is in no sense a mere shout of empty and superficial praise. It sounds forth praise from the heart of a world that has discovered the cost to God of the world's redemption, that has in fact glimpsed that in the heart of the Living God there is a Cross. Consequently it summons us in our turn to praise God, not only with our lips, but with our lives. These are to be poured out in sacrificial service through the power, the "horn" of God's Holy Spirit in our hearts. In this way we join in praise with all God's creatures everywhere, both now and in all eternity. The total pattern of God's redemptive plan of activity has been glimpsed and fitted into the liturgy of Israel. What, then, is there left for not just Israel, but for *everything that breathes*, except to shout the one comprehensive word "Hallelujah!"

APPENDICES

	RSV Text	Footnote
16:2	I have no good apart from thee	Jerome, Tg.: The meaning of the Hebrew is uncertain
16:4	Those who choose another god multiply their sorrows	Cn: The meaning of the Hebrew is uncertain
18:35	thy help	Or *gentleness*
19:4	their voice	Gk, Jerome; compare Syr.: Heb. *line*
22:20	my life	Heb. *my only one*
27:2	uttering slanders against me	Heb. *to eat up my flesh*
29:1	heavenly beings	Heb. *sons of gods*
30:12	that my soul	Heb. *that glory*
31:6	Thou hatest	With one Heb. MS., Gk, Syr., Jerome: Heb. *I hate*
38:19	without cause	Cn: Heb. *living*
40:2	desolate pit	Cn: Heb. *pit of tumult*
40:6	thou hast given me an open ear	Heb. *ears thou hast dug for me*
41:1	the poor	Or *weak*
41:3	thou healest all his infirmities	Heb. *thou changest all his bed*
45:4	and to defend	Cn: Heb. *and the meekness of*
45:13	people with all kinds of wealth. The princess is decked in her chamber with gold-woven robes	Or *people. All glorious is the princess within, gold embroidery is her clothing*
46:1	very present	Or *well proved*
50:14	offer to God a sacrifice of thanksgiving	Or *make thanksgiving your sacrifice to God*
51:10	right	Or *steadfast*
52:1	against the godly	Cn; compare Syr.: Heb. *the kindness of God*

55:22	your burden	Or *what he has given you*
59:7	snarling with	Cn: Heb. *swords in*
59:9	I will sing praises to thee	Syr.: Heb. *I will watch for thee*
60:4	bow	Gk, Syr., Jerome: Heb. *truth*
60:6	in his sanctuary	Or *by his holiness*
66:12	to a spacious place	Cn; compare Gk, Syr., Jerome, Tg.: Heb. *saturation*
68:35	in his	Gk: Heb. *from thy*
71:3	a strong fortress	Gk; compare 31:3: Heb. *to come continually thou hast ₁commanded*
73:26	strength	Heb. *rock*
75:9	I will rejoice	Gk: Heb. *declare*
76:4	the everlasting mountains	Gk: Heb. *the mountains of prey*
80:15	planted	Heb. *planted and upon the son whom thou hast reared for thyself*
89:7	great and terrible	Gk, Syr.: Heb. *greatly terrible*
89:16	and extol	Cn: Heb. *are exalted in*
89:50	the insults	Cn: Heb. *all of many*
91:9	Because you have made the Lord your refuge	Cn: Heb. *Because thou, Lord, art my refuge; you have made*
97:10	The Lord loves those who hate evil	Cn: Heb. *You who love the Lord hate evil*
100:3	and we are his	Another reading is *and not we ourselves*
107:17	sick	Cn: Heb. *fools*
109:6	bring him to trial	Heb. *stand at his right hand*
110:3	upon the holy mountains	Another reading is *in holy array*
138:2	thou hast exalted above everything thy name and thy word	Cn: Heb. *thou hast exalted thy word above all thy name*
139:24	the way everlasting	Or *the ancient way*
145:13	The Lord is faithful . . . all his deeds	These two lines are supplied by one Heb. MS., Gk and Syr.

Appendix 2. A LIST OF PSALMS ARRANGED BY KIND OR THEME TO FACILITATE FURTHER STUDY

As is proper in a "daily study" commentary, readers have been taken through the Psalms in the order that we have them in the Bible. There is method in the Biblical arrangement (see especially the Introduction to this volume), but it is not easily discerned, and it is not at all like the arrangement we are used to in modern hymnals. For future study readers may like to have by their side an arrangement along "hymnal" lines, one, that is, which brings together psalms that strike a similar mood or that develop themes or provide similar insights into God's ways with men. It is hoped that the following guide will be of help to them.

Psalms that begin with the worshipper's complaint but, as he thinks more deeply about God's nature, lead him on to praise: 3, 4, 5, 11, 13, 17, 22, 25, 28, 31, 41, 51, 69, 70, 71, 77, 86, 102.

Psalms in which the nation or the worshipping community complain to God but are likewise led through complaint to praise: 12, 14, 44, 60, 64, 74, 85, 90.

Psalms for the blackest days when faith and hope come hard: 6, 10, 22, 38, 39, 53, 55, 79, 88, 120, 123, 130, 137, 140, 142, 143.

Psalms which breathe a spirit of confidence and trust in time of trouble: 16, 23, 27, 32, 40, 42, 43, 46, 52, 56, 57, 61, 62, 63, 73, 75, 91, 112, 115, 131.

Psalms of thanksgiving in which the individual or the community looks back on God's mercy and guidance: 9, 18, 30, 34, 67, 89, 92, 116, 118, 124, 126, 136, 138.

Psalms which praise God for his own qualities and in which the worshipper's needs are given second place
—the greatness and majesty of God: 68, 76, 113, 147, 148, 149, 150
—God the King and Judge: 47, 50, 82, 93, 96, 97, 98, 99
—the God of nature: 8, 19, 29, 65, 104, 114
—the God of history: 78, 80, 81, 103, 105, 106, 135
—the faithfulness and providence of God: 33, 36, 103, 107, 111, 117, 136, 139, 145, 146.

Psalms which allude to the Temple and its worship: 24, 42, 43, 50, 66, 68, 92, 95, 96, 100, 116, 118, 134, 149, 150.

Pilgrim psalms and psalms about the holy city: 46, 48, 84, 87, 121, 122, 125, 133.

Psalms about the Davidic king: 2, 20, 21, 45, 72, 89, 101, 110, 132, 144.

Psalms about the "good life" and its opposite: 1, 15, 19, 26, 37, 49, 73, 112, 127, 128, 133, 141, and above all the "Great Psalm" 119.

Psalms which offend the Christian conscience and which are better avoided: 7, 35, 54, 58, 59, 83, 94, 108, 109, 129. (There are vindictive and cruel notes sounded in not a few other psalms—e.g. 17, 55, 68, 69, 79, 137, 139—but in these psalms such notes are counterbalanced by more positive and appealing notes.)

FURTHER READING

A. A. Anderson, *The Book of Psalms*, 2 volumes (New Century Bible) (Oliphants, 1972)

E. M. Blaiklock, *Psalms for Living*, Vol. I; *Psalms for Worship*, Vol. II (Scripture Union, 1977)

J. H. Eaton, *Psalms, Introduction and Commentary* (Torch Bible Commentaries) (SCM Press, 1967)

J. H. Eaton, *Kingship and the Psalms* (Studies in Biblical Theology) (SCM Press, 1976)

John Hargreaves, *A Guide to the Psalms* (TEF Study Guide 6) (SPCK, 1973)

A. R. Johnson, *The Cultic Prophet in Ancient Israel* (University of Wales Press, 1962)

Derek Kidner, *Psalms*, 2 volumes (Tyndale Old Testament Commentaries) (Inter-Varsity Press, 1973–75)

J. A. Lamb, *The Psalms in Christian Worship* (The Faith Press, 1962)

Sigmund Mowinckel, *He That Cometh* (Basil Blackwell, 1956)

R. E. Prothero, *The Psalms in Human Life* (J. Murray, reprinted 1905)

A. B. Rhodes, *Psalms* (Layman's Bible Commentaries) (SCM Press, 1964)

J. W. Rogerson and J. W. McKay, *Psalms*, 3 volumes (Cambridge Bible Commentary on the NEB) (CUP, 1977)

Artur Weiser, *The Psalms: A Commentary* (Old Testament Library) (SCM Press, 1962)

Claus Westermann, *The Psalms: Structure, Content and Message* (Augsburg Press, 1980)